# HISTORY OF
*United States Naval Operations*
## IN WORLD WAR II

★

V O L U M E   T H R E E

# The Rising Sun in the Pacific
*1931–April* 1942

# HISTORY OF UNITED STATES NAVAL OPERATIONS IN WORLD WAR II

## By *Samuel Eliot Morison*

Also
*Strategy and Compromise*

*Admiral Thomas C. Hart* USN
Commander in Chief United States Asiatic Fleet

HISTORY OF UNITED STATES NAVAL
OPERATIONS IN WORLD WAR II
*VOLUME III*

# The Rising Sun in the Pacific

## 1931 - *April* 1942

BY SAMUEL ELIOT MORISON

*With Illustrations*

CASTLE BOOKS

HISTORY OF UNITED STATES NAVAL OPERATIONS IN WORLD WAR II

*The* RISING SUN IN THE PACIFIC
*1931 – April 1942*
VOL. III

ISBN: 0-7858-1304-7

*To*

*The Memory of*

JAMES FORRESTAL

*Under Secretary of The Navy*

August 1940 to May 1944

*Secretary of The Navy*

May 1944 to September 1947

*Secretary of National Defense*

September 1947 to March 1949

All hidden things the endless flowing years
Bring forth, and bury that which all men knew.
Falters the firm resolve and plighted word;
And none may say "It cannot happen here."

— SOPHOCLES, Ajax, 646–649

# Preface[1]

THIS volume is the first of nine that will cover the operations of the United States Navy in the war against Japan. Like all others in the *History of United States Naval Operations*, it is written for the general reader rather than the professional sailor.

Americans cannot with impunity deny the importance of warfare in their history. But the history of warfare loses most of its significance unless we know what the fighting was about. That is why considerable space is devoted to "incidents" that really began the war in the Pacific, and to the internal conflict within Japan which was largely responsible for turning one of America's traditional friends into an implacable enemy. On the other hand, little space is given to the question of who was responsible on our side for the surprise at Pearl Harbor. For the Joint Congressional Investigating Committee has published forty volumes on this subject, and has issued a thorough, painstaking report which is readily available.

Admiral William James RN some years ago published a book on the American War of Independence with the mordant title "The British Navy in Adversity." A subtitle of this volume might well be "The United States Navy in Adversity." After sustaining the most shattering blows in its history, the Navy suffered a series of reverses at Wake Island, in the Philippines and along the Malay Barrier, with the relief of only minor tactical victories such as the action off Balikpapan and the Halsey-Doolittle strike on Tokyo. These first five months of the war in the Pacific are neither pleasant to investigate nor inspiring to read about, except possibly for our

[1] See also the Introduction to Volume I of this History for statement of scope and purpose of this work, and the methods followed by the writer.

late enemies and present friends, the Japanese; but I would be faithless to my trust if I glossed them over. And I owe it to the brave men who held this succession of Thermopylaes against an enemy of overwhelming strength to record their efforts with the same care and detail that I devote to the victories that follow.

Writers like Gilbert Cant, Fletcher Pratt, Walter Karig and the anonymous authors of the O.N.I. Combat Narratives, who wrote books covering this part of the war while it was still being fought, have my sincere admiration. But, in order to make this History approach nearer to finality (that goal which historians, like the lover on Keats's Grecian urn, may win near yet never, never attain), I had to wait until data of enemy origin could be collected and digested. Shortly after Japan surrendered, a determined effort was made to get at this information. Many Japanese records were sent to the National Archives in Washington, after the war. Some of them, translated by members of the Office of Naval Intelligence or of the Combat Intelligence section of Cominch or by Lieutenant Roger Pineau USNR of my staff, have been most helpful. But much of our information on the Japanese side comes from interrogations of Japanese officers, or reports reconstructed by them from memory and from their personal diaries.

A joint Army-Navy organization known as USSBS (United States Strategic Bombing Survey) began rounding up and interrogating Japanese officers and key civilians, before the end of 1945. Rear Admiral R. A. Ofstie, the senior naval member of USSBS, had charge of interrogating the naval officers. Although he and his staff entertained considerable skepticism as to the value of information obtained in this way they found out, by asking questions to which the answers were already known, that the Japanese officers were telling the truth, or as much of it as they could remember; most of them were even eager to volunteer information. From the material so obtained, Admiral Ofstie selected and published two volumes of *Interrogations of Japanese Officials*, besides the valuable *Campaigns of the Pacific War* based upon them. Other interrogations, quoted here as USSBS No. so-and-so, exist only in mimeographed sheets. In addition the Allied Translator and Interpreter Section (ATIS) of General MacArthur's staff translated many important Japanese documents, naval and otherwise. This organization was of great assistance to us by translating selected documents.

I have made one visit to Japan in quest of further information, Lieutenant Pineau has gone three times, and Lieutenant Commander Henry Salomon Jr. USNR, then one of my assistants, once. General MacArthur and members of his staff received us in the most friendly manner and allowed us to use the invaluable services of ATIS. Encouraged by the General, several officers of the Japanese Navy reconstructed reports of naval operations especially for this work. Rear Admiral Sadatoshi Tomioka, Captain Toshikazu Ohmae, Commander Masataka Chihaya and Commander Moriyoshi Yamaguchi and others worked long and faithfully to this end and have so continued by answering questions addressed to them by letter.

Another group of American officers working with Japanese coöperation, the Joint Army-Navy Assessment Committee (Rear Admiral Jerauld Wright, chairman) produced a highly valuable work: *Japanese Naval and Merchant Shipping Losses During World War II by All Causes.*[2] This is the source for all my statements of losses inflicted on the enemy. But I do not claim that we have secured all existing Japanese information. Additional data are certain to turn up from time to time.

In the spelling of foreign names, I admit inconsistency. Most American geographers have adopted the names used by the sovereign power of the given place. Thus, Formosa becomes Taiwan; Foochow, Minhow; Surabaya, Soerabaja; Sunda Strait, Stratt Soenda. I cannot go along with them. British and American seamen have been familiar with Pacific waters for two centuries or more; their Anglicized place names, in Admiralty and United States charts, are familiar to English-speaking sailors, and have even entered literature through the works of Conrad, Hergesheimer,

---

[2] Published Feb. 1947, by Superintendent of Documents, U. S. Government Printing Office, Washington, D.C.

and many others. It seems reasonable, however, to use the local spelling for small ports and inland places, instead of attempting to Anglicize them in conformity with the others. Thus, I say Badung Strait, but spell Bandoeng as the Dutch do.

In addition to work performed by the above-mentioned assistants, Lieutenant Albert Harkness Jr. USNR did the basic research for Parts II and IV. Mr. Donald Martin, formerly Chief Yeoman USNR, compiled the U. S. Task Organizations. Most of the typing was done by Yeomen Herbert M. Donaldson and Antha E. Card.[3] The charts are by Jane M. Donnelly (Specialist Wave USNR), Robert M. Berish (Yeoman 3rd class) and David C. Redding (Fireman 1st class) temporarily attached to my staff for that purpose.

James Forrestal, Under Secretary of the Navy when the war broke out, was the first, after President Roosevelt and Secretary Frank Knox, to approve this project; and in the early years of the war, he saw to it that I was given the assistance and the facilities to launch it properly. His interest in the work continued after he became Secretary of the Navy and Secretary of National Defense. Mr. Forrestal devoted his unusual knowledge and gave all his tremendous energy to the cause of national defense, and died in the service of his country. Deeply grateful for his confidence in me, I have dedicated this volume to his memory.

During the war and after, I have incurred debts of gratitude to many others, too numerous to mention here; but I must particularly thank Forrestal's successors, the Honorable John L. Sullivan and the Honorable Francis P. Mathews; two successive Chiefs of Naval Operations, Fleet Admiral Ernest J. King and Fleet Admiral Chester W. Nimitz; two successive Directors of Naval History, Rear Admiral Vincent R. Murphy and Rear Admiral John B. Heffernan; Admiral Thomas C. Hart, Admiral Raymond A. Spruance, Rear Admiral William R. Furlong and Captain Ralph C. Parker. The Honorable Joseph C. Grew, former American Ambassador to Japan, and the Honorable Eugene H. Dooman,

---

[3] Harvard University contributed by enabling me to retain the valuable services of Miss Card as secretary after she left the Navy.

former Counsellor of the Embassy at Tokyo, have generously
assisted me in collecting and interpreting data for the diplomatic
history prior to the outbreak of war.

SAMUEL E. MORISON

HARVARD UNIVERSITY
7 *December 1947*


During the six years since the first edition of this volume appeared, officers of the United States Navy and Mr. K. W. L. Beze-
mer, historian of the Royal Netherlands Navy, have supplied corrections and emendations, as have the official historians of the
United States Army under Colonel Kent Roberts Greenfield, and
of the Air Force under Dr. Albert F. Simpson. All corrections and
additions were checked and collated by Captain John W. McElroy
USNR, who was detailed by Admiral Heffernan for this purpose.
But I hope that any further errata will be called to my attention.

S.E.M.

ON BOARD YAWL *Emily Marshall*
*25 August 1953*

# Contents

## PART IV

### DEFENSE OF THE MALAY BARRIER
#### January–March 1942

# List of Illustrations

*(All photographs not otherwise described are Official United States Navy)*

# List of Charts

# Abbreviations

Officers' ranks and bluejackets' ratings are those contemporaneous with the event. Officers and men named will be presumed to be of the United States Navy unless otherwise stated; Naval Reservists are designated USNR.

RN, Royal Navy
RNN, Royal Netherlands Navy
RAN, Royal Australian Navy
USA, United States Army
USMC, United States Marine Corps; USMCR, Reserve of same

Other abbreviations used in this volume: —

Abda — American-British-Dutch-Australian Command
AM — Minesweeper
Anzac — Australia-New Zealand Area Command
AP — Transport; APD — Destroyer converted to transport
ATIS — Allied Translator and Interpreter Section of General Headquarters (General MacArthur's command)
Batdiv — Battleship Division
BB — Battleship
Buships — Bureau of Ships
CA — Heavy Cruiser
Cardiv — Carrier Division
C. in C. — Commander in Chief
Cincpac — Commander in Chief, Pacific Fleet
CL — Light Cruiser
C.O. — Commanding Officer
Com before cardiv, desdiv, etc., means Commander Carrier Division, Commander Destroyer Division, etc.
Cominch — Commander in Chief, United States Fleet
CNO — Chief of Naval Operations
CM — Minelayer
CTF — Commander Task Force
CV — Aircraft Carrier; CVS — Seaplane Carrier
CVL — Light Aircraft Carrier
DD — Destroyer
Desdiv — Destroyer Division
Desron — Destroyer Squadron
H.M.S. — His Majesty's Ship
H.N.M.S. — Her Netherland Majesty's Ship
H.M.A.S. — His Majesty's Australian Ship
*Inter. Jap. Off.* — U.S.S.B.S. *Interrogations of Japanese Officials,*
2 vols., 1946

N.A.S. — Naval Air Station
Opnav — Chief of Naval Operations
O.N.I. — Office of Naval Intelligence
PC — Patrol Craft
P.H. *Attack* — *Pearl Harbor Attack. Hearings before the Joint Committee* (in 40 Parts, Washington 1946)
P.H. *Report* — *Investigation of the Pearl Harbor Attack. Report of the Joint Committee* (79th Cong. 2d Sess., Doc. No. 244, 1946)
R.A.F. — Royal Air Force
R.N.Z.A.F. — Royal New Zealand Air Force
SS — Submarine
TF — Task Force
TG — Task Group
U.S.A.A.F. — United States Army Air Forces
U.S.S. — United States Ship
USSBS — United States Strategic Bombing Survey
VB — Bombing plane or squadron
VF — Fighting plane or squadron
VT — Torpedo plane or squadron
WDC — Washington Document Center
WDI — War Department Intelligence
YP — Patrol Vessel

U.S. aircraft designations that appear in this volume are: —

A–24, Army version of the SBD
B–17, Flying Fortress, Army four-engine heavy bomber, land-based
B–18, Bolo, Army two-engine medium bomber, land-based
B–25, Mitchell, Army two-engine medium bomber, land-based
B–26, Marauder, Army two-engine medium bomber, land-based
F2A, Buffalo, Navy single-engine fighter, land- or carrier-based
F4F–3, F4F–4, Wildcat, Navy single-engine fighter, land- or carrier-based
J2F, Duck, Navy single-engine utility seaplane, tender-based
OS2U, Kingfisher, Navy single-engine float plane, carried by battleships and cruisers
P–35, Army single-engine pursuit plane, land-based
P–40, Warhawk, Army single-engine pursuit plane, land-based
PBY–5, Catalina, Navy two-engine patrol bomber, seaplane, tender-based
SBD–2, SBD–3, Dauntless, Navy single-engine scout and dive-bomber, carrier-based
TBD–1, Devastator, Navy single-engine torpedo-bomber, carrier-based

## PART 1
## *Panay* through Pearl

# CHAPTER I
# *Hakko Ichiu*
## *1920–1940*

### 1. *The Background*

*From whence come wars and fightings among you? Come they not hence, even of your lusts that war in your members? Ye lust, and have not: ye kill, and desire to have, and cannot obtain: ye fight and war, yet ye have not . . .*

SAINT JAMES may not have been the brightest of the Twelve Apostles, but in these trenchant words he announced a fundamental cause of all war which is particularly applicable to World War II. Two nations which regarded themselves as "have nots" fought and made war to obtain what they wanted and, owing to the weakness or shortsightedness of their immediate neighbors, won a series of astounding victories. But their own cruelty and oppression aroused the rest of the world against them, and in the end they had less than nothing.

No historian, however, may assume the complete righteousness of his nation, or the inevitability of a war. He must ask himself whether a wiser statesmanship might not have averted, or at least postponed, a conflict which brought so much misery to the world, burdened his own country with responsibilities it never wished to assume, and opened up a dark prospect for the future of civilization. For an historian of the United States Navy a brief inquiry into the causes of the war in the Pacific is peculiarly appropriate; since an officer of that Navy first cracked the shell around Japan, upon that Navy fell the first fury of the enemy attack, and by that Navy

— alone, or as a spearhead for other armed forces — Japan was utterly defeated.

The Japanese and American peoples had very different sets of values, each derived from a long past; yet their interests did not clash and their formal relations remained generally cordial for over fifty years. Through numerous writings and personal contacts Americans had learned to appreciate the peculiar virtues of the Japanese and they in turn regarded the United States as their best friend in the outside world. The work of Commodore Perry and Townsend Harris in bringing Japan out of a precarious isolation into the comity of nations, even saving her perhaps from dismemberment by European powers, was generously appreciated in Japan and often acknowledged. In the Russo-Japanese War American opinion was uniformly anti-Russian, and the mediation of President Theodore Roosevelt probably saved Japan from defeat. The United States and Japan were associates in World War I and, although acute differences between them developed at the peace conference, both countries made concessions. Japan gave up Shantung and the United States placed the Philippines on the road to independence. The naval limitation treaties, with their nonfortification clauses, seemed to postpone indefinitely all causes of conflict. Economic relations between the two countries were mutually profitable; each produced raw materials and manufactures that the other wanted. No American group or set of interests wanted war with Japan; on the contrary, aversion to such a war was so strong that only a long series of provocations, culminating in the treacherous attack on Pearl Harbor, made war possible.

Why, then, did Japan attack America? The immediate occasion, as we well know, was the Far Eastern policy of the United States, seeking first by persuasive diplomacy and finally by economic sanctions to restore peace and union to distracted China, as against a Japanese policy that aimed to conquer and control that immense country. Yet that does not answer the question. Why did Japan wish to control China? Not from any vital pressure such as over-population [1] but from inability to make a competent synthesis between power and responsibility. Japan was the only important nation in the world in the twentieth century which combined modern industrial power and a first-class military establishment with religious and social ideas inherited from the primitive ages of mankind, which exalted the military profession and regarded war and conquest as the highest good. True, the country possessed an intellectual élite who had accepted the Christian ethic if not the Christian religion, and attempted to guide the Japanese nation into the ways of peace; but those Western ideals vaguely comprehended under the term "democracy" had made so little dent on the people at large that they were swept away by a self-conscious and active group of military extremists.

The crucial decade was that of the 1920's, and the field of conflict was Japan itself. Japanese militarists, seeing their traditional primacy undermined by civilian elements, and their dreams of conquest vanishing, deliberately provoked the "Manchuria Incident" to reëstablish their power. When *Hakko Ichiu* — "bringing the eight corners of the world under one roof," — the probably mythical utterance of the possibly mythical Emperor Jimmu around the year 600 B.C., was resurrected in 1931 as a slogan of national policy, it was a signal that the old Japan had won against

[1] Although Japan was a thickly inhabited country with some 73,000,000 people in 1941 in an area less than that of California, the country was prosperous, like England earlier, owing to its immense export trade. Taking 100 as index of industrial production in 1929, that of the U.S. fell to 53 in the 1930's and rose to 126 in 1940; that of Japan fell only to 92 in 1931 and rose steadily to 194 in 1940 (*Statistical Yearbook of League of Nations*, 1940–41). Underpopulated Manchuria. publicized as a "breathing space" in 1931, attracted only 301,700 Japanese immigrants in the next 6 years, and the great majority of these were middle class — teachers, technicians, shopkeepers and railway officials (*The Manchukuo Yearbook 1942*, p. 117). The much greater peasant emigration to Manchuria was Chinese. When the Japanese annexed a country they moved in as a governing class, monopolizing the professions and the more lucrative jobs. Thus, in Korea in 1945 only 150 of the 3000 physicians in the American zone were Koreans, the rest Japanese; and the highest ranking Korean who could be found to run the railroads was an assistant deputy stationmaster. As a final refutation to the over-population argument, one may point to the fact that Java, the principal objective of the Japanese southward thrust in 1941–42, had a much denser population than Japan itself.

the new, and that any nation that did not like it would have to "put up or shut up."

## 2. *The Army and Japanese Policy*

Although foreign diplomatic representatives had to deal with the Foreign Office, it was the Army that made Japanese foreign policy before 1920 and after 1931. The Japanese Army, to which the Imperial Japanese Navy was a junior and (in popular estimation) inferior service, had a peculiar place in Japanese life. The darling of the nation, it was representative of the nation to a far greater degree than the Diet. Universal military service for twenty years (of which two were spent in active service and the rest in various reserve forces) was the rule for all men. As early as 1927, 30 per cent of the officers came from the lower middle class, and the proportion constantly rose. Yet the upstarts vied with descendants of the Samurai in promoting *Bushido*, the traditional "way of the warrior." Every Japanese was proud to serve in his armed forces and ambitious to die for the Emperor, when he would become one of the demigods or spirits that guarded his native land. The Army was too sacred even to be made fun of. The G.I. gripes to which we are accustomed, "Sad Sack" cartoons and poking fun at the "brass hats," were unthinkable in Japan.

The Japanese constitution of 1889 embodied the doctrine of "imperial command," the principle that the Emperor alone had the prerogative of determining the size and strength of his armed forces. This doctrine, completely alien to American tradition, was natural and proper for Japan. It was a means of rallying the military class to westernization. It was a shield against European imperialism. As the imperial command principle evolved in practice, the Army obtained control of the government whenever it chose to exert its prerogative. The system was sanctioned by success. Ten years after the 1894-95 war with China, in which Japan won Formosa, she challenged and defeated a major power, Russia. In

1910 Japan annexed the ancient kingdom of Korea, which she had pledged herself to protect. It is probable that early in the century the elder statesmen of Japan had laid down a long-term policy aimed at liquidating all European concessions in China and eliminating all European colonies in East Asia. The only difference between their policy and that of the Army was one of ways and means, and of timing. Tojo and Shimada carried forward a policy of conquest inherited from more moderate predecessors, whose faces were turned, though less boldly, in the same direction.

In 1914 Japan entered the World War on the side of Great Britain and France, in order to obtain the German colonies in the Far East. With no fighting worth mentioning, she took possession of the German concession of Tsingtao on the Shantung Peninsula, the Marianas (except Guam, which the United States had purchased in 1899), the Carolines (including Yap, the Palaus and Truk) and the Marshalls. As early as 1915, in the "Twenty-one Demands" made to China, the Japanese government showed what was in its mind: a virtual protectorate of Japan over China, with complete direction of her military, political and industrial life, and full opportunity to exploit. This was the first important violation of the "Open Door" to China, the American policy in the Far East to which all major European nations, and Japan herself, had subscribed. The powers protested and Japan nominally withdrew the Twenty-one Demands, but waited for a good opportunity to apply them again.

At the Peace Conference of 1919, Japan received a mandate to all former German possessions in the Pacific north of the Equator. The Wilson Administration has been criticized for "permitting" Japan to retain those strategic positions, the recovery of which cost us so much blood and effort. But no other course was possible. Japan had seized them as legitimate war booty while the United States was still neutral, and she was determined to keep them, although willing to observe the responsibilities of a mandatory power. The only way to break the Japanese hold on these islands was to go to war over them; and war for such an objective would have been unthinkable, even if their strategic importance in an air age could have been foreseen.

Having obtained what it wanted in the Pacific Islands, the Japanese Army turned against Russia, temporarily weakened by the Soviet Revolution. Only the fact that the intervention in Siberia was an Allied affair, the United States participating, prevented the Japanese Army from setting up a vassal state like Manchukuo in eastern Siberia.[2] And the refusal of the Diet in 1922 to vote the desired military credits forced the Army to withdraw, and liquidate the Siberian adventure.

That refusal, a very courageous stand for a Japanese Diet to take, marked a new era in Japanese history which unfortunately lasted less than ten years. The prestige of democracy at the close of World War I, the belief that European imperialism was no longer to be feared, the collective security promised by the League of Nations, brought about for the first time a public opinion in Japan that demanded social and economic reform, parliamentary government, close collaboration with the Western powers, and supremacy of the civilian over the military elements. Something like a two-party system was established. Military budgets were repeatedly cut, and the savings turned into social enterprises. Japan had a permanent seat in the League of Nations, and fulfilled her international obligations scrupulously.

A liberal Japanese government accepted the 5–5–3 ratio at the Washington Conference of 1921–22, returned the Shantung Peninsula to China and signed the Nine-Power Treaty of 6 February 1922. Therein Japan agreed with the United States and seven other powers to safeguard the rights and interests of China, respect its sovereignty, independence, territory and administrative integrity, maintain the Open Door principle, refrain from creating spheres of influence or seeking special privileges, and in other ways enable that distracted republic to settle its affairs without outside interference. Japan also signed the Kellogg-Briand Pact for the outlawry of war.

[2] W. S. Graves *America's Siberian Adventure.*

Looking backward, we can see that the only hope of preserving peace in the Pacific was to encourage and support the liberal elements of Japan responsible for these agreements and concessions. A very wise, understanding and tactful attitude was called for by all the Western powers. Did American policy fill the bill? Not altogether. The traditional friendship appeared to be cemented by an outpouring of American sympathy and financial relief after the Tokyo earthquake of 1923. But all that capital of good will was quickly dissipated when the American Immigration Act of 1924 excluded Japanese completely from entering the United States. If Japan had been given a quota like other nations, only 150 to 200 persons could have been admitted annually, a mere drop in the bucket; and Japan demanded no more, since that would have placed her on the same basis as "white" nations. But this absolute exclusion, placing Japan in the same category with other orientals, deeply offended her national pride, built up bitter hatred, and discredited the liberal policy of coöperating with the Western powers.

The other great error was the insistence of Great Britain and the United States on naval limitation. If the naval limitation treaties of 1921 and 1930 were a crime against American defense,[3] they were a tragic mistake in their effect on the internal struggle in Japan. Naval limitation by treaty violated the doctrine of imperial command, and rendered the militarists desperate. It became clear to them that if civilians were allowed to determine naval strength by international treaties, and if the Diet were allowed to hamstring the armed forces by meager appropriations — as was being done in the United States and Great Britain — their millennial supremacy would soon be a thing of the past, and their plans for expansion by conquest must be permanently shelved. The military elements knew perfectly well that the limitation treaties left Japan in a very advantageous position as regards security; it was the principle of the thing and its political consequences that they dreaded. And the deceptively small end of the ratio that Japan received enabled the militarists to tell the ignorant masses that the Americans were

[3] See Commodore Knox's Introduction to Volume I of this History.

trying to keep them forever inferior.[4] Hence "5–5–3" became a jingo slogan, like our old "54–40 or Fight."

Thus the long-run effect of these well-meant efforts by the Anglo-American powers to prevent an armaments race merely turned Japanese opinion against them, and provoked reactionary, militarist elements in Japan to desperate measures, in order to create a state of national emergency which would overwhelm the civilian and liberal elements of the nation.

An ideological movement deliberately promoted to prepare the way for an overthrow of liberalism and representative government was already under way.

### 3. Kodo-Ha *and the* "*Manchuria Incident*"

This was an Oriental version of National Socialism, sometimes called the "Showa Restoration," [5] sometimes *Kodo-Ha* or "the Way of the Emperor," and by other names as well. Essentially a lower middle class and junior officer movement, its basic motives were hatred of the rich who were getting richer, hatred of the white man and his industrial civilization, an ardent desire to restore military supremacy at home and to make conquests abroad. Numerous secret societies, of which the Black Dragon was the most notorious although not the most powerful, furthered the movement. Ikki Kita's *Reconstruction Program for Japan,* which came out in 1920, was the Japanese *Mein Kampf.* He proposed the abolition of the Diet, a distribution of private property, nationalization of important industries, suppression of all political criticism, a reconstruction of the government so that there would be no barriers between "the nation" (i.e., the Army) and the Emperor, the "freeing" of 700,000,000 "brethren" in India, China, the Philippines and European Asiatic

[4] Ellis M. Zacharias *Secret Missions* (1946) p. 26.
[5] Showa, "enlightened peace," was the name chosen by Hirohito at his accession in 1926, by which he would be known after his death. The "Showa Restoration" meant that under Hirohito's aegis a new polity would be adopted, which would parallel the Meiji Restoration of 1868 by destroying the power of the big capitalists and all Western influences.

colonies, and a Japanese hegemony of the Far East which in turn would lead to *Hakko Ichiu*, the hegemony of the world.[6] The government tried to suppress Kita's book as a troublemaker, but it circulated widely and had a tremendous influence in the Army and among the people. Naval limitation and the American Immigration Act fanned the movement white-hot.

The militarists planned a *coup d'état* in 1923. The Tokyo earthquake prevented this, and their next opportunity came in 1931. Following the explosion of an alleged bomb on the tracks of the South Manchuria Railway on 18 September 1931, General Hayashi, a *Kodo* man who commanded the Japanese armed forces in Korea, moved his Kwantung Army into Manchuria without the permission of his government. Neither the Foreign Office nor the War Department knew anything about the "incident" until after it had occurred. The Foreign Minister had to accept the accomplished fact and explain it as best he could to the world. A state of war with China followed, and this gave the military a legal and constitutional control over the Japanese government.

Mr. Henry L. Stimson, Secretary of State in the Hoover Administration, promptly protested against the Japanese invasion of Manchuria; the League of Nations invoked the Kellogg-Briand Pact and appointed the Lytton Commission to study the situation and report. On 7 January 1932 Secretary Stimson announced what is known as the "nonrecognition policy." The United States would not recognize any "situation, treaty or agreement" brought about by the use of force. And, in an open letter of 23 February 1932, Mr. Stimson invited the nations of the world to follow suit. Tokyo replied by formally recognizing the independence of "Manchukuo," and setting up a puppet Manchu emperor. China countered with an anti-Japanese boycott; Japan landed sailors and soldiers in Shanghai, drove Chinese forces thence with a maximum of savagery and destruction, and, having saved her "honor," withdrew at the end of May. The Lytton Commission reported at the end of September,

[6] Hugh Byas *Government by Assassination* (1942) pp. 86–88. Other movements more or less similar to Kita's are there described.

condemning the Japanese action in Manchuria. Japan replied by withdrawing from the League of Nations. In the meantime, the militarists had consolidated their power by the simple means of getting rid of inconvenient persons; during the first half of 1932 the Minister of Finance, the chief manager of the Mitsui interests, and the seventy-five-year-old Prime Minister were assassinated. It was even planned to kill United States Ambassador Joseph Grew and Charlie Chaplin (then visiting Tokyo), in the hope of provoking a war with the United States and thus riveting military control on the government.

Throughout the discussions that preceded the war, the Japanese government and press so continually harped on their desire for "peace" that many well-meaning Americans, who chose to shut their eyes to actual events, were deceived. Even the Imperial Edict of 8 December 1941, announcing the opening of war to the Japanese people, threw the blame on Great Britain and the United States for placing obstacles "in the way of peaceful commercial endeavors of the Empire," and declared the objective of the war to be "everlasting peace in East Asia." [7] This was not hypocrisy. The Japanese simply put a different meaning on "peace" from that of any Western power. To them it meant complete control — military, political and economic — of all Oriental countries by a Japanese ruling class, a control imposed by force and terror if not abjectly accepted by other orientals. It meant exactly what Ikki Kita wrote, "A feudal peace obtained by the emergence of the strongest country, which will dominate all others of the world." It meant *Hakko Ichiu.*

## 4. *From Incident to Incident, 1935–1937*

A curious tension developed because, purely by chance, American newspapers printed on 30 December 1934, alongside the Japanese denunciation of the naval treaties, a somewhat grandiloquent

[7] "Japan's Decision to Make War" ATIS Enemy Publications No. 6 Appendix I.

From "Photographic History of Naval Strategy"
compiled by Imperial Naval Headquarters

Admiral Osami Nagano

Chief of the Naval General Staff

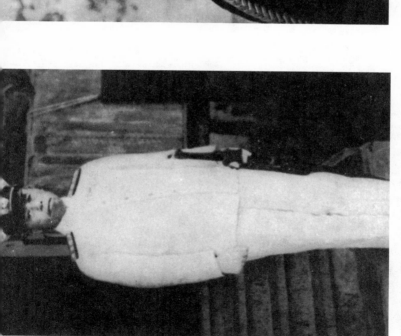

Admiral Isoroku Yamamoto

Commander in Chief Combined Fleet

*Japanese Naval Commanders*

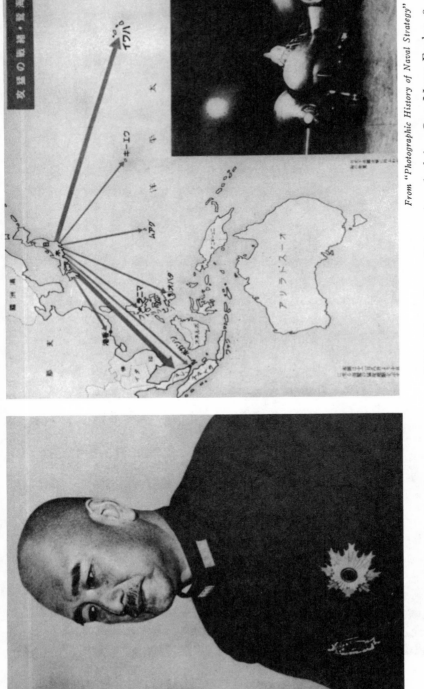

From "Photographic History of Naval Strategy"

"This Chart Shows Points Attacked by Our Navy Eagles, 8–10 December. Left to Right: Hong Kong, Kota Bharu, Singapore, Manila, Davao, Guam, Wake, Hawaii." *Insert:* "One of the Raging Eagles of Our Navy Leaving for a Moonlight Attack"

Admiral Shigetaro Shimada
Navy Minister 1941

program for the forthcoming United States Fleet Problem of 1935. It was announced as "the greatest game of mock naval warfare ever staged on the face of the globe," operating in a triangle "containing five million square miles of ocean" between the Aleutians, Pearl Harbor and Midway Island. There was an immediate uproar from peace societies and well-meaning individuals to the effect that this was a "minatory gesture" directed at Japan. When Admiral J. M. Reeves, Commander in Chief of the Fleet, visited Mr. Roosevelt in January 1935, the President told him that he was considerably annoyed by this criticism, but refused to interfere when the Admiral assured him that the Fleet would not operate within 2000 miles of Japan. A public announcement to that effect was made in early April, along with a statement that Commander in Chief Asiatic Fleet would pay a courtesy visit to Yokohama on 3 May. Midway Island, one of the focal points of the maneuvers, lies only a few miles east of the International Date Line, and the western Aleutians are west of it. Admiral Reeves could have sent his ships across long. 180° without passing the 2000-mile limit, and intended so to do. Nevertheless, after deployment was already under way, he received an order from the Secretary of the Navy that no ship must cross the 180th meridian.

The refusal of Japan's Finance Minister, a respectable octogenarian, to sanction a further increase of Army appropriations was a signal for his assassination by Army extremists, together with that of Admiral Saito, Lord Keeper of the Privy Seal, and of General Watanabe, the Inspector General. The Prime Minister, Admiral Okada, was also marked down, but the murderers shot his brother-in-law by mistake. As one might expect, this affair was very discouraging to moderate statesmen. The Genro selected the next cabinet, Hirota's, which took office in March 1936, and Hirota at once began preparations for full-scale war with China. Conversion of light industry to heavy war industry was speeded up, producers of steel and munitions were exempted from direct taxation and liberally supplied with loans, a five-year program in warship construction was started. When Hirota balked at the vastly increased military budget, a new cabinet was formed under General Hayashi which lasted until June when Prince Konoye, who deplored these trends but was unable to resist the militarists, became Premier.

When the Army was ready, it invaded China proper. That was the famous "China Incident" of 7 July 1937, a cooked-up clash between Japanese troops on maneuvers and a Chinese outpost on the Marco Polo Bridge near Peiping.

Prince Konoye declared on 27 July, "In sending troops into North China, of course, the government has no other purpose . . . than to preserve the peace of East Asia" (peace, of course, in the Japanese sense); and again, "Japan never looks upon the Chinese people as an enemy." [8] Such talk sounded like gross hypocrisy, especially in China where the Japanese military organized battues of unarmed peasants and in general conducted themselves with a savagery worthy of Genghis Khan. But it made sense to the Japanese. Assuming their divine mission to rule East Asia and thus bring about a "feudal peace" based on the hegemony of the Emperor, Chinese resistance was a sin against the light, and those who failed to coöperate in the beneficent work of conquest had to be liquidated. Such is the philosophy of absolutism everywhere.

For two years the American government concentrated on diplomatic efforts to "bring Japan to her senses," and restore peace in China. The attempt proved to be futile, but that is not to say that it was foolish. There was always hope that the increasing difficulty and expense of making war on China would discredit the Army and bring back a comparatively liberal government, as had happened in 1920 with respect to the Siberian adventure. Moreover, President Roosevelt, Secretary Hull and everyone else in a responsible position knew that the American people would never go to war merely to save China from conquest or partition. John Citizen was sorry for John Chinaman and mistrusted the Japs, but he felt that if 450,000,000 Chinese could not defend themselves against 73,000,000 Japanese there was nothing he should or could do about it.

[8] *Pearl Harbor Report* p. 2.

President Roosevelt might, to be sure, have declared that a state of war existed and so invoked the Neutrality Acts and prevented the export to Japan of scrap iron, aviation gas and other war munitions with which she was building up forces that were eventually to be used against us. But any such embargo must, according to the Neutrality Acts, be applied impartially; and if so applied would have hurt China, whose war industries and merchant marine were rudimentary, far more than Japan. Mr. Grew, moreover, warned the Administration repeatedly that if and when Japan was denied access to petroleum and steel products in the United States, or to oil, rubber, tin and other strategic materials in the British and Netherlands East Indies, her armed forces would go down there and take them.[9]

No peaceful effort was neglected to stop the Chinese war; but peaceful efforts were insufficient. The United States with eighteen other nations took part in a conference at Brussels in 1937 to consider ways and means to end the war. Japan refused to participate. The Conference issued a declaration reaffirming the principles of the Nine-Power Treaty, to which Japan was a signatory; it proposed a suspension of hostilities and offered mediation to bring about a settlement. Japan replied that the China Incident was her exclusive affair.[10]

Although the Japanese Foreign Office probably did its feeble best to dissuade the Army in China from molesting Americans and their property, these warnings were consistently disregarded. As Mr. Grew wrote in 1941, American churches, hospitals, universities and schools throughout China had been bombed despite flag markings on their roofs; American missionaries and their families had been killed; and there could be no doubt that these attacks were planned, because the Japanese Army had been furnished with maps showing the locations. There were two or three hundred "accidents" of this kind; so many that the Chinese said that the most dangerous spot in an air raid was an American mission. The

[9] *Ten Years in Japan* p. 272.
[10] *Peace and War, U.S. Foreign Policy 1931–1941* (1943) pp. 50–52.

Japanese obviously were trying to drive American missionary, educational, medical and cultural activities out of China permanently.[11]

Even the sinking of a United States ship and the deliberate shooting-down of survivors failed to arouse the American people from their dream of peace.

## 5. *The Sinking of* PANAY, *12 December 1937*

U.S.S. *Panay* was one of five small, shoal-draft river gunboats that had been built about ten years earlier, primarily for patrolling the Yangtze in order to protect American commerce and American nationals during the Chinese civil war.[12] They were used to being fired upon (and seldom hit) by irresponsible guerilla bands of Chinese,[13] but what happened to *Panay* was deliberately planned by responsible Japanese officers.

On 21 November 1937, when Japanese forces were approaching Nanking, Chiang Kai-shek's foreign office notified the American Embassy that it must prepare to evacuate. The Ambassador and most of the personnel left next day in U.S.S. *Luzon;* the rest stuck it out for another week, when they decided to depart in *Panay*. Ambassador Grew so notified the Japanese government on 1 December. On the 11th the gunboat embarked the American officials together with a number of civilians, and started upriver, escorting three Standard Oil barges that also wished to escape. Two British gunboats and a few other British craft followed the same course. For two miles this little flotilla was fired upon repeatedly by a shore battery commanded by Colonel Hashimoto, one of the ringleaders in the assassinations and a prominent *Kodo* man. His object was to provoke the United States into a declaration of war, which would eliminate civilian influence from the Japanese gov-

---

[11] Grew *Report from Tokyo* p. xv; *Ten Years in Japan* p. 231.

[12] *Panay* of 450 tons was 191 ft. long and carried two 3-inch and ten .30-cal. machine guns.

[13] *Annual Report of Navy Department* 1930 p. 99.

ernment and complete the "Showa Restoration." The shooting was so wild that *Panay* and her convoy, making slow speed against the current, pulled out of range without suffering a hit. An advanced Army unit notified naval authorities that Chinese troops were fleeing the capital in ten ships.

At 1100 next morning (12 December 1937) *Panay* and the three tankers anchored near Hoshien, upstream from Nanking. American flags were hoisted on their masts and painted on their awnings and topsides. The day was clear, sunny and still. *Panay's* crew ate their Sunday dinner and secured. No guns were manned or even uncovered. Shortly after 1330, three Japanese Navy bombing planes flew overhead and released eighteen bombs, one of which disabled *Panay's* forward 3-inch gun, wrecked the pilothouse, sick bay and fire room, wounded the captain (Lieutenant Commander J. J. Hughes) and several others. Immediately after, twelve more planes dive-bombed and nine fighters strafed, making several runs over a space of twenty minutes. She fought back with her .30-cal. machine guns. By 1405 all power and propulsion were lost, the main deck was awash and, as Captain Hughes saw that his ship was going down, he ordered her to be abandoned. Japanese planes strafed the boats on their way to shore, and even combed the reeds along the riverbank for survivors. Two of the three oil barges were also bombed and destroyed. The *Panay* survivors, kindly treated by the Chinese, managed to get word through to Admiral Yarnell and were taken on board U.S.S. *Oahu* and H.M.S. *Ladybird* two days later. Two bluejackets and one civilian passenger died of their wounds; eleven officers and men were seriously wounded.[14]

Mr. Grew, who remembered the *Maine*, at first expected his country to declare war. But the promptness and apparent sincerity with which the Japanese government and people apologized and expressed their readiness to make what reparation they could,

[14] Account by Mr. George Atcheson Jr., Second Secretary of the American Embassy, who was a passenger; report of Court of Inquiry held by order of Admiral Yarnell on Board U.S.S. *Augusta* off Shanghai 23 Dec. 1937, printed in *Foreign Relations, Japan 1931–1941* I 532–47.

turned away wrath. The Japanese official inquiry resulted in the face-saving explanation that the attack was all a mistake; ships emblazoned with American flags had been mistaken for Chinese at 600 yards' range; it was just too bad. A United States Naval Court of Inquiry at Shanghai brought out unmistakable evidence that the sinking was deliberate. But the United States government was so anxious to avoid war that it accepted the "mistake" theory, together with an indemnity. When it did so, a sigh of relief passed over the length and breadth of America.[15] In a Gallup poll conducted during the second week of January 1938, 70 per cent of the American voters who were interviewed and had an opinion on the subject favored a policy of complete withdrawal from China — Asiatic Fleet, Marines, missionaries, medical missions, and all.[16]

Apparently no American except Mr. Grew remembered the *Maine*.

[15] Same, p. 559; Grew *Ten Years in Japan* pp. 232–42. The allegations of Hashimoto's responsibility were obtained by Mr. Hallett Abend of the *New York Times* and other American newspaper correspondents, and transmitted to me by Admiral Yarnell in 1947. *Note:* But for an excellent Japanese account of this affair, see Commander Okumiya "How the *Panay* Was Sunk," U. S. Naval Institute Proceedings pp. 587–96 (June 1953). The author, whose plane squadron led the dive-bombing attack, makes out a good case for the fliers who neither recognized *Panay* nor were informed of the gunboat's presence in the vicinity. The strike was made on the basis of army intelligence, not on the orders of Colonel Hashimoto; the Japanese naval aviators thought they were bombing enemy troops escaping up-river in Chinese merchant ships.

[16] The vote was about 3 to 1 for complete withdrawal in eight West Central States; 2 to 1 in New England and the Pacific Coast. *American Institute of Public Opinion*, 16 Jan. 1938.

# CHAPTER II

# The Two Navies

## *1931–1941*

### 1. *The Imperial Japanese Navy*

JAPAN held the small end of the 5–5–3 ratio set by the Washington Naval Conference of 1921 until the London Conference of 1930, when she acquired equality in submarines and had her cruiser ratio raised to 3.5. By the time of the second London Conference in 1935, the militarists who objected to limitation in principle, as contrary to the doctrine of imperial command, were in the saddle. They therefore insisted on equality, or what they called a "common upper limit" of construction, knowing full well that this would be inacceptable as it would make the Japanese Navy overwhelmingly superior in the Pacific. Rejection of this demand by the other powers gave Japan an excuse to withdraw from the negotiations on 15 January 1936. The original Naval Limitation Treaty had only a year more to run, so the principle of imperial command was now restored. Japan promptly took advantage of her freedom.

Comparative tonnage of the United States, British, Japanese and other Navies in 1922, 1936 and 1941 demonstrates the phenomenal rise of the Japanese Navy in relative strength. At the earlier date it had only 547,000 tons of combat shipping as against 1.1 million for the United States and 1.4 million for the Royal Navy. But in nineteen years Japan almost doubled its combat tonnage, while the British Empire and the United States had increased by only 37,000 and 218,000 tons respectively.[1] By 1941 the Japa-

[1] Table in Volume I of this History, p. lxi; see this volume, p. 58, for comparative numbers in 1941.

nese Navy was more powerful than the combined Allied Fleets in the Pacific. And, having received the best of upkeep and lavish modernization, it was in a better state of readiness for combat.

The Commander in Chief of the Navy, as of the Army, was the Emperor; but the Supreme War Council formulated policy in his name.[2] This council, over which the Emperor presided, comprised the War and Navy Ministers, the chiefs of the General Staff and of the Naval Staff, all field marshals of the Army and fleet admirals of the Navy, as well as other high officers appointed by the Emperor. In time of war a smaller council called Imperial Headquarters was created in order to exercise supreme military command. Corresponding to our Joint Chiefs of Staff, it had the same membership as the Supreme War Council except that the field marshals and fleet admirals and some of the special appointees were excluded. While the Supreme War Council determined basic policies and objectives, and allotted men and matériel, Imperial Headquarters drew up strategic plans and coördinated the activities of both armed forces. It was the Supreme War Council that made the final decision to go to war with the United States and Great Britain. The Chief of the Naval General Staff, who corresponded to our Chief of Naval Operations, was a member both of the council and of Imperial Headquarters, on the same footing as the chief of staff (Army). As such he expressed his opinion as to exact requirements of men and matériel in a given operation, and he had the right to call a meeting of the Supreme War Council to have such matters decided.

The Naval General Staff was organized much like our Office of the Chief of Naval Operations, with War Plans and other sections. Naval operation plans originated either in the Naval General Staff or at Combined Fleet Headquarters, but were discussed by both organizations before the final plans were formulated. If a plan required Army participation, the Army General Staff would be consulted before the Chief of the Naval General Staff gave his final

[2] This information is based on the Japanese Historical Research Department's reply to an USSBS query.

approval. Similarly an Army plan for an amphibious operation was discussed with the Naval General Staff before final approval; but the Japanese Navy complained that in these plans for joint operations it was all "give" on their side and "take" by the Army.

The two armed forces met in these high levels of command, but there was little love between them even there, and no contact in lower echelons. In China, Army and Navy learned by practice to conduct amphibious operations successfully when there was little opposition. In general, however, relations between the two armed services were coldly formal rather than cordial.[3]

Although the Japanese are a maritime people, the Imperial Navy was a relatively new force without deep roots in national history and tradition, such as the Army had. Most Japanese naval vessels in the war with Russia were British built and designed; training methods and organization were on British models. But, from the beginning of World War I, Japan built about half of her naval vessels in the four main naval construction yards,[4] and let out the rest to private shipyards. These firms and navy yards turned out excellent ships, but made no attempt to devise mass-production methods of construction, or to provide against the special difficulties of replacing wartime losses when handicapped by material shortages.

While there was nothing remarkable about the design of the earlier Japanese battleships, except that they were generally faster than their opposite numbers in the United States Navy, *Yamato* and *Musashi*, laid down in 1937 and completed in 1941 or early 1942, were the largest and most heavily armored warships in the world, with a standard displacement of 63,700 tons, an overall length of 863 feet and an 18.1-inch main battery.[5]

[3] Ellis M. Zacharias *Secret Missions* (1946) p. 33.
[4] Yokosuka, at the mouth of Tokyo Bay; Kure on the Inland Sea; Sasebo on the western side of Kyushu, and Maizuru on the Japan Sea.
[5] Length and standard displacement have been worked out by the Bureau of Ships from the blueprints of *Yamato* obtained in Japan. Full load displacement was about 75,500 tons. Compare our *Iowa* class, none of which were commissioned before 1943; standard displacement 45,000 (full load 52,000), length 887 ft., 16-inch main battery.

Japan early became interested in ship-based air power. Treaty provisions prohibited her from constructing new carriers during the 1920's, but there were two conversions (*Kaga* and *Akagi*) corresponding to our *Lexington* and *Saratoga*, besides a number of smaller ones and, after 1936, new carriers from the keel up. At the outbreak of war the Japanese Navy had 10 carriers as against our 8, of which 3 were in the Pacific. And one of the disagreeable surprises of the war was the superior performance of Japanese carrier-borne plane types, especially the "Zeke" fighters and the "Kate" torpedo-bombers.

Before 1931 the Japanese Navy had a smaller fleet train than that of the United States because it did not expect to fight far from home, but after hostilities opened with China large numbers of small transports, patrol craft and gunboats were built to give a proper organization for amphibious warfare. Most of the large vessels of the merchant marine were capable of quick conversion to transports, seaplane tenders, oilers, and the like.

In their cruisers the Japanese emphasized speed, which was attained by long hulls, light armor protection and tremendous horsepower — 152,000 in *Tone*. For instance, heavy cruiser *Atago*, completed in 1930, designed for a top speed of 34¼ knots, had turret-face plates less than 2 inches thick, compared with 5 or 6 inches on the turret faces of our *Pensacola* class. They also carried a more powerful armament than the United States heavy cruisers.

The most original Japanese efforts in warship construction are seen in their destroyers. The *Fubuki* class (completed 1928–32) led the world's navies in design and armament. The *Fubukis* inaugurated twin-mounted 5-inch 50-cal. guns in enclosed mounts,[6] shields for torpedo tubes, and high, all-steel bridges.

---

[6] It is stated in certain reference books that these were dual-purpose, because after 1930 their highest elevation was increased to 75° which made them excellent anti-aircraft weapons. In the U.S. Navy the eight destroyers of *Farragut* class, completed in 1934–35, carried four open single-mount dual-purpose 5-inch 38's; the *Porter* class of 1935–36 carried twin-mounted but single-purpose guns. All subsequent U.S. destroyers had a dual-purpose main battery but the enclosed twin-mounts did not appear until the middle of the war.

In submarines the Japanese ran the gamut from 20-ton midgets to submersible transports 400 feet long, displacing 3560 tons, intended for supplying islands that were otherwise cut off. The combat submarines, fleet submarines of over 1000 tons, were called the I-class; the smaller ones, the RO-class. Considerable ingenuity was shown in designing the seaplane-carrying submarines which were able to project plane reconnaissance as far as Puget Sound.

Torpedo development was an outstanding technical achievement of the Japanese Navy. As a result of research between 1928 and 1933, first an oxygen-enriched and then a completely oxygen-fueled torpedo was invented. Postwar studies by our experts found that the Japanese Type 95 Model 2 torpedo (24-inch) had a speed of 49.2 knots with a range of 5760 yards, and carried a 1210-pound explosive charge. And they credited the Japanese claim that their Type 93 Model 1 torpedo could do 49 knots with a range of 22,000 yards.[7] Moreover, the Japanese Navy fired torpedoes freely in practice and at maneuvers, thus improving them constantly; while the United States Navy had to economize when testing warheads and exploders, and never found out what was the matter with its torpedoes until the war had been going on many months.

Elaborate precautions had to be taken in handling oxygen-fueled torpedoes, but the risk was justified by their effectiveness. The writer was pleased to observe, however, that Japanese "fish" were not 100 per cent perfect. The one that hit the square stern of a cruiser in which he was serving, and hung there several minutes without exploding, was the subject of a special vote of thanks — to the ship's chaplain.

Two other classes of matériel in which the Japanese had a definite superiority were pyrotechnics and optics. Their starshells and parachute flares were brighter and more dependable than ours;

[7] U.S. Naval Technical Mission to Japan Report. The best destroyer and submarine torpedoes that we had at the beginning of the war were 21 inches in diameter, capable of 46 knots for 4500 yards. Japanese aërial torpedoes could be launched at altitudes up to 1000 feet and at plane speeds of 250 knots and upwards

their binoculars were so much better, especially for night work, as to be eagerly sought after by American officers and bluejackets. Their naval officers were excellent navigators. High-speed night movements of large fleets in the restricted waters of the Solomon and Philippine Archipelagos were accomplished with few navigational mishaps.

The rapid expansion of the Japanese Navy after 1930 forced the government to resort to conscription.[8] Physical standards were high, training was thorough and realistic, and life in a Japanese man-of-war was Spartan compared with that of the American bluejacket or the British tar.

Peacetime procurement of officer material for the Japanese Navy was similar to that in the United States, and both basic and technical training schools were similarly arranged; Eta Jima in Hiroshima Bay was the Nipponese Annapolis. During the war, as with us, personal qualifications and standards were greatly reduced. But the Navy, being much smaller than the Army, managed to keep the social standards of its officer corps fairly high.

In recent years [stated a Japanese Navy Department pamphlet of 1937] the activities of the Fleet have been as follows. Leaving home ports the latter part of January and carrying out intensive training for the greater part of the year in the stormy Pacific or in out-of-the-way gulfs where human habitations are extremely scarce, with hardly a day of rest other than two or three days at anchor for recreation after . . . sometimes more than a month of operating. . . . There are no Saturdays or Sundays, especially when under way, where one drill follows another — literally a period of no rest and no sleep. This is because if we are not under way we cannot carry out actual battle training, and so with a tenacious and tireless spirit we are striving to reach a superhuman degree of skill and perfect fighting efficiency.[9]

[8] A comparative table of 1932 shows that Japan had on board 6 battleships and 4 battle cruisers, only 1000 fewer men than the U.S.N. had in 15 battleships. Her heavy cruisers carried an average of 692 men each, as against 517 for that type in the U.S.N. Each Navy then had 72 destroyers in full commission, but the Japanese destroyers carried 9547 men, the U.S. DDs 7773. U.S. Naval Attaché Tokyo, Report No. 183, 8 Dec. 1932.

[9] Translation by Lt. J. Finnegan and Lt. M. R. Stone, attached to Report No. 187 of U.S. Naval Attaché, Tokyo, 6 July 1937.

This statement is no exaggeration. The Japanese Navy conducted its battle training by preference in remote waters where it would not be observed, and where the men would be hardened by exposure to the elements. That this rigorous and realistic training under combat conditions paid off, was all too evident in the first months of the war. If men were killed or lost in these exercises, the press was not allowed to mention it. In contrast, the United States Navy normally carried out peacetime maneuvers and exercises in southern waters or where fine weather prevailed. Extra precautions had to be taken to avoid casualties and consequent unwelcome publicity.

By April of each year this period of tough training was completed and the Combined Fleet relaxed for two months, making a short cruise along the coast of China. The second half of the year was again devoted to divisional, type and fleet training, and the year was concluded with a Fleet Problem, similar to ours.[10]

Japanese fleet organization was frequently changed, but certain general principles were constant. Everything except Naval Forces in China (which correspond to our Asiatic Fleet) was included in the Combined Fleet; and this was divided into a Battle Force and a Scouting Force stationed in home waters, a Blockade and Transport Force in readiness for overseas operations, a Submarine Force, a Carrier Fleet, and two small fleets allotted to specific areas. Fourth Fleet, based at Truk, was charged with the defense of the Mandates. On 24 July 1939 the Navy announced to the press somewhat truculently that a new Northern or Fifth Fleet, just organized, watched over the Kuriles. At all times Commander in Chief Combined Fleet shifted ships from one fleet to another in accordance with operational necessity. The Combined Fleet also acted as the first line of defense or offense, behind which the smaller fleets could operate with relative impunity.

The following table is a reasonably approximate composition of the Combined Fleet shortly before Japan went to war with the United States.

[10] Report of U.S. Naval Attaché, Tokyo, 13 May 1940.

# COMBINED FLEET, JULY 1941 [11]

Admiral Isoroku Yamamoto, Commander in Chief, in *Nagato*

## FIRST FLEET OR BATTLE FORCE

Admiral Yamamoto, based at Hiroshima Bay

| | |
|---|---|
| BB | NAGATO, MUTSU, YAMASHIRO (Batdiv 1) |
| BB | FUSO, ISE, HYUGA (Batdiv 2) |
| BB | HIEI, KONGO, KIRISHIMA, HARUNA (Batdiv 3) |
| CA | KAKO, FURUTAKA, AOBA, KINUGASA (Crudiv 6) |
| CL | ABUKUMA with 12 destroyers of FUBUKI and SHIGURE classes (Desron 1) [12] |
| CL | SENDAI with 15 destroyers of FUBUKI class (Desron 3) |

## SECOND FLEET OR SCOUTING FORCE

Vice Admiral Kondo, based at Hainan

| | |
|---|---|
| CA | TAKAO, ATAGO, CHOKAI, MAYA (Crudiv 4) |
| CA | MYOKO, NACHI, HAGURO (Crudiv 5) |
| CA | KUMANO, MOGAMI, MIKUMA, SUZUYA (Crudiv 7) |
| CL | JINTSU and 16 destroyers of ASASHIO and KAGERO classes (Desron 2) |
| CL | NAKA and 12 destroyers of SHIGURE and ASASHIO classes (Desron 4) |

## THIRD FLEET OR BLOCKADE AND TRANSPORT FORCE

Vice Admiral I. Takahashi, based at Formosa

| | |
|---|---|
| CL | NATORI and 12 destroyers of MUTSUKI and KAMIKAZE classes (Desron 5) 6 submarines and tender, and 46 transports, 6 minelayers, 12 minesweepers, 6 gunboats, 12 patrol craft [13] |

## FOURTH FLEET

Vice Admiral S. Inouye, based at Truk

| | |
|---|---|
| CL | TENRYU, TATSUTA, KASHIMA |
| CL | YUBARI and 8 destroyers of KAMIKAZE and MUTSUKI classes (Desron 6) 16 submarines and 2 tenders, 41 transports, 7 minecraft, 15 gunboats, 3 patrol craft, 1 survey ship |

## FIFTH FLEET

Vice Admiral B. Hosogaya, based at Maizuru or Ominato

| | |
|---|---|
| CL | TAMA, KISO and an unknown number of destroyers |

## SIXTH FLEET OR SUBMARINE FLEET

Vice Admiral M. Shimizu, based at Kwajalein

40 submarines of I-class with suitable tenders

---

[11] Based on CNO Intelligence Report, Ser. 54–41.

[12] The Japanese Navy almost invariably used an old or small light cruiser as flagship of a destroyer squadron.

[13] Japanese PCs were usually converted destroyers similar to our APDs, and often used as such — that is, as small, fast transports.

## CARRIER FLEET

Vice Admiral C. Nagumo, based at Kure and carrying about 500 planes

| | | | | |
|---|---|---|---|---|
| CV | KAGA, AKAGI (Cardiv 1) | | CVL | RYUJO, HOSHO (Cardiv 3) |
| CV | SORYU, HIRYU (Cardiv 2) | | CVL | ZUIHO, TAIYO (Cardiv 4) |
| CV | ZUIKAKU, SHOKAKU (Cardiv 5) | | | |

organized 1 Sept. 1941

16 destroyers of latest types (Desdivs 7, 17, 23)

## COMBINED AIR FORCE [14]

Based at Kanoya Naval Air Station

11th Air Fleet, based at Formosa: 150 VF, 120 VB, 40 miscellaneous types
21 and 22 Air Flotillas: based in Indochina, 200 VF, 180 VB and VT
In Japan and training: 100 VF, 70 VB and VT, 450 trainers, 60 miscellaneous
Not allocated: 70 VF, 50 VB and VT, 60 trainers, 40 miscellaneous
11th and 12th Seaplane Tender Divisions: 8 tenders, 70 seaplanes
Combined Fleet: 80 seaplanes

To sum up: in every important branch, including the air arm, and in all major ship types; in gunnery, navigation, ship handling, tactics and in fighting spirit, the Japanese Navy was a worthy antagonist. Never, since 1814, had the United States Navy been up against so tough, well-trained or powerful a fighting force. But no Navy can be better than its high command, or endure without a firm industrial base. Stupidity characterized the strategy by which the Japanese Navy was directed, and the supporting industrial base was fatally weak.

## 2. *The United States Navy in the Pacific*

Since 1922 the policy of the United States Navy had been to keep the major part of the United States Fleet in the Pacific Ocean. Undoubtedly the main reason was the unspoken conviction of every senior naval officer that the next war would be with Japan, the only maritime power likely on any near or remote contingency to challenge the United States.

On 1 April 1931, following the scrapping and economy wave of

---

[14] Shore-based land and seaplanes, with great mobility of organization. Units were detached to work with other forces, and returned to the Combined Air Force pool when mission fulfilled. Various air squadrons and groups frequently split into smaller units and scattered over wide areas. The strength here given is of 1 Dec. 1941 (USSBS 414, Navy No. 86, plate 80–81 to Annex A).

President Hoover's administration, the United States Navy comprised 15 battleships, 3 aircraft carriers (*Langley, Saratoga* and *Lexington*), 18 cruisers, 78 destroyers, 55 submarines and 115 smaller vessels such as tugs, tenders, gunboats and subchasers.[15] These were divided unequally between two Fleets: the United States Fleet and the Asiatic Fleet.

The United States Fleet comprised (1) the Battle Force, including the newer battleships, the carriers, one light cruiser division and three or four destroyer squadrons, in the Pacific; (2) the Scouting Force, comprising the rest of the cruisers and destroyers, besides a Training Squadron consisting of three old battleships and eight destroyers, operating in the Atlantic and Caribbean; (3) the Submarine Force, divided between the two oceans; and (4) the Base Force, or Train (auxiliaries), similarly divided.

The much smaller Asiatic Fleet comprised the South China Patrol (19 destroyers based at Chefoo), the Yangtze River Gunboat Flotilla (of which *Panay* was one) based at Shanghai, 12 submarines and a few auxiliaries. This Fleet had existed under one title or another for over a century,[16] and was still serving its original purpose of protecting American commerce against pirates, and a good deal else. A civil war had been going on in China for several years, and each principal European power as well as Japan and the United States provided naval protection for its own commerce and nationals. Yangtze gunboats convoyed American merchantmen up and down that great artery, temporary Naval Armed Guards were provided for unescorted merchant vessels, destroyers landed bluejackets to protect American property and persons in seaports disturbed by civil commotion. Commander in Chief Asiatic Fleet, who received the temporary rank of four-star admiral in order to be on the same level with the commanders of the British, French and Japanese Asiatic Fleets, also controlled the 4th Regiment United

---

[15] "Annual Report of Chief of Naval Operations for Fiscal Year 1931," printed in *Annual Reports of Navy Department* for that fiscal year. This, and the 1932 one, were the last CNO reports to be printed.

[16] East India Squadron, 1835; Asiatic Squadron, 1866; Asiatic Fleet, since 1902 (except 1907–10).

States Marines stationed in the International Settlement at Shanghai, and a Marine brigade stationed at Peiping as legation guard.

The Asiatic Fleet, or part of it, usually spent a few months of every year in Philippine waters and paid courtesy visits to Japan, Singapore, Hanoi, Hong Kong, Batavia and other Far Eastern ports. Service in this fleet had its compensations, for it meant "seeing the world" for bluejackets, good career background for officers, foreign travel and exotic experiences for Naval families ashore.

In the spring of every year there took place a fleet concentration and a tactical maneuver known as a Fleet Problem, sometimes in the Caribbean but more often in the eastern Pacific. On such occasions the Scouting Force came through the Panama Canal to join the Battle Force, or vice versa.[17] It was perhaps to implement Mr. Stimson's nonrecognition policy that the concentration of 1932 was extended for two weeks, to 28 May, after the normal seven weeks had elapsed; that the Scouting Force remained in the Pacific after the exercises were over; and that all fleet aircraft not attached to Pearl Harbor or the Canal spent the summer at San Diego undergoing tactical training in connection with the carriers *Langley*, *Saratoga* and *Lexington*.

At all times the Navy, conscious that it was an instrument of national policy and the servant of the American people, was very careful to avoid giving provocation to Japan. All fleet exercises and maneuvers were held on the eastern side of the International Date Line, although Wake Island, Guam, the Philippines and the western Aleutians lay west of that line and Midway Island not far east of it. The usual amenities between navies of friendly nations were observed. Almost every year one or more naval vessels paid courtesy visits to Yokohama or Nagasaki; Japanese warships were regularly and vociferously welcomed by the Nipponese population at Honolulu and San Francisco, although with somewhat less enthusiasm

[17] In 1931 the Fleet Concentration and Fleet Problems were held in Panama Bay; in 1932 in the Pacific, in 1933 between Hawaii and the West Coast; in 1934 on both sides of the Canal; in 1935 between Puget Sound, Hawaii and the Aleutians; in 1936 in the Panama-Pacific area; in 1937 in the Hawaiian area; in 1938 in the Hawaii-Pacific area; in 1939 in the Caribbean, and in 1940 in the Hawaii and Northeastern Pacific areas.

by the local authorities. American naval officers got on fairly well with Japanese naval officers, who, as a former admiral on the Asiatic station expressed it, were "mostly gentlemen, a very different breed from the narrow-minded boors who commanded the Japanese Army." A large proportion of them spoke English.

The United States Navy pursued a policy of detailing a few officers to Japan each year to study the Japanese language and people, but in 20 years this program netted only 36 language officers, a number inadequate for the task. This lack was filled by the Navy Language School, established in October 1941, which in a surprisingly short time qualified hundreds of men and women to work in the Japanese language.

At the time of the Manchuria Incident, the Navy was still struggling to preserve its standards in the face of limitation treaties, inadequate appropriations for personnel, upkeep and gunnery, and the indifference of presidential administrations and public.[18] A revival began in 1933 when President Franklin D. Roosevelt, shortly after his first inauguration, proposed that the Navy be built up to treaty strength. In June he allotted depression emergency funds to revive the defunct shipbuilding industry and start a number of ships. Next year Congress, by passing the Trammell-Vinson Act, provided for the replacement of obsolete vessels by new construction and a gradual increase of ships and planes to full treaty strength. Even this modest goal could be attained only if Congress made the necessary annual appropriations. That it did, without authorizing a corresponding increase in personnel. In 1935 the Navy, with only 6121 line and 1942 staff officers and 82,500 enlisted men, had to operate ships with about 81 per cent of their full complement.[19] And although the Naval Limitation Treaties expired in 1936, as desired by Japan, the United States continued to live up to them.

Under an appropriation of 17 May 1938 several new battleships and carriers were laid down. In June, Great Britain, France and the

---

[18] See Commodore Knox's Introduction to Volume I this work.
[19] *Annual Report of Secretary of the Navy for Fiscal Year 1935.*

United States signed a protocol raising the limit of battleship tonnage from 35,000 to 45,000 tons, thus making "gangway" for the *Iowa* class; but Japan in great secrecy had already laid down the 63,700-ton *Musashi* and *Yamato*. In 1939 *Yorktown* and *Enterprise* joined the United States Fleet. *Wasp* was under construction, and *Hornet's* keel was laid; battleships *North Carolina* and *Washington* were being built and four more battleships had been started. Thirty-one destroyers and six submarines were under construction. The United States Navy was decidedly looking up, although "treaty strength" as authorized in 1934 would not be attained until 1944.[20]

In August 1939, when Admiral Leahy was relieved as Chief of Naval Operations by Admiral Stark, he could look back with some satisfaction at the increase of naval strength during the two and a half years of his incumbency. But, as he wrote in his last report, "The Navy must be sufficiently strong in every essential element, and it must be adequately trained," in order to take the offensive in the event of war and "defeat the enemy Fleet wherever it can be brought to action." In several respects the Navy was not well-rounded. Authorized enlisted personnel, already 100,000 in mid-1937, was increased only by 10,000 during the next two years. Very few fast, modern auxiliaries had been finished, although five seaplane, submarine and destroyer tenders had been started and two more fast oilers of the successful *Cimarron* class were expected shortly.[21] But the chief worry that Leahy bequeathed to his successor was the subject of bases.

\* \* \*

[20] How gradual was the build-up may be seen by the list of new ships commissioned in each fiscal year (ending 30 June of year named). *1934:* cruisers *New Orleans, Minneapolis, Astoria, San Francisco;* destroyer *Farragut. 1935:* cruiser *Tuscaloosa,* 6 destroyers of *Farragut* class, 1 floating dry dock. *1936:* cruiser *Quincy,* 2 destroyers of *Porter* class, 4 submarines. *1937:* cruiser *Vincennes,* 22 destroyers of *Mahan* and *Porter* classes, one each of *Fanning* and *Craven* classes, gunboats *Erie* and *Charleston,* 6 submarines, 1 cargo ship, 3 fleet tugs. *1938:* carriers *Enterprise* and *Yorktown;* cruisers *Philadelphia, Brooklyn, Savannah, Nashville, Honolulu;* 12 destroyers (8 of *Craven* class, 2 of *Somers,* 1 *Fanning,* 1 *McCall*); 6 submarines. *1939:* cruisers *Wichita, Boise, Phoenix, St. Louis;* 8 destroyers (4 of *McCall* class, 3 of *Somers,* 1 of *Sims*); 4 submarines, 2 minesweepers, 1 cargo ship, 1 fleet tug.
[21] The Navy on 1 July 1939 had only two transports, three cargo ships, three oilers and one ammunition ship in commission.

It was probably a good thing in the long run that the United States Navy was so ill-provided with bases in the Pacific, in comparison with the Japanese and British Navies. Want of them made American ships by necessity more self-sufficient. Nevertheless, failure to develop adequately what bases we had meant a rapid withdrawal of American sea power from the western Pacific when the Japanese struck.

Congress in May 1938 directed the Secretary of the Navy to appoint a board of five or more naval officers to investigate and report on the need of additional submarine, destroyer, minecraft and naval air bases in the United States and its possessions. This board, which took its name from the chairman, Rear Admiral A. J. Hepburn, made a quick but thorough survey and reported on 1 December of the same year. The Hepburn Report was the point of departure for the extensive base-development plan on both oceans that began in 1939 and was greatly accelerated by war.

The Navy had outgrown all its shore clothes, but the need for additional land facilities for aircraft was most urgent. The Hepburn Board recommended the establishment of naval air and submarine bases as follows:

In Alaska: patrol-plane and submarine bases at Kodiak and Dutch Harbor; patrol-plane base at Sitka. At that time the only military or semi-military establishments in the Aleutians were a naval radio station and a small Coast Guard base at Dutch Harbor.

On Oahu: the Ford Island Naval Air Base at Pearl Harbor to be enlarged,[22] and an additional base for patrol-plane operations to be established at Kaneohe, since Pearl Harbor was inadequate for landing and takeoff.

Midway and Wake Islands to be developed as patrol-plane and submarine bases, and the lagoons dredged to accommodate large tenders and tankers.

Guam, "at present practically defenseless against determined at-

---

[22] Formerly shared with the Army, this base had been allocated wholly to the Navy in 1935, but as the Army had not yet completed Hickam Field, its planes and personnel were still there in 1939.

tack by any first-class power based in the western Pacific," could, the Board predicted, by adequate air, anti-air, coast defense and submarine protection "be made secure against anything short of a major effort," and with a moderately strong garrison could hold out long enough "for adequate support to arrive." [23]

These observations about Guam can be best understood in the light of the then existing plan for United States armed forces in case war broke out in the Pacific. American Army and Navy planners had long agreed that the Philippines were indefensible against a long-sustained Japanese attack, but the United States forces must endeavor to hold Manila Bay and its approaches while the Fleet fought its way thither by or through the Japanese-mandated islands, an operation that was expected to take several months at least. Obviously a strong air and submarine base in Guam, neutralizing the near-by Saipan, would be of tremendous assistance in this defensive phase of the war; it might even prevent a Japanese southward thrust through the Philippine Sea.

In other words, a strong Guam in American hands would be a serious breach in the great L-shaped system of Pacific islands — Bonins, Marianas, Carolines and Marshalls — then controlled by Japan. The Japanese Navy might rule the waves up to long. 180° or even eastward; but Guam could still be reinforced by submarines and by air, using the steppingstones of Midway and Wake. Moreover, predicted the Hepburn Board, "Guam is adapted naturally to development as a major advanced fleet base." Such development, urged both by Army and Navy in 1919, was forbidden by the Washington Treaty of 1922; that treaty had been denounced by Japan, and was no longer binding.

Congress eventually met the Hepburn Board's recommendations as to Alaska, Oahu, Midway and Wake; but the development of Wake lost much of its purpose since nothing was done about Guam. A bill carrying a modest appropriation of $5,000,000, for dredging

[23] Hepburn Report 27 Dec. 1938, printed as 76th Cong. 1st Sess., House Doc. No. 65. The report also recommended that Johnston, Palmyra, Canton and Rose Islands (the last in Samoa) be developed to permit tender-based patrol-plane operation, and contained other recommendations for bases in the Atlantic.

Apra Harbor for a submarine base and providing a few additional facilities, was defeated by the House of Representatives on 23 February 1939 by a vote of 205 to 168.[24] Several of the Congressmen who voted against it gave as their reason the fear of provoking or appearing to challenge Japan. Undoubtedly they expressed American public opinion correctly. The United States, to avoid stirring up Japan, refrained from protecting her own possessions, while the Japanese were fortifying the former Mandates and practicing total war on the Chinese.

If Admiral Hepburn's suggestions had been carried out promptly and the inherent strategic capabilities of Guam developed the whole pattern of the war might have been altered.

[24] *Congressional Record*, 76th Cong. 1st Sess., LXXXIV Part 2 p. 1842.

CHAPTER III

# Greater East Asia

## *1938–1940*

### 1. *Moral Embargo and Southward Swing*

THE RAPE of Nanking — which followed the sinking of *Panay* — shocked the civilized world, but nothing was done about it. Almost every week, news reached Mr. Grew of fresh outrages against American persons and property in China; the Japanese government either denied that they were done by Japanese soldiers, or expressed its sorrow and assurance of no repetition.

Six months after the *Panay* sinking, on 11 June 1938, Secretary Hull made a strong public statement reproving the air bombing of innocent civilians which was constantly practiced by the Japanese Army in China. And on 1 July he announced the so-called "moral embargo" on the export of planes to Japan. The Department of State declared that the United States government was "strongly opposed to the sale of airplanes or of aeronautical equipment" to any nation then making a practice of bombing civilians from the air.[1]

Japanese ingenuity was able to cope with aëronautics, but not with oil or iron ore. In petroleum products particularly, Japan was exceedingly vulnerable; almost her entire supply had to be imported. Why, then, did the United States government allow exports of oil and scrap to continue? For several reasons. On the legal level, any such restriction would have violated the existing commercial treaty with Japan. On the level of broad policy, any drastic action would have united Japan behind the militarists, and

[1] *Foreign Relations, Japan 1931–1941* II 201.

destroyed our hope that the unexpectedly stout resistance of Chiang Kai-shek would discredit them and bring liberal elements back into power. Mr. Grew warned his government in 1938 that if Japan were deprived of oil she would move south and take what she wanted in Borneo and Sumatra. Consequently, neither an oil embargo nor any other economic sanction should be imposed until and unless the United States was "prepared to see them through to their logical conclusion, and that might mean war." [2]

The United States government was faced with the dilemma of conniving at Japanese aggression by allowing oil exports to continue, or risking war if it cut them off. The Japanese government was faced with a similar dilemma: it must have oil for conquest, or conquer more territory to obtain oil. For the time being, it subsidized the synthetic oil industry, dug hundreds of wells (very few of which struck oil), built thousands of storage tanks, and imported huge quantities from the United States as a reserve. In 1940 the combined imports of crude and refined oils totaled 37,160,000 barrels. [3]

Prince Konoye, the Japanese Prime Minister, announced on 22 December 1938 the basis on which Japan expected to make peace with China. He began with the unpromising statement that Japan would carry on military operations for the "complete extermination" of the Kuomintang government, and at the same time establish a "New Order in East Asia." China must accept the "independence" of Manchukuo, submit to Japanese military occupation, and permit the establishment of an economic protectorate. [4]

Within a week, Chiang Kai-shek refused to make peace on this basis of dismembering his country and dissolving his government. Prince Konoye was then replaced by the zealous Hiranuma, who formed a cabinet with two extremist generals in key positions. Hachiro Arita, the Foreign Minister, initiated negotiations with the European Axis with a view to a definite military and political alliance in case either side came into conflict with Russia. That country

[2] Diary for 5 Dec. 1938 in *Ten Years in Japan* p. 272.
[3] *Oil in Japan's War* (Oil and Chemical Division USSBS) Feb. 1946.
[4] *Foreign Relations, Japan* I 482–83.

Photo by one of the survivors

U.S.S. Panay Settling in the Yangtze

was causing the Japanese militarists considerable apprehension, because the Soviets had a military force ready and available for action. Several big border clashes had occurred, and in these the Japanese Army was badly beaten by the Russians, with considerable loss. Although the *Kodo* men in the Army were willing to provoke a war with the United States, of whose capacity to project power across the Pacific they were scornfully contemptuous, they feared Russia and wanted assurance of Axis support before starting the "New Order in East Asia." Their chance would come soon.

In late February 1939, a few days after the Guam appropriation had been defeated in Congress, Hiroshi Saito, former Japanese Ambassador at Washington, died in the United States. As a goodwill gesture the Department of State conceived the bright idea of sending Saito's ashes home on a warship. Ironically enough, the ship chosen for this mission was the heavy cruiser *Astoria*, Captain Richmond Kelly Turner, which the Japanese Navy subsequently sank in the Battle of Savo Island; and her commanding officer became one of the most tough and capable enemies of Japan.

U.S.S. *Astoria* embarked the honorable ashes at Annapolis in mid-March, and arrived at Yokohama 17 April 1939. The remains were duly interred with impressive ceremonies, accompanied by an official good-will demonstration which Mr. Grew with some difficulty kept within reasonable bounds; for a group of prominent Japanese were endeavoring to interpret this American gesture as an official condonation of everything that Japan had done in China.[5] War Minister Itagaki, who almost never visited an embassy, attended the dinner that the Grews gave for Captain Turner, and the Tokyo press and public boiled over with appropriate emotion. But neither ambassadorial terrapin nor *Astoria's* mission had the slightest effect on the Japanese military. During the next two months there were even more outrages than usual against American persons and property in China.

While *Astoria* was at sea on her pious mission, Japanese troops occupied the strategic island of Hainan in the South China Sea.

[5] Letter of Mr. Grew to the writer.

For Hainan contained a valuable deposit of iron ore and it was a good jumping-off place for an attack on Malaya. Next, Japan announced that she had annexed the small Spratly or Sinnan Islands off Indochina, hitherto claimed by France. Both annexations suggested that the master militarists of Japan were contemplating a change of direction in their program of expansion. Foreign Minister Arita denied that any "South Sea Advance" was contemplated; but it had already started.[6]

These latest annexations probably had something to do with a quick transfer of United States naval strength from the Atlantic to the Pacific. In 1939, for the first time since the "Manchuria Incident," the annual Fleet Problem and concentration took place in the Caribbean. These maneuvers were to be followed by a visit to New York for the opening of the World's Fair; but, greatly to the disappointment of all hands, festivities were canceled and the Fleet departed for the West Coast, speeding through the Canal on 20 April en route to Hawaii.

It cannot be said that the return of the Fleet had any more effect on the Japanese military than the return of Saito's ashes. The important power fact in the Pacific that year was a military stalemate in China. The last important conquests of the Japanese Army were Canton and Hankow in October 1938. Chiang Kai-shek's government had retired to Chungking on the upper Yangtze and was putting up a heroic and effective resistance. This led to a certain loss of face by the Japanese Army, and an appreciable rise in the influence of the Japanese Navy.

Although Yamamoto and other admirals were in sympathy with the Showa Restoration movement, most high naval officers appear to have been opposed to the China Affair. They believed, naturally, that Japan's destiny lay on the sea and that she should get possession of the Netherlands East Indies, with their wealth in strategic resources and people, before attempting to bring so vast a country as China under control. But they had to admit that a southward expansion could only be carried out at the risk of war

[6] *Foreign Relations, Japan 1931–1941* II 4–5, 277–80. Hainan occupied 3 Feb. 1939; Spratlys annexed 30 Mar. 1939.

with Great Britain and probably with the United States. Accordingly China was picked on as the first victim. Now that China was proving recalcitrant to conquest, why not swing south and take the risk? Everyone knew that England and America were reluctant to fight.

The first move in that direction came in 1938 when the Japanese Army in a series of amphibious operations occupied the shores of the South China Sea, seeking to shut China off from the ocean. Hainan put the cork in that bottle. In May and June 1939 the Japanese Army was active in the Shanghai International Settlement, seeking to make life there intolerable for the American and European residents; and in June it began blockading the British and French concessions at Tientsin.

By the time that American public opinion had reached the point of wishing to do something substantial to check Japan and help China,[7] the Japanese air force stepped up its attacks on Chungking, Chiang Kai-shek's capital. In the air raids of 6–7 July 1939, bombs fell on an American church near the Embassy and close aboard the river gunboat U.S.S. *Tutuila*. President Roosevelt believed that the time had come to impose economic sanctions. To clear the way, it was necessary to denounce the 1911 Treaty of Commerce with Japan. That was done on 26 July 1939, which meant that after 26 January 1940 the President and Congress could dictate the terms upon which Japan might continue to trade with the United States.

American public opinion approved this step with hardly an important dissent; even Senator Borah agreed.[8] The Japanese govern-

[7] A Gallup poll in early June 1939 showed 74 per cent of voters interviewed in sympathy with China, 66 per cent in favor of an American boycott of Japanese goods, 72 per cent in favor of an embargo on arms and munitions to Japan. – *Public Opinion News Service* 16 June 1939. A poll in mid-July (same periodical 23 July) on question "How far do you think the United States should go to protect American interests in China?" resulted in 6 per cent for fighting Japan, 18 per cent for protesting, 51 per cent for stopping export of war materials to Japan and 25 per cent for doing nothing.

[8] A Gallup poll of about 25 Aug. (*P.O. News Service* 30 Aug.) showed 81 per cent approving the denunciation of the treaty, and 82 per cent in favor of an embargo on "war materials" when the treaty expired. This vote has been cited as proof that the people were ahead of their government by at least a year; but of course the voters were not told, and could not be told, that an almost certain consequence of the embargo that they wanted was war with Japan.

ment, accustomed to merely verbal protests, was taken by surprise, but countered with the sarcastic assumption that the American government merely planned to negotiate a new commercial treaty which would "frankly recognize" the "new situation . . . now fast developing in East Asia." [9]


## 2. *Effects of the European War in the Pacific* [10]

Before the treaty expired in January 1940, Europe had gone to war.

In April 1939, six months before war broke out, Hitler went fishing for an unconditional military pact between Germany, Italy and Japan, which would bring all three into any war that one of them started. General Itagaki, War Minister in the Hiranuma cabinet, and the *Kodo* men in general, were all for it; but the Imperial court, Big Business, Navy Minister Yonai and Admiral Yamamoto, were against it. They foresaw that any such pact might involve Japan in war with Great Britain and the United States, and they succeeded in stalling the negotiations. Hitler and Ribbentrop, exceedingly annoyed at this outcome, threatened to find another ally; and Hitler's nonaggression pact of August 1939 with Stalin was, in part, his "answer" to Japan.

This desertion of the Anti-Comintern Treaty by Hitler, without even consulting his Far Eastern partner, was naturally resented in Japan. It exposed her to a greater concentration of troops on the Manchurian frontier, possibly to a Russian invasion of Mongolia. And there were other factors as well that produced a marked swing of Japanese opinion in favor of the Western Powers during the first

[9] *Foreign Relations, Japan 1931–1941* II 190.
[10] "The Japanese Policy 1936–45 under the Aspect of German-Japanese Relations," a memoir written for General MacArthur's Command shortly after V–J day by Counselor Boltze and First Secretary Marchtaler of the German Embassy, Tokyo, with "Remarks" and "Comments" on same by H. G. Stahmer and Eugen Ott, former German Ambassadors to Japan, and "Personal Statement" by Ott. (Translations prepared under direction of Maj. Thomas Sheehan Jr. USA at Tokyo.) These documents give a valuable inside view of German-Japanese diplomacy.

six months of the European war. A German military mission had trained the Chinese Army in the tactics that had thwarted the Japanese, and the German Foreign Office had frequently urged Japan to liquidate the China Affair, having more important work for her in view. Hitler had given broad hints that Germany expected to enjoy an "Open Door" to China in the future, and his shrill shrieks about lost colonies and the Treaty of Versailles gave some reason to fear that if he won the European war he would demand restitution of the Carolines, Marshalls and Marianas.

On the other hand, strong forces pulled Japan into Hitler's orbit. There was an ideological affinity between Nazi doctrine and Japanese polity. The Army extremists were strong for a German alliance, thinking it would frighten America and Britain into keeping hands off East Asia, where Great Britain and France had valuable possessions that they coveted. So, on the whole, a German victory held out greater promise to the Japanese war lords. Any break-up of the British and French Empires would mean rich pickings for Japan; and by the time the Germans were in a position to challenge, Japan would have absorbed these areas and be in a good position to resist. Certain Japanese political leaders, notably Matsuoka, favored concluding a full-fledged alliance with the Axis in order to divide the expected loot in advance. Others advised playing a lone hand in order to avoid a break with the United States and Great Britain. All agreed to take advantage of any weakness on the Allied side.

There was no doubt as to where the interests of the United States lay. It was clearly our duty to prevent any formal alliance between Japan and the Axis, which would give her the same opportunity to expand southward, at the expense of the Allies, as her alliance with the same Allies had afforded in 1915, at the expense of Germany. Mr. Grew was instructed accordingly, and in sundry confidential talks with Japanese statesmen urged them to maintain a strict neutrality. The Japanese generally countered with the hint that, if the democracies wanted neutrality, they must give Japan a free hand in China and abandon Chiang Kai-shek to his fate.

After all, the entire coast of China by 1940 was held by the Japanese Army, so that aid could no longer be sent to China except over the Burma Road. Why not be realistic and accept the inevitable? Why not recognize Japan's "Monroe Doctrine of the Pacific"? In the meantime, outrages against American persons and property in China continued without abatement, and every section of China seized by Japanese armies was at once closed to the trade of other powers.

The Yonai Cabinet, formed early in 1940, wished to conciliate the United States, and German diplomats frequently warned Japanese officials against challenging a country of such vast military and economic potentiality. But, as the same diplomats remarked in 1945, "all efforts made by the successive Japanese governments to improve relations with America and Britain were doomed to failure because Japan, far from restoring the sovereignty and integrity of China, only asked for recognition of the situation she had established in China, in open violation of existing treaties."

On 6 January 1940 Admiral James O. Richardson relieved Admiral Claude C. Bloch as Commander in Chief United States Fleet, and hoisted his flag in U.S.S. *Pennsylvania* at San Pedro Harbor. He was somewhat disturbed to find that a considerable detachment of the Fleet, consisting of cruisers and destroyers, had already been sent to Hawaii. American newspapers of 31 March 1940 announced that the fleet maneuvers that spring would take place in the Hawaiian area.

The reception of this announcement in Japan was significant. In 1935, when maneuvers had been held much farther to the westward, the Japanese government and press had kept silent, letting the American pacifists work for them. But in 1940 the Tokyo papers reacted in a resentful and defiant manner, declaring that the maneuvers were planned as a demonstration against Japan. And on 4 April the Navy Ministry spokesman announced to the press that if the maneuvers crossed the International Date Line they would be regarded as a "brandishing of the big sword" near Japanese territory.

On 2 April the rest of the United States Fleet departed from West Coast ports for the Hawaiian Islands, where it conducted Fleet Problem XXI, well to the eastward of the 180th meridian. Although the Fleet was scheduled to return to its West Coast bases on 9 May, the Chief of Naval Operations (Admiral Stark) on the 7th ordered it to remain two weeks longer, and shortly after informed Admiral Richardson that he would be based at Pearl Harbor until further notice.

In reply to Richardson's question from Pearl Harbor, "Why are we here?" Stark wrote on 27 May 1940, "You are there because of the deterrent effect which it is thought your presence may have on the Japs going into the East Indies." [11]

The timing of this fleet movement was determined by events in Europe, and the repercussion in Japan. On 15 April 1940 Foreign Minister Arita, doubtless tipped off by the Germans on impending events, hinted that his country's policy had broadened out from a mere liquidating of the China Incident to a "Greater East Asia Co-Prosperity Sphere." What he grandiloquently termed "relations of economic interdependence and of co-existence and co-prosperity" between Japan and the Netherlands East Indies must be maintained, whatever happened to their home country. Mr. Hull took prompt notice of this in a press release declaring that any armed intervention in the Dutch colonies "would be prejudicial to the cause of stability, peace and security" in the entire Pacific. The Japanese government decided to commit no overt act, but sent economic missions to Batavia which became increasingly exigent and arrogant.

On 10 May German armies crashed into the Low Countries, and on the 14th swung on France. One month later they were in Paris, and within ten days Pétain had surrendered. No one knew what advantage Japan would take of this situation, but everyone expected the worst. General Marshall on 7 June 1940 warned Hawaii to be

[11] Interrogation of Admiral Richardson in *Pearl Harbor Attack* Part 1 pp. 253–341; documents, including his correspondence with Admiral Stark, in Part 14 pp. 923–1000.

on the alert "against an overseas raid from the west by a hostile Nation." Admiral Richardson instituted a plane patrol to westward of Oahu that covered considerably more ocean than did the one subsequently set up by Admiral Kimmel.[12] Great Britain, momentarily expecting a German invasion, consented under pressure from Japan to close the Burma Road for three months on 18 July.[13] That was one of Chiang Kai-shek's two remaining connections with the outside world, the other being Hanoi, the port of French Indochina.

The fall of Holland and of France opened up new opportunities for easy Japanese conquest, enticing and fatal as those which led Napoleon and Hitler to their doom. Immediately one began to hear more of the Southward Advance and "Greater East Asia," which diverted public attention from the sorry mess that the Japanese Army had made of China.[14] Even moderates, pro-Allies and high ranking naval officers, believing German invincibility to be proved, urged their government to emulate Hitler and take a fat slice of the French and Dutch Empires for Japan.

The moderate Yonai ministry fell, and on 22 June a new one was formed under the smooth Prince Konoye. General Hideki Tojo, an old Kwantung Army man and prominent *Kodo* militarist, became Minister of War; the energetic, ambitious and ardently pro-German Yosuke Matsuoka was appointed Minister of Foreign Affairs. Matsuoka had lived several years in the United States. Americans had always told him they would never go to war again, and he believed them.

Konoye at once set about organizing a "New Structure" in Japan. This was, in effect, the Japanese version of totalitarianism that had long been planned and promoted under the name "Showa

[12] "Narrative Statement of Evidence" I 156–61; *Pearl Harbor Attack* Part 39 p. 338.

[13] *Peace and War* pp. 94–95. At the end of that period, when the back of the air blitz in Britain had been broken, she felt strong enough to reopen the Burma Road.

[14] Eugen Ott, German Ambassador to Japan at the time, said after the war that one of the main reasons for the Japanese attack on the U.S. was this. "In Nationalist circles the war in China was considered to have reached a stalemate. . . . The only hope of a successful conclusion . . . lay in possible Japanese successes in a more inclusive Pacific war."

Restoration." The government gradually assumed complete control over operations and profits of the Zaibatsu, the big financial and
industrial interests. All political parties were suppressed on the
theory that the entire nation was united in loyalty to the Emperor;
laborers were required to work long hours in war industries; all
luxuries and many pleasures were forbidden — even geisha girls
were denied the privilege of having a telephone! Mr. Grew interpreted all this as preparation for an early move on Indochina,
whose northern provinces offered a new base of attack on Chungking.[15]

He was right. As a result of heat applied by Hitler at Vichy, and
under the sorry pretense of "protecting" Indochina from invasion,
Marshal Pétain on 30 August 1940 consented to a Japanese military
occupation of, and construction of airdromes in, northern Indochina.[16] This was the first formal breach of the *status quo* in East
Asia since the outbreak of war in Europe.

On 27 September 1940 Japan formally joined the Axis by the
famous Tripartite Pact, a treaty of alliance with Germany and
Italy. Japan recognized the Hitlerian "New Order in Europe";
Germany and Italy recognized "the leadership of Japan in the establishment of a New Order in Greater East Asia." Each would
assist the other if "attacked by a power at present not involved in
the European war or in the Sino-Japanese conflict."[17] That power,
of course, was the United States. By the threat of a two-ocean war,
both governments hoped to frighten the United States into remaining neutral, and Matsuoka also expected that the Tripartite Pact
would stifle American protests against Japanese expansionist policy.
Japan, he predicted, now united with two nations of "the same
aspirations and policy," would "go fearlessly forward." *Hakko
Ichiu* seemed to be just around the corner.

Both Prince Konoye and Admiral Yamamoto did their best to

[15] Grew Diary for 1 Sept. 1940, *Ten Years in Japan* pp. 327–28.
[16] *Foreign Relations, Japan 1931–1941* II 289–97.
[17] *Foreign Relations, Japan* II 165–67. It was by virtue of this pact that Germany
and Italy declared war on the United States immediately after the Pearl Harbor
attack.

prevent this tie-up with the Axis; but they had to go along. Shortly
after the pact was concluded, Admiral Yamamoto made a statement
to Prince Konoye that has often been quoted in more or less
garbled form but is best read in the Japanese-schoolboy translation
of the Prince's memoirs: —

If I am told to fight regardless of consequence, I shall run wild considerably for the first six months or a year, but I have utterly no confidence for the second and third years. The Tripartite Pact has been
concluded and we cannot help it. Now that the situation has come to
this pass I hope you will endeavor for avoidance of an American–
Japanese war.[18]

Admiral Richardson, Commander in Chief United States Fleet,
was not the type of naval officer who simply does what he is told
and asks no questions. He regarded Japanese expansion and other
events in the Orient as of slight concern to the United States. He
had written to Admiral Stark before departing San Pedro that the
Chief of Naval Operations should repeatedly impress on the President that a war with Japan would last five to ten years, and that
our old war plan was defective and obsolete. He objected to basing
the Fleet permanently at Pearl Harbor; not only because he regarded the security of the Western Hemisphere as "the paramount
thing," but because he disliked Pearl for logistic reasons. The harbor would be badly congested unless the unprotected Lahaina
Roads were used for overflow; an additional sea voyage of 2000
miles would be required for the inadequate fleet train to bring out
recruits, equipment and supplies; morale would be impaired by
keeping the men at a distance from their homes.[19] If there were
danger of war with Japan, the Fleet could be readied more
promptly for combat through the superior facilities of Pacific

[18] Memoirs of Prince Konoye (translation from extracts printed in *Asahi Shim-
bun* 20–31 Dec. 1945, issued by Okuyama Service, Tokyo, 1946). Another
version of what the Admiral said was reported by Admiral Toyoda after the war
as, "We can carry through for one year, some way; but after that I don't know."
*Inter. Jap. Off.* II 325.
[19] *Pearl Harbor Attack* Part 14 pp. 924–27, 935–36. Honolulu was and remained an unsatisfactory liberty port for bluejackets. White women were few in
number, and the shopkeepers gypped the men even more unmercifully than those
of Norfolk, Virginia. Admiral Richardson made it clear in the Pearl Harbor Inquiry that he had never advocated withdrawal from Pearl because of danger of
air attack, only for logistic reasons.

Coast bases. The Admiral felt so strongly about this that he visited Washington in July and again in October 1940 to press his views on the President, the State Department, and everyone he could lay hold of. He told the President that the military masters of Japan would fear a prepared and well-serviced Fleet on the West Coast more than an undermanned and unprepared Fleet at Pearl Harbor. Mr. Roosevelt replied that he knew that the presence of the Fleet at Hawaii "has had and is now having a restraining influence on Japan." Mr. Cordell Hull and others in the Department of State emphatically agreed.[20]

Admiral Richardson was relieved on 1 February 1941 by Admiral Husband E. Kimmel. On the same day the United States Fleet was renamed the Pacific Fleet, and that Fleet stayed at Pearl. Obviously, if Admiral Richardson's views had prevailed, the Pacific Fleet might not have been the victim of a surprise attack. The Japanese would hardly have sent their carrier force as far as the West Coast. Yet, even though the Fleet was based at Pearl Harbor on 7 December 1941, it need not have been surprised there. Moreover, the mere fact of having the Fleet there from May 1940 meant that this Hawaiian port was immensely improved as a fleet base and infinitely better prepared for hostilities. In one year from June 1940 the civilian force of the Pearl Harbor Navy Yard was more than doubled and the naval personnel augmented many times; hundreds of acres of land were purchased for enlargement; housing facilities for naval and civilian personnel were constructed; a new dry dock was started; foundries were equipped to turn out castings of any size, and complete machine- and toolshops were set up, rendering the Yard almost independent of the mainland. How much if any of this would have been done if the Fleet had been withdrawn to the West Coast, is still a matter of opinion.

[20] *Pearl Harbor Attack* Part 1 pp. 263–66, 282, 297–98. According to Admiral Richardson, the President at this luncheon on 8 Oct. 1940 said that the United States would not go to war with Japan if the Japanese attacked Thailand, the Kra Isthmus or the Dutch East Indies, and that he doubted that even if they attacked the Philippines we would enter the war, but that the Japs might make "mistakes" which would bring us in. But Admiral Leahy, who was present at the luncheon, remembered no such statement and indicated that if Japan had then invaded the Philippines, the President would have recommended declaring war. Same, p. 356.

# CHAPTER IV

# Last Year of "Peace" in East Asia

### October 1940–November 1941

## 1. *Staff Conversations and the Basic Strategic Decision*

THE TRIPARTITE PACT of 27 September 1940 as good as told the world that Japan intended to pursue her southward advance, confident that Germany would come to her aid in the event of a head-on collision with the United States.

It was generally believed in America that Hitler was pushing Japan into war with Great Britain and the United States. If the postwar statements of German diplomats may be believed, pressure in that direction was exerted only around July 1940, when Hitler and Ribbentrop urged Matsuoka to attack British possessions in the Far East. Nine months later they urged Matsuoka to take on Russia first. Instead, Matsuoka promptly concluded a neutrality pact with Russia.

As soon as Hitler declared war on Russia, his diplomatic efforts in Japan were directed toward persuading her to invade Siberia. No Japanese government wanted any part of that. From June 1941 Hitler ceased to count in the formation of Japanese policy; the German Embassy in Tokyo was not kept informed about the last negotiations with the United States — and the attack on Pearl Harbor took it, too, by surprise.

Informal staff conversations as to what the Western powers would do if attacked by Japan began even earlier than the similar conversations with respect to Germany. These conferences consumed much time and thought, but had no substantial results. In contrast to the Atlantic war, where the United States and Royal

Navies coöperated as virtual allies before the German declaration and knew exactly what each had to do thereafter, the three future allies in the Pacific failed to coöperate before 8 December 1941, and did so "too little and too late" thereafter.

The first Anglo-American staff conversations respecting the Pacific were an indirect result of the China Incident and the completion of the Anti-Comintern Pact in October 1937. President Roosevelt and Mr. Hull, foreseeing the United States' being involved in a two-ocean war, instructed Admiral Leahy, then Chief of Naval Operations, to draw up a war plan based on that contingency. On the assumption that the British would be our ally in any war against Japan and Germany, Captain Royal E. Ingersoll, then Director of the War Plans Division, was detailed to find out from his opposite number in the Royal Navy, Captain Tom Phillips, what the Royal Navy contribution would be. At London in January 1938 they agreed to recommend coöperation in case of war on the basis of the Royal Navy's basing a battle force on Singapore if the Japanese moved south, with the United States Fleet concentrating at Pearl Harbor.[1] In May 1939, when the British government believed that war with Germany and Italy was close, it sent an officer to Washington to reconsider the situation. He informed our War Plans Division that, owing to the necessity of watching the Mediterranean, it would be impossible to send a battle force to Singapore. He suggested that the United States undertake to defend the Malay Barrier, the string of islands from the Kra Isthmus to Timor. Nothing was then decided; but the Joint Planning Committee of the United States Army and Navy drew up a new War Plan (Rainbow 1) on the assumption that no Battle Fleet of the Royal Navy could be counted on in the Pacific.

During the preliminary Anglo-American staff conversations at London in September 1940, and the more formal ones at Washington in January–March 1941,[2] a divergence of views developed

[1] Admiral Ingersoll's testimony about this conference is in *Pearl Harbor Attack* Part 9 pp. 4272–80.
[2] See Volume I of this work, pp. 38–55.

between the British and American delegations on methods of holding a defensive position in the Pacific against Japan. The controversy turned largely on Singapore. The British believed that Singapore was essential to the defense of the Malay Barrier and of the Empire; without it, the lifelines through the Indian Ocean to Australia and New Zealand would be severed. They were very insistent that the United States divide its Pacific Fleet in order to defend Singapore. The American delegation, in which Rear Admiral R. K. Turner was the Navy spokesman, doubted the premise and resisted the demand. It believed that Singapore was not essential for the defense of the Malay Barrier or the imperial lifeline; that Singapore could not be defended if Japan seized Indochinese airfields within bombing distance; [3] and that to detach warships to Singapore, or to reinforce the Asiatic Fleet at the expense of the Pacific Fleet, would merely offer the Japanese Navy an opportunity to defeat the United States Navy in detail.

As a result of this stalemate, "It was agreed that for Great Britain it was fundamental that Singapore be held; for the United States it was fundamental that the Pacific Fleet be held intact." [4]

The Australian delegation declined to take any part in the naval defense of Singapore and proposed to concentrate the small Australian Navy in focal areas in the Tasmanian Sea. They had good reason for this in the operations of German commerce raiders. One of these, the *Komet* or *Schiff 45,* had made the Northeast Passage with Russian icebreaker assistance, debouched into the Pacific via Bering Strait on 5 September 1940 and, in concert with *Schiff 36,* which came out by way of Cape Horn and the Tasmanian Sea, sank some 60,000 tons of shipping near Australia before

[3] Another factor, to which Admiral Turner with rather unusual tact did not refer, was this: When the Luftwaffe seriously damaged H.M.S. *Barham, Warspite* and *Illustrious* by dive-bombing at the end of 1940 and beginning of 1941, the Admiralty asked permission to have them repaired in United States Navy Yards. Admiral Stark asked, Why not at Singapore? The British then admitted they had neither the personnel, the spare parts, nor the machine tools to effect major repairs of capital ships at Singapore. So why fight for Singapore?
[4] Minutes of the Washington Staff Conversations, 10 Feb. 1941.

returning home around Africa.[5] Raider operations, moreover, were an additional argument for strong escort-of-convoy to Singapore.

Finally the British agreed, in case of war with Japan, to send at least six capital ships to defend Singapore if the United States Navy would assist the Royal Navy in watching the Mediterranean. That arrangement was in the course of being carried out when the surprise attack on Pearl Harbor altered everything.

On 27 March 1941 this staff conference at Washington concluded the "ABC–1 Staff Agreement," which incorporated the basic strategic decision of the war.[6] Assuming that the United States and Great Britain would do their utmost to dissuade Japan from further aggressive moves that would render war inevitable, this agreement declared that, in any event: —

The Atlantic and European area is considered to be the decisive theatre. The principal United States military effort will be exerted in that theatre, and operations of United States forces in other theatres will be conducted in such a manner as to facilitate that effort. . . .

If Japan does enter the war, the military strategy in the Far East will be defensive. The United States does not intend to add to its present military strength in the Far East but will employ the United States Pacific Fleet offensively in the manner best calculated to weaken Japanese economic power, and to support the defense of the Malay barrier by diverting Japanese strength away from Malaysia. . . .[7]

In other words, the United States was pledged to "help beat Hitler first," even if Japan attacked her first; and to employ a *strategic* defensive. This, it must be emphasized, did *not* mean a

[5] Admiral P. Wenneker (former German Naval Attaché at Tokyo) Memorandum "German-Japanese Naval Operations in World War II" 3 May 1946; news story by J. G. Lucas in Washington *Daily News* 29 Oct. 1947, based on an article by Rear Admiral Eyssen, former C.O. of *Komet*. In addition, *Schiff 41* operated in the Eastern Indian Ocean in the summer of 1941, sank H.M.A.S. *Sydney* and went down herself; and *Schiff 16*, which operated in the Indian Ocean in 1940–41, claims to have sunk 145,000 tons of shipping.
[6] See Volume I of this work, pp. 46–49.
[7] Facsimile of original text in *Pearl Harbor Attack* Part 15 p. 1491. The identical words were incorporated in the Joint Army and Navy Basic War Plan "Rainbow 5," printed in Part 32 p. 70.

"holding operation," as was often said at the time and since.[8] It meant much more than merely holding what we had: a series of *tactical* offensives, as the following summary of the staff agreement makes clear: —

*The Pacific Ocean Area.*[9]
1. The United States Pacific Fleet will
   *a.* Support Allied operations for the defense of the Malay Barrier by diverting enemy strength through attacks on the Marshall Islands, and raids on sea communications and positions.
   *b.* Support British naval forces south of the equator and west to long. 155° E.
   *c.* Protect Allied territory and sea communication in the Pacific.
   *d.* Prepare to capture the Marshalls and Carolines.
2. The United States Army, in conjunction with the Pacific Fleet and Army Air Force, will
   *a.* Hold Oahu.
   *b.* Defend the Panama Canal and the Pacific Coast of the United States and Canada, including Alaska.
   *c.* Support the republics of the West Coast of South America.

Since this area was now an undivided responsibility of the United States, no combined planning was necessary. The Joint Army and Navy Board drafted its own War Plan ("Rainbow 5"), which called for an immediate attempt to capture positions in the Marshalls. As the Japanese attack on Pearl Harbor rendered this plan obsolete, it need not detain us here.

The staff agreement also contained the following stipulation: —

*Far East Area.*[10] Coördination in the planning and execution of the operations by the military forces of the United States, British Common-

---

[8] "It would be a grave error for anyone to get the idea that the war in the Central Pacific was to be purely defensive. Far from it." Admiral Turner at the Hart Inquiry (Same, Part 26 p. 265).

[9] Defined in same, Part 15 p. 1511, as all of the Pacific north of the equator and east of long. 140° E or south of the equator and east of long. 180°, plus Japan.

[10] Limited on the east to long. 141° E and on the west to long. 92° E (the meridian of Aykab, Burma); on the north to lat. 30° N (mouth of the Yangtze) and on the south to lat. 13° S. *Pearl Harbor Attack*, Part 15, p. 1502. Thus India and Australia were excluded; the one because the United States wanted no part in the defense of India, and the other because Australia declined to take part in the defense of the Malay Barrier, other than Singapore.

wealth and Netherlands East Indies in the Far East will, subject to the approval of the Dutch authority, be effected as follows (summary only): —

1. Collaboration in the formation of strategic plans.
2. Each country will be responsible for the defense of its own territory.
3. The British Commander in Chief, China, will be responsible for strategic direction of the naval forces of the three powers, except that Commander in Chief, United States Asiatic Fleet, will be responsible for naval defense of the Philippines.[11]

The real planning problem was what to do about the regions known to be coveted by Japan, where everyone expected her to strike first. The vital planning conference for the Far East took place at Singapore between 21 and 27 April 1941. Presided over by the British Commander in Chief Far East (Air Chief Marshal Sir Robert Brooke-Popham), it was attended by Commander in Chief China (Vice Admiral Sir Geoffrey Layton RN), Chief of the General Staff Netherlands East Indies (Major General H. ter Poorten), representatives of the Australian, New Zealand and British Indian armed forces, and Captain William R. Purnell, Admiral Hart's chief of staff.[12]

Obstacles to arriving at a working "ADB" (American-Dutch-British Commonwealth) War Plan for the Far East were insuperable. At the Washington staff conferences earlier in the year, there had been but one uncertain factor, whether or not the United States would go to war with Germany and Italy. Great Britain had been at war for eighteen months, and the United States was already on a "short of war" basis, so that definite plans leading from one status to the other could be drafted at once. But in the Far East at the time of the Singapore Conference everything was fluid and uncertain except the fact of Japan's war with China. Would Japan con-

[11] Same, p. 1502.
[12] *Pearl Harbor Attack* Part 15 p. 1554 ff. The other American delegates were Col. A. C. McBride USA, Assistant Chief of Staff to General MacArthur, Capt. A. M. R. Allen USN, and Lt. Col. F. G. Brink USA, the U.S. Naval and Military Observers at Singapore. There had already been two Anglo-Dutch planning conferences at Batavia in Nov. 1940 and Jan. 1941, which Capt. Purnell attended as an observer.

tinue her southward advance, and at whose expense? If she did, where would she strike first — at Manila or Hong Kong, at Thailand or the Malay Peninsula, at Borneo or some of the Dutch possessions? Nobody then believed the Japanese to be capable of more than one or possibly two such thrusts at a time, although attacks on Portuguese Timor or French New Caledonia were regarded as distinct probabilities.[13]

This list does not exhaust the uncertainties. Supposing Japan attacked British, Dutch or French possessions, would the United States consider it a *casus belli?* Even President Roosevelt knew no answer to that question, and Captain Purnell could only guess. Mr. Roosevelt by that time believed that the United States should oppose, with force, if necessary, any Japanese advance into Malaysia. He believed that if Japan were permitted to monopolize the immense resources of tin, oil and rubber in this region she would become well-nigh invincible. But he could not be certain of obtaining a declaration of war from Congress on that issue, which would certainly have been interpreted as "sending American boys to support tottering colonial empires." And finally, supposing Japan launched her initial attack on the Philippines, would the British and the Dutch declare war, or endeavor to buy more time with neutrality? Neither Sir Robert Brooke-Popham, nor Admiral Layton, nor General ter Poorten knew the answer to that.

There was also the stumblingblock of Singapore. The British had given up trying to persuade the United States to divide the Pacific Fleet, but their naval thinking about the Far East pivoted around Singapore. They wished to employ the British Far Eastern Fleet, the Royal Netherlands Navy, and whatever American ships they could get, in escorting troop and supply ships through the Indian Ocean to Singapore, and covering the sea lanes to Australia and New Zealand. But the two British commonwealths concerned proposed to keep their own navies in home waters for local defense, and the Dutch promised to release only one cruiser, two destroyers

[13] Same, pp. 1559, 1564. Pearl Harbor, as outside the Far East, was not discussed.

and two submarines to operate under a unified command.[14] Captain Purnell pointed out that overemphasis on escort-of-convoy would deprive naval striking forces of their necessary punch to break up Japanese amphibious and fleet attacks; the British-Dutch concept of operations, emphasizing local defense and escort, seemed to him defensive almost to the point of defeatism.[15] If the United States were to assist in defense of the Malay Barrier, the best strategy, in his opinion, would be an attack by the Pacific Fleet on the Marshall Islands, thus forcing the Japanese Navy to shift weight to the north and east. Sound strategy indeed; but the Japanese Navy broke it up on 7 December.

Consequently the ADB Conference at Singapore dissolved on 27 April 1941 after a week's session and agreeing upon a combined operating plan of local defense forces only in case war came with Japan.

The conference also made certain recommendations to the governments represented, of which the most important was to fight Japan in any one of the following contingencies: —

A "direct act of war" by Japanese armed forces against American, British or Dutch territory.

A movement of Japanese forces into Thailand west of the meridian of Bangkok or south of the Kra Isthmus.

Occupation of Portuguese Timor or the Loyalty Islands off New Caledonia.[16]

The "ADB Plan," as the conclusions and resolutions of the Singapore Conference were called, disappointed both the American and the British Chiefs of Staff. Admiral Stark and General Marshall definitely rejected it on 3 July 1941 for several reasons, but mainly because the whole thing pivoted on Singapore. They notified the British Chiefs of Staff that an earlier permission, given to Admiral Hart to operate his Fleet under British strategic directions, was revoked.[17] Nevertheless, on 5 November 1941 the United States

[14] Same, p. 1570.
[15] Conversations with Admirals Purnell and Hart.
[16] *P. H. Attack* Part 15 pp. 1564–67.
[17] Same, pp. 1677–79.

Chiefs of Staff passed on to President Roosevelt the exact recommendations made by the Singapore Conference as to the three contingencies, any one of which should be met by an American declaration of war on Japan.[18]

## 2. *Naval Movements*

The decision to base the United States (after 1 February 1941 the Pacific) Fleet at Hawaii had been made in May 1940; but that Fleet was anything but static. In April 1941, at the time the ADB Conference was breaking up, there was an amusing contest of wills and wits between the Chief of Naval Operations and the Department of State.

At the request of that Department, the Navy sent four cruisers and a destroyer squadron to visit New Zealand, Australia, Fiji and Tahiti, in order to demonstrate to Japan our solidarity with the British Commonwealth and hearten our Antipodean friends, who felt forgotten and virtually abandoned by Mother England. Admiral Stark hated to interrupt training schedules, but he complied, and the visits turned out to be a great success, even from the viewpoint of training.[19] But the President alarmed the Chief of Naval Operations by announcing that he wished to send more ships out — "to keep them popping up here and there, and keep the Japs guessing." Admiral Stark regarded this suggestion, which he attributed to the State Department, as childish. Accordingly, he drew up a plan to send a carrier force northwestward from Hawaii, which he hoped would "give the State Department a shock which might make them haul back." It did. The Department begged the President not to let the Navy do anything so alarming to Japan,

---

[18] Same, Part 14 p. 1062. The U.S. Chiefs of Staff were known as the Joint Chiefs of Staff after 8 Feb. 1942.

[19] *Pearl Harbor Attack* Part 26 pp. 267, 340. The ships were U.S.S. *Chicago, Portland, Brooklyn, Savannah* and Desron 3, under command of Rear Admiral John H. Newton. When the writer was on board *Brooklyn* late in 1942 the officers and men were still talking about wonderful receptions they had had, especially in Auckland.

and no more was heard of sending warships dashing around the Pacific merely to say "Boo!" to the Japs.[20]

Although it had been anticipated at the Washington staff conversations in February 1941 that the United States would send a detachment of the Pacific Fleet to the Atlantic whenever war with Germany seemed imminent, in return for the Royal Navy's sending a force of equivalent strength to base on Singapore,[21] the move came earlier than was anticipated, and for different reasons. New naval construction was unable to keep pace with the enlarged needs of the Atlantic Fleet, now that participation in escort-of-convoy and the occupation of strategic islands had been decided on; and the U-boats had moved into the Central Atlantic with a consequent rise of merchant ship sinkings.

After considerable debate and hesitation, Admiral Stark ordered the transfer of battleships *Idaho, Mississippi*, and *New Mexico*, carrier *Yorktown*, light cruisers *Brooklyn, Philadelphia, Savannah* and *Nashville* and two destroyer squadrons, from the Pacific to the Atlantic Fleet. The transfer was effected between April and June 1941. By midsummer oilers *Cimarron, Sangamon* and *Santee*, three transports and a few other auxiliaries had also been transferred to the Atlantic in order to cover the occupation of the Azores, for which Iceland was substituted.[22] This reduced the strength of the Pacific Fleet by about 20 per cent, and left it inferior to the Japanese Navy in every category of combat ship.

The following table shows the comparative naval strength in

[20] Letters of Admiral Stark in *Pearl Harbor Attack* Part 16 pp. 2163–64. More in Navy's "Narrative Statement of Evidence" I 260–66. The President's later proposal to Admiral Hart to operate river gunboats as picket boats in the South China Sea did not stem from the same idea, but from a desire to supplement the work of our patrol planes in reporting Japanese ship movements. A suggestion was made at the Pearl Harbor Inquiry that this was an intentional provocation; but naturally the United States Navy has a right to send its ships anywhere on the high seas.

[21] The reasons for making this roundabout exchange were: (1) Singapore was not equipped to service American warships; and (2) the United States high command did not believe that Singapore could be defended.

[22] See Vol. I pp. 56–7 for Admiral Stark's view of the critical situation in the Atlantic and his letters in *Pearl Harbor Attack* Part 16 pp. 2161–69. The Orders and lists of ships are in Part 11 pp. 5502–06; correspondence of Rear Admiral R. K. Turner with Rear Admiral V. H. Danckwerts RN on the transfer in Part 19 pp. 3457–61.

the Pacific (including British ships in the Indian Ocean) as of 1 May 1941, subsequent to this detachment: —

NAVAL COMBATANT STRENGTH, PACIFIC OCEAN, 1 MAY 1941 [23]

|  | UNITED STATES PACIFIC FLEET | ASIATIC FLEET | ROYAL NAVY | ROYAL NETH. NAVY | TOTAL POTENTIAL ALLIES | JAPANESE NAVY (7 DEC.) [24] |
|---|---|---|---|---|---|---|
| Battleships | 9 | — | 1 | — | 10 | 10 |
| Carriers | 3 | — | 1 | — | 4 | 10 |
| Heavy Cruisers | 12 | 1 | 4 | — | 17 | 18 |
| Light Cruisers | 9 | 2 | 13 | 3 | 27 | 17 |
| Destroyers | 67 | 13 | 6 | 7 | 93 | 111 |
| Submarines | 27 | 28 | — | 15 | 70 | 64 |

## 3. *Economic Sanctions*

Admiral Stark's Memorandum on National Policy which he presented to Secretary Knox on 12 November 1940 recommended a "diminution of the offensive military power of Japan, with a view to the retention of our economic and political interests in the Far East." [25]

The one way to do this, short of war, was to deny Japan the oil and other war materials then being purchased in abundant quantities from the United States; and that was just what he meant. He conceded that the probable consequence would be a Japanese attack on the Dutch East Indies, and he was unwilling to take that risk until the United States was ready to fight. America was becoming more and more uneasy over her moral position. She was protesting against aggression in the Far East while selling the material means of conquest to Japan. She was allowing Japan to bid against American armed forces in the home market for steel, oil and other strategic items.

Economic sanctions began, as we have seen, with the "moral

[23] *Pearl Harbor Attack* Part 15 p. 1903; prepared by O.N.I. in Nov. 1945. Those of R.N. light cruisers and destroyers are estimates.
[24] Figures furnished by the Japanese Navy Minister to USSBS in Nov. 1945. Allied estimates for 1 May were 7 carriers and 100 destroyers, otherwise the same.
[25] See Volume I of this work, p. 42.

embargo" of July 1938 against the export of planes and their equipment to countries engaged in bombing civilians. In early February 1940, Senator Pittman of Nevada introduced a resolution calling for an embargo on war materials to Japan. A Gallup poll taken in the same month showed 75 per cent of the voters interviewed, and expressing an opinion, to be in favor of an embargo on "arms, airplanes, gasoline and other war materials." [26] The government, knowing full well that anything so drastic would precipitate war, waited for an opportunity to do it gradually and in such a manner as to afford a minimum of irritation to Japan.

The opportunity came in July 1940 when Congress passed an "Act to Expedite the Strengthening of the National Defense," which authorized the President "to prohibit or curtail the exportation of any military equipment or munitions, . . . or machinery, tools or material or supplies necessary for the manufacture, servicing or operation thereof," whenever he determined such action to be "necessary in the interest of national defense." In the same month Congress passed the Two-Ocean Navy Bill. [27] Selective Service (the Army draft) was already before Congress, the destroyers-naval bases deal with Britain was just over the horizon; and American industry, with much hesitation and reluctance, yet convinced of the necessity, began to convert from peace to war production. Whilst the main and declared purpose of the National Defense Act was to keep strategic materials and supplies at home, the broad powers that it gave the President made it possible for him to implement national policy by giving export licenses in favor of our friends and denying them to our prospective enemies. In practice the licenses were only accorded in favor of the British Commonwealth, China, the Netherlands East Indies, and resistant groups in Europe. This saved Japan's "face" but was equally effective in gradually denying her access to American markets for war materials.

[26] *Public Opinion News Service* 14 Feb. 1940.
[27] See Volume I pp. 27–8.

The dates and rough classification of the principal prohibitions follow: — [28]

*5 July 1940.* Various strategic minerals and chemicals; aircraft engines, parts and equipment.

*26 July 1940.* Aviation motor fuel and lube oil; certain classes of iron and steel scrap.

*30 September 1940.* Every kind of iron and steel scrap.

The Gallup poll on this showed 96 per cent of those expressing an opinion approving, and 90 per cent favoring a complete embargo on all war materials.[29] Japan protested against it as an "unfriendly act" on the naïve ground that for some years she had been the "principal buyer of American iron and steel scrap." When the Japanese Ambassador called at the Department of State to express this view, Mr. Hull remarked "that it was unheard of for one country engaged in aggression and seizure of another country . . . to turn to a third peacefully disposed nation and seriously insist that it would be guilty of an unfriendly act if it should not cheerfully provide some of the necessary implements of war to aid the aggressor nation in carrying out its policy of invasion." [30]

On 8 November 1940 the Emperor approved the appointment as Ambassador to Washington of Admiral Kichisaburo Nomura, a former foreign minister and man of high personal character who was known to be opposed to a breach with the United States. At the same time the Japanese began an intensive militarization of the Marshall and Caroline Islands, building airfields, seaplane bases and fortifications.[31]

Between 10 December 1940 and 10 January 1941 embargoes were imposed on additional metals, ores and manufactures.

On 27 January Mr. Grew confided to his diary: "There is a lot of talk around town to the effect that the Japanese, in case of a break with the United States, are planning to go all out in a surprise mass

[28] Full details in *Foreign Relations, Japan* II 211–65.
[29] *Public Opinion News Service* 20 Oct. 1940.
[30] *Foreign Relations, Japan* II 227.
[31] *P. H. Attack* Part 26 p. 227. The Japanese insisted at the war guilt trials in 1947 that they built no defenses in the Mandates until after war began. We have plenty of evidence to the contrary.

attack at Pearl Harbor. Of course I informed our government." [32]
Actually this was the very time when Admiral Yamamoto began
planning the Pearl Harbor attack.

On 7 February Mr. Grew observed that Japan was continuing
her "nibbling policy" in a southward direction, this time by taking
advantage of an undeclared war between Thailand and French
Indochina. The Thai government was trying to pluck a few feathers
from the beaten Gallic cock. Japan mediated in the dispute and
obtained early in March 1941 a settlement much to her own interest. Thai secured some of her "lost provinces," and Japan, as the
price of saving the rest of them for France, exacted of Vichy a
monopoly of the Indochinese rice crop and the right to occupy
the airport at Saigon, within bombing distance of Singapore.

This gave Japan a stranglehold on the whole of Indochina.
American public opinion, as tested by the Gallup poll, took another
move forward. Around 10 March 1941, a bare majority of the
voters consulted and expressing an opinion were willing to accept
the risk of war to prevent Japan from taking Singapore and the
Netherlands East Indies.[33] Next day, the first Lend-Lease Bill became law.

On 13 April 1941 Foreign Minister Matsuoka concluded with
Molotov a Russo-Japanese nonaggression pact. Stalin consented
because he was already expecting an attack by Germany; Japan
wanted it to secure her Manchurian frontier and to release forces
for the southward advance.

During the spring Japan poured troops into Northern Indochina
in preparation for taking the rest of that colony at one gulp. On
2 July the government called up between one and two million con-

[32] *Ten Years in Japan* p. 368. Grew's dispatch is reproduced in the Navy's
"Narrative Statement of Evidence," I 259. The Division of Naval Intelligence
"places no credence in those rumors," stated Admiral Stark when communicating
it to Admiral Kimmel.

[33] *Public Opinion News Service* 14 Mar. 1941. In late July the proportion willing to risk war "to keep Japan from becoming more powerful" had risen to 51
per cent, with 31 per cent opposed and 18 per cent undecided; and six weeks later
the *pros* had risen to 70 per cent and *cons* fallen to 18 per cent. But around 12 Nov.,
with Pearl Harbor only three weeks away, the *pros* on the same question had
fallen to 64 per cent and the *cons* risen to 25 per cent. Same, 3 Aug., 7 Sept.,
14 Nov. 1941.

scripts, recalled all its merchant ships from the Atlantic, and adopted other measures indicating warlike intentions. On 25 July the Japanese Minister of Foreign Affairs informed Mr. Grew that Vichy had consented to admit Japan to a joint protectorate of French Indochina.[34] This meant that Japan was free to extend her military occupation over the entire colony, which was done forthwith. It also completed the left curve of a strategic horseshoe around the Philippines.

This time the American reply came quickly, and in deeds, not words. On 26 July 1941 President Roosevelt issued an executive order freezing Japanese assets in the United States.[35] His intention was to choke off Japanese–American trade, including the highly important oil exports. No Japanese vessels were allowed thenceforth to discharge cargo in United States ports, and those already in our ports had to depart in ballast.

## 4. *The Impact of Oil*

Up to this time there had been only a "moral" restriction on the export of petroleum products to Japan other than high octane gas and aviation lube oil. American shipowners had been "morally" dissuaded from carrying fuel oil to Japan, but immense quantities were still going there in Japanese and neutral tankers. Now all that stopped. And the freezing of Japanese assets, which was also done by Great Britain and the Dutch, had a restrictive effect on procurement of oil in the Netherlands East Indies. A Japanese economic mission had extracted from Dutch oil interests a promise to deliver a large amount of petroleum products for cash; but the only place where Japan had cash was in the United States. Deprived of this resource for foreign exchange, Japanese tankers were forced to lay up for weeks in harbors of Borneo or Sumatra while their captains waited for money from home.[36]

[34] *Foreign Affairs, Japan* II 318–22.
[35] Same, pp. 266–67.
[36] Statement by Admiral Hart to the writer. Even Germany froze Japanese assets unless used to purchase German goods.

The oil embargo and assets-freezing order of 26 July 1941 made war with Japan inevitable unless one of two things happened, and neither was humanly possible. The United States might reverse its foreign policy, restore trade relations and acquiesce in further Japanese conquests; or the Japanese government might persuade its army at least to prepare to evacuate China and renounce the southward advance. Small chance of that at a time when the Australians and the Dutch were virtually helpless, when the German Army, apparently irresistible, was sweeping into Russia and Rommel had pushed back the British to the suburbs of Alexandria. No measure short of war could then have diverted the Japanese militarists from seizing their "golden opportunity" for expansion. Any temporary concession, however welcome to liberal Japanese civilians, would surely have been disregarded by an Army which, as the facts show, would accept no compromise that did not place America in the ignominious role of collaborating with conquest.

In any case Japan had to make up her mind quickly because the oil embargo and the freezing of her assets in the United States threatened a general impoverishment of her economy. Shortly she would lack fuel oil for normal domestic consumption, let alone naval operations.[37] The No. 1 industrial planner of Japan declared he could produce enough for domestic needs by synthetic processes if given time and money; but the military would grant him neither.[38]

Japan imported about 88 per cent of all oil products consumed in the country and about 80 per cent of the total came from the United States. During the last few years the government had been stockpiling oil as fast as possible, and in the year ending 31 March 1941, imports reached an all-time high with 22,850,000 barrels of crude oil and 15,110,000 barrels of refined products. This was

[37] According to the USSBS publication *Oil in Japan's War*, Japanese oil wells and synthetic plants combined, "in the year of Pearl Harbor," produced only 3,103,000 barrels, less than 12 per cent of the annual civilian and military consumption without counting on war with the United States. Note that an oil barrel contains 42 U.S. gallons or 35 Imperial gallons. To convert barrels of crude (36 gravity API) or fuel (16 gravity API) oil to metric tons of 2204.6 lbs., divide by 7 and 6.7 respectively. To convert barrels of 60 gravity gasoline to metric tons, divide by 8.5.

[38] Konoye Memoirs in *Pearl Harbor Attack* Part 20 p. 4012.

about enough for one year of war, although it might be stretched if civilian consumption were still further curtailed.

Other strategic items such as rubber, scrap iron, tin and tungsten would dwindle; but oil was paramount. With the synthetic process ruled out, Japan must get more oil in order to conquer, or conquer in order to get more oil;[39] and the Roosevelt Administration had determined to shut off oil. The American people were tired of placating Japan with oil and scrap, conniving at an aggressive policy against friendly nations. There was no doubt about their feelings in the matter. But they did not yet understand, and of course the Administration could not tell them, that shutting off oil made one of two things inevitable: war with Japan, or an easy Japanese conquest of areas which would make that nation well-nigh invincible.

So, beginning with the assets-freezing order, both countries intensified their military preparations. On 26 July 1941 President Roosevelt signed an order nationalizing the armed forces of the Philippine Commonwealth, and appointing Field Marshal Douglas MacArthur of the Philippine Army, Commanding General United States Army Forces Far East. The Japanese Army planners were busy drafting plans for major strikes against the Malay Peninsula, the Philippines and Pearl Harbor, as well as minor ones against Hong Kong, North Borneo, Guam and Wake. The United States Navy made no new war plan, but the country accelerated industrial and military preparation all along the line.

## 5. *The Final Negotiations*[40]

Diplomatic negotiations during the four months of "peace" that remained after the oil embargo were little more than sparring for

[39] *Oil in Japan's War* Appendix pp. 12, 15.

[40] The most detailed narrative of the diplomacy of this period is in Appendix D of *Report of Joint Committee on P. H. Attack* pp. 291–468. This is superior to the one in *Foreign Relations, Japan* because it takes into account the Japanese end of the negotiations as obtained from decrypted dispatches between Tokyo and its Washington Embassy, military moves of the Japanese, and many matters of which the State Department was ignorant. The texts of the Japanese dispatches, in *P. H. Attack* Part 12, and Prince Konoye's Memoirs in same Part 20, are most important.

time. Civilian elements in the Japanese government wanted time to find a solution that would satisfy the militarists, who in turn needed a few months to train the carrier air groups to destroy the United States Pacific Fleet. America wanted time for new naval construction, for manufacture of munitions and implements of war, and to reinforce the Army in the Philippines. Nevertheless, the negotiations were sincere on both sides. The Japanese diplomats, and probably even the Foreign Minister and Prince Konoye, did not know what their own military were up to. The President and Secretary Hull wished to explore every possibility and seize every occasion that might alter the Japanese internal situation in the direction of peace.

During these negotiations both sides frequently and loudly proclaimed their desire for "peace" in Asia, but they were using the word in two different senses. The Americans meant a cessation of Japanese military operations in China and elsewhere. The Japanese meant the peace that would ensue when they were dominant and impregnable in Greater East Asia — the peace of *Hakko Ichiu.*

Ambassador-Admiral Nomura, *persona grata* to the State Department, had been in Washington since 14 February 1941. The first proposal he transmitted to Mr. Hull was a settlement on the basis of the "Konoye Principles" of December 1938 — a very unpromising beginning. Nevertheless, in view of the need for time, and the desire "to avert, or at least to delay as long as possible, any Japanese move which would result in a war on two oceans," the United States government explored "every possible means, starting with the Japanese proposals, of coming to an agreement." [41]

Nomura had many friends in Washington. Admiral Stark had several long talks with him and believed that he earnestly desired to avert a crisis.[42] He did; but, as an agent of a government that made no proposals possible for the United States to accept, he had no chance of success.

In mid-July, however, one personal obstacle to peace was re-

[41] *Foreign Relations, Japan* II 335.
[42] To Admiral Richardson 4 Apr. 1941. *P. H. Attack* Part 16 p. 2161.

moved from power. Yosuke Matsuoka, the megalomaniac Minister of Foreign Affairs, had lately been throwing his weight about so inconsistently, now demanding war on Russia, and again seeking to provoke the United States, that he had lost the confidence of the Emperor, the Prince and General Tojo. He was allowed to resign on 16 July 1941, ten days before the oil embargo and assets-freezing.[43] Mr. Grew believed that his successor, Admiral Toyoda, as well as the Premier, desired a new orientation of Japanese policy. Konoye so states in his memoirs, but he was unable to stop the occupation of southern Indochina; and, as for Toyoda, the German diplomats revealed that he was made Foreign Minister because, as "old school Navy" and, since his retirement, a leading figure in the Zaibatsu, he was counted on to make a favorable impression on the Americans. But he lost no time in sending a very tough message to the Japanese Ambassador at Washington which American cryptographers placed in Mr. Hull's hands on 4 August. Japan "must take measures to secure the raw materials of the South Seas. Our Empire must immediately take steps to break asunder this ever-strengthening chain of encirclement" by "England and the United States, acting like a cunning dragon seemingly asleep. That is why we decided to . . . occupy that territory [Indochina]. . . . All measures which our Empire shall take will be based upon a determination to bring about the success of the objectives of the Tripartite Pact." [44]

No promise of peace here. The last clause meant that Japan would make war on the United States if Germany did; and war with Germany seemed very near in August 1941.

The next Japanese proposal, which Admiral Nomura presented orally to Mr. Hull on 6 August, was fully in accord with Toyoda's attitude. The United States must restore free trade with Japan, "suspend its military measures in the southwestern Pacific" (meaning the reinforcement of the Philippines), discontinue aid to China

[43] Memoirs of Prince Konoye, translation in *P. H. Attack* Part 20 pp. 3992–97. The whole ministry resigned, to save Matsuoka's face, but Konoye immediately reconstructed another, his third, with but one change.

[44] *P. H. Report* pp. 297–98.

and to British and Dutch possessions in the Far East, recognize Japan's special military, political and economic status in Indochina, and put pressure on Chiang Kai-shek to negotiate. In return for these concessions, Japan merely promised to make no further military advances outside Indochina, to evacuate that French colony after "settlement of the China Incident," and to guarantee the neutrality of the Philippines "at an opportune time," provided Japanese subjects were given the same rights and privileges therein as American citizens.[45]

At this time President Roosevelt was on his way to the Atlantic Conference at Argentia. There he and Mr. Churchill agreed to take parallel action in warning Japan to the effect that "any further encroachment by Japan in the southwestern Pacific would produce a situation" in which their governments "would be compelled to take countermeasures even though these might lead to war" between their countries and Japan.[46]

The President and the Prime Minister agreed, however, that the President should see Nomura immediately upon his return to Washington, and pursue the thin ray of hope held forth in the Japanese note of 6 August.

Even before the Atlantic Conference, the Japanese government had suggested a Pacific Conference between President Roosevelt and Prince Konoye. The latter's feeling that Nomura had bungled matters, his knowledge that time was running short, and a sincere desire to get something fixed up before the militarists got out of hand were the main motives. Konoye apparently hoped that he

[45] *Foreign Relations, Japan* II 549–50; Prince Konoye's résumé in *P. H. Attack* Part 20 p. 3998. The difficulty of translating Japanese is illustrated by the second condition. The one quoted in the text above is as Mr. Hull received it. Two translations of Konoye's Memoirs give it thus: "America will remove her armaments in the Southwest Pacific," and "The U.S. shall disarm herself in the Southwest Pacific areas." What the Japanese intended was "no reinforcement of the Philippines."

[46] Mr. Sumner Welles's Notes on the Atlantic Conference, printed in *P. H. Attack* Part 4 pp. 1784–92. Mr. Roosevelt's warning, 17 Aug., is in *Foreign Relations, Japan* II 556. Apparently the British government never issued the parallel warning but Mr. Churchill, in a speech to Parliament a few days later, made it clear that if the United States went to war with Japan, England would follow.

could bring home from a personal conference with Mr. Roosevelt a formula that would appease the militarists and postpone war.

Accordingly on 17 August, the very day that the President returned to Washington from Argentia, Nomura laid the Pacific Conference proposal before him. Mr. Roosevelt's first reaction was favorable, for he excelled in personal diplomacy and knew it. Mr. Hull, however, was much more reserved, and persuaded the President to make only a qualified acceptance, provided "there could be reached a meeting of minds on fundamental principles" which would make such a meeting worth while.[47]

Prince Konoye, in conversation with Mr. Grew at a private dinner in Tokyo on 6 September, indicated that the minds had met. He said that he and his government "conclusively and wholeheartedly agreed with the four principles enunciated by the Secretary of State as a basis for rehabilitation of relations," although their implementation would take time. These were in principle (1) respect for the territorial integrity and sovereignty of all nations; (2) noninterference in the internal affairs of other countries; (3) equality, including the Open Door; (4) alteration of *status quo* in the Pacific only by peaceful means.[48]

Possibly Mr. Hull would have done better to have accepted Konoye's word and called the Pacific Conference. But, in the light of what Japan had done and continued to do, he could only regard Konoye's acceptance of his "four principles" as insincere. He would have had no doubt about it had he known what we now know from Konoye's memoirs. The Prince had already assured General Tojo and the Navy Minister that in conference with President Roosevelt he would "insist, of course, on the firm establishment of the Greater East Asia Co-Prosperity Sphere" and a revision in Japan's favor of the Nine-Power Pact guaranteeing the integrity of China.[49] Moreover, on 6 September 1941 (the same

[47] *Foreign Relations, Japan* II 346; Masuo Kato *The Lost War* pp. 31–34; Konoye Memoirs.
[48] *Foreign Relations, Japan* II 332, 349; Grew *Ten Years in Japan* p. 426.
[49] P. H. *Attack* Part 20 p. 3999; deleted in the Okuyama Service translation.

day as Konoye's dinner with Grew) the following resolutions presented by the Army were adopted at a meeting of the Imperial Conference, presided over by the Emperor: —

1. Determined not to be deterred by the possibility of war with America and England and Holland, and in order to secure our national existence, we will proceed with war preparations so that they will be completed approximately toward the end of October.
2. At the same time we will endeavor by every possible diplomatic means to have our demands agreed to by America and England.
3. If by the early part of October there is no reasonable hope of having our demands agreed to . . . we will immediately make up our minds to get ready for war against America and England and Holland.

A list of "Japan's minimum demands and maximum concessions," of which the following is a summary, was also adopted: —

1. United States and Great Britain must let Japan settle "China Incident," must close Burma Road and give no more assistance to Chiang Kai-shek.
2. There must be no increase of British or American military forces in the Far East, even in their own possessions.
3. No interference with Japanese-French relations as to Indochina.
4. American coöperation for obtaining needed raw materials, by restoration of free trade and assisting Japan "to establish close economic relations with Thai and the Netherlands East Indies."
5. Japan will not use Indochina as a base for operations against any country except China and will evacuate Indochina "as soon as a just peace is established in the Far East."
6. Japan will guarantee the neutrality of the Philippines.[50]

Thus the military gave the Japanese government about six weeks to reach a peaceful settlement, and dictated the terms. These amounted, in effect, to America's becoming a sort of sleeping partner in Japan's "Greater East Asia" and leaving China to her fate.

[50] Konoye Memoirs in *P. H. Attack* Part 20 p. 4022. Konoye states that the Emperor, much displeased with the attitude of Tojo, the Navy Minister and the Army Chief of Staff, insisted that diplomatic means be exhausted before the last resort. These "minimum demands" were practically identical with "Proposal B" which Nomura was instructed to present to the U.S. on 5 Nov. *P. H. Attack* Part 12 pp. 96–97.

If the Pacific Conference had been held, Prince Konoye might have agreed to evacuate China and Indochina in return for a restoration of trade; but the military in that event would certainly have overthrown his government and probably assassinated him.[51]

The reason for the Supreme War Council's deadline of six weeks may be summed up in one word, oil. Crude oil inventories had dwindled alarmingly since the beginning of the year 1941, from over 20,000,000 barrels on 1 April to 15,000,000 on 30 September; refined oil inventories had been kept steady owing to increased production by the refineries, but could not long be maintained.[52] Thus, every month that Japan delayed striking would make her oil situation worse. She was eating her own tail. If Konoye and the diplomats could persuade America to reopen the pipeline, well and good. If not, the armed forces must seek oil to the southward.[53]

President Roosevelt and his advisers knew nothing of the deadline. They observed the feverish haste of the Japanese Ambassador to get something decided, and guessed that Prince Konoye was under some sort of pressure. Mr. Hull, in his conversations with Nomura, talked no more of principles but concentrated on trying to elicit "clear-cut evidence" that Japan "really wished to abandon the course of aggression which it had been following and to revert to a peaceful program and peaceful methods." [54] So he informed the Japanese Ambassador on 20 October.

By this time the deadline set by the Imperial Council on 6 September had been passed. On 12 October Prince Konoye conferred with General Tojo, the War Minister, Admiral Oikawa, the Navy Minister, Admiral Toyoda, the Foreign Minister, and one or two

---

[51] His predecessor, Premier Hiranuma, just escaped assassination on 14 Aug. 1941, the provocation being that he had opposed the Tripartite Pact; and an attempt to assassinate Konoye was made about the same time.

[52] USSBS *Oil in Japan's War* Appendix pp. 13, 14.

[53] Konoye Memoirs in *P. H. Attack* Part 20 p. 4012. Admiral Nagano, Chief of Naval General Staff, at the Imperial Conference likened Japan to a patient who was certain to die if you did nothing, but might be saved by a dangerous operation.

[54] *Foreign Relations, Japan* II 354. Kato (p. 50) is in error in stating that the U.S. government formally rejected the proposed Konoye-Roosevelt meeting. It was never rejected but kept in view as long as the Konoye Cabinet stood, hoping that a formula for negotiation could be agreed upon.

others. Oikawa wanted negotiations to continue. Toyoda told Tojo that there was no hope of a diplomatic settlement with America unless Japan yielded on China. Tojo said that was impossible, and the meeting broke up without a decision. Two days later Konoye met Tojo alone, and, after warning the General of the danger of challenging America to war, asked his consent to withdraw troops from China. Tojo refused because, he said, any such concession would encourage the United States to make further demands, and to terminate the "China Incident" would undermine Army morale and cause Japan to lose face throughout the Orient. Further, Tojo believed that if it came to war with America, Japan would win.

So there was nothing for Konoye to do but resign. The Army exercised its constitutional prerogative of forming a new ministry; and, because it would not accept as premier any civilian whom the Emperor cared to appoint, Tojo was given that high office. The Tojo Cabinet was formed on 18 October, the General retaining the war ministry and the home office as well as taking the premiership. Admiral Shimada became Navy Minister and a rather innocuous diplomat named Togo the head of foreign affairs.

Both Togo and Shimada were relatively moderate men who still hoped to avert war with the United States. The Admiral, like many flag officers of the Imperial Navy, had traveled extensively and respected American industrial and naval power. But he was powerless to control events. Although the high naval command was responsible for the plan of attacking Pearl Harbor, it was loath to risk all by putting that plan into execution, and even submitted as a condition of executing both this and the other planned attacks that the Navy be given a large share in the national oil reserves. Tojo yielded that point and thus the last naval argument for delay or postponement was lost.[55]

On 10 November General Terauchi, commanding the Southern Army, and Admiral Yamamoto concluded a "Central Agreement" which outlined a detailed and stupendous scheme of conquest, in substance as follows: —

[55] Kato p. 42.

1. Simultaneous landings of amphibious forces in Luzon, Guam, the Malay Peninsula, Hong Kong, and Miri, British North Borneo. All except the last to be preceded by air attacks.

2. Carrier air attack on the United States Pacific Fleet at Pearl Harbor.

3. Rapid exploitation of initial successes by the seizure of Manila, Mindanao, Wake Island, the Bismarcks, Bangkok and Singapore.

4. Occupation of the Dutch East Indies and continuation of the war with China.[56]

Mr. Grew of course did not know exactly what was going on, but he had a very good idea of it. In a telegram of 3 November he warned Mr. Hull that Japan's resort to measures which would make war with the United States inevitable might come "with dramatic and dangerous suddenness." [57]

General Tojo's accession actually delayed the final showdown about six weeks. On 5 November, Foreign Minister Togo, in a dispatch "of utmost secrecy" which the American cryptographers soon deciphered, told Nomura that it was "absolutely necessary" to come to an agreement with the United States by the 25th.[58] That was Tojo's new deadline. In conversation both with his colleagues and with the diplomatist Saburo Kurusu, whom he sent to Washington on 5 November to help Nomura, Tojo professed to believe that Roosevelt would not dare to precipitate war with Japan; by taking a strong attitude a settlement ought to be reached without the necessity of evacuating China. Kurusu had an American wife, and Tojo expected that if anyone could persuade the American government to backtrack he could. On the very day that Kurusu saw Tojo, the detailed plans for Pearl Harbor were completed; but neither he nor Nomura knew anything about them.

President Roosevelt asked the opinions of members of his Cabinet on 7 November whether the American people "would support a strike against Japan" in the event that she attacked British Malaya

[56] *The Campaigns of the Pacific War* pp. 43–48.
[57] *P. H. Report* p. 336; dispatch of 17 Nov. in *P. H. Attack* Part 14 p. 1055.
[58] *P. H. Report* p. 335, and *Attack* Part 14 p. 1055.

or the Dutch East Indies. The Cabinet was unanimously of the opinion that they would.[59]

Kurusu flew to Washington and first saw Mr. Hull on 15 November. "Exploratory conversations" were accelerated. Proposals and counterproposals were made, but no common basis of agreement could be found. The two Japanese envoys warned their government that the American temper was rising and begged Tojo for some measure of concession, which the Premier curtly refused. Finally, on 20 November, Nomura presented a note which his Foreign Minister told him should be regarded as "our absolutely final proposal," an "ultimatum." It was identical with the formula approved by the Imperial Council at Tokyo on 5 November: — [60]

1. Neither Japan nor the United States will move armed forces into Southeastern Asia [61] or the South Pacific Area, except that Japan may increase her forces in northern Indochina.

2. Japan will withdraw troops from southern to northern Indochina as soon as an agreement is made with the United States, and will evacuate Indochina altogether when peace is concluded with China or "an equitable peace" is made in the Pacific area.

3. The United States and Japan will "coöperate" in securing commodities for themselves from the Netherlands East Indies.

4. The United States and Japan will release each other's assets, and the United States will "supply Japan a required quantity of oil."

5. The United States will cease helping China.[62]

---

[59] *P. H. Report* p. 171.

[60] Same, p. 360.

[61] Emphasis on "southeastern" because the Japanese Army was then planning a drive from northern Indochina into Yunnan Province in order to sever the Burma Road. On 30 Oct. Chiang Kai-shek made an urgent plea to Great Britain and the United States for air assistance to prevent this. Mr. Hull submitted this proposal to the Army-Navy Joint Board, which on 5 Nov. strongly opposed weakening our air forces in the Philippines to help China, and begged that no action be taken for several months to provoke war. *P. H. Report* pp. 337–44.

[62] *Foreign Relations, Japan* II 755–56; *Report* pp. 333, 361. Paragraph 5 reads: "The Government of the United States undertakes to refrain from such measures and actions as will be prejudicial to the endeavors for the restoration of general peace between Japan and China." This meant, however, discontinuing aid to Chiang Kai-shek, as Kurusu orally explained to Hull.

Mr. Hull correctly diagnosed this proposal as a bid for American connivance, through restoring the flow of oil and releasing assets, at a complete crushing of China by Japan; "an abject surrender of our position under intimidation." [63]

Admiral Stark, who was in close touch with diplomatic developments, sent the following message to Admiral Hart at Manila and Admiral Kimmel at Pearl Harbor on 24 November: —

"Chances of favorable outcome of negotiations with Japan very doubtful. This situation coupled with statements of Japanese Government and movements of their naval and military forces indicate in our opinion that a surprise aggressive movement in any direction including attack on Philippines or Guam is a possibility. . . . Utmost secrecy necessary in order not to complicate an already tense situation or precipitate Japanese action." [64]

"The situation was critical and virtually hopeless," said Mr. Hull in retrospect. We wanted time; Japan was pressing for a showdown. "We had reached the point of clutching at straws."

The straw selected was a proposal of a "temporary arrangement or *modus vivendi* to tide over the immediate crisis." Delay might prevent a breach, might possibly produce another government crisis in Japan. Admiral Stark and General Marshall begged for more time. Some 21,000 troops were to sail from the United States for the Philippines on 8 December, an Army contingent was at sea near Guam, and the Marines were just pulling out of Shanghai. The longer the delay, the better the chance of defending the Philippines. Stark and Marshall supported the recommendation of the ADB Conference that military action against Japan be undertaken only if Japan "attacks or directly threatens" American, British or Dutch territory, or advances into Thailand, Timor or New Caledonia. [65]

[63] *P. H. Report* pp. 34, 362.
[64] *P. H. Attack* Part 4 p. 1751.
[65] Joint Memorandum of Marshall and Stark to the President, *Report* pp. 174–75. It is dated 27 Nov. 1941 but was actually drafted before the rejection of the *modus vivendi* was known to them. Marshall and Stark, however, had frequently pleaded with the President for some such arrangement since 5 Nov. if not earlier. Same, pp. 340–42.

The Department of State, after consultation with the President, Admiral Stark and General Marshall, accordingly completed on 25 November the draft of a three-months' *modus vivendi*, of which the following is a summary: —

1. Mutual declaration of peaceful policy.
2. No further advances by force or threat of force.
3. Withdrawal of Japanese troops from southern to northern Indo-china; a reduction of those in the latter region.
4. Resumption of American trade with Japan, oil to be on "a monthly basis for civilian needs."
5. Pious hope that Japan would negotiate with Chiang Kai-shek on "principles of peace, law, order and justice." [66]

The proposed *modus vivendi* was submitted to the representatives of China, Great Britain, Australia and the Netherlands at Washington. The Chinese government "violently opposed the idea." Winston Churchill called it "Thin diet for Chiang Kai-shek." Several Americans, cognizant of the terms, well said that they amounted to "selling China down the river." The other governments consulted were lukewarm or unfavorable. The President decided, as Mr. Hull advised him, "that the conclusion with Japan of such an arrangement would have been a major blow to Chinese morale. . . . The slight prospects of Japan's agreeing to the *modus vivendi* did not warrant assuming the risks involved in proceeding with it. . . ." [67]

There were indeed insuperable objections against making the offer. As Mr. Stimson observed, any such concession at that point would have been derogatory to the honor of the United States, a blow to American as well as Chinese morale, a signal to the world that our Far Eastern policy was words and nothing else. General Marshall, admitting that his viewpoint was "materialistic," begged for this or any temporary agreement to save time; and so, with

[66] Same, pp. 35–36.
[67] Mr. Hull in *P. H. Report* p. 36. Details of the discussion of the *modus vivendi* are in same, pp. 364–81, 393. The only civilian of any consequence who was in favor of this stop-gap proposal was Lord Halifax. In an intercepted Japanese dispatch quoted in same, pp. 37–38, Tojo on 20 Nov. had already categorically rejected the essential idea of the *modus vivendi*.

less insistence, did Admiral Stark. But Japan could use time too; and time may be bought too dear. The proposed *modus vivendi* was not a way of living, but the way of Munich.

Mr. Hull had already caused to be prepared, as a counterproposal to the Japanese ultimatum of 20 November, an "Outline of Proposed Basis for Agreement between the United States and Japan." Dated 26 November, it was presented to Kurusu and Nomura on the same day. This long document, a summary of which follows, outlined steps to be taken by both governments to bring about permanent peace in the Pacific: —

1. A nonaggression pact among Great Britain, China, Japan, the Netherlands, Russia, Thailand and the United States, and an agreement to respect the territorial integrity of Indochina.
2. Evacuation by Japan of China and Indochina.
3. Mutual renunciation of extraterritorial rights in China.
4. Japanese recognition of the Chungking government.
5. A new Japanese-American trade agreement on most-favored-nation basis, with raw silk on the free list; reciprocal unfreezing of assets.
6. Stabilization of the dollar–yen exchange.[68]

Neither Mr. Hull nor anyone else in the American government believed that Tojo would accept this. They knew that he was poised to strike; but where? They knew that his deadline was only three days off.[69] Evidence of Japanese ship and troop movements to the southward was accumulating — but no hint of the Pearl Harbor Striking Force, which had already set sail on its deadly mission. On the 25th, Mr. Stimson heard from Army Intelligence that a Japanese fleet of 30 to 50 ships, carrying five divisions of troops, had been sighted off Formosa. This was Admiral Ozawa's expeditionary force against the Malay Peninsula.[70] Actually Nomura and Kurusu, even before they saw the "Proposed Basis for Agreement," had cabled Tokyo that their negotiations had failed.[71]

[68] *Foreign Relations, Japan* II 373–75; *P. H. Report* pp. 382–84.
[69] Tojo on 22 Nov. extended his deadline from the 25th to the 29th, according to a dispatch to Nomura which was decrypted and delivered to Mr. Hull and the President next day. Same, p. 32.
[70] *P. H. Report*, pp. 375, 379–80, 403–09.
[71] Same, pp. 385–86.

On 27 November Admiral Stark sent his famous "war warning" message — an unprecedented phrase — to Admirals Hart and Kimmel: —

This dispatch is to be considered a war warning. Negotiations with Japan looking toward stabilization of conditions in the Pacific have ceased. An aggressive move by Japan is expected within the next few days. The number and equipment of Japanese troops and the organization of naval task forces indicates an amphibious expedition against either the Philippines, Thai or Kra Peninsula or possibly Borneo. Execute appropriate defensive deployment preparatory to carrying out the tasks assigned in WPL 46.[72]

The American note of 26 November was not an ultimatum. Tojo admitted at his trial that it was largely a rewriting of the Nine-Power Treaty of 1922, to which Japan was a party.[73] An ultimatum means a final demand as alternative to war; and President Roosevelt did not propose to recommend a declaration of war if Japan merely refused to negotiate on the basis of this note. He might have asked Congress for a declaration of war if Japan had invaded Malaya, the Philippines or the Dutch East Indies; but there would have been no war, at least not in 1941, if Japan had merely kept what she had already taken and desisted from further aggression. That was what Prince Konoye proposed at a solemn "senior statesmen's conference" with the Emperor on 30 November, at which the final war decision was made. Konoye pled to "proceed as we were, with broken economic relations but without war." Mr. Suzuki, president of the national planning board, supported him. Tojo refused even to consider this alternative. "If we were to proceed with broken economic relations," he said, "the final consequence would be gradual impoverishment." Suzuki had earlier assured Konoye that he could increase domestic production of oil and other materials if allotted a small part of what a Pacific war would cost. But, he remarked, "Opening hostilities is a matter of domestic politics" — a remark "with much meaning," recorded Ko-

[72] *P. H. Attack* Part 14 p. 1406. WPL 46 was the naval part of the Rainbow 5 War Plan.
[73] *N. Y. Times* 7 Jan. 1948.

noye. Of course that was the nub of it; had been all along. Only by war could Tojo and the Showa Restoration crowd rivet their control on Japan.[74]

On 29 November, his deadline date, Tojo made a bellicose speech about nations throwing obstacles in the way of the East Asia Co-Prosperity Sphere, and the need of purging Anglo-American influence from Asia.[75] That was the theme song of the Japanese government's official reply to the American proposals of 26 November. The "Proposed Basis of Agreement" convinced Tojo and the Army that nothing was to be gained by further negotiation. Actually the Pearl Harbor Striking Force had already sailed.

On 1 December a Cabinet Council met in the Imperial presence and ratified Tojo's decision to make war on America, Great Britain and the Netherlands. Operation plans for the three-pronged attack were activated the same day and on the 2nd the Pearl Harbor Striking Force was notified that the planned "X-day," 8 December, was confirmed. It was arranged that Nomura and Kurusu would present the Japanese reply to the 26 November proposals half an hour before the attack began. But there was still a loophole to peace if President Roosevelt had cared to use it. The Pearl Harbor Striking Force was subject to recall, and doubtless would have been recalled if Mr. Hull had cabled Tokyo, "We give up — have it your own way — oil exports start next week," or words to that effect. One may always have peace at some price.

Since his aircraft carriers would not be ready to strike until 8 December, Tojo on 30 November informed the Japanese press that Nomura was still negotiating. He notified Nomura not to break off, and on 2 December ordered the Washington embassy to burn all codes except the one necessary to decrypt the final note, which would be presented when the attack planes were already in the air. On the same day the Japanese consul at Honolulu was directed to

[74] Konoye Memoirs in *P. H. Attack* Part 20 pp. 4012–13. The point is important, as American pacifists have echoed the Japanese militarists' claim that war was "necessary" when oil was cut off; that it was we who "provoked" Pearl Harbor. Here Japan's civilian premier and No. 1 production planner admit that it was not necessary.

[75] *P. H. Report*, p. 401.

send daily reports of warships in Pearl Harbor, and advise whether they were provided with protective nets.[76]

On 6 December President Roosevelt played his last card for peace — a personal message to Emperor Hirohito, begging him for the sake of humanity to withdraw the military and naval forces from southern Indochina which threatened the Philippines, Malaya, Thailand and "the hundreds of islands of the East Indies." Hirohito did not want war with the United States, but he wanted still less to lose his throne. Showa Restoration would have been turned into Showa Deposition if he had refused to go along with Tojo at this point. So he said nothing.

On Sunday morning, 7 December 1941 — the "day that will live in infamy" — the Japanese Ambassadors, as instructed by their government, asked for an interview with Mr. Hull at 1300 in order to read Tojo's reply to the proposals of 26 November. That time had been selected because it was just twenty minutes before the scheduled hour (0750 Honolulu time) of the attack on Pearl Harbor. Owing, it seems, to a delay by the embassy staff in deciphering and translating this note, the interview was postponed until 1400. Mr. Hull had already been handed a copy of Admiral Kimmel's message, "Air attack on Pearl Harbor. This is not a drill," but he thought it might be a mistake; and having no official word of war he believed he should hear what Nomura and Kurusu had to say. So he received them at 1420.

It seems hardly necessary to repeat the text of the final Japanese note, of which Mr. Hull remarked spontaneously after a quick reading that in fifty years of public service he had "never seen a document that was more crowded with infamous falsehoods and distortions." [77]

It was now 0900 December 7 in Hawaii. The first sad and bloody hour was over. The burned and shattered bodies of more than a thousand Americans lay strewn along airfields, on charred decks, or trapped beneath the waters of Pearl Harbor.

[76] Same, p. 196; *P. H. Attack* Part 31 pp. 3249–50.
[77] *Foreign Relations, Japan* II 787.

# CHAPTER V

# The Attack on Pearl Harbor[1]

## 7 December 1941

### 1. *The Plan, January–November 1941*

East Longitude dates, Tokyo time (Zone minus 9).

THE JAPANESE ATTACK on Pearl Harbor was but a part, and in their estimate not the most important part, of a comprehensive plan for the Greater East Asia War. Formulated bit by bit, this plan was finally brought together at a Supreme War Council on 6 September 1941. Not Pearl, but pearls of greater price were the objective: populous islands fabulously rich in natural resources and strategic materials, possession of which would enable the Japanese to dominate East Asia and, finally, the world. As Admiral Yamamoto put it in his "Top Secret Operation Order No. 1" issued to the Combined Fleet on 5 November 1941, Japan intended "to drive Britain and America from Greater East Asia, and to hasten the settlement of the China Incident. . . . When Britain and America have been driven from the Netherlands Indies

[1] The 40 volumes or "Parts" of the Joint Congressional Investigation (cited here as *P. H. Attack*), are mainly concerned with the question of surprise; the *Report* contains one of the best accounts of the genesis and execution of the attack from Japanese sources. Other important accounts are *The Campaigns of the Pacific War* (1946) and ATIS Research Reports nos. 131 and 132: *Japan's Decision to Fight* and *The Pearl Harbor Operation*, 1 Dec. 1945. "The Japanese Plan for Attack on Pearl Harbor," prepared by Combat Intelligence, is also valuable. Of the USSBS Interrogations of Japanese Officers who were at Pearl Harbor, those of Captains Fuchida and Watanabe are printed in *Interrogations of Japanese Officials*, but two important ones are not included: Fuchida's "recheck" (USSBS 103, 28 Nov.) and that of Fleet Admiral Osami Nagano, Chief of Naval General Staff (USSBS 498, 30 Nov. 1945). Much of the same material with additional details is in *P.H. Attack* Part 13 p. 413 and ff.

and the Philippines, an independent, self-supporting economic entity will be firmly established. The vast and far-reaching fundamental principle, the goal of our nation — *Hakko Ichiu* — will be demonstrated to the world." [2]

The comprehensive war plan was this: First, without a declaration of war, to invade Thailand,[3] destroy the United States Pacific Fleet and deliver air strikes on the Malay Peninsula and Luzon. After the initial surprise, to effect conquest of the Philippines, Borneo, British Malaya (including Singapore) and Sumatra. When these were secure, Japanese amphibious forces would converge on the richest prize, Java, and mop up the rest of the Dutch islands. Intensive development of Netherlands East Indies resources would begin at once, and to secure these new possessions a "ribbon defense" or defensive perimeter would be established, running from the Kurile Islands through Wake, the Marshalls and around the southern and western edges of the Malay Barrier to the Burmese-Indian border.[4]

Although the Japanese knew that America had ample resources to stage a comeback, they expected that, with Australia and New Zealand isolated, and the Japanese Navy operating from interior lines, any attempt of the British and American Navies to break through the defensive perimeter could be beaten back for eighteen months or two years. By that time, it was hoped, the English-speaking powers would be so stricken by fighting a two-ocean war as to be ready to make peace on the basis of Japan's retaining most of her conquests. She could then proceed at leisure to the complete subjugation of China. Over half the world's population would then be under the economic, political and military control of the Son of Heaven. If not eight corners of the world, five at least would be under the "one roof" as Emperor Jimmu once predicted.

---

[2] *Japan's Decision to Fight* p. 7.

[3] Thailand had been infiltrated and the government suborned in advance; it issued an order to its troops to cease firing about three hours after the attack began on 8 December.

[4] It was also planned to detail a naval striking force to break up all sea communications westward and southward from Hawaii, Panama, and the West Coast of South America, but that part never materialized.

No such vast plan of quick conquest had ever been formulated in modern history. Apparently it never occurred to the average Japanese that there was anything morally wrong with it. Japan's divine mission to realize *Hakko Ichiu* was taken for granted, and so all means to that end were proper. Surprise attacks, regardless of plighted word, were part of *Bushido*, the code of the warrior. The earlier wars of Japan on Russia and China had begun that way and both had been successful; Heaven obviously approved.

The place of the Pearl Harbor attack in this comprehensive scheme was purely and simply to eliminate the United States Pacific Fleet so that it could not interfere with the numerous amphibious operations necessary to conquer the "Southern Strategic Area." It was "a strategic necessity," said Admiral Nagano. We shall examine that concept later.

Up to about 1940 the Japanese planned in the event of war with the United States to keep their Combined Fleet in home waters. The high command either knew or guessed correctly that the United States naval plan was to fight its way across the Pacific via the Marshalls and Carolines, taking Truk en route, in order to relieve the Philippines. The Japanese proposed to make this voyage very unpleasant for the United States Fleet, by submarine attacks and land-based or tender-based air attacks mounted from sundry airfields and lagoons in the Marshalls and Carolines. Whatever ships survived would be pounced upon by an overwhelmingly superior Combined Fleet in the Philippine Sea, and there annihilated. That was sound strategy; fortunately for us, the Japanese abandoned it for something more spectacular and less effective.

Admiral Isoroku Yamamoto was fifty-seven years old in 1941. An early champion of air-sea warfare and a brilliant tactician, he was well known personally to a number of United States naval officers, who regarded him as highly capable, intelligent, alert, aggressive and dangerous. Their respect for him was enhanced by his brilliance as a poker player; and he also played better bridge and chess than most good players of those games. He was the first Japanese naval officer to foresee the possibilities of carrier-based air power.[5] In 1937 the official Japanese doctrine for the employment of carriers was the same as ours had been: they were supposed to provide an "air umbrella" for a striking force of battleships. Whether or not it was due to knowledge of our successful Fleet Problem, of attacking Pearl Harbor by carrier-based air approaching from the north, Admiral Nagano could not (or would not) say after the war; but he admitted that from us Japan learned a better employment for the flat-tops; namely, *to project fire power deep into enemy territory.*[6] This concept became Japanese naval doctrine in 1938. Japan then began building 30,000-ton 34-knot carriers like *Shokaku* and experimenting with suitable plane types to operate from them. By December 1941 there were ten Japanese carriers in commission, with well-trained air groups. The United States Navy had only eight carriers, three of them in the Pacific Fleet.

In January 1941 Admiral Yamamoto ordered his own staff and Rear Admiral Onishi, chief of staff of the Eleventh Air Fleet, to study his concept of a surprise carrier strike on Pearl Harbor and work out details. No one else was taken into the secret until late August, when Yamamoto summoned to Tokyo all fleet commanders and key members of their staffs for a series of war games, in which members of the Naval General Staff joined. That was the first that Admiral Nagano, Chief of the Naval General Staff, knew about it. The war games were held on a game board at the Naval War College, Tokyo, similar to the one at our Newport institution. After the attacking team in this war game "lost" two out of its six carriers, several members of Nagano's staff regarded the proposal as too risky and speculative. They saw no sense in stirring up the United States; let Japan concentrate on taking the rich southern islands and, if America intervened, carry out the old plan to pound the Pacific Fleet on its passage, and annihilate it in waters

[5] E. M. Zacharias *Secret Missions* pp. 91–94; Capt. Layton in *P. H. Attack* Part 26 p. 235.
[6] "Our principal teacher in respect to the necessity of emphasizing aircraft carriers was the American Navy," said Admiral Nagano. "We had no teachers to speak of besides the United States in respect to the aircraft themselves." USSBS 498 p. 4.

near Japan. Nagano himself seriously doubted whether a carrier strike could succeed in so late and stormy a season as December. But he was overruled by Yamamoto and others, who argued that the United States was bound to come in anyway. Japan had the ships and planes to strike Pearl simultaneously with the southward advance, so why not pull off both operations simultaneously before the Pacific Fleet was alerted? By 13 September the staff study which became the basis of the Combined Fleet Secret Operation Order No. 1 of 5 November was completed.

Certain officers on the planning staff became so enthusiastic as to urge that the surprise attack be followed by an amphibious force to seize Oahu, and so deny Pearl Harbor to the United States for the duration. But Japan could spare neither the transports nor the merchant ships and tankers for the necessary follow-up and support of an invasion so far from home. All she had were needed for the conquest of the Southwest.

Once the Pearl Harbor attack was decided on, the question of approach was threshed out. The northern route, the one actually chosen, passed through stormy waters which would complicate the problem of fueling at sea. A central course heading east from Japan and passing southward of the line Midway–Oahu, and a southern course through the Marshalls, were suggested. Either would take the Striking Force through calmer waters and so facilitate fueling. But the danger of detection by merchant ships would be much greater than on the northern route and neither lay outside the possible range of American patrol planes based on Wake, Midway, Palmyra and Johnston Islands. Consequently, to insure secrecy, it was decided to accept the risk of stormy weather and a route was laid out between the Aleutians and Midway. In case these waters should be too rough for fueling en route, the destroyers were to be left behind.

After 15 September there were numerous conferences on the plan between the Navy and Army General Staffs. And the Advance Expeditionary Force of 27 large I-class submarines, five of them carrying midget submarines on deck, was brought into the

*Photo brought from Japan by Rear Admiral Shafroth*

Japanese Miniature Mock-up of Pearl Harbor

*Japanese official photograph*

Battleship Row at the Beginning of the Attack

t to Right: *Nevada; Arizona* and *Vestal; Tennessee* and *West Virginia; Mary-* *d* and *Oklahoma; Neosho; California.* Geyser subsiding from hit on *West* *ginia;* white disks in mid-channel indicate bomb drops; torpedo tracks visible. ves outboard of *Oklahoma* and *California* indicate that they have been tor- pedoed. Bomb hit, *California.* Smoke in distance: Hickam Field

*Pearl Harbor Setup*

*"Banzai!"* 7 December

A torpedo-armed "Kate" starting her take-off

*Air Attack*

picture. The midgets had been training for such work for at least a year before the Pearl Harbor attack was planned.[7]

Specific training for Pearl Harbor by the carriers and their air groups started in September. An unfrequented island in Japanese waters doubled for Oahu as a practice target for bombing.[8] Particular attention was given to dropping torpedoes in shoal water such as that of Pearl Harbor, and special fins were installed on the aërial torpedoes so that they would not "porpoise" or hit the bottom. These were counted on to strike the initial and lethal blows; but high-level bombers and dive-bombers were also provided for a follow-up, as well as fighter planes to protect the bombers from interception, and destroy grounded planes and kill personnel. The 423 planes on board the six carriers, a large complement for that period, included air groups of two other carriers as well. Of these 423 planes, 30 were used for combat air patrol over the fleet, 40 were in reserve on the day of the attack, and 353 were flung at Oahu. Of them, about 100 were "Kates" for high-level bombing, 40 were "Kates" especially equipped for torpedo-bombing, 131 were dive-bombing "Vals" and 79 were "Zeke" fighters. The cruisers and battleships provided 13 float planes for reconnaissance and combat air patrol.[9]

On 5 October a meeting of about one hundred officer pilots of the carrier air groups was called on board *Akagi* anchored off Shibushi in Ariake Bay, Kyushu. These aviators were told under seal of high secrecy that they had been selected to destroy the

[7] Documents on Japanese midget submarine operations in *P. H. Attack* Part 13 pp. 414, 487–96. Mr. Eugene H. Dooman informs me that a few days after the Pearl Harbor Attack he saw at Tokyo a Navy press release stating that the midgets had been training for it at least six years, and that theirs was the original attack plan to which the carriers were later added.

[8] I do not know how to reconcile this with the statement in Commander Minobi's book of 1942, summarized in Zacharias *Secret Missions* 114, to the effect that a full-scale mock-up of Pearl Harbor was constructed on Shioku (*sic*) Island, for the carrier planes to practice on, as early as 1928; or how to reconcile Minobi's statement with Nagano's that the plan was not even formulated until 1941. I suspect that Minobi was boasting, and that the only mock-up was the miniature one shown overleaf, which was constructed after the attack in order to take movies of it.

[9] Fuchida Interrogation (USSBS 603) pp. 3, 13; *The Campaigns of the Pacific War* pp. 15–18, 23–24. Corrections by Capt. Ohmae.

American Fleet at Hawaii on or about 8 December. Admiral Yamamoto urged them to hit hard, promising that the United States would be unable to recover before Japan occupied the Philippines, the Malaya Peninsula and the Netherlands East Indies.[10] The pilot who reported this meeting rejoined carrier *Kaga* at Saeki on the Kyushu side of Bungo Channel, where his air group practiced until 7 November. They were better trained than any Japanese carrier group later in the war.

By the end of October, plans for the simultaneous attacks were practically completed, and on 5 November the basic operation order was issued from Admiral Yamamoto's flagship *Nagato* at Saeki.[11] In Tokyo two days earlier Yamamoto met Admiral Nagano, chief of the naval general staff, who made his final decision in favor of the operation on 3 November.

On 7 November Yamamoto set 8 December as approximate date (Y-day) because it was Sunday. He was cognizant of Admiral Kimmel bringing most of the Fleet into Pearl Harbor every week end. And on the same day, 7 November, he delegated responsibility for the Pearl Harbor Striking Force to Vice Admiral Chuichi Nagumo, its commander.

Admiral Nagumo's first operation order was issued from his flagship *Akagi* at Saeki on 10 November. On or about that day the chief of staff of the Combined Fleet, Admiral Ugaki, gave the flag officers of the Striking Force an oral explanation of what it was all about. As Yamamoto's chief yeoman remembered this speech, it went as follows: —

A gigantic fleet . . . has massed in Pearl Harbor. This fleet will be utterly crushed with one blow at the very beginning of hostilities. . . . If these plans should fail at any stage, our Navy will suffer the wretched fate of never being able to rise again. The success of our surprise attack on Pearl Harbor will prove to be the Waterloo of the war to follow. For this reason the Imperial Navy is massing the cream of its strength in ships and planes to assure success.

It is clear that even if America's enormous heavy industry is imme-

[10] Interview with Lt. Cdr. Y. Shiga 13 Oct. 1945, *P. H. Attack* Part 13 p. 645.
[11] Same, pp. 431–41, and annexes through p. 484.

diately converted to the manufacture of ships, planes and other war materials, it will take at least several months for her manpower to be mobilized against us. If we insure our strategic supremacy at the very outset . . . by attacking and seizing all key points at one blow while America is still unprepared, we can swing the scales of later operations in our favor.

Heaven will bear witness to the righteousness of our struggle.[12]

## COMPOSITION OF PEARL HARBOR
## STRIKING FORCE [13]

Vice Admiral C. Nagumo (Commander in Chief First Air Fleet)

AIR ATTACK FORCE, Admiral Nagumo

| Carrier Division 1 | | Carrier Division 5 | | Carrier Division 2 | |
|---|---|---|---|---|---|
| CV | AKAGI | CV | SHOKAKU | CV | HIRYU |
| CV | KAGA | CV | ZUIKAKU | CV | SORYU |

*Screen*, Rear Admiral S. Omori in CL ABUKUMA

Destroyer Squadron 1

| DD | TANIKAZE | DD | HAMAKAZE | DD | KAGERO |
|---|---|---|---|---|---|
| DD | URAKAZE | DD | KASUMI | DD | SHIRANUHI |
| DD | ISOKAZE | DD | ARARE | DD | AKIGUMO |

SUPPORT FORCE, Vice Admiral G. Mikawa

| Battleship Division 3 | | Cruiser Division 8 | |
|---|---|---|---|
| BB | HIEI | CA | TONE |
| BB | KIRISHIMA | CA | CHIKUMA |

*Ship Lane Patrol*, Captain K. Imaizumi

Submarines *1–19, 1–21, 1–23*

*Midway Neutralization Unit*, Captain K. Konishi [14]

| DD | SAZANAMI | DD | USHIO |
|---|---|---|---|

*Train*

Eight Tankers and Supply Ships

[12] ATIS *Japan's Decision to Fight* pp. 10–11. Other Japanese deny the speech was made.
[13] *The Campaigns of the Pacific War* p. 21.
[14] According to same, p. 20, this Unit departed Tokyo Bay independently about 1 December, and arrived Midway the night of the 7th. Its route is unknown.

## 2. *Outward Passage of the Striking Force*

In the Japanese Air Attack Force *Akagi* ("Red Castle") and *Kaga* ("Increased Joy") had been converted respectively from a battle cruiser and a battleship, but were of smaller tonnage than our *Lexington* and *Saratoga*. *Hiryu* ("Flying Dragon") and *Soryu* ("Green Dragon"), completed in 1938, were 728 feet long and displaced about 17,500 tons; although rated as light carriers, they were much larger than our *Wasp* and *Ranger* class. The two largest, *Shokaku* ("Soaring Crane") and *Zuikaku* ("Happy Crane") were new carriers from the keel up, 826 feet long. The two battleships, of the 14-inch gunned *Kongo* class, were over twenty-five years old, but had recently been modernized, and with a speed of 30 knots they were much faster than American battlewagons of the same date. *Tone* and *Chikuma* were the two latest 8-inch gunned cruisers, post-treaty, and so bigger (14,070 tons) and faster (35 knots) than ours. The screen destroyers with deceptively sentimental names (*Kasumi* means "Mist of Flowers," *Shiranuhi*, "Phosphorescent Foam" and *Tanikaze* "Valley Wind") were of the newest, 1900-ton *Asashio-Kagero* class with eight 24-inch torpedo tubes and six 5-inch 50-cal. guns in covered mounts, paired.

These fine fighting ships will turn up again and again in the Pacific War; but, with the exception of a single destroyer, lucky *Ushio*, every one was sunk by gunfire, torpedoing, or air bombing before the end of hostilities — four of the carriers at Midway, the other two in 1944, and the two battleships at Guadalcanal.

This Striking Force sortied from Kure naval base on the Inland Sea of Japan in echelons, between 10 and 18 November, 1941. Foul weather clothing and special weatherproof gun tarpaulins were issued, and the men guessed that Dutch Harbor was the destination. All ships kept strict radio silence from the moment of departure, but the rest of the Fleet, at Kure, kept up a large volume of radio communication so that American listeners-in would not notice any diminution of radio traffic from the Inland Sea. This ruse, like the others, worked well. The Pacific Fleet Intelligence Officer at Pearl Harbor noticed that no call signs of two carrier divisions were on the air, but Admiral Kimmel did not regard this as significant.

By 22 November the Striking Force had rendezvoused in Tankan Bay (Hitokappu Wan) on Etorofu, biggest of the Kurile Islands. There were no installations at this desolate bight except a wireless station, one small concrete pier and three fishermen's houses. The ground and the hills behind the harbor were covered with snow. It was an ideal spot for a secret rendezvous.

Thousands of drums of fuel oil which had been sent up ahead were stowed in every vacant space of the carriers and even topside in case it proved too rough to fuel at sea. The last provisions were taken on board. On 2 December after departing Tankan Bay the destination was announced to all hands, to their vast delight. "An air attack on Hawaii! A dream come true," wrote Seaman Kuramoto. "What will the people at home think when they hear the news? Won't they be excited! I can see them clapping their hands and shouting with joy! We would teach the Anglo-Saxon scoundrels a lesson!" [15]

In no account by any Japanese, participant or not, was there any trace of compassion for the American sailors, soldiers and civilians who were to be massacred without a chance to fight back. No sentiment other than hatred was expressed for the nation that had assisted Japan to emerge from a sterile isolation and first welcomed Japan to the family of nations. On the contrary, this was the little fellow's dream come true of getting back at the envied occidental, showing the world that the sons of Nippon were second to none. Japanese nature is probably no worse than other human nature; but the docility of the people, their willingness to let leaders think for them, made them particularly susceptible to hate propaganda. Every sailor and aviator in the Striking Force appears to have been inspired with a personal grudge against the unsuspecting enemy.

[15] Translation of Kuramoto's "The Southern Cross," telling his own experiences, in *P. H. Attack* Part 13 p. 516.

No comparable armed expedition in history ever set forth better informed as to what it was about to do and why; or so full of black, bitter hatred against victims marked down for destruction.

On 25 November Admiral Yamamoto issued his order to the Striking Force to sortie next day, to "advance into Hawaiian waters, and upon the very opening of hostilities attack the main force of the United States Fleet in Hawaii" and deal it a mortal blow. "The first air raid is planned for the dawn of X-day — exact date to be given by a later order."

"Should the negotiations with the United States prove successful, the task force shall hold itself in readiness forthwith to return or reassemble."

At 0600 November 26 the "magnificent air fleet set out" from Tankan Bay "through thick fog and stormy waves."[16]

The six carriers steamed in two parallel columns with a battleship at the rear of each, two destroyers on the left flank and the three submarines on the right flank, and a heavy cruiser several miles away on either flank. The rest of the destroyers steamed in line several miles ahead in order to detect shipping. Orders were given to sink at sight any American, British or Dutch merchant ship encountered, and to place a boarding party on any neutral to prevent radio transmission; but only one vessel, a Japanese, was met on the outward passage.

The Striking Force followed a rhumb line southeasterly to lat. 43° N, long. 159°30′ E, thence due east to a designated refueling area around long. 170° E set for 3 December.[17] The slow speed of the oilers, as well as the need to conserve fuel, restricted the average speed of advance. A careful watch was kept on radio transmissions from Pearl Harbor, to judge whether the secret had leaked out, but everything was normal. Yamamoto had ordered the Striking Force to abandon its mission and return if discovered prior to

[16] *P. H. Attack* Part 13 p. 516.
[17] These data on the course were furnished by the Japanese themselves. A track based on their original chart, in *P. H. Attack* Part 21 Item 15, is the basis of ours.

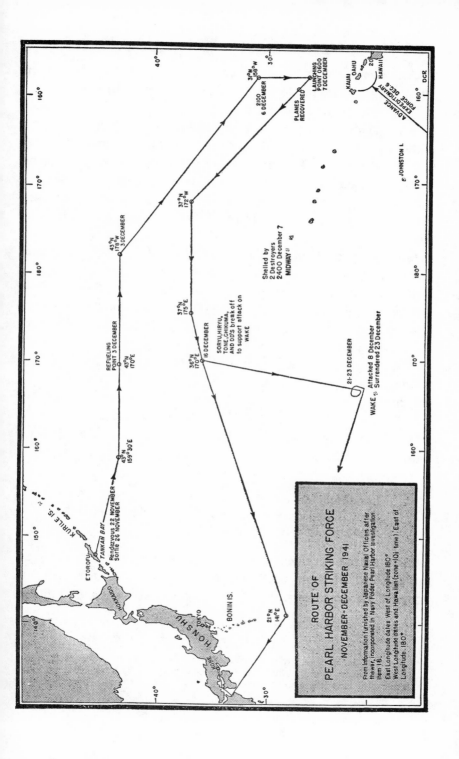

ROUTE OF
PEARL HARBOR STRIKING FORCE
NOVEMBER-DECEMBER 1941

From information furnished by Japanese Naval Officers after
the war, incorporated in Navy Folder Pearl Harbor investigation
Item 18.

East Longitude dates West of Longitude 180°
West Longitude dates and Hawaiian (zone +10½ time) East of
Longitude 180°

6 December. If discovered 7 December (East Longitude date) Admiral Nagumo would decide whether or not to attack.[18]

Their good luck escaping detection was due partly to weather: gales, moderate to high seas, and thick fog. Signal flags were blown to tatters, men were washed overboard, lookouts became exhausted. Towing spars were streamed in order to insure position keeping. Whenever weather permitted, anti-aircraft gunnery practice was conducted, and the aviators pored over maps and intelligence material until they knew the geography of Oahu better than any native Hawaiian.

On 1 December, as we have seen, the Cabinet Council ratified Tojo's decision to commence hostilities on the 8th. On the 2nd, Admiral Yamamoto from his flagship in the Inland Sea broadcast the phrase *Niitaka Yama Nobore* (Climb Mount Niitaka), the prearranged code for "Proceed With Attack," and confirmed 8 December as X-day.

The Striking Force darkened ship and set Condition Two — the second degree of readiness for action — on 2 December. The sea moderated sufficiently for a successful refueling along the course of advance on the 3rd. On the evening of the next day the force reached a position about 900 miles north of Midway, where course was changed to the southeastward.

> At this point we may shift our narrative to West Longitude dates and Hawaiian (Zone plus 10½) time. The Japanese continued to use the dates and time zone of their homeland.[19]

Early on the 6th the latest and most accurate data on ships present at Pearl Harbor were received on board the carriers from Imperial Headquarters, Tokyo — seven battleships, seven cruisers,

---

[18] "Japanese Plan for the Attack," p. 8.

[19] Hawaii did not change to war (or summer) time (Zone plus 9½) until 9 February 1942. In December Hawaiian time was 19½ hours earlier than the Japan time (Zone minus 9) used by the Striking Force, and 5½ hours earlier than Washington time (Zone plus 5). For instance, 0300 December 8, Japan time, was 0730 December 7 at Hawaii; 1300 December 7 at Washington, and 1800 December 7 at Greenwich.

but no carriers. The mimeographed chart with which each pilot had been provided was corrected accordingly.[20]

At 2100 that evening the Striking Force reached the meridian of Oahu — long. 158° W — at a point about 490 miles north of the island.[21] All hands on the carriers who could be spared from duties below were summoned to the flight decks, the actual "Z" flag which had been displayed from Admiral Togo's flagship before the Battle of Tsushima in 1905 was hoisted to the masthead of *Akagi*, and air group commanders made speeches. It was a moment of great emotion. Course was altered to due south and all combat ships bent on 26 knots, leaving the train to seek a new rendezvous. Through a dark and thick night, with a mounting sea, the carriers charged toward their launching point, lat. 26° N, long. 158° W, about 275 miles north of Pearl Harbor.

The heavy cruisers pushed on ahead of the carriers' launching position and catapulted four float-type "Zeros" at about 0600 to reconnoiter Pearl Harbor and report whether the Pacific Fleet was really there. There it was — all except those prize targets, the three carriers. If the Fleet had taken alarm and sortied, the Japanese planes had fuel enough to pursue it 150 miles to the southward of Pearl Harbor; or, if it could not be located by the reconnaissance planes, the Striking Force had orders to scout around the Islands and select a new launching point. But everything went according to plan.

Admiral Nagumo reached his launching point slightly before 0600; and, as the planes hit Oahu "right on the nose," it is evident that his fleet navigating officer had done an excellent job of dead reckoning. For several days there had been little or no opportunity to check the flagship's position from the heavenly bodies, but the proper allowances for current and leeway had been made, and the

---

[20] Fuchida Interrogation USSBS 603 p. 7. This is probably more reliable as to source of the information than Lt. Cdr. Shiga's printed in *P. H. Attack* Part 13 pp. 645-47.

[21] The track chart furnished by the Japanese is obviously inaccurate as to the last leg, showing the turning point too far north. The turn must have been at about lat. 30° N.

ships arrived on time at the designated spot on the ocean where winged death was to be released.

In the darkness before dawn there was a heavy overcast at about 6000 feet, a moderate sea running that made the flight decks pitch badly, and a fresh northeast tradewind blowing. The carriers commenced launching the first wave immediately: 40 "Kates" armed with deadly aërial torpedoes, 49 more equipped as high-level bombers, 51 "Val" dive-bombers and 43 "Zeke" fighters took off and orbited south of the force, waiting for their group commander's signals to go.[22] Again emotion welled high in the breasts of the Japanese. Aviators were exalted with their "divine mission"; ground crews and sailors off watch gathered on the flight decks and shrilled their *Banzais* into the gray dawn.

A magnificent sunrise greeted the flyers as they sped toward their objective at an altitude of 3000 meters above the surface of the sea. When the flight commander's navigator believed they were near Oahu, they ducked under the overcast, and at a few minutes before 0740 sighted the coastline. The Waianae and Koolau Mountains were wreathed in clouds, but their southern slopes stretching to Pearl Harbor and Honolulu were perfectly clear.

"Pearl Harbor was still asleep in the morning mist," wrote Commander Itaya, who led the first formation of planes. "It was calm and serene inside the harbor, not even a trace of smoke from the ships at Oahu. The orderly groups of barracks, the wriggling white

[22] Fuchida Interrogation USSBS 603 p. 3.

Early in the war, nicknames of boys and girls were assigned by us to the different types of Japanese planes: —

"Kate" (Type 97 Mark–3) was the standard carrier-borne torpedo-bomber, single engine, normal cruising speed 166 m.p.h., range at that speed loaded, 1060 miles, crew of two or three. It carried one 1760-lb. torpedo or the equivalent in bombs and was armed with three 7.7 mm. machine guns.

"Val" (Type 99 Marks–1 and –2) was the standard carrier-borne Japanese dive-bomber, single engine, normal cruising speed 190 m.p.h., range at that speed, loaded, 1095 miles, crew of two. With two bomb carriers under each wing it could carry 1078 lbs. of bombs, and was armed with three 7.7 mm. machine guns.

"Zeke" (Type Zero Mark–1) was the standard one-man fighter plane both for carriers and shore bases. Normal cruising speed 240 m.p.h., range, loaded, at that speed 790 miles (1030 miles at 171 m.p.h.). Carried two 7.7 mm. and two 20-mm. machine guns. (Information from *Japanese Aircraft and Armament*, issued by office of Assistant Chief of Air Staff, Intelligence, No. 44, 11 March 1944.)

line of the automobile road climbing up to the mountain-top; fine objectives of attack in all directions. In line with these, inside the harbor, were important ships of the Pacific Fleet, strung out and anchored two ships side by side in an orderly manner." [23]

It was now 0750 December 7. The hour of doom had struck for the old Battle Force Pacific Fleet, for scores of Army and Navy planes in Oahu, and for over two thousand of their officers and men.

## 3. *The Advance Expeditionary Force* [24]

An integral though inconspicuous component of the attack on Pearl Harbor was the Advance Expeditionary Force of 27 aggressive submarines. This force was charged with the triple mission of reconnaissance, transmitting information to the Striking Force, and torpedoing ships that escaped the air attack. Three more with the Striking Force and two far-ranging scouts joined later.

Most of the participating submarines were of the long-range I-type, displacing 1955 tons surfaced, 320 feet long, and with a cruising range of 12,000 miles at 14 knots. Eleven of them were equipped with small planes secured abaft the conning towers; five others bore midget submarines 41 to 45 feet long, carrying two small torpedoes and propelled by storage batteries. These five midgets and their two-man crews were called the "Special Naval Attack Unit." They were secured to the mother ships by heavy clamps and connected with them by an access hatch as well as by telephone and battery-charging leads. As sacrifice missions make a special appeal to the Japanese conception of courage and loyalty, there was intense competition for these jobs, and Lieutenant Iwasa, who conceived the idea, was allowed to carry it out.

The large submarines sortied from Kure and Yokosuka on 18–20 November and called at Kwajalein for fuel and supplies.

[23] *The Pearl Harbor Operation* p. 15.
[24] Data from various Japanese sources printed in *P. H. Attack* Part 13 pp. 414, 487–501; *The Pearl Harbor Operations* pp. 17–24, with pictures of the midget heroes.

*I-26* and *I-10* broke off, one for the Aleutians, the other to watch
Samoa and the Fijis; the rest pressed on to Hawaii. On or about 5
December (West Longitude date) they took up prearranged scouting and patrolling sectors on segments of circles drawn from Pearl
Harbor as a center, the nearest 8½ miles and the farthest 100 miles
from the harbor mouth. What the Japanese Navy's Office of Public Relations described as "the glorious, incomparable, strong attack upon Pearl Harbor by the Special Naval Attack Unit . . .
at the time of the iconoclastic blow against outrageous America
which disregarded our great motive and mission of world peace" [25]
was launched shortly after midnight 6–7 December by casting off
the five midgets from their mother ships.

Ensign R. C. McCloy USNR of U.S.S. *Condor,* one of two small
converted minesweepers that were conducting a routine sweep
of the harbor entrance, made the first enemy contact of the war.
At 0342, four full hours before the air attack, he sighted the periscope of a midget submarine less than two miles outside the harbor
entrance buoy, and passed the word by blinker signal to destroyer
*Ward,* then on night patrol.[26] After *Ward* had been searching for
over two hours, a Navy Catalina sighted the same or another
midget at 0633 and dropped smoke pots on the spot. The submarine
was apparently trailing U.S.S. *Antares* (a repair ship engaged in
towing an empty steel barge toward Pearl Harbor) in the hope of
slipping through the gate under the protection of the barge's
wake.[27] *Ward,* being close by at the time, attacked the midget at
0645 and sank it with gunfire and depth charges. At 0654 *Ward*
radioed in code to Commandant 14th Naval District: "We have
attacked, fired upon and dropped depth charges on a submarine operating in the defensive sea area." This was the first message sent out
by anyone about the contact. Owing to a delay in decoding by a not

---

[25] *Pearl Harbor Operations* p. 18.
[26] *P. H. Attack* Part 37 pp. 1222, 1282–90, 1298–99.
[27] Same, p. 1283. *Ward* and *Condor* radio communications between 0520 and
0534 were overheard and logged by the Bishop's Point Radio Station (Part 37
p. 703) but nobody thought to relay this to headquarters.

very bright yeoman, the 14th Naval District duty officer (Lieutenant Commander Harold Kaminsky) did not receive it until 0712.[28] He passed the word to Admiral Bloch, who immediately ordered the ready-duty destroyer (U.S.S. *Monaghan*) to get under way and assist *Ward*, and the stand-by destroyer to get up steam. Between 0720 and 0725 Bloch's office notified Commander V. R. Murphy, the Cincpac staff duty officer who (after sundry delays owing to telephone switchboard congestion) called the Commander in Chief. Admiral Kimmel said "I will be right down," and it was in response to this call that he was on his way to headquarters when the air bombs began to drop.[29]

Owing to an unexplained and almost incredible laxness, the gate in the anti-torpedo net, which had been opened for the entry of the two minesweepers at 0458, was not closed until 0840.[30] Consequently, at least one midget succeeded in entering the harbor. Destroyer *Monaghan* disposed of it, as will subsequently be related. Another ran on a reef to the eastward of the entrance channel, was spotted there by destroyer *Helm* and fired on at 0817; it slipped off the ledge, submerged and evaded searchers, but owing to damage was beached on the windward side of Oahu, off Bellows Field, where the skipper surrendered.[31] A chart of Pearl Harbor recovered from this boat shows a navigation track indicating that it intended to make the circuit of Ford Island.[32] The fate of the other two midgets is uncertain; probably they were finished off in one or more of the anti-submarine attacks reported by U.S.S. *St. Louis, Blue, Ramsay* and *Breese*. At any rate, all five of the participating midgets were lost to the Japanese without having caused any direct damage.

Aggressive patrolling and depth-charging by destroyers and

---

[28] 14th N.D. Control Post Watch Officer's Log, in Same, Part 24 p. 1649. But *Ward's* log (Part 37 p. 1290) says the dispatch was sent by voice transmission at 0645. Cf. Part 36 pp. 276–77 and Part 26 p. 135.
[29] Testimony of Kaminsky and Murphy before Roberts and Hart Commissions, *P. H. Attack* Part 23 pp. 1035–41, Part 26 pp. 209–10.
[30] Quartermaster's log of the net tender in Same, Part 38 Items 133–34.
[31] *P. H. Attack* Part 16 pp. 2016–22.
[32] Reproduced in Walter Karig *Battle Report* I Plate V.

other ships on patrol completely nullified the work of the big, 1900-ton submarines. They did not torpedo a single one of the very numerous ships entering and departing from Pearl Harbor and Honolulu. In groups the twenty I-boats deployed south of Oahu returned to Kwajalein by mid-January, but seven were ordered to the West Coast to join scouts *I-26* and *I-10* already there. En route, just as bombs fell on Pearl Harbor, *I-26* had sunk a small merchant-man; others sank a few more off California and Oregon.

Thus the Advance Expeditionary Force failed completely. It did little damage, but lost all five midget submarines and one large one, *I-70*, sunk by a plane from U.S.S. *Enterprise.*

## 4.  *The Air Strikes of 7 December* [33]

### *a.*  The Surprise

Sunday 7 December 1941, the "day that will live in infamy," dawned bright and fair over Pearl Harbor. According to the Nautical Almanac the time of sunrise was 0626; but at that season day comes up from over Mount Tantalus and Mount Olympus, which were carrying their usual nightcap of tradewind clouds. So it was almost 0700 when the sun actually appeared, heightening the green of the canefields that stretch up the slopes above Aiea, deepening the blue of the lochs, as the arms of Pearl Harbor are called. Even for Oahu, favored by nature throughout the winter, this was an uncommonly beautiful, peaceful and bright Sabbath morn. Every so often a cloud broke loose from the Koolau Mountains and floated lazily over the harbor in the light N to NE tradewind. On board

---

[33] The best general narrative of what happened at Pearl Harbor and the Naval Air Station is the official Cincpac Report to the Secretary of the Navy dated 15 Feb. 1942. This is followed almost word for word in the Statement made 15 Nov. 1945 by Rear Admiral T. B. Inglis, Chief of Naval Intelligence, before the Joint Congressional Committee, printed in part in *P. H. Attack* Part 1 pp. 42–49, and separately with a useful "Navy Folder" of charts and tables. Awards and citations for acts of individual heroism will be found in Walter Karig and Welbourn Kelley *Battle Report — Pearl Harbor to Coral Sea* (1944) pp. 330–37.

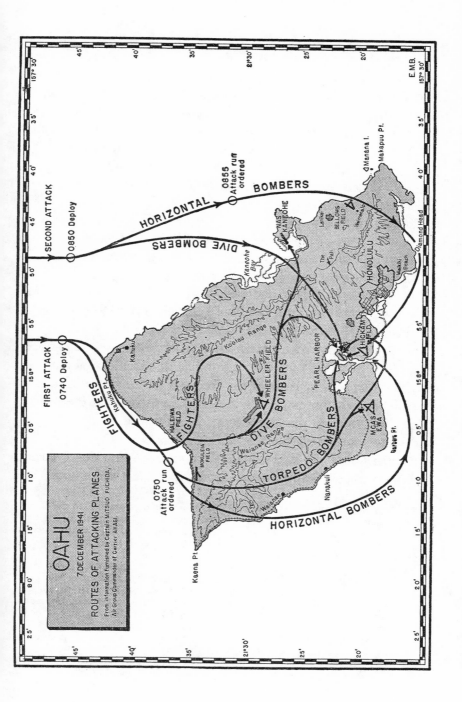

OAHU
7 DECEMBER 1941
ROUTES OF ATTACKING PLANES
From information furnished by Captain MITSUO FUCHIDA,
Air Group Commander of Carrier AKAGI.

SECOND ATTACK
0850 Deploy

HORIZONTAL BOMBERS
0855 Attack run ordered

DIVE BOMBERS

FIRST ATTACK
0740 Deploy

FIGHTERS

0750 Attack run ordered

FIGHTERS

DIVE BOMBERS

TORPEDO BOMBERS

HORIZONTAL BOMBERS

Kaena Pt.
Kahuku Pt.
Kahuku
Koolau Range
Kaneohe Bay
Kaneohe
The Pali
HONOLULU
Waikiki Beach
Diamond Head
Makapuu Pt.
Manana I.
Bellows Field
Lanikai
Kailua
NAS KANEOHE
HICKAM FIELD
PEARL HARBOR
WHEELER FIELD
HALEIWA FIELD
MOKULEIA FIELD
Waianae Range
Waianae
Nanakuli
MCAS EWA
Barbers Pt.

157° 30'
45'
40'
35'
21° 30'
25'
20'
E.M.B.
157° 30'
35'
40'
45'
50'
55'
158°
05'
10'
15'
20'
25'
3.5'
21° 30'
25'
20'

ships the forenoon watch was piped to breakfast, while the men they were to relieve concluded the various duties of a Sunday morning watch, cleaning brass and wiping dew off the machine guns, of which about one in four were fully manned — for the Fleet never wholly relaxed and "Condition 3" of readiness was always set in harbor.[34] The sound of church bells at Honolulu, ringing for eight o'clock mass, came over the harbor, whose calm surface was only lightly rippled by the breeze. Many officers were at breakfast in their wardrooms, others were just rising; and seamen who had finished breakfast were lounging on deck talking, reading or writing letters home. Among the 70 combat ships and 24 auxiliaries in the harbor,[35] only one, destroyer *Helm*,[36] was under way. As the hour for morning colors (0800) approached, sailors in white uniforms removed the jack and ensign from their lockers, the signal bridge was ready to hoist the Blue Peter or "Prep" flag, and boatswains were all set to pipe the preparatory signal at 0755.

Sharp-eyed Boatswain's Mate Milligan of destroyer *Allen* noticed twenty to twenty-five planes orbiting at an altitude of about 5000 feet at 0730; but, in view of the frequent air attack drills held of late, he thought nothing of it. Apparently these were the "Vals," which had reached the target first, owing to their superior speed, and were waiting for the torpedo-carrying "Kates."

Rear Admiral W. R. Furlong, Commander Mine Force Pacific Fleet, was pacing the quarterdeck of U.S.S. *Oglala* tied up outboard

---

[34] *P. H. Attack* Part 1 p. 34. This bore little resemblance, however, to the Condition 3 of wartime. The main and 5-inch batteries were not manned at all; the plotting room, directors and ammunition supply were not manned; and, in the machine guns that were manned, the ready ammunition was in locked boxes and the Officer of the Deck had the keys.

[35] Eight battleships, 2 heavy cruisers, 6 light cruisers, 29 destroyers, 5 submarines, 1 gunboat, 9 minelayers (8 of them converted destroyers), 10 minesweepers (4 of them converted destroyers) and 24 auxiliaries (10 tenders, 3 repair ships, 2 oilers, 2 ocean-going tugs) and 1 each of the following types: hospital, hydrographic survey, store issue, target, ammunition, submarine rescue and the *Argonne*. ("Navy Folder," Item 9.)

[36] *Helm* got under way from East Loch at 0726 and at 0755 was just entering West Loch for deperming. She commenced sortieing at once, shot down a plane before passing through the gate, and fired at the midget submarine on Tripod Reef.

of cruiser *Helena* at Pier 1010, in an excellent position to survey what followed. A few seconds short of 0755 he noticed a plane flying low over Ford Island from the northeast. Then he heard the explosion of a bomb on the seaplane ramp at the south end of the island, saw dust and debris arise, but thought it an accidental drop by one of our own planes.[37] The plane turned up the main channel between his ship and Ford Island, and he saw the "meatball" insignia painted on its side. He called for General Quarters and, realizing he was the S.O.P.A. (senior officer present afloat) in Pearl Harbor, had the signal hoisted: "All Ships in Harbor Sortie." [38]

Almost simultaneously with the fall of the first bomb, the signal tower at Pearl Harbor telephoned to Admiral Kimmel's headquarters, "Enemy air raid — not drill." At 0758 Rear Admiral Patrick N. L. Bellinger from his headquarters on Ford Island broadcast a message that shook the United States as nothing had since the firing on Fort Sumter: —

AIR RAID, PEARL HARBOR — THIS IS NO DRILL.[39]

The Sabbath calm was rudely broken by bomb explosions, by the hoarse klaxon sounding General Quarters on every vessel; presently by the sharp bark of 5-inch anti-aircraft guns and the nervous chatter of machine guns. Colors were raised defiantly and the Battle of Pearl Harbor was on. In one split second, the United States passed from a precarious neutrality to full-fledged belligerency; 7 December was the first of 1364 days of war.[40]

[37] The same explosion was observed from many other ships. Some gave the time a little earlier and some a little later, but the majority have it coincide with the preliminary signal for morning colors.
[38] Admiral Pye was ashore and Rear Admiral Kidd in *Arizona* was Furlong's junior. The senior member of Admiral Pye's staff on board *California* made the same signal a few minutes later. It was belayed after Phase I, owing to the fear that mines had been sowed in the harbor.
[39] *P. H. Attack* Part 26 p. 135. This was followed "a few minutes later by a similar message" from Admiral Kimmel. (Part 1 p. 43; Kimmel's broadcast, sent at 0800, said, "This is not a drill" — Part 23 p. 935.) When this was brought to Secretary Knox in Washington he exclaimed, "My God! This can't be true, this must mean the Philippines!" (*Report*, p. 439.)
[40] V–J Day: 2 Sept. 1945.

## *b.* Attacks on Battleship Row [41]

Although there were 94 ships of the United States Navy in Pearl Harbor to choose from, the Japanese knew exactly what they wanted. Eight battleships were the priority targets; and the aviators, well-briefed with the latest clandestine information from the Japanese consul at Honolulu, and supplied with accurate charts, knew that they were tied up singly or in pairs to the great mooring quays [42] along the southeast shore of Ford Island. Four separate torpedo-plane attacks were made before 0825 — the major one by 12 "Kates," which swung in from the southeast over Merry Point, split up and launched their specially fitted shoal-water torpedoes at altitudes between 40 and 100 feet above the water. The second torpedo attack by 3 planes was made on the same battleships; the third, by a single plane, was directed at cruiser *Helena;* the fourth, of 5 planes which came in from the northwest, attacked the ships moored to the berths on the north side of Ford Island, two or three

[41] The Cincpac official Report, and the Navy Statement, divide the air attack on Oahu into five phases, as follows: —

*Phase I:* 0755–0825. Torpedo and dive-bomber attacks on battleships, and strafing attacks on Naval Air Station (Ford Island), Ewa (Marine Airfield), Kaneohe (Naval Patrol Plane Station), Hickam, Wheeler and Bellows Fields (Army Air Force).

*Phase II:* 0825–0840. Lull.

*Phase III:* 0840–0915. High-level bombing attacks on Pearl Harbor.

*Phase IV:* 0915–0945. Dive-bombing attacks on Pearl Harbor.

*Phase V:* 0945 on. All planes withdraw.

It has seemed best in this presentation to start with Phase I, but carry through the story of each ship or station attacked, even if it overlaps into later phases.

Phase I was executed by the first wave of planes from the Japanese carriers, which according to Captain Fuchida, senior officer of the attack group and an actual participant, consisted of 40 "Kates" armed with torpedoes, 50 "Kates" doing high-level bombing, 50 "Val" dive-bombers, and 50 "Zeke" fighters. The few attacks in Phase II were apparently by laggards from the first wave. Phases III and IV were executed by the second wave from the carriers, comprising 50 high-level "Kates," 80 "Vals" and 40 "Zekes." (*Interrogations of Japanese Officials* I 23. These figures are accepted in *The Campaigns of the Pacific War,* although they vary considerably from those given in "Navy Folder" Item 11, which are apparently the contemporary estimates by U.S. forces of number of planes sighted over Pearl Harbor only, not counting those that struck the airfields.)

[42] These, technically known as "interrupted quays," were pairs of hexagonal concrete pillars embedded in the harbor bottom, with fenders and timbers at waterline level, and bollards for the ships' lines topside.

Ford Island early in the attack

wo "Kates" are flying over the harbor. Geyser from torpedo hit on *Oklahoma*, hich is already listing. At left, smoke arising from bomb hits on *Raleigh* and *Utah*

*West Virginia* sinking alongside *Tennessee*
Survivor being rescued by motor sailing launch

*Pearl Harbor, 7 December*

After her magazine exploded
(Stern of *Tennessee* at left)

Blown in half

*Death of* Arizona, 7 *December*

of which were normally occupied by carriers.[43] From within five minutes of the first torpedo attack, the battleships were also combed fore and aft by dive-bombers, which in that position were very difficult to get at with the few anti-aircraft guns then mounted on battlewagons. Both "Kates" and "Vals," after launching torpedoes and dropping bombs, flew back over their targets, strafing viciously to kill the men. Half an hour after the battle opened, *Arizona* was a burning wreck, *Oklahoma* had capsized, *West Virginia* had sunk, *California* was going down, and every other battleship (except *Pennsylvania* in dry dock) had been badly damaged. By 0825 the Japanese had accomplished about 90 per cent of their objective — they had wrecked the Battle Force of the Pacific Fleet.

Let us take up the events on each ship, one by one.[44] *West Virginia*, the youngest battleship present — eighteen years old on 1 December — was one of the first and hardest hit, and also one of the last to be returned to active duty. "Wee Vee," as her crew called *West Virginia*, took six or seven torpedoes on her port side — four of them on the armor belt amidships when she was listing heavily — and, for good measure, two bombs, one of which started a fire. The first torpedoes hit before 0756.

Two fortunate circumstances, one due to training and the other to chance, saved *West Virginia* from the fate of battleships that received fewer hits. A group of her younger officers, Lieutenant C. V. Ricketts and three lieutenants junior grade, H. B. Stark, F. H. White USNR and R. R. Beecham, discussing an air raid on the Fleet, and damage control measures thereby required, acted promptly and decisively. The officer of the deck, Ensign Roman L. Brooks, saw the first bomb hit the hangar on

---

[43] It was thought that the aviators expected to find carriers there, but the Striking Force had already been informed that the carriers were out. A chart recovered from a midget submarine did show *Saratoga* in one of these berths, but the midget subs had no information later than November. (*P. H. Attack* Part 31 Items 57, 58.)

[44] The following account is based primarily on the Action Reports of individual ships; and on the BuShips War Damage Reports on them, valuable correctives to early estimates. The writer has also obtained much information from individuals who were on board at the time, and from a Report by an officer in charge of salvage, Capt. V. D. Chapline "Pearl Harbor a Year Later" 14 Dec. 1942.

Ford Island and thought that it was an internal explosion on board *California*, which was in his line of vision thither. He promptly gave the order "Away Fire and Rescue Party!" This immediately started *West Virginia* personnel topside on the run and saved hundreds of lives. Lieutenant White, one of the first to reach the deck, saw a "Kate" in the act of launching, and gave the general alarm before the first torpedo hit.

These torpedo hits knocked out all power, light, communications, and the anti-aircraft guns on the port side. The ship listed so rapidly that the guns on the starboard side, which opened fire within two minutes, could only be served by organizing a double row of ammunition passers, one to pass and the other to hold up the passer.

Lieutenant Commander J. S. Harper, at Central Station, gave the order to counterflood promptly, but it never reached the repair parties because the telephones had gone silent with the loss of power — installation of sound-powered telephones had not been completed. Lieutenant C. V. Ricketts, although on the sick list, started counterflooding on his own initiative, with the aid of Boatswain's Mate Billingsley, who knew how to operate the gear. This counterflooding, together with the retarding force of the wire cables between *West Virginia* and *Tennessee*, corrected a 28-degree list to 15 degrees, and allowed her to sink bodily until the

### KEY TO CHART OF PEARL HARBOR
#### (Reading NW to SE in nests of ships)

1 Destroyer-minecraft *Ramsay, Gamble, Montgomery*
2 Destroyer-minecraft *Trever, Breese, Zane, Perry, Wasmuth*
3 Destroyers *Monaghan, Farragut, Dale, Aylwin*
4 Destroyers *Henley, Patterson, Ralph Talbot*
5 Destroyers *Selfridge, Case, Tucker, Reid, Conyngham;* tender *Whitney*
6 Destroyers *Phelps, MacDonough, Worden, Dewey, Hull;* tender *Dobbin*
7 Submarines *Narwhal, Gudgeon, Dolphin, Tautog;* seaplane tenders *Thornton, Hulbert*
8 Destroyers *Jarvis, Mugford* (inside *Argonne* and *Sacramento*)
9 Destroyer *Cummings;* destroyer-minelayers *Preble, Tracy, Pruitt, Sicard;* destroyer *Schley;* minesweeper *Grebe*
10 Minesweepers *Bobolink, Vireo, Turkey, Rail, Tern*

Other auxiliaries, not shown, were moored up West Loch. There were also several tugs and yard craft, not shown, in the area of the chart.

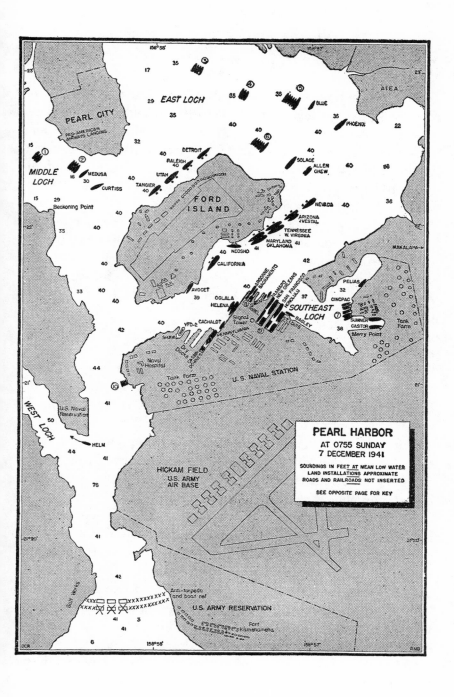

PEARL HARBOR
AT 0755 SUNDAY
7 DECEMBER 1941

SOUNDINGS IN FEET AT MEAN LOW WATER
LAND INSTALLATIONS APPROXIMATE
ROADS AND RAILROADS NOT INSERTED

SEE OPPOSITE PAGE FOR KEY

turn of the port bilge hit bottom, and so saved the ship from capsizing.

In the meantime Captain Mervyn S. Bennion had been disemboweled by fragments from a bomb that exploded on *Tennessee* alongside. His last order was to Ricketts and White to leave him, which they refused to do; Chief Pharmacist's Mate Leak administered a hypodermic, and he was moved to another part of the bridge. His only thought was for the ship and crew, and he kept asking what was going on until he died.

Within a few minutes of opening fire the ready ammunition for the anti-aircraft guns was expended. Ricketts and Ensign Ford organized an ammunition-passing team which continued to operate when the ship was all aflame topside, for *Arizona's* forward magazines had exploded, showering burning debris on *West Virginia's* decks.

For an hour and a half all hands stood by to fight fires and only the wounded were evacuated. During much of this time the ship was being dive-bombed and strafed. Anti-aircraft gunners stood to their guns despite the list. At 0940 the ship was on fire from the bow to turret No. 1, flames shooting up to the foretop, curiously sparing that end of the bridge where Captain Bennion's body lay. About a hundred men, blown overboard or injured and fallen overboard, were in imminent danger from burning oil, or drowning; but most of these were saved by boats from other ships, notably by a motor launch from the repair ship *Rigel*.

At about 1005, when all power was lost and the ship rested on the bottom and fire swept her superstructure, the damage control officer ordered Abandon Ship. Survivors went over the side into boats or swam to Ford Island or to the *Tennessee*. Some crossed to her by walking tightrope on a 5-inch gun, and remained there to help her gunners. Senior officers then organized a working party which returned on board and, with the aid of others who reported, brought all fires under control during the afternoon.

"Throughout the entire action," reported Commander Hillenkoetter, "there was never the slightest sign of faltering or of cowardice. The actions of the officers and men were wholly commendable; their spirit was marvelous; there was no panic, no shirking nor flinching, and words fail in attempting to describe the truly magnificent display of courage, discipline and devotion to duty of all." Highly commended was Chief Boatswain's Mate L. M. Jansen, commander of *YG–17*, who brought his "honey barge" (garbage lighter) alongside and helped fight the fires until quenched, then he performed the same service for *Arizona*.

*West Virginia* lost two officers and 103 men killed or missing out of 87 officers and 1454 men "on board 1 December"; and additional 52 men were wounded but recovered.[45] These casualties were light, in view of the heavy damage sustained by the ship, because of the excellent discipline of the crew and the prompt alert.

*Tennessee* (Captain C. E. Reordan), twenty-one years old, and one of five turbo-electric-drive battleships, was moored inboard of *West Virginia* and so protected by her from aërial torpedoes. She received two bomb hits very early in the action. The first, which detonated on the center gun of turret No. 2, is the one that killed Captain Bennion of *West Virginia;* the other hit turret No. 3, pierced the 5-inch armor and exploded inside, fortunately with a low order detonation.[46] Most of her damage, however, came from fires started by flaming debris or burning oil from *Arizona,* moored only 75 feet astern. *Tennessee's* crew were able to handle their own fires and render assistance to the other battleship as well. Fire fighting continued all that day and the next night, the men taking time out only for coffee and sandwiches. Casualties in this ship were light: 5 men killed or missing, 1 officer and 20 men wounded, out of 94 officers and 1372 men on board 1 December.

[45] These and the casualty figures for the other battleships are the revised official ones compiled in Casualty Section, Welfare Division, Bureau of Naval Personnel. The figures of total on board include Marines and flag personnel. Men who died of wounds on or before 16 Dec. 1941 are included with the killed and missing. The number of men who died after 16 Dec. 1941 from wounds received on 7 Dec. has never been compiled.

[46] By piecing together fragments, it was found that these bombs were really converted 16-inch armor-piercing shells weighing between 1500 and 2000 lbs. The story that they were a job lot purchased from the British before the war is not correct.

Although *Tennessee's* power plant remained intact, the ship was so wedged in by the sunken *West Virginia* that it was very difficult to move her. As early as 20 December she got under way, in company with *Maryland* and *Pennsylvania*, and was given a complete overhaul and modernization at the West Coast battleship repair center at Bremerton, Puget Sound.

Battleship *Arizona*, moored astern of *Tennessee*, took the worst beating of any ship in the Fleet, suffered the largest number of casualties, and became a total loss. Although moored inboard, she did not enjoy much protection, for the outboard berth was occupied by the repair ship *Vestal*, beyond which her bow projected about 100 feet. The repair ship remained there during the attack on *Arizona*, took two bomb hits which caused serious flooding, but got under way around 0845 and saved herself by beaching on Aiea Shoal.

*Arizona* barely had time to sound General Quarters, man battle stations, and set Condition Zed (complete watertight integrity) when she received several lethal torpedo and bomb hits. One torpedo passed ahead of *Vestal* and hit under turret No. 1; but the thing that broke her up was a heavy bomb that hit beside the second turret, penetrated the forecastle, and exploded in one of the forward magazines before it could be flooded — so fast the action occurred. This explosion completely wrecked the forward part of the ship. Flames shot five hundred feet into the air; scores of men, including Rear Admiral Isaac C. Kidd, who was on the signal bridge, and Captain Franklin Van Valkenburgh, who was on the navigation bridge, were killed. This happened, apparently, before 0756. Shortly after, a second bomb went right down the stack, a third hit the boat deck, a fourth the face-plate of No. 4 turret; and four more struck the superstructure between the bridge and the tripod mast. *Arizona* listed radically but settled so fast that she did not capsize. A hideous business altogether — over a thousand men burned to a crisp or trapped below until they drowned. Machine guns continued firing at planes until the heat of the flames drove the men from their guns, and all able-bodied survivors remained on board fighting fires and evacuating the wounded until 1032, although for half an hour earlier she looked like one mass of flames. *Arizona* lost almost four fifths of her complement — 47 officers and 1056 men killed or missing, 5 officers and 39 men wounded, out of 100 officers and 1411 men on board 1 December.

*Nevada,* moored next astern of *Arizona* at the easternmost berth in battleship row, was lucky in that she had no ship tied up alongside to restrict her movements, and she was superbly handled by Lieutenant Commander Francis J. Thomas USNR, the senior officer on board at the time. The anti-aircraft battery, directed by Ensign J. K. Taussig, Jr., even after he had been severely wounded, opened fire promptly and accurately. The 5-inch battery on the port side, commanded by Ensign T. H. Taylor, shot down one and possibly two of the torpedo-bombers that made for the ship; .50-caliber machine guns accounted for another which splashed off her port quarter. It was probably due to this good shooting that *Nevada,* despite her exposed position, suffered only one torpedo hit, and that well forward. The torpedo tore a hole 45 feet long and 30 feet high, flooding many compartments but leaving the power plant intact. Around 0825 the ship was subjected to a severe dive-bombing attack, which resulted in two or three hits. Thomas, the acting commanding officer, then decided, in spite of the enormous hole made by the torpedo hit, to stand out. Chief Boatswain E. J. Hill jumped onto the mooring quay, cast off the lines under strafing fire, and swam back to the ship just as she was getting under way.[47]

Shortly before 0900 Rear Admiral Furlong in *Oglala,* having observed explosions in the main ship channel which looked like magnetic mines, signaled *Nevada* to go around the north side of Ford Island; but she was already committed to the southerly course and passed right over the scene of the explosions without damage. A flight of "Val" dive-bombers making for *Pennsylvania,* seeing a battleship under way, concentrated on her instead, and, when *Nevada* had reached a point opposite the floating dry dock, she

[47] He was blown overboard by a bomb later in the morning when directing the anchoring detail, and was killed.

looked like a goner. The spray from exploding near-misses almost concealed her from view and she received more hits here, too. Admiral Furlong hailed two tugs and ordered them to assist the battleship, fearing she might be sunk in the channel; they went alongside, pushed her clear, helped her extinguish fires (for her fire mains had been ruptured by bombs) and beached her on hard bottom at Waipio Point, opposite the southern end of Ford Island, around 0940. There the ship's crew brought fires under control and secured.

*Nevada* had taken at least five bomb hits in addition to the torpedo. The forward part of the ship was pretty thoroughly wrecked, the superstructure was mostly destroyed and the navigation bridge and charthouse deck were completely burned through. But the engineering department was intact. Three officers and 47 men were killed or missing, 5 officers and 104 men wounded, out of 94 officers and 1390 men on board 1 December. *Nevada* was floated on 12 February 1942, proceeded to Puget Sound after temporary repairs, and rejoined the Fleet before the end of 1943.

The remaining pair of battleships, moored to the next berth forward, was *Maryland* and *Oklahoma*. The latter, in the outboard position, was hit very early in the fight. A few moments after the first bomb was seen to explode on the southwest end of Ford Island, and almost simultaneously with the call to General Quarters, *Oklahoma* was struck by three torpedoes in rapid succession and took a list of 25 to 35 degrees. There was no time to set Condition Zed, to counterflood, or to take other measures to prevent capsizing; and the rapid listing prevented all but one or two machine guns from firing. Captain H. D. Bode was ashore. Within a few minutes the Executive Officer, Commander Jesse L. Kenworthy, Jr., decided after a quick conference with Lieutenant Commander William H. Hobby, the First Lieutenant, to abandon ship. The word was passed and the men were directed to go over the ship's starboard side as she rolled. Two more torpedo hits above the armor belt were received as she started to capsize; the men were strafed as they crawled over, and explosions from high-level bombers hit all

*Nevada* in her gallant sortie

*Oklahoma* capsized, *Maryland* alongside; *West Virginia* and *Arizona* burning

*Pearl Harbor, 7 December*

General view of the attack, near the end

*California* listing and sinking; *Neosho* backing away
Signals order certain ships to sortie

*Pearl Harbor, 7 December*

around. *Oklahoma* only stopped rolling when her masts caught in the mud of the harbor bottom. Within twenty minutes of the start of the attack she was capsized to 150 degrees with the starboard side of her bottom above water and a portion of the keel clear. "The conduct of the crew was excellent throughout," and many climbed on board *Maryland* to assist fighting her anti-aircraft batteries. Twenty officers and 395 men were killed or missing, 2 officers and 30 men wounded, out of 82 officers and 1272 men on board.

*Maryland*, protected from torpedoes by *Oklahoma*, was the luckiest battleship. Just as the attack started, Seaman L. V. Short broke off addressing Christmas cards to operate a machine gun, and got him a torpedo plane before it could launch. Only 2 officers and 2 men were killed or missing, and 14 men wounded, out of 108 officers and 1496 men on board. The only damage to the ship was caused by a fragmentation bomb that detonated on the forecastle awning ridgerope, and by one of the 16-inch armor-piercing kind which entered the forecastle below the waterline and detonated in the hold. The Navy Yard completed temporary repairs on *Maryland* by 20 December without taking her into dry dock, and she was the first of the Battle Fleet to return to active service, in February 1942.

Skipping oiler *Neosho*, which got under way promptly and received no hits, we come to *California*, flagship of Vice Admiral W. S. Pye, at the southernmost berth. Although the last of the battleships to be hit, she was less prepared than any for the blows. Her material condition as to watertight integrity was bad; [48] too

[48] It is a well-known fact, although never publicly admitted, that battleships carrying admirals' flags, although taut and smart in appearance, were commonly inferior to others in readiness and material condition because (1) of a practice of "marking them up" — that is, overlooking shortcomings at material inspections, in order not to mortify or annoy the admiral; and because (2) admirals and their staffs demanded lots of "spit and polish." In the case of *California*, a material inspection was about to be made, and normal preparations required thorough ventilation of the tanks and voids. This explains the fact, reported by the commanding officer, that six manhole covers to the double bottom were off, and the securing nuts of 12 others slacked away. (BuShips War Damage Report *California*, 28 Nov. 1942; Capt. J. W. Bunkley Report on Damage Control to CNO, 26 Jan. 1942.)

many of her officers were ashore; and some of those on board failed to act quickly or intelligently. There was a delay both in sounding General Quarters and ordering Condition Zed set.

At 0805, before Condition Zed could be executed, even so far as the bad material condition of the ship permitted, and just as the machine-gun battery opened fire, two deep-running torpedoes hit *California* below the armor belt, one just forward of the bridge and the other aft, below turret No. 3. Their effect, owing to the "unbuttoned" condition of the ship, proved to be far-reaching and disastrous. She began listing to port. Prompt though unorthodox counterflooding, directed by Ensign Edgar M. Fain USNR, prevented her from capsizing, but the rupture of oil tanks by the forward torpedo let salt water into the fuel system and, before it could be cleared, light and power were lost. It was now 0810; all anti-aircraft batteries were blazing away, ammunition supply being kept up by hand. At 0825 a bomb exploded below, setting off the anti-aircraft ammunition magazine, spreading blast and fire in the ammunition passageway, and killing about 50 men; a second bomb ruptured the bow plates.

Owing to herculean efforts by the damage control party, light, power and water pressure were restored at 0855, the men concentrated on fighting fires which they successfully brought under control; and *California* was ready to get underway by 0910, using four boilers. But before Captain Bunkley, who in the meantime had come aboard, could issue orders to unmoor, burning oil from the battleship to windward floated down and engulfed the stern. So at 1002 the captain ordered Abandon Ship. Shortly after the wind blew this pool of burning oil clear, and at 1015 the captain ordered all hands to return on board. Not everyone obeyed.

Although minesweepers *Vireo* and *Bobolink* closed the battleship and applied their pumps, and numerous "handy billies" (portable gasoline-driven pumps) were obtained from other vessels, *California* slowly settled. Her bulkheads were so leaky that the water entering the great gashes made by enemy torpedo hits could not be isolated;[49] they were simply pumping Pearl Harbor through the ship. Prompt work by divers might have kept her afloat, but as it was she slowly settled into the mud, and did not reach her final position, with only the superstructure above water, until late Wednesday night, 10 December. Six officers and 92 men were killed or missing, 3 officers and 58 men wounded, out of 120 officers and 1546 men on board. Refloated 24 March 1942, *California* proceeded to Bremerton under her own power and rejoined the Fleet in time for the Marianas operation.

The only other ship moored to this side of Ford Island was the twenty-three-year-old seaplane tender *Avocet*, converted from a minesweeper. Her two 3-inch 50-cal. guns opened fire about seven minutes after the start of the action, and winged one "Kate" that had turned away after torpedoing *California*. This plane was seen to burst into flames and crash near the Naval Hospital.

## c. Northwest of Ford Island

The fourth group of torpedo planes, which came in at 0800, made for the other side of Ford Island where seaplane tender *Tangier*, target ship *Utah* and light cruisers *Raleigh* and *Detroit* were moored. *Tangier*, first in this row to open fire, escaped altogether and at about 0840 inflicted considerable damage on an attacking wave of dive-bombers. Her 3-inch battery shot the tail off one and her machine-gun battery claimed "assists" on two more — one which lost control and crashed the starboard crane of seaplane tender *Curtiss*, and one which splashed near the Pan American dock at Pearl City.[50]

The old battleship *Utah*, converted to a target ship, was com-

---

[49] "This progressive flooding was caused by a combination of battle damage, non-closure of watertight fittings, and rupture of ventilation ducts." (Capt. Bunkley's Report of 26 Jan. 1942.)

[50] One of the touching incidents of the attack was afforded by a troupe of Hawaiian girls in native costumes who in the midst of the battle calmly appeared at the Pan American dock for the customary *Alohas* and gifts of *lei* to departing clipper passengers. They were told that their services were no longer required, and sadly they departed.

pletely defenseless. Within five minutes of the beginning of this attack she took two torpedo hits, and listed so rapidly that the senior officer on board ordered "All hands on deck and abandon ship over starboard side." As the crew crawled over, some of them coming out through ports in the captain's cabin, the "Kates" returned and strafed them. By 0812 *Utah* was bottom up, a total loss.

Light cruiser *Raleigh*, lying at the berth next ahead of *Utah*, was gallantly and efficiently served by Captain R. B. Simons and a crew commanded largely by ensigns. All her batteries were firing when a torpedo struck outside No. 2 fireroom, completely flooding it and the forward engine room. Prompt counterflooding and jettisoning of topside weights, and running additional lines to the mooring floats, prevented her from capsizing. In the later dive-bombing attack, one armor-piercing bomb went right through this thin-plated ship and exploded on the harbor bottom. Nevertheless she helped to shoot down several planes. The executive officer, coming on board at 1000, found all hands "in high spirits," although the ship was in momentary danger of capsizing, "apparently only hoping that the enemy would return so that they could have another crack at them." *Raleigh* floated and was successfully repaired at Pearl Harbor by mid-February. Light cruiser *Detroit*, the last ship in this row, was near-missed by a torpedo and suffered no damage.

These four ships on the north side of Ford Island had plenty of support from the destroyers moored in four "nests" in East Loch, from tender *Curtiss* and repair ship *Medusa* at the entrance to Middle Loch, and from the minecraft moored to the northwestward of them. The destroyers, as ordered by their type commander, Rear Admiral Draemel, at 0828, made every effort to get under way and sortie. These ships, while lighting off boilers and getting up steam, blazed away at flying targets. *Aylwin* opened up at 0758 and got under way an hour later, pursued by her commanding officer in a motor launch; but the squadron commander refused to let her slow down to pick him up and Ensign Stanley Caplan USNR, senior officer on board, exercised the command "superbly . . . for 33 hours during war operations of the severest type."

*Monaghan,* the ready destroyer in East Loch which had been ordered to sortie and support *Ward* two minutes before the attack opened, was the first away at 0827. She had a very eventful trip down-harbor. Only eight minutes after casting off mooring pendants, steaming at low speed north of Ford Island, a signalman noticed that tender *Curtiss* was flying a signal indicating presence of an enemy submarine. The midget was sighted two minutes later, under fire from *Curtiss* and *Medusa.* It launched a torpedo which missed *Curtiss* and hit a dock at Pearl City. The two auxiliaries checked fire when the destroyer was about to foul their range and enjoyed a few minutes' relaxation as they applauded the fine seamanship and attack technique exhibited by Lieutenant Commander Burford and his merry men of the *Monaghan.* Her first shot was an "over" that ricocheted into a derrick barge moored off Beckoning Point. She then made ready to ram. The midget fired a torpedo at *Monaghan* which missed and detonated against the shore. *Monaghan* rammed at 0843, passed over the midget, depth-charged it twice and sank it. But the destroyer was now making such speed that she was unable to clear the shore. Just as the crew were about to make suitable acknowledgment of *Curtiss's* cheers, *Monaghan's* bow fouled the unfortunate derrick barge, now ablaze and a serious explosive hazard. While she was backing away from this unwanted and mutually embarrassing contact, a second submarine alarm sounded, and one shot was fired at what proved to be a black harbor-buoy. *Monaghan* then stood out of the harbor and "remainder of day was spent in organizing and clearing ship."

*Curtiss* was not through. One of her guns, as well as those on other ships (including destroyer *Blue,* now steaming down-harbor a short distance behind *Monaghan*), at 0905 hit a "Val" pulling out of a dive over Ford Island. The pilot either lost control or decided to inaugurate suicide tactics; his plane crashed the tender's starboard side and started a fire. Before that was brought under control, several planes attacked *Curtiss* and one of their bombs exploded in the hangar, starting more fires, killing 20 men and wounding 58. But the tender had the satisfaction of seeing one of the planes under fire from her machine guns disintegrate in the air. And within half an hour the fire on board was quenched.

Two nests, each containing four old destroyers converted to minecraft that were moored northwest of *Medusa* in Middle Loch, also got into this action with their anti-aircraft guns and probably contributed to the shooting down of two or three planes. Most of these ships got under way between 0915 and 1000 and stood out of the harbor, where they patrolled and swept during the rest of the day and most of the next.

The five destroyers of Division 1, moored northeastward from Ford Island alongside tender *Dobbin*, were the target of dive-bombing attacks at 0910 and 0945. In the first attack three men were killed and several wounded on the tender; the second (before which *Phelps* had slipped her mooring and got under way) was broken up by concentrated fire from the ships.

## d. At the Navy Yard

Now let us turn our attention to the opposite side of the main channel, over against battleship row. Minelayer *Oglala*, as we have seen, was moored outboard of light cruiser *Helena* at pier 1010. To Admiral Furlong it seemed "some time" after the first bomb dropped — but actually it was within three minutes, and probably less — that a lone torpedo plane crossing the southern end of Ford Island made for this unequal pair. The "fish" passed under *Oglala's* keel and hit *Helena* on the starboard side almost amidships, just as the crew was running to battle stations. One engine room and one boiler room were flooded, wiring to the main and 5-inch batteries was severed, but prompt action by the engineers in starting and cutting in the forward diesel generator made power available to all gun mounts within two minutes. *Helena's* main and 1.1-inch anti-aircraft batteries were so effective that most of the follow-up dive-bombers sheered off from her midship section and made their drops from points well forward or aft.

"Every man and officer observed on this ship conducted himself

The dry dock after the attack
*Pennsylvania, Downes* (left) and *Cassin* (right)

*Shaw* burning in the floating dry dock

*Pearl Harbor, 7–8 December*

A diver emerging from sunken ship

The capsized minelayer *Oglala*

*Destruction and Salvage*

in a meritorious and exemplary manner. . . . Had not a single order been issued — and very few had to be in fact — it is believed that every job would have been carried out by someone who saw the need for the task. This reveals the intelligent discipline that is standard throughout the ship," proudly reported the Commanding Officer, Captain R. H. English. *Helena* was so promptly buttoned up that she did not sink; temporary repairs were started at Pearl Harbor and finished at Mare Island, and this cruiser became a tower of strength to the South Pacific Force in the Guadalcanal campaign.

Little *Oglala*, the "egg-layer" alongside, was not so lucky. The torpedo that exploded against *Helena* ruptured her hull so that the fire room flooded rapidly and had to be abandoned; and at about 0800 a bomb fell right between the two ships and exploded. As all power was lost and the auxiliary submersible pumps were unable to check flooding, the crew, helped by a tug and a motor launch, secured her to the pier abaft *Helena* during a severe strafing attack by fighter planes. Flooding continued, the ship careened and at 1000 capsized. Salvage operations on her were successful.

*Pennsylvania*, flagship of the Pacific Fleet, was in the permanent dry dock next to pier 1010, facing shoreward, with destroyers *Cassin* and *Downes* occupying the space at the head of the dock. These three had a special fight of their own. During the first phase they were attacked by dive-bombers and "Zekes" that had just made passes at near-by Hickam Field. On board the battleship all anti-aircraft batteries were promptly manned and rapidly brought into action; her 3-inch 50s "fired fast, quietly and efficiently," reported the skipper of *Cassin*. The two destroyers could return only machine-gun fire at first, because their main batteries had been partially taken apart for ordnance alteration; but sailors were sent scurrying to the Navy Yard shop for missing parts, the guns were put together under heavy strafing fire, and by 0820 they were firing, too. Both destroyers and *Pennsylvania* were handicapped by the fact that a bomb severed their power cables from the yard.

At 0840 the second attack of 50 high-level "Kates," 80 dive-bombing "Vals" and 40 "Zekes," launched from the Japanese carriers about an hour after the first, began to come in. The high-level bombers crossed and recrossed their targets from various directions at 10,000 to 12,000 feet altitude, inflicting serious damage on several ships with their converted 16-inch armor-piercing bombs. Up to this time it had been mostly take and no give for the Fleet; but the fifteen-minute lull before 0840 gave time to replenish ammunition supply, organize defense, and give something back.

About 0900 when *Nevada* on her sortie was off 1010 dock, she attracted the worst of a dive-bombing attack that was initially directed at *Pennsylvania*. Several of the "Vals," however, refused to be diverted. One of them dropped a bomb that hit destroyer *Shaw* in the floating dry dock only a few yards to the westward, and caused a spectacular explosion. Another dropped an incendiary bomb that hit the dock between *Cassin* and *Downes*. Oil tanks were ruptured and flames began rising and spreading over both ships, which had to be abandoned. Their crews, including many men who had been severely burned, concentrated on fighting the fires with yard hoses, under severe strafing fire. At 0906 *Pennsylvania* suffered a hit which penetrated her boat deck and detonated in the casemate of a 5-inch gun.

In the meantime Captain Cooke of *Pennsylvania* had ordered the dry dock to be flooded, hoping to quench the flames; but this did not mend matters because burning oil rose on top of the water. At 0930 magazines and torpedo warheads started to explode in the unfortunate destroyers and *Cassin* rolled over onto *Downes*. "The conduct of the men was superb, particularly the quiet overall supervision by Chief Boatswain's Mate J. T. Scrattin, who seemed to be everywhere at the same time directing closure and abandoning," reported the skipper of *Cassin*. "The ship was lost, but the Commanding Officer has naught but praise for the officers and men of the crew . . . who . . . showed they were real shipmates with a concern for each other's safety," wrote the skipper of *Downes*. And neither ship was a total loss. Their engines and other "innards" were salvaged and shipped to Mare Island where new hulls were built around them; *Cassin* and *Downes*, phoenix-like, again took the water in 1943. *Pennsylvania*, owing to the bomb hit that exploded below, lost 2 officers and 16 men killed and 30 men wounded, out of 81 officers and 1395 men on board, but suffered no great damage. She left the dry dock on 12 December and proceeded to the West Coast for overhaul.

Destroyer *Shaw*, in the near-by floating dry dock, whose bow had been blown off by the bomb hit, was fitted with a temporary wooden bow, sent to the West Coast for permanent repairs in February 1942 and, with the same commanding officer and sixty of her old crew, was in time to see action off Guadalcanal that year.[51] The floating dry dock was ready for service before the end of January.

The considerable concentration of cruisers, repair ships and destroyers at the docks and piers of the Navy Yard east of Pier 1010 received very little attention from the attacking planes, but, as all the combat ships there were being repaired, they were the less ready to fight. Their batteries were not manned quickly enough to shoot at the initial wave of torpedo-bombers, which was unfortunate because some of these "Kates" chose points close astern of *Argonne*, *Ramapo* and *Sacramento* from which to launch torpedoes at the battleships. On the deck of *Ramapo* were four motor torpedo boats loaded for transportation to Manila. These opened fire at the planes on their own initiative and contributed to the shooting down of one. A fragmentation bomb exploded about halfway between *Rigel* and heavy cruiser *New Orleans*, puncturing many small holes in the ship and injuring a number of men, but killing nobody. Light cruiser *Honolulu* received damage from a near miss but was restored to the Fleet a month later. Her sister ship *St. Louis*, moored outboard of her, got under way at 0931 and stood out to sea. Half an hour later, when she was just inside the channel entrance, two torpedoes were seen coming toward her from outside

[51] There is a good account of *Shaw* by Stanley Bailey in San Francisco *Chronicle* 4 July 1942.

but they hit a reef and exploded there. *St. Louis* sighted the midget submarine that did this, took it under fire and probably sank it.

## *e.* On Airfields and Air Stations

Comparing the losses of planes and ships in the Battle of Pearl Harbor, air power suffered relatively greater losses than sea power. Ships could and did fight back, even if surprised, but closely parked planes, when suddenly attacked from the air, are completely defenseless. Ground crews and grounded pilots at the several airfields in Oahu fought back valiantly with anything they had, wrenching guns from planes and mounting them on work benches or even ashcans; but, by the time these improvised defense measures went into effect, American air power in Oahu had been almost wiped out.

The Naval Air Station on Ford Island was headquarters of Navy Patrol Wing 2, commanded by Admiral P. N. L. Bellinger, and the parking and repair place for all carrier planes in the area not on board their ships. One of the Catalinas on dawn patrol took part, as we have seen, in the attack on the midget submarine outside Pearl Harbor around 0700. Its coded message to that effect was not decoded and received by the staff duty officer at Ford Island until 0735, and the operations officer had just drafted a plan for an air search for other submarines when the first bomb dropped on Ford Island, at 0755. While the torpedo-bombers concentrated on the battleships, a flight of "Vals" worked over the air station to such good purpose that within a few minutes 33 of the Navy's best aircraft, almost half the total, were destroyed or badly damaged. The one combat plane available for instant use was launched with difficulty, owing to the wreckage on the runway, and sent to search a sector between 280° and 300° by Admiral Bellinger, who arrived at the operations office during the first attack. A few remaining planes of the utility squadron were sent up as well.

During the attack, Ford Island received some welcome reinforcements in the shape of a number of Dauntless dive-bombers (SBDs) belonging to U.S.S. *Enterprise*, then about 200 miles from

Oahu. Two planes, one piloted by Commander H. L. Young of the carrier's air group, took off at 0615 in order to land a passenger at Ford Island; the rest were launched at 0637 with orders to conduct air search ahead of the carrier. Commander Young, when closing the shore at 0820, noticed planes circling the Marine airfield at Ewa but supposed them to be United States Army aircraft, and continued his flight. Just as he was wondering what the antiaircraft fire from Pearl Harbor was about, he and his wing man were attacked from the air by "Zekes." He evaded them but, with insufficient fuel to return to his carrier, had to run the gantlet of ships' and Ford Island anti-aircraft fire (the gunners being too excited to observe his recognition signals), and landed about 0835 with several bullet holes through his wings. Ten minutes later, Lieutenant Commander Hopping brought in the rest of Squadron 6. Thirteen of them came down safely. At noon, nine of these were sent out to search the sector 333° to 30° from Pearl Harbor, and the other four to investigate reports of Japanese ships off Barbers Point, variously described by excited observers as carriers, transports and landing craft. When six of the SBDs returned after nightfall, with fuel tanks almost dry, four were shot down by our own anti-aircraft fire because communications at Ford Island had been so impaired by bombing that one gun which did not get the word started a panic of firing. Five planes managed to return aboard *Enterprise;* two were shot down by the Japanese.[52] From one of these, when attacked by several enemy planes and by "friendly" anti-aircraft too, Lieutenant C. E. Dickinson Jr. bailed out, made his way to Ford Island and immediately manned another plane and participated in the search.

A half hour's drive from the suburbs of Honolulu up the beautiful Nuuanu Valley takes one to the Pali, the cliff where Kame-

[52] *Enterprise* Air Group (Cdr. H. L. Young) Action Report 15 Dec., enclosing Action Report of VS–6 (Lt. Cdr. H. L. Hopping). Hopping's figures differ from Young's; I have assumed that the three he marks missing were among those shot down over Ford Island in the evening. The Marine Corps Monograph on the attack on Ewa Field (see below) states that 10 planes from *Enterprise* landed there during the Japanese attack, were refueled and took off. But Hopping states that only one of his planes landed at Ewa.

hameha I forced his enemies to leap down to their destruction. From this point one gains a superb view — one of the world's finest — of the windward coast of Oahu from Kualoa Point to Makapuu. Conspicuous in the center is the rugged Mokapu Peninsula which protects the southern bight of Kaneohe Bay, and where a United States Navy Seaplane Base had recently been established. This was the main center for land-based patrol planes, as Ford Island was for carrier-based planes. Three squadrons of Catalinas, 33 of them in operating condition, were based at Kaneohe on 7 December, and only three of them were out on patrol at 0755 when a squadron of Japanese dive-bombers, specially briefed for Kaneohe, struck.

"Val" dive-bombers came down low to shoot up the Catalinas, most of which were parked on the concrete. Having done all the destruction they could, these planes withdrew to the north. At about 0820 another squadron appeared over Kaneohe and began bombing and strafing. One hangar received a direct hit which destroyed four Catalinas inside; another hangar was set afire and burned to the ground. These planes strafed the pilots and ground crews who were around their planes, attempting to launch or to salvage them. At 0930 eighteen more "Vals" bombed a hangar. The men bravely set up machine guns right in line with the drop, and shot down two Japanese planes. As the last enemy aircraft were departing for their carriers, some of them flew over Kaneohe for a final strafing at 1000. In all 27 of the 36 PBYs were destroyed, and 6 others were damaged; only the 3 Catalinas out on patrol were saved. In no other target struck by the enemy did destruction so nearly approximate 100 per cent.[53]

At the Marine Corps Air Station at Ewa (pronounced "Evva") [54] a mile and a half from the waters of West Loch and two miles from the ocean, were based 49 planes — 11 Wildcat fighters, 32 scout bombers and 6 utilities, of Marine Corps Air Group 21, a

[53] "Navy Folder" Items 12 and 16; Compatwing 1 (Capt. K. McGinnis) Action Report 1 Jan. 1942.
[54] Same, and Action Report by Col. Claude A. Larkin USMC, 30 Dec. 1941, are principal sources for this attack.

rear echelon for the Marine Air squadrons stationed at Midway and Wake. They, like the Army planes at Wheeler and Hickam Fields, were alerted against sabotage only and drawn up wing tip to wing tip on Ewa Field. The officer of the day, in the mess hall at 0755, heard the roaring of aircraft engines, stepped outside and spotted two formations of Japanese torpedo bombers flying parallel with the coast from Barbers Point toward Pearl Harbor, and 21 "Zeke" fighters coming in over the mountains. He was running to the guardhouse in order to sound the alarm when the "Zekes" hit. They swooped as low as 20 feet from the ground, attacking individual parked planes with short bursts of incendiary, explosive and armor-piercing bullets. For 20 to 25 minutes they made repeated passes and succeeded in completely destroying or severely damaging 9 Wildcats, 18 scout bombers and all 6 utilities. A second attack by "Zekes" and "Vals" which came in ten to fifteen minutes later found so many planes already out of action that it concentrated on buildings and installations, including the Marines' hospital tents, and on strafing the men. By this time the Marines had organized their defense, dragging one SBD plane to a good position to use as a machine gun mount, breaking out spare machine guns from ordnance rooms and wrenching them off damaged planes to set up elsewhere. They were able to keep the would-be strafers at a healthy distance, shot down one plane and hit a number of others. A third attack by 15 "Zekes" was rendered ineffectual by the defensive gunfire. Only four men were killed or fatally wounded in the three attacks.

A substantial number of the Japanese fighter planes and dive-bombers were initially directed to the two principal Army airdromes, Wheeler Field in the center of the island and Hickam Field at Pearl Harbor, in order to insure that no intercepting planes took the air. That precaution was unnecessary. The Army planes, alerted against sabotage only, were parked in close order so that guards could be thrown around them. At Hickam, an Army chaplain was just preparing his altar for an outdoor mass when the planes struck. He made for a near-by machine gun, planted it atop the altar and blazed away at them. But, despite this and many other instances of heroic improvised defense, 18 planes and the principal installations were destroyed by the dive-bombers and fighter planes before 0900. At Wheeler Field, where planes were parked with wing tips touching and in lines only 15 to 20 feet apart, 25 dive-bombers attacked at about 0802 and destroyed most of the grounded planes. Bellows Field in the eastern part of the island, where a number of P–40s were based, was pretty much wiped out by nine "Zekes" shortly after 0900. Haleiwa Field on the north coast was the only one of the four Army fields in Oahu to escape attack.

The losses of Army planes may best be seen in a table: —

ARMY PLANES ON OAHU BEFORE AND AFTER ATTACK OF
7 DECEMBER [55]

|  |  | BEFORE ATTACK | | AFTER ATTACK | |
|  |  | Usable [56] | Under Repair, etc. [57] | Usable [56] | Under Repair, etc. [57] |
| --- | --- | --- | --- | --- | --- |
| Bombers | B–17 | 6 | 6 | 4 | 4 |
| " | B–12A | 1 | 2 | 1 | 2 |
| " | B–18 | 21 | 12 | 11 | 10 |
| " | A–12 | 2 | 0 | 0 | 0 |
| " | A–20 | 5 | 7 | 5 | 5 |
| Fighters | P–40 | 64 | 35 | 36 | 30 |
| " | P–36 | 20 | 19 | 16 | 19 |
| " | P–26 | 10 | 4 | 4 | 4 |
| Reconnaissance | | 11 | 2 | 9 | 4 |
| Trainer, Utility | | 3 | 1 | 1 | 1 |
| *Total* | | 143 | 88 | 87 | 79 |

At Haleiwa, the small unattacked field, two flights consisting of four P–40s and one P–36 each were made between 0815 and 1000. These claimed to have shot down seven Japanese planes at the cost of one of their own. Bellows Field was unable to get a plane in the air until 0950, or Hickam until 1127.

The infantry and artillery components of the Oahu garrison — which had a total strength of some 60,000 officers and men — were largely in two concentrations, Schofield Barracks in the center of the island, and Fort Shafter between Pearl Harbor and Honolulu,

[55] Compiled from *P. H. Attack* Part 1 p. 54.
[56] A majority of the "usable" planes were as yet unarmed.
[57] Including overhaul and inspection.

although many small detachments were located all around the island. It naturally took more time for them to assume their battle stations than for bluejackets in a ship; and their deployment according to the existing defense plan, in expectation of an invasion, was not complete until the late afternoon.

In and around the Pearl Harbor Navy Yard were about a dozen Army anti-aircraft installations. Few of these were manned when the blitz struck, and none had ready ammunition; [58] the Japanese air commander stated that none opened fire until nearly the close of the attack. Thus the Army contribution to the defense of the Fleet was practically zero.

## *f.* Conclusion

By ten in the morning the battle was over; last enemy planes rendezvoused over northern Oahu, and returned to their carriers.

Never in modern history was a war begun with so smashing a victory by one side, and never in recorded history did the initial victor pay so dearly for his calculated treachery. There is some question, however, whether the aviators were directed to the right targets, even from the Japanese point of view. They knocked out the Battle Force and decimated the striking air power present; but they neglected permanent installations at Pearl Harbor, including the repair shops which were able to do an amazingly quick job on the less severely damaged ships. And they did not even attempt to hit the power plant or the large fuel oil "tank farm," filled to capacity, whose loss (in the opinion of Admiral Hart) would have set back our advance across the Pacific much longer than did the damage to the Fleet. [59]

[58] It was explained at the Congressional inquiry that anti-aircraft ammunition was regularly returned to depots after practice as it was apt to disintegrate or get dusty if kept at the anti-aircraft positions, where ready boxes or magazines had not yet been provided. After 7 Dec. the Navy took over these positions, manned them from the sunken battleships and set up 10 new emplacements of 4 guns each. The Army did not take over the land defense of Pearl Harbor until 20 May 1942. (Conversation with Rear Admiral Furlong.)

[59] Letter in *Washington Post* 18 Jan. 1946.

Whatever one may conclude about responsibility for the armed forces not being well alert, there is no doubt that the men of the Fleet fought intelligently and courageously, despite the normal percentage of key officers and chiefs on week-end liberty. Splendid leadership and initiative were shown by the junior officers on whom the initial responsibility fell. As soon as news of the attack got around, cars and taxicabs were commandeered and everyone on leave hastened to landings where small craft were constantly plying to and fro, in complete disregard of the bombing and strafing, bringing the wounded to the hospital and taking men out to their ships. There are many stories illustrating the eagerness of officers to get on board. Ensign George G. Ball of the minecraft *Perry*, at breakfast with his parents at Wheeler Field when the enemy struck there, jumped into his car and raced down the mountain road, strafed en route by Japanese fighter planes, all of which missed him. At Pearl City he commandeered a boat to go on board his ship, found that he was senior officer and handled her admirably the rest of the day. Ensign W. H. Sears USNR, a turret officer of *West Virginia*, jumped aboard a boat at the Navy Yard that took him to the cruiser *Phoenix* instead of to Ford Island. Shortly after, the cruiser got under way to sortie. Finding that the captain had no need of a turret officer, Ensign Sears dived overboard as *Phoenix* was steaming by the burning *West Virginia* and swam to his own ship.

The American casualties of the day were as follows: —

| | KILLED, MISSING AND DIED OF WOUNDS | WOUNDED |
|---|---|---|
| Navy [60] | 2,008 | 710 |
| Marine Corps [61] | 109 | 69 |
| Army [62] | 218 | 364 |
| Civilians [63] | 68 | 35 |
| *Total* | 2,403 | 1,178 |

[60] Revised figures in Navy Bureau of Medicine, 1947. These are much less than were originally reported by Secretary Knox on 15 Dec. 1941.

[61] Casualty Statistics at Marine Corps Headquarters, 1947.

[62] Office of the Adjutant General of the Army, 1947.

[63] Deaths from University of Hawaii War Depository; wounded from the local press of 8 Dec. 1941.

The United States Navy lost about three times as many men in this one treacherous attack as it lost by enemy action in two previous wars — Spanish–American and World War I.

## 5. *Responsibility and Repair*

It is no part of this writer's purpose to set himself up as a one-man court of inquiry on a subject that has consumed months of time by six boards or courts of inquiry and filled forty volumes of print — the question of who was responsible for United States forces' being caught napping at Pearl Harbor. Nevertheless, in writing a book such as this it is impossible to avoid reaching an opinion on the subject, a statement of which is the readers' due.

Anyone who ponders the problem of Pearl Harbor should keep in mind certain basic factors.

First, a carrier-borne air strike is the most difficult of all forms of attack to detect, because even a large fleet of ships makes a very small spot on a big ocean. United States carrier forces obtained surprise time after time during the war. The Halsey-Doolittle raid on Tokyo was a surprise to the authorities there, even though the carriers had been reported by picket boats; Admirals Halsey, Wilson Brown, Frederick Sherman and Charles Pownall delivered a series of surprise attacks on Japanese-held islands during the first two years of the war; Halsey's spectacular raids on Okinawa, the Philippines and Indochina in 1944–45 caught the enemy flat-footed; and off Luzon in October 1944, reconnaissance planes from Mitscher's and Ozawa's carriers searched for each other a full day without finding anything. So there is nothing astonishing about the Pacific Fleet's failing to detect the approach of a Japanese striking force, at a time when it was unalerted by war or even by a breach of diplomatic relations.

They might, nevertheless, have prepared for the possibility; and their failure so to do is the essence of the charge. Mr. Seth W. Richardson, general counsel for the Joint Congressional Investigation Committee in 1946, has pointed out the strange fact that throughout the first eight months of 1941, Army and Navy commands in Washington and Hawaii were much concerned with the danger of an air attack upon Pearl Harbor, but that after August that probability appears to have faded from the mind of every military man or civilian in a position of high responsibility; even, by his own admission, from that of the Director of Naval Intelligence, Rear Admiral T. S. Wilkinson, who had one of the best brains in the armed forces.[64]

Admiral Stark warned the commandants of all naval districts on 1 April to be particularly on their alert during week ends.[65] Frequent communications between Secretaries Knox and Stimson, between General Marshall and Admiral Stark in Washington with General Short and Admiral Kimmel in Oahu, "discussed and detailed all possible phases of the peril surrounding Pearl Harbor from an enemy air attack." Brigadier General F. L. Martin, commanding the Army Air Forces, and Rear Admiral "Pat" Bellinger, commanding the Naval Air Arm in Hawaii, issued a secret joint report on 31 March in which they stated that "the most likely and dangerous form of attack on Oahu would be an air attack launched from carriers," and that if launched at dawn there was a high probability of its being delivered as a complete surprise. And on 20 August General Martin advised General Short that the most probable approach of a Japanese carrier force would be from the northwestward.

The Basic Navy War Plan (WPL–46 or Rainbow 5), issued 26 May 1941, explicitly envisaged the probability of a surprise attack on the Fleet at Pearl. The Pacific Fleet's own operation plan, promulgated 21 July by Admiral Kimmel, stated that the enemy's initial action would be "possibly raids or straight attacks

[64] S. W. Richardson "Why Were We Caught Napping at Pearl Harbor?" *Saturday Evening Post* 24 May 1947 pp. 20–21, 76–80. Admiral Turner afterwards said that he was "not in the least" surprised (*P. H. Attack* Part 26 p. 273) but his actions on and before 7 Dec. suggest that he was, although unlike Admirals Stark and Wilkinson he did expect an attack on the Philippines. Wilkinson, it should be said, was not confronted with the problem before mid-October, when he became Director of Naval Intelligence.
[65] Navy "Narrative Statement of Evidence" I 267.

on Wake, Midway, or other United States outlying possessions." [66]

Yet, despite all these estimates, advices and warnings, the danger seemed to pass from the minds of responsible officers after August. "Personally I do not believe the Japs are going to sail into us," wrote Admiral Stark to Admiral Kimmel on 17 October 1941.[67] Cincpac's war plans officer, Captain Charles H. McMorris — the famous "Soc" McMorris who later won the Battle of the Komandorski Islands and became a sheet anchor to Admiral Nimitz — told Kimmel and Short in a conference on one of the first three days of December that there would "never" be an attack on Pearl Harbor by air.[68]

Despite the 27 November war warning from Washington, the major part of the Pacific Fleet was moored in Pearl Harbor over the week end of 6–7 December, normal peacetime liberty was granted to officers and men, the Army continued to operate aircraft warning and search radar on a training basis only, and failed to have ready ammunition at the anti-aircraft batteries in vital points around the harbor. All but a handful of the Army and Navy planes on Oahu were grounded or moored, and the few on patrol were searching to the southward when the attack came.

Why, then, did this "unwarranted feeling of immunity from attack," as Admiral King described the state of mind at Hawaii, prevail over the earlier alerts and apprehensions?

Mr. Richardson has furnished at least part of the answer. Everyone underestimated the enemy's capabilities. "The basic trouble was that the Navy failed to appreciate what the Japanese could and did do," said Admiral King.[69] Few officers believed the Japanese capable of mounting more than one major naval or amphibious operation at the same time. Nor, for that matter, did the British and Dutch officers who canvassed the probabilities with Captain Purnell at the ADB Conference in April.

[66] Same, I, 216–17. Rainbow 5 is printed in full in *P. H. Attack,* Part 26 Appendix.
[67] Same, Part 32 p. 108.
[68] Same, Part 22 p. 526.
[69] Quoted in Zacharias *Secret Missions* p. 268.

From mid-October on, a spate of information on Japanese troop and ship movements flowed in on American intelligence centers. Everything, apparently, was moving southward. All indications pointed to an amphibious expedition against the Philippines, Thai, the Kra Isthmus or possibly Borneo, as the Stark war warning of 27 November said; and the patrol planes sent out by the Asiatic Fleet to search the South China Sea actually picked up Admiral Kondo's amphibious force en route to the Gulf of Siam in early December. It looked as if the whole Japanese Navy, with the important exception of the newer battleships and most of the carriers, assumed to be in the Inland Sea, was convoying troop transports south to overwhelm the Malay Peninsula.[70] Nobody in high places believed that the Japanese could mount an independent carrier striking force. It was assumed that they would need all they had to furnish air cover for the southward advance, and the two carriers (*Ryujo* and *Hosho*) reported to be in the Marshalls were estimated to be guarding the eastern flank of the southward movement.[71] Naval Intelligence lost track of four carriers during the three weeks preceding 7 December, as Admiral Kimmel was informed by his intelligence officer on the first;[72] but there was no reason for him to assume from that purely negative evidence that the carriers were steaming toward Pearl. They might have been at Kure, not "talking" on waves we could pick up — which is just what the Japanese wished us to think.

Thus, the very size and complexity of the Japanese southward swing in October–November, and the ample knowledge we obtained of it, led the top military minds to conclude that Hawaii was safe for the time being.

---

[70] Captain E. T. Layton's summary of information received in *P. H. Attack* Part 26 pp. 230–32; dispatches, p. 487. Office of Naval Intelligence summary of 1 Dec., in Same, Part 36 p. 231. This summary was sent out that day to the Fleet by air mail.

[71] It is still unexplained why no high-ranking American commander regarded the Japanese concentration in the Marshalls as a threat to Oahu. Probably they regarded it as defensive, in case we declared war and attempted to execute Rainbow 5.

[72] Layton's testimony in Part 36 p. 128; *Report* p. 135.

An understandable manner of thinking is to plan for the most probable emergency, and not for all possible ones which may arise; military writers often warn against this common human failing.[73] To explore everything an enemy may do, and make a correct estimate of each possibility, often seems an endless task. Hence military planners are apt to base their war plans upon what they think the enemy will probably do.

If an underestimate of the enemy's capabilities was one cause of the curious attitude that reigned at Pearl Harbor in early December, an overestimate of his intelligence was at least equally responsible. This was well stated by Captain Vincent R. Murphy, assistant war plans officer to Admiral Kimmel, at the Hart Inquiry in 1944: —

QUERY. What were your views, at that time, with respect to such a surprise air attack?

ANSWER. I did not think that such an attack would be made. I thought that it would be utterly stupid for the Japanese to attack the United States at Pearl Harbor. . . . I thought that the Japanese could probably have gone into Thailand and Malaya, and even the Dutch East Indies. . . . I did not think they would attack at Pearl Harbor because I did not think it was necessary for them to do so, from my point of view. We could not have materially affected their control of the waters that they wanted to control, whether or not the battleships were sunk at Pearl Harbor. In other words, I did not believe that we could move the United States Fleet to the Western Pacific until such time as auxiliaries were available, as the material condition of the ships were improved, especially with regard to anti-aircraft, and until such time as the Pacific Fleet was materially re-enforced. I thought it would be suicide for us to attempt, with an inferior fleet, to move into the Western Pacific.[74]

[73] Admiral E. C. Kalbfus *Sound Military Decision* (1942 ed.) p. 140: "In his estimate, however, the commander's interest is not confined to what the enemy will *probably do; probabilities are subject to change,* and do not, therefore, cover the whole field of capabilities. The commander is not exclusively interested in what the enemy *may intend to do,* or even in what the enemy may be known, at the time, to intend to do; such *intentions are also subject to change.* The commander is interested in *everything that the enemy can do* which may materially influence the commander's own courses of action."

[74] *P. H. Attack* Part 26 p. 207.

And so it would have been, as the fate of *Prince of Wales* and *Repulse* indicates. The Pacific Fleet was too weak in many types, especially destroyers and auxiliaries, too deficient in anti-aircraft protection, to go tearing into waters covered by enemy land-based air power. The Rainbow 5 War Plan, which would have gone into effect upon declaration of war if the Pearl Harbor attack had not taken place, called for the Fleet to capture Japanese positions in the Marshalls and Carolines, including Truk, before proceeding to the relief of the Philippines or elsewhere. Prewar estimates of the time it would take for the Pacific Fleet to accomplish this vary from six to nine months; but even at the most optimistic the Japanese could have conquered everything they wanted in the Philippines and Malaya by leaving Pearl Harbor alone and relying on submarines and aircraft in the Mandates to deal with our Pacific Fleet. United States naval officers assumed that the Japanese high command had enough strategic sense to appreciate this, and the Department of State supposed that there was sufficient political wisdom in the Japanese government to avoid an act of unqualified aggression that would bring America, angry and united, into the war.

Thus, the surprise attack on Pearl Harbor, far from being a "strategic necessity," as the Japanese claimed even after the war, was a strategic imbecility. One can search military history in vain for an operation more fatal to the aggressor. On the tactical level, the Pearl Harbor attack was wrongly concentrated on ships rather than permanent installations and oil tanks. On the strategic level it was idiotic. On the high political level it was disastrous.

The military atmosphere in Oahu during the three months preceding the attack was neither careless nor complacent, but tense and energetic. Admiral Kimmel, a conscientious, capable and hard-working officer, was obsessed with the urgent problem of training. Trained officers and men were constantly being drafted out of the

Fleet in order to make skeleton crews for new ships being constructed in the United States, and raw replacements were constantly
coming in. These men had to be incorporated in ships' and patrol
plane squadrons' rosters, and trained. Then, too, there were vital
matériel shortages, especially in anti-aircraft guns, aircraft bombs,
fuel oil and planes. Kimmel was on the horns of a dilemma: he
might keep his command in a state of constant alert, which would
expend precious matériel, exhaust the men and undermine their
morale; or he might concentrate on training at the expense of
alertness. The oil reserves at Pearl were far from sufficient to keep
the Fleet constantly at sea, and the total capacity of all naval and
commercial tankers available to bring oil out to Pearl was only
760,000 barrels: about nine days' fuel for the Fleet on a war basis.[75]
If all available planes had been used to maintain a 360-degree search,
pilots and bombardiers could not have received the necessary training to cover the Fleet in its westward advance to the Marshalls,
and many of the planes would have cracked up before they could
be so used.

General Short had a similar problem. The Alert No. 1 that he
maintained, even after Washington's war warning of 27 November, was an alert against ground sabotage only. The Army Air
Force had been assigned the task of ferrying Flying Fortresses to
the Philippines, and had to furnish the crews. Only six of these
B–17s were in Oahu for training purposes. If the Army went to
Alert 3, the alert against enemy air attack, training would have to
stop, and there would have been no crews ready to carry out the
ferrying operations, which the War Department considered very
important, since it anticipated an attack on the Philippines but
not on Pearl.[76] Therefore, since Washington believed, and the Intelligence officers in Hawaii advised them, that there was only a
remote possibility of an attack on Pearl Harbor, Kimmel and Short

[75] In the first nine days after the attack "we pumped into the Fleet 750,000
barrels" — testimony of Vice Admiral W. L. Calhoun, Commander Service Force
Pacific Fleet, at Navy Court Inquiry, *P. H. Attack* Part 32 p. 593.
[76] General Walter C. Short's testimony at Naval Inquiry. Same, p. 185.

concentrated on training at the expense of alertness. That was a tragic mistake, but an honest one.

It may be noted that the command set-up was defective, both at Pearl Harbor and at Washington, for coping with this situation. Admiral Kimmel took too much on himself. By a long-standing agreement incorporated in the official publication *Joint Action of Army and Navy*, the Army in Oahu was responsible for the safety of ships in harbor. The Navy's share in that defense was properly the responsibility of Admiral Bloch, commandant of the 14th Naval District. Admiral Bloch, not Admiral Kimmel, was the opposite number to General Short in Oahu. Kimmel might have exercised his command and training functions at sea with the Pacific Fleet, and made Bloch his deputy ashore for coöperating with the Army in the defense of Oahu. But Kimmel stayed ashore, and, despite his preoccupation with training, he was constantly going over Bloch's head or interfering with his functions.[77] The result would possibly have been the same in any case, since Bloch took the same view of probable Japanese action as Kimmel; but the actual set-up be-deviled the command situation in the important field of air reconnaissance, dividing responsibility among three flag officers of the Navy and two general officers of the Army.

The same may be said of the customary restrictions on the Office of Naval Intelligence at Washington. That office, to the head of which there was appointed on 15 October 1941 Rear Admiral Theodore Stark Wilkinson, did a thorough job of gathering intelligence about the enemy; but it was not allowed to evaluate,[78] much less to disseminate, the information so gathered. Evaluating this material (which included the decrypted dispatches between the Japanese government and its agents abroad), predicting future movements of the Japanese Navy, and deciding who should be let in on this information, was the responsibility of the war plans officer (Rear Admiral Richmond K. Turner) on Admiral Stark's

[77] This was a difficult situation for Admiral Bloch, who was a former Commander in Chief of the Fleet and Kimmel's senior.

[78] Excepting what Admiral Wilkinson called the "static" part — facts and figures about Japanese armed forces, industry, etc.

staff.[79] Admiral Wilkinson was "ordered not to develop the enemy intentions," [80] although his office contained several officers trained in the Japanese language, including the circumlocutory manner of Japanese writing that is lost in translation. Again, as Admiral Wilkinson made the same underestimate of the enemy's capabilities and overestimate of his common sense as did everyone else,[81] the result might have been the same if he had been made responsible.

In Washington the President, the Secretaries and all top-flight Army and Navy officers made the same mistake in concluding that, when and if the Japanese struck they would strike to the southward, not at Oahu. Some even thought they would by-pass the Philippines. By a curious paradox it was the officers in possession of the whole available intelligence picture who drew the wrong conclusion; subordinate and junior officers who had but a part of it were the ones who put little pieces together and, too late to give adequate warning, pointed to 0730 December 7 as the hour of destiny. Kimmel and Short might have been favored by Washington with more intelligence data, such as the decrypted dispatch from the Japanese government to its consul at Honolulu asking for the mooring and berthing plan at Pearl;[82] but they received enough information about code-burning and the like in Japanese consulates to have been more alert than they were.

After every allowance is made for the insistent training problem and the failure of Washington to let the Hawaiian commands have all the intelligence in their possession, the fact remains that Pearl Harbor was the most important United States base in the Pacific and that war was imminent, as everyone who read the newspapers

[79] This set-up is described in detail in Admiral Wilkinson's testimony in the Hart and Hewitt inquiries, *P. H. Attack* Part 26 pp. 299 *ff.*, and Part 36 pp. 229 *ff.*, and repeated at greater length in Part 4 pp. 1723 *ff.*

[80] *P. H. Attack* Part 4 p. 1853.

[81] Same, p. 1757.

[82] *P. H. Attack* Part 2 p. 794; see testimony in Part 4 pp. 1746–48. The *Report of Joint Committee*, p. 190, after a thorough consideration of this particular message in comparison with similar ones from Japanese consuls at Bremerton, Panama, etc., states: "We are unable to conclude that the berthing plan and related dispatches pointed directly to an attack on Pearl Harbor, nor are we able to conclude that the plan was a 'bomb plot' in view of the evidence indicating it was not such."

knew. It was an outpost, too, where military men are supposed to be alert at all times, like a sentry walking his post.[83] Admiral Kimmel need not have had so rigid a schedule of arrivals and departures that the Japanese could count on the battleships being in port Sun-

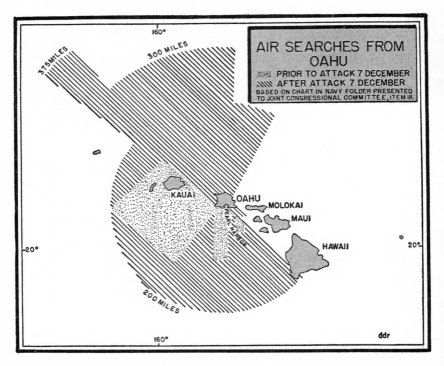

day morning. Normal week-end leaves and liberties need not have been granted when war was likely to break out any day. Distant air reconnaissance might have been very much better, as it became immediately after the heavy losses on 7 December. More planes

[83] The Secretary of War expressed this well in the Pearl Harbor Investigation: "The outpost commander is like a sentinel on duty in the face of the enemy. His fundamental duties are clear and precise. He must assume that the enemy will attack at the time and in the way in which it will be most difficult to defeat him. It is not the duty of the outpost commander to speculate or rely on the possibilities of the enemy attacking at some other outpost instead of his own. It is his duty to meet him at his post at any time and to make the best possible fight that can be made against him with the weapons with which he has been supplied." *P. H. Attack* Part 11 p. 5428.

might and would have been patrolling if both services had not been maintaining their Sabbatical rest. And two unmistakable shadows of events to come, in the darkness before the fatal dawn, were disregarded by lower echelons.

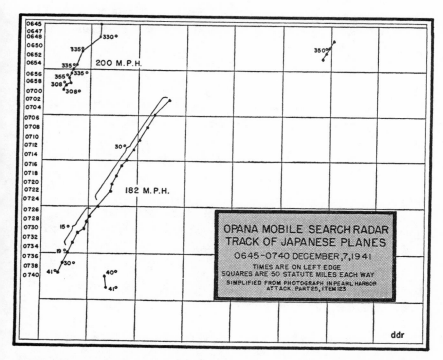

OPANA MOBILE SEARCH RADAR
TRACK OF JAPANESE PLANES
0645-0740 DECEMBER 7, 1941
TIMES ARE ON LEFT EDGE
SQUARES ARE 50 STATUTE MILES EACH WAY
SIMPLIFIED FROM PHOTOGRAPH IN PEARL HARBOR
ATTACK. PART 25, ITEM 123

The three small naval vessels (*Condor, Antares* and *Ward*) that had been concerned with hunting a midget submarine off the harbor from 0350 on, made no report of it to shore until the midget was sunk, and the naval radio station that listened in on their conversation failed to pass the word.

The Army, too, failed miserably in its handling of the six mobile search radars with which Oahu had been supplied. The one set up at Opana on Kahuku Point, the northern extremity of Oahu, was operated on a "training" basis, more or less as play, only from 0400 to 0700 every morning. The story is well known how the Army private who was being trained by another private soldier in the operation of the Opana unit continued to search for half an hour after 0700 because the breakfast truck was late; how he picked up on his screen the approaching carrier planes, 132 miles to the northward, tracked them for several minutes, reported what he saw to the watch officer at the central station — a young lieutenant under training — who did nothing about it because he was expecting a flight of our own B-17s. Less known is the fact that this was the second time within half an hour that the same two operators had reported, only to be laughed, or yawned, off. From 0645 to 0700 they tracked one of the cruiser float planes that was reconnoitering ahead of the bombers, and reported it properly; the watch officer heard but did nothing.[84] As Admiral King commented, an "unwarranted feeling of immunity from attack . . . seems to have pervaded all ranks at Pearl Harbor, both Army and Navy."

On any reasonable condition of alertness not incompatible with training schedules the naval command should have been alerted by 0600 owing to the midget submarine contact, for midgets were known to portend something bigger. And the whole island should have been alerted by 0700 through the Army radar contact on the planes. That would have given fifty minutes' warning. Many aircraft might have taken the air to intercept the bombers; others could have been dispersed on the ground; ships in the harbor could have been at General Quarters and getting up steam, if not under way. As we have seen, the first torpedo plane attack came in so low, and the bombers launched their torpedoes so close to ships on both sides of the harbor, that even with ten or fifteen minutes' warning the anti-aircraft gunners could have opened fire in time to have protected the battleships. As it was, the torpedo-bombers swept with impunity past men-of-war just waking up to a leisurely peacetime Sunday morning routine.

The failure to provide anti-torpedo nets or baffles about the

[84] Information from Rear Admiral Inglis, Director of Naval Intelligence. This was partially brought out at the Congressional Investigation (*P. H. Attack* Part 1 pp. 39-40) but glossed over. The radar plot of the Opana detector is reproduced in Same, Part 25 Item 123. The B-17s actually came in only five minutes behind the first wave of enemy planes, and on a bearing only 3° different. Part 32 p. 186.

battleships is equally notorious. The British torpedo plane attack on the Italian Fleet at Taranto in November 1940 had proved that aërial torpedoes could be rigged to run true in shoal water. The Chief of Naval Operations called this fact to the attention of Admiral Kimmel on 17 February 1941. Admiral Bloch replied a month later that the installation of baffles for the moorings in Pearl Harbor would narrow the ship channel and so restrict boat traffic that he would not recommend it; to which Admiral Kimmel added that "until a light, efficient net that can be laid temporarily and quickly" were developed, he preferred that "no anti-torpedo nets be supplied this area." [85] So that matter was left hanging in the bight.

The most measured and magistral comment on responsibility for the surprise was made by Admiral King in his endorsement, dated 6 November 1944, on the Report just made by the Naval Court of Inquiry.[86] We shall quote a few of the most trenchant extracts from this document: —

"It is evident, in retrospect, that the capabilities of Japanese aircraft torpedoes were seriously underestimated."

Admiral Kimmel "was not on entirely sound ground in making no attempt at long-range reconnaissance, particularly as the situation became more and more tense in the few days immediately preceding the Japanese attack. . . . There were certain sectors more dangerous than others which could have been covered to some extent."

"Army and Navy aircraft on the ground, and naval patrol planes moored on the water, were not in condition to take the air promptly. Some patrol plane squadrons were in 'day-off for rest' status; some patrol planes were in the air for local patrol and exercise; 50 per cent were on four-hours' notice. This is further indication of the lack of appreciation of the imminence of attack, and led to the destruction of large numbers of United States aircraft."

Admiral King was equally severe on the failure of Admiral Stark to report promptly to Hawaii the fact that the Japanese had broken off negotiations and might be presumed to be about to commence

---

[85] *P. H. Attack* Part 32 p. 226.
[86] Printed in full in *P. H. Attack* Part 39 pp. 335–45; most of it in *N. Y. Times* 30 Aug. 1945 p. S–53.

war immediately. The 14th and last part of the final Japanese note, declaring "it is impossible to reach an agreement through further negotiations," was decrypted and available at the Navy Department by 0800 December 7. It was brought by Admiral Wilkinson to Admiral Stark's office about 0915, and at 0950 to the Department of State where the Secretary was conferring with Mr. Knox. Almost simultaneously it was known at the Navy Department that Tokyo had ordered Nomura to deliver this note to Mr. Hull at 1300. A naval communications officer, when delivering this decrypted dispatch to Mr. Knox and Mr. Hull, pointed out that 1300 in Washington was about sunrise at Honolulu. General Marshall, when he returned from his horseback ride about 1130, read the two dispatches, concluded that something important was going to happen at 1300 and proposed to Admiral Stark that they send a special war alert to the interested commands, including Panama, San Francisco, Manila and Pearl Harbor. Admiral Stark demurred, as he thought there had been too much crying "Wolf!" General Marshall, however, decided to issue the warning on his own hook, and drafted it at once, Stark concurring: —

The Japanese are presenting at 1 P.M. Eastern Standard Time today what amounts to an ultimatum. Also they are under orders to destroy their code machine immediately. Just what significance the hour set may have we do not know, but be on the alert accordingly.

Owing to various delays in communication, this message, though filed in Washington at noon (0630 in Hawaii), was not delivered to General Short's signal office at Fort Shafter, Honolulu, until after the attack was over.[87]

Admiral King, remarking justly that "even two hours' advance warning would have been of great value in alerting planes and in augmenting the condition of readiness existing on board ship" concluded that there was a "lack of efficiency in Admiral Stark's organization." [88]

This writer believes that Admiral King was a bit hard on Admiral

[87] *P. H. Report* pp. 221–25.
[88] *P. H. Attack* Part 39 pp. 340, 344.

Yard workmen hauling out trapped men through hole cut in bottom

The line of bents

*Salvage of* Oklahoma

Half-righted

Alongside battleship *Wisconsin*, 1944

*Salvage of* Oklahoma

Stark. Hindsight makes the hour of delivery deeply significant; but to infer before the event that it meant a carrier plane strike on Pearl Harbor at that hour was not logical, nor did General Marshall's message just quoted convey any such inference. The late drafting of that warning was due less to inefficiency in Admiral Stark's office than to the efficiency of General Marshall's horse in keeping him so long at his Sunday morning exercise.

At the Joint Congressional Investigation, Admiral Wilkinson was asked, "Did you have any information, written or oral, prior to the actual attack, which specified Hawaii as a point of attack?" To which the former Director of Naval Intelligence replied, "Not the slightest." [89]

That denial was completely borne out by the investigation. Nobody in Washington could warn Hawaii of something he neither knew nor suspected. And, in view of the disinclination of Kimmel and Short to interrupt normal training schedules and Sabbatical rest, in view of their belief (which Washington shared) that the Japanese were moving all available naval forces southward, in view of the fact that the "surprise aggressive movement in any direction is a possibility" message of 24 November and the "war warning" message of 27 November and the code-burning message of 3 December had failed to impress them with the necessity for alertness against air attack, it is highly improbable that the additional bits of information not sent would have done so, or that Marshall's warning just quoted, if sent and transmitted in time to be in their hands by 0600, would have been of any avail.

General MacArthur made affidavit that the same dispatches from the War Department that were sent to General Short, all of which were available to Admiral Kimmel, gave him "ample and complete information and advice for the purpose of alerting the Army Command in the Philippines on a war basis, which was done prior to 7 December 1941." [90] Yet, as we shall see, although General MacArthur received news of the attack on Pearl Harbor before

[89] *P. H. Attack* Part 4 p. 1754.
[90] *P. H. Attack* Part 35 p. 85.

the Japanese struck Luzon, he was no more successful than General Short in protecting his command area from the enemy.

Admiral King concluded: —

The Navy cannot evade a share of responsibility for the Pearl Harbor incident. That disaster cannot be regarded as an "Act of God" beyond human power to prevent or mitigate. It is true that the country as a whole is basically responsible in that the people were unwilling to support an adequate army and navy until it was too late to repair the consequences of past neglect in time to deal effectively with the attack that ushered in the war. It is true that the Army was responsible for local defense at Pearl Harbor. Nevertheless some things could have been done by the Navy to lessen the success of the initial Japanese blow. Admiral Stark and Admiral Kimmel were the responsible officers. . . .

The derelictions on the part of Admiral Stark and Admiral Kimmel were faults of omission rather than faults of commission. In the case in question, they indicate lack of the superior judgment necessary for exercising command commensurate with their rank and their assigned duties, rather than culpable inefficiency. . . . Appropriate administrative action would appear to be the relegation of both of these officers to positions in which lack of superior judgment may not result in future errors.[91]

That action was taken by Secretary Forrestal respecting both admirals, and also by Secretary Stimson with respect to General Short.

The Joint Congressional Committee a year later, after the most exhaustive investigation in our history, one which uncovered considerable information from enemy sources that was not available to other courts of inquiry, did little more than confirm the opinion of the Commander in Chief of the Fleet as to the Navy's share in responsibility for being taken completely by surprise.[92]

\*      \*      \*

[91] *P. H. Attack* Part 39 pp. 343–44.
[92] It may be well to mention a few of the loose charges made at the time and talked about even today, although the various courts and committees proved them to be unqualifiedly false: —
(1) That Admiral Kimmel and General Short seldom conferred on the problem of defense and were hardly on speaking terms; (2) That hundreds of officers and men of the Fleet were absent from duty because suffering from hangovers on Sunday morning 7 December; (3) That many Japanese in Honolulu had advance notice of the attack, coöperated with it and committed sundry acts of sabotage;

The ways and means by which four of the five battleships sunk in Pearl Harbor were raised, and four of them (together with the three damaged but not sunk) were restored to the Fleet, bears out Admiral Furlong's motto for the Pearl Harbor Navy Yard: "We keep them fit to fight." Captain Homer N. Wallin was the officer chiefly responsible for these praiseworthy salvage operations.[93] For want of space we shall confine ourselves to those on the *Oklahoma* and *West Virginia*.

*Oklahoma*, toughest and most spectacular of the salvage jobs, was not only sunk but capsized, with keel in air and masts crumpled in the mud. Under the direction of Chief Watertender R. H. Snow, a scale model, inverted in exactly the position of the ship, was constructed so that divers could orient themselves to an upside-down interior. Divers sealed the great apertures that the torpedoes had torn in her hull, and opened other vents for the water to flow out, so that by the forcing in of air the 29,000-ton ship was given a positive buoyancy of 18,800 tons. In *Oklahoma*, as in all the sunken ships, decomposed organic matter from the provisions, clothing and bodies of the victims generated a gas so deadly that even when water was freed from the compartments men had to work with gas masks. This preparatory work took over a year to accomplish.

When buoyancy was restored to *Oklahoma*, the next problem was to right her. In order to distribute the strain fore and aft, 21 triangular timber frames 40 feet high, of the type known as "bents,"

---

(4) That the Australian government had prior knowledge of the attack and warned Washington; (5) That the cruiser *Boise* had contacted the Japanese carrier fleet and given similar warning; (6) That President Roosevelt, or the Secretaries of War and of the Navy, or General Marshall or Admiral Stark, or any of them, had had positive information of the impending attack on Pearl Harbor by an "East Wind, Rain" or other decrypted dispatch and deliberately suppressed this information in order to let the attack develop and bring the United States into the war.

[93] Capt. Wallin "Report of the Repair and Salvage of Naval Vessels Damaged at Pearl Harbor," 13 July 1942; and "Rejuvenation at Pearl Harbor," U.S. Nav. Inst. *Proceedings* LXXII 526 (Dec. 1946) p. 1521; Rear Admiral William R. Furlong's official report; article prepared by Robert Trumbull for *New York Times* Dec. 1943 but never published; F. H. Whitaker "The Salvage of U.S.S. *Oklahoma*," *Transactions* of Society of Naval Architects and Engineers LII (1944). Admiral Furlong has supplemented these accounts by oral explanations and it is he who supplied us with the photographs.

were erected on her capsized bottom. From the steel cap at the apex of each bent, six heavy steel cables led to pad-eyes welded into the inverted vessel's starboard side along a line where the greatest leverage could be exerted. And also, from each cap, two steel cables led to an enormous 16-sheave burton tackle whose pendant was geared at 8000-to-1 ratio to a 5-horsepower electric winch firmly embedded in a deep concrete foundation on Ford Island.

When everything was set, in March 1943, the twenty-one small motors pulled the big ship over to a 90-degree position in a little over one hundred hours. The bents and cables were then removed, a new hold taken by the cables topside, and she was righted completely.

*Oklahoma* had now passed her twenty-seventh birthday. The raising of her was necessary to clear the harbor, but so much new construction had come out that the Navy Department did not wish to spend more money on her rehabilitation. Sold to a wrecking company as junk, she sank when being towed to the West Coast after the war was over.

*West Virginia* was perhaps the most successful example of rehabilitation. The six or seven torpedoes that hit her had blown out a series of gashes 120 feet long and 12 to 15 feet high; one of the bomb hits had pushed the third, second and main decks down so that they came together ten feet below the original third-deck level. Inside it looked as if a giant had crumpled the ship and then lighted a torch to the remains; and her bottom was wrinkled and bent where it struck the harbor bottom. But she lay almost on an even keel.

As the great slash in her port side was too large for patching, the engineers built a series of huge cofferdams, 50 feet deep, which were weighted, lowered and bolted to the hull by divers so that they formed one big outer wall. At the bottom, where a snug fitting of timbers to the jagged edges of steel was impossible, the gap was sealed with tremic cement, the kind that hardens under water. This battleship was pumped out, raised, and cleaned largely by her

Slash made by Japanese torpedoes

In dry dock, showing cofferdams over slashes

*Salvage of* West Virginia

Port side, in dry dock

Refloated, 1943, but without new batteries installed

*Salvage of* West Virginia

own crew with the aid of civilian technicians, since the common workmen of the Navy Yard blenched at the indescribable filth and grisly human remains in her wrecked and soaked interior. On 17 May 1942 she floated and was towed into the Navy Yard dry dock for temporary repairs. The General Electric Company, which had built the motors and generators, sent fifty specialists to assist more than a hundred Pearl Harbor electricians in the complex task of rewinding all main generators and motors.

In due course *West Virginia* proceeded under her own power to Bremerton for a modernization which made her practically a new ship. As the work was frequently interrupted by other tasks of higher priority, she was not ready to rejoin the Fleet until the middle of 1944. Her new construction was all welded instead of riveted, and the saving in weight raised her waterline by 2½ inches. Her deck and turret armor was doubled in thickness, her water-tight integrity greatly improved. A new ventilation system, new fire mains and new fuel oil-lines were built, as well as "blisters" on both sides, to afford greater stability and anti-torpedo protection. These increased her beam from 98½ to 114 feet, so that she could no longer pass through the Panama Canal. Her main battery had to be regunned. But, of all the improvements that came about through war experience, the most impressive is the additional anti-aircraft armament, as shown in this before-and-after table: —

ANTI-AIRCRAFT ARMAMENT OF U.S.S. *WEST VIRGINIA*[94]

|  | On 7 December 1941 | After Rehabilitation |
|---|---|---|
| 5-inch | 8  5"25s single mounts, open | 16  5"38s, twin-mounted, covered |
| 3-inch | 4  3"23s | None |
| Large machine guns | None; mounts only for 4 1.1" quads. | 64  40-mm. in 16 quads. |
| Small machine guns | 10  .50 cal. | 82  20-mm. |

*Nevada* served as Rear Admiral Morton Deyo's flagship in the Normandy invasion and returned to the Pacific in time to help pound Iwo Jima. *West Virginia, Maryland, California, Tennessee*

[94] Data furnished by an officer who remained with her throughout the war.

and *Pennsylvania* crossed the enemy's "T" at the Battle of Surigao Strait and subsequently participated in the Okinawa operation, where *Nevada* joined them and where they were more or less damaged by kamikaze and other air attacks. *West Virginia* had the proud privilege of entering Sagami Bay, Japan, with the occupation force on 27 August 1945.

## PART II
# The Philippines and Near-by Waters[1]

*All dates are East Longitude, and local times are used;*
*those in the Philippines are Zone minus 8*

[1] This Part, for which Lieutenant Albert Harkness Jr. USNR did the basic research, owes much to Admiral Thomas C. Hart, Commander in Chief United States Asiatic Fleet, who prepared a "Narrative of Events Asiatic Fleet . . . to 15 February 1942" in 1942, and a "Supplementary Narrative" in 1946. In addition he gave much time to the writer, who wishes to express his gratitude as well as his admiration for the candor with which the Admiral has told the story of his command, excusing nothing, laying no blame on others, but pointing out the factors which rendered his mission hopeless. Several other officers who served in the Asiatic Fleet have read the following chapters and made corrections or suggestions; and Lieutenant Commander Henry Salomon Jr. USNR, who procured the material of enemy origin in Japan, contributed to their final form.

# CHAPTER VI

# The Rising Cloud

## 1940–1941

### 1. *Plans, Preparations and Personalities*

A POSITION of responsibility without power is an anomaly in military as well as political science; yet that was exactly the situation of America in the Philippines. She was responsible for their defense until such time as the Philippine Commonwealth became independent, but her armed forces deployed in the Pacific lacked the power to defend them against a determined attack by Japan.

This basic fact had long been admitted by American war planners of both services. It was largely a matter of distance; one could demonstrate the proposition with a map of the Pacific and a pair of dividers. Takao, the great Japanese base in southern Formosa, lies only 270 miles from Aparri, the northernmost airfield on Luzon, and only 482 miles from Manila. But Manila lies 6200 miles from San Francisco by the Great Circle route that skirts Japan, and 4800 miles from Honolulu, via Guam. Moreover, these routes were boxed in for 2000 miles from Manila by Japanese-held islands so that they were certain to become unusable in time of war. Geography, and Japanese prescience in taking the Marianas, Carolines and Marshalls, doomed the Philippines to isolation from their legal sovereign and protector.

In the Philippine Islands the political situation was somewhat anomalous. The United States had pledged its word to give them independence in 1945, and had set up a Commonwealth that was not prepared to undertake its own defense. The grant of autonomy and promise of independence had drawn off almost all the anti-American feeling; economic relations with the United States were highly advantageous; and politically conscious Filipinos, who had been subjected to Western culture for almost four centuries, regarded the Japanese as an inferior breed of heathen whose Greater East Asia propaganda was a subject for ridicule.

Conditions being what they were, the basic Army-Navy war plan, which had been on the books substantially since 1921, envisaged the following strategy: —

Assuming that one of the first acts of war by Japan would be an invasion of the Philippines, the brunt of their defense would fall on the United States Army garrison and the Philippine Army. If, despite their efforts, the enemy could not be held off, the two armies would retire to the Bataan Peninsula and thence hamper and delay the Japanese advance. For the main objective in this war plan was to hold Manila Bay at all costs until reinforcements could arrive from the United States.

In this delaying action, the United States Pacific Fleet was to play no part. That Fleet would then be fighting its way across the Pacific, in order to secure a sea lane for troop reinforcements and begin a reconquest of the islands from Manila Bay. All naval action during the defensive and delaying phase must be performed by the Asiatic Fleet. Since it was admitted that this minor (not to say minuscule) force could be pounced on by the Japanese Combined Fleet and made a mouthful of, it was planned to retire its major striking elements, the cruisers and destroyers, to the Indian Ocean, leaving only submarines, patrol wings of Catalina flying boats, and small craft to help the Army repel troop landings and protect local shipping.

General Douglas MacArthur is the greatest single figure in the military history of the Philippines. His name will be forever associated with the heroic defense of Bataan, the long and patient build-up in Australia, the glorious return in October 1944, and the liberation of the Archipelago. In 1935, after he had completed a five years' term as chief of staff of the United States Army, Mac-

Arthur received an appointment as military adviser to the Philippine Commonwealth. With a small staff of United States Army officers he set about organizing armed forces for the nascent Republic. When commissioned Field Marshal of the Philippine Army in 1937 he retired from the United States Army but retained his position as United States Military Adviser.

The General brought to his new task a wide knowledge of the Philippines, where both he and his father, General Arthur MacArthur, had been United States military commanders. He knew and loved the islands and their people. An optimist by nature, he believed that a relatively small but well trained Philippine Army, if assisted by the Asiatic Fleet, could hold off a Japanese invasion until the basic war plan was executed and reinforcements could arrive by way of Australia, if not in the wake of the Pacific Fleet.

General MacArthur's opposite number on the naval side was Admiral Thomas C. Hart, who on 25 July 1939 relieved Admiral Yarnell as Commander in Chief of the Asiatic Fleet.[1] Small, taut, wiry and irascible, Admiral Hart had the reputation in the Navy of being very much of a strict disciplinarian. He was respected as a student of the art of war and as an administrator. During the years 1931–40 the main function of the Asiatic Fleet was to protect American interests in China. As war clouds gathered in the Far East, the Admiral wished to shift his base from Shanghai to Manila, where he could coördinate the Fleet's activities with General MacArthur's command and with potential allies. Although the Department of State objected to this as a "retreat" which would encourage Japanese aggression, the Chief of Naval Operations wisely left the decision to Admiral Hart, ordering him to remain at Shanghai unless "compelling reasons" demanded a withdrawal. Hart judged the reasons to be compelling, and in the autumn of

---

[1] Thomas Charles Hart, born Michigan 1877, Naval Academy '97. Served in the Spanish–American war, rose to command of a submarine division in 1916, and took two such divisions into European waters in World War I, during which he rose to the rank of captain. Attended courses at Army and Naval War Colleges; C.O. *Mississippi* 1925; Comsubdivs Atlantic Fleet, 1927; Rear Admiral, 1929; Superintendent of the Naval Academy, 1931; Com. cruisers Scouting Force, 1935; General Board, 1936.

1940 sailed in flagship *Houston* with most of his small fleet to Manila Bay. Rear Admiral Glassford, Commander Yangtze Patrol, remained at Shanghai to operate the river gunboats. In June 1941, Admiral Hart set up headquarters in the Marsman Building on the Manila waterfront.

Conditions in the Philippines, as the Admiral found them, were disheartening. The Commonwealth authorities, like those of the United States, were emotionally unprepared for war, and the United States High Commissioner, the Honorable Francis B. Sayre (so it appeared to Admiral Hart) believed that war could be averted by not thinking about it. Mr. Sayre suddenly changed his attitude, however, in July 1941, publicly admitted the gravity of the situation, and coöperated with the armed forces to the best of his ability.

The Washington staff conference in January–March 1941, which made the basic strategic decision of the war, made Admiral Hart responsible for the naval defense of the Philippines as a sort of enclave inside the Far Eastern Area, over which the British Commander in Chief China was to have the general strategic direction of the naval forces of the three powers. Admiral Hart was represented by his chief of staff, Captain William R. Purnell, at the ADB Conferences at Singapore in April. As we have already seen, the numerous uncertainties in the Far Eastern situation prevented this conference from making any definite arrangements for a combined command or operating plan.

In the new war plan (Rainbow 5 or WPL 46), officially adopted in May 1941, Admiral Hart found the rôle of the Asiatic Fleet unchanged. It must support the Army in the defense of the Philippines "so long as that defense continues," but could shift base of operations to a British or Dutch port at the commander's discretion. Whatever forces he might shift south would fall under British command, and their task would then be to support the British and Dutch Navies in the defense of the Malay Barrier — Sumatra, Java, Bali, Lombok, Soemba, Flores and Timor.

In July 1941 the Japanese occupied Indochina, virtually completing their encirclement of the Philippines; and, as retaliation, the United States froze Japanese assets. At this new turn of events, the War Department decided to augment ground forces in the Philippines to 200,000 men. Field Marshal MacArthur's Philippine Army, absorbed into the United States Army on 27 July, supplied about half this number; the balance, 75,000, were to be sent out from the United States. MacArthur was recalled to active duty, promoted Lieutenant General by the same presidential order of 27 July, and ordered to command United States Army Forces Far East, as his mixed force was named. He believed that these forces could be brought up to the 200,000 mark by about 1 April 1942 when he estimated that hostilities would begin.[2] But the Navy could promise no reinforcement to Admiral Hart, whose staff planners had to work on an "as is" basis, with the ships, planes and facilities actually on hand.

In July or early August the Army General Staff at Washington underwent a change of heart about the defense of the Philippines. Instead of assuming a retreat to Bataan as inevitable, they began to think that if enough reinforcements could be sent to Luzon and if a powerful, well-rounded air force could be built up, it might be possible to hold the entire Archipelago, except Mindanao and Palawan, and so check the Japanese southward advance. This change was brought about in part by General MacArthur's infectious optimism, in part by the apparent success of Flying Fortresses lend-leased to the Royal Air Force in bombing Germany. If MacArthur's army could be built up to 200,000, and if enough B-17s could be flown in,[3] Luzon and the Visayas might become a self-sustaining fortress from which the South China Sea could be blockaded. This new concept was the reason why the Army urged delay on the State Department and the President. On 6 October 1941

[2] General Jonathan Wainwright *General Wainwright's Story* (1946) pp. 12–13.
[3] B-17s, moreover, could be sent to the Philippines by the Fiji–New Caledonia–Australia route even if the Japanese captured Guam and Wake.

the Secretary of War told the Secretary of State, "We need three months to secure our position." [4]

Admiral Hart, as a junior partner in this defensive scheme, learned only by accident what was in the Army's mind; he fell in, enthusiastically, with the new MacArthur-Marshall plan. On 27 October he suggested to the Navy Department that the Asiatic Fleet concentrate in Manila Bay instead of moving its main strength south, as the existing war plan required when hostilities were imminent. He pointed out that the expansion of the Army Air Force made it probable that Manila Bay would be fairly secure from attack; that we had a moral obligation to abandon no territory voluntarily; and that so little progress had been made in combined planning that to send the Asiatic Fleet south might be worse than useless. This radical proposal required a prompt reply, but the Admiral received none until 20 November, and that was a flat negative from the Secretary. Frank Knox was right, as the Admiral admits with his usual candor; but the delay in answering was unfortunate because, while waiting for it, Hart shelved his plans for deployment to the southward. In consequence the sudden outbreak of war caught several auxiliary vessels crowded along the waterfront of Cavite.

Upon receipt of the Department's negative on 20 November, Hart began to deploy his Fleet. On 24 November he sent four destroyers with their tender *Black Hawk* to Balikpapan on Makassar Strait, and light cruiser *Marblehead* with four other destroyers to Tarakan on the Celebes Sea. *Houston*, flagship of Task Force 5, proceeded to Iloilo, to await the new striking force commander, Rear Admiral Glassford, who arrived at Manila from his Yangtze command on 5 December.

Months after he had requested permission to do so, the Department ordered Admiral Hart to withdraw remaining forces from

[4] Hon. Henry L. Stimson's Diary, communicated by his biographer, Col. Mac-George Bundy. Dr. Louis Morton and Capt. Bernhardt Mortensen USA, of the Historical sections of the War Department, and of the A.A.F., have helped us to prepare parts of this chapter relating to the Army, but they are not responsible for the conclusions.

China. He decided to pull the Marines out first and the gunboats later. Two "President" liners were chartered and first went to Shanghai to remove elements of the 4th Marines and attached naval personnel. Then *President Harrison* was turned around for Chinwangtao, the nearest port to embark the Marine detachments from Pekin and Tientsin. Overhauled by a Japanese cruiser on 8 December, she ripped her bottom open on the China coast reefs to avoid falling into enemy hands.[5]

Four river gunboats remained in Chinese waters. U.S.S. *Wake*, the smallest, was left at Shanghai, stripped down and equipped for demolition, as a station ship and radio outlet for the few Americans who remained; the Japanese took her over on 8 December. *Tutuila* could not come down-river because of the Japanese blockade and so was turned over to the Chinese Navy under lend-lease. Admiral Glassford's flagship *Luzon*, and *Oahu*, *Tulsa* and *Asheville*, made the voyage to Manila without incident. *Mindanao*, a river gunboat with some three feet of freeboard, was held at Hong Kong awaiting word of how the others fared in the autumn monsoon on the South China Sea. She weighed anchor just in time and made Manila safely.[6]

In the meantime there was plenty for the Asiatic Fleet to do at Manila. The Navy and War Departments ordered all protective mine fields in Manila Bay to be planted on 15 July, and Subic Bay was mined too. On 22 July the floating dry dock *Dewey* moved from Olongapo, a place regarded as indefensible, and moored at Mariveles.

A dispatch indicating a grave turn in United States–Japanese relations caused High Commissioner Sayre to call a conference with General MacArthur and Admiral Hart on 27 November. All three agreed as to their general responsibilities and the importance of inspiring confidence at lower levels.[7] On the Japanese side, everything was set for the invasion. On the 26th, there had been a con-

[5] The Japanese captured the whole crew, salvaged the ship and operated her as *Kachidoki Maru* until torpedoed by U.S.S. *Pampanito* on 12 Sept. 1944.
[6] Hart Report p. 27 and Lt. Cdr. W. B. Porter "Gunboat Saga" *U.S. Naval Institute Proceedings* LXX (Apr. 1944) p. 421.     [7] Hart Report.

ference of flag officers on board Vice Admiral Takahashi's flagship *Ashigara* off Formosa to discuss the operation.[8]

Admiral Hart had been working for months on the joint air defense of Manila Bay, and so had General Brereton, Army Air Force Commander under General MacArthur. A counteroffensive of land-based planes seemed the only solution. But who should command it, and how should it be comprised? The first question was resolved on the basis of coöperation; the second was more difficult. Army Air was building up so rapidly, in fighters particularly, that it hardly knew from day to day what component it could supply; and the Army Air Force command was under such strain from this rapid expansion that it had no time to prepare for joint communications with submarine or surface ships, or to train the newly arrived B–17 pilots in ship recognition. Finally, almost at the last minute, Army and Navy made a joint plan for air patrol. Flying Fortresses, because of their greater speed and higher ceiling, were sent to patrol the two northern sectors which touched Formosa, while Catalinas made flights along the Indochinese coast. Neither acquired any information of value before war broke.

The new naval commander at Singapore, Vice Admiral Sir Tom Phillips RN, one of the youngest and most able flag officers in the Royal Navy, arrived in Manila on 5 December to confer with Admiral Hart and General MacArthur. They took care to keep this visit secret, lest the Japanese suspect something was up; that was a pity, because the enemy was already poised to strike, and Phillips would have enjoyed Manila in the last days of peace. The bright tropical city with its white concrete buildings and broad boulevards, accented by the great green bay and the ancient walled city, where East and West had been meeting for the better part of four centuries, had a peculiar charm until it was befouled and battered by the Japanese.

Phillips, who had held the first Anglo-American staff conversa-

---

[8] Philippine Force Order No. 1 found in cruiser *Nachi*, sunk in Manila Bay, 1944, ATIS Extensive Translation No. 39 of 22 Apr. 1945. "Japanese Navy Plans and Orders 1941–44," in 12 vols.

tions with Admiral Ingersoll almost four years earlier, had just come to Singapore as commander of a nucleus battle force consisting of H.M. battleship *Prince of Wales* and battle cruiser *Repulse*. Although he was responsible for the defense of Singapore, he saw eye to eye with Admiral Hart as to its indefensibility against a well directed attack, and agreed that Manila Bay would make a better base for offensive naval operations. But it was obvious that British naval forces could not move up from Singapore to Manila Bay until and unless air protection were greatly increased. For the time being, the only thing to decide was how many destroyers Admiral Hart would allocate to the Singapore force in his southern deployment. He agreed to send four, if the Royal Navy would add three then stationed at Hong Kong.

While they were conferring, a report came in that a large Japanese convoy known to have been in Camranh Bay, Indochina, had put out to sea and was heading for the Gulf of Siam. Obviously, this was no time for Admiral Phillips to be in Manila. As Hart bade farewell to Phillips on the evening of 6 December he said, "I have just ordered my destroyers at Balikpapan to proceed to Batavia on the pretext of rest and leave. Actually they will join your force." [9] But by the time they were ready to proceed, there was no more force, or Phillips.

## 2. *Composition and Deployment of Naval Forces* [10]

### *a.* American
### (as of 8 December 1941)

[Contrary to our usual practice, the United States Asiatic Fleet has been arranged in order of deployment, so that the reader may know where each ship was at the opening of hostilities.]

[9] Hart interview, and stenographic notes of conference. Hart was very favorably impressed with Phillips and would have urged Washington to nominate him for area commander had he lived.

[10] Information from vessels' logs, "Roster of Asiatic Fleet and Station"; Comsubs Asiatic Fleet to Cominch and CNO 1 Apr. 1942; "War Activities Submarines, U.S. Asiatic Fleet, 1 Dec. 1941–1 Apr. 1942" pp. 1–21.

*The highest ranking naval officers at Manila on 8 December were:* —

Admiral Thomas C. Hart, Commander in Chief United States Asiatic Fleet.
Rear Admiral William R. Purnell, Chief of Staff Asiatic Fleet.
Rear Admiral William A. Glassford, Commander Task Force 5.
Rear Admiral Francis W. Rockwell, Commandant 16th Naval District and Commander Philippine Coastal Frontier.
Colonel Samuel L. Howard USMC, Commander 4th Marine Regiment.

## FORCES AT MANILA BAY AND OLONGAPO

Destroyer Division 59, Cdr. P. H. Talbot

| | |
|---|---|
| POPE | Lt. Cdr. W. C. Blinn |
| PEARY [11] | Lt. Cdr. H. H. Keith |
| PILLSBURY [11] | Lt. Cdr. H. C. Pound |
| JOHN D. FORD | Lt. Cdr. J. E. Cooper |

*Submarines*

Commander Submarines Asiatic Fleet, Capt. W. E. Doyle [12]

| | | | |
|---|---|---|---|
| S-37 | Lt. J. C. Dempsey | SKIPJACK | Lt. C. L. Freeman |
| S-38 | Lt. W. C. Chapple | SNAPPER | Lt. Cdr. H. L. Stone |
| S-40 | Lt. N. Lucker Jr. | STINGRAY | Lt. Cdr. R. S. Lamb |
| S-41 | Lt. G. M. Holley | STURGEON | Lt. Cdr. W. L. Wright |
| PORPOISE | Lt. Cdr. J. A. Callaghan | SARGO | Lt. Cdr. T. D. Jacobs |
| PIKE | Lt. Cdr. W. A. New | SAURY | Lt. Cdr. J. L. Burnside |
| SHARK [13] | Lt. Cdr. L. Shane, Jr. | SPEARFISH | Lt. R. F. Pryce |
| TARPON | Lt. Cdr. L. Wallace | SCULPIN | Lt. L. H. Chappell |
| PERCH | Lt. Cdr. D. A. Hurt | SAILFISH | Lt. Cdr. M. C. Mumma Jr. |
| PICKEREL | Lt. Cdr. B. E. Bacon Jr. | SWORDFISH | Lt. Cdr. C. C. Smith |
| PERMIT | Lt. Cdr. A. M. Hurst | SEADRAGON [13] | Lt. Cdr. W. E. Ferrall |
| SALMON | Lt. E. B. McKinney | SEALION [13] | Lt. Cdr. R. G. Voge |
| SEAL | Lt. Cdr. K. C. Hurd | SEARAVEN | Lt. Cdr. T. C. Aylward |
| | | SEAWOLF | Lt. Cdr. F. B. Warder |

*Submarine Tenders and Repair Ships*

| | |
|---|---|
| CANOPUS | Cdr. E. L. Sackett |
| HOLLAND | Capt. J. W. Gregory |
| OTUS [14] | Lt. Cdr. J. Newsom |

[11] Under repair.
[12] Capt. John Wilkes was appointed in his place on 10 Dec. 1941.
[13] Under overhaul.
[14] *Otus*, a former Lykes liner, came to Manila in mid-1941 to complete conversion at Cavite. Conversion was incomplete when war broke out but *Otus* was useful as a supply ship.

### Gunboats

Inshore Patrol, Cdr. K. M. Hoeffel

| | |
|---|---|
| ASHEVILLE | Cdr. Hoeffel |
| TULSA | Lt. Cdr. T. S. Daniel |
| OAHU | Lt. Cdr. D. E. Smith |
| LUZON | Lt. Cdr. G. M. Brooke |
| MINDANAO 15 | Lt. Cdr. A. R. McCracken |
| ISABEL | Lt. (jg) F. W. Payne Jr. |

### Seaplanes

Patrol Wing 10, Capt. F. D. Wagner

28 PBYs, 4 J2Fs, 1 OS2U, based on tenders

| | |
|---|---|
| LANGLEY | Cdr. F. B. Stump |
| CHILDS | Lt. Cdr. J. L. Pratt |

### Minesweepers, Lt. Cdr. E. R. J. Griffin

| | |
|---|---|
| LARK | Lt. Cdr. H. P. Thomson |
| WHIPPOORWILL | Lt. Cdr. C. A. Ferriter |
| TANAGER | Lt. Cdr. E A. Roth |
| QUAIL | Lt. Cdr. J. H. Morrill |
| BITTERN | Lt. T. G. Warfield |

### Tankers

| | |
|---|---|
| PECOS | Lt. Cdr. E. P. Abernathy |
| TRINITY | Cdr. W. Hibbs |

### Salvage Vessels and Tugs

| | |
|---|---|
| PIGEON | Lt. R. E. Hawes |
| NAPA | Lt. N. M. Dial |
| *Keswick* | (Civilian vessel under naval control) |

Floating Dry Dock DEWEY      Lt. Weschler

4th Marine Regiment and Navy Yard Marines

## FORCES ELSEWHERE IN THE PHILIPPINES

Heavy Cruiser HOUSTON (flagship TF 5) Capt. A. H. Rooks, at Iloilo
Light Cruiser BOISE,16 Capt. S. B. Robinson, at Cebu
Submarine *S-36*, Lt. J. R. McKnight Jr., off Lingayen
Submarine *S-39*, Lt. J. W. Coe, at Sorsogon Bay, Luzon
Station Ship GOLD STAR, Cdr. J. W. Lademan Jr., at Malangas
Four PBYs based on tender WILLIAM B. PRESTON, Lt. Cdr. E. Grant, at Davao
Four OS2Us based on tender HERON, Lt. W. I. Kabler, at Palawan

15 En route from Hong Kong.
16 *Boise*, belonging to the Pacific Fleet, had recently escorted an Army transport bringing reinforcements to Manila. Admiral Hart was humorously accused of "shanghaiing" her to reinforce his Fleet.

## FORCES IN BORNEO

### AT TARAKAN

Light Cruiser MARBLEHEAD          Capt. A. G. Robinson

Destroyer Squadron 29, Capt. H. V. Wiley

PAUL JONES [17]                   Lt. Cdr. J. J. Hourihan

Destroyer Division 58, Cdr. T. H. Binford

| | |
|---|---|
| STEWART | Lt. Cdr. H. P. Smith |
| BULMER | Lt. Cdr. L. J. Manees |
| BARKER | Lt. Cdr. L. G. McGlone |
| PARROTT | Lt. Cdr. E. N. Parker |

### AT BALIKPAPAN

Destroyer Division 57, Cdr. E. M. Crouch [18]

| | |
|---|---|
| WHIPPLE | Lt. Cdr. E. S. Karpe |
| ALDEN | Lt. Cdr. L. E. Coley |
| JOHN D. EDWARDS | Lt. Cdr. H. E. Eccles |
| EDSALL | Lt. Cdr. J. J. Nix |

Tender BLACK HAWK [19]            Cdr. G. L. Harris

## *b.* Japanese
## (as of 8–25 December 1941) [20]

All important Japanese naval operations affecting the Philippines were effected by the Third Fleet. This was primarily an amphibious fleet with a supporting force of carriers, cruisers and destroyers. The Second Fleet, under Vice Admiral Kondo in heavy cruiser *Atago*, covered the invasion from a distance and some of its destroyers were assigned to bolster support for the surprise forces. Special task forces were organized for the various missions which

[17] Operated with Desdiv 59 in Philippines most of the time.
[18] These ships departed for Batavia 7 December but their orders were changed when *Prince of Wales* and *Repulse* were sunk.
[19] *Black Hawk* was Capt. Wiley's administrative flagship.
[20] Based on Combined Fleet Top Secret Operation Order 1 dated 5 Nov. 1941 on board flagship *Nagato* in Saeki Bay, O.N.I. Intelligence Report "Japan, Navy, Organization, Fleet" 14 Jan. 1942; ATIS doc. 19692 Interrogation of Vice Admiral Shiraichi, USSBS No. 33 (Navy No. 7) and Lt. LaRocque's answers to Mr. Salomon's queries, 8 July 1946. At best the results of reconciling the various sources are only approximate.

the Third Fleet undertook. In the Philippines campaign these consisted intially of one Main Force, four Surprise Attack Forces, a Southern Philippines Support Unit, and a Minelaying Force.

Lieutenant General M. Homma was the Joint Commander in Chief of all invasion forces for the Philippines, but apparently Admiral Takahashi had a free hand in directing naval and amphibious forces until the General came ashore on 24 December.

## JAPANESE INVASION FORCES FOR THE PHILIPPINES

### SECOND FLEET
Vice Admiral N. Kondo

#### DISTANT COVER FORCE, Admiral Kondo [21]

| | | | |
|---|---|---|---|
| CA | ATAGO | BB | HARUNA |
| CA | TAKAO | BB | KONGO |

About 10 destroyers of Desrons 4, 5 and 8

### THIRD FLEET
Vice Admiral I. Takahashi

#### CLOSE OR NORTHERN COVERING FORCE, Admiral Takahashi

| | | | | |
|---|---|---|---|---|
| CA | ASHIGARA | CL | KUMA | Converted seaplane tenders |
| CA | MAYA | DD | ASAKAZE | SANYO MARU |
| | | DD | MATSUKAZE | SANUKI MARU |

#### THIRD SURPRISE ATTACK FORCE (*Batan I.*), Rear Admiral S. Hirose

| | | | |
|---|---|---|---|
| DD | YAMAGUMO | Torpedo Boats | 2 Minesweepers |
| | | CHIDORI | 2 Converted Gunboats, 9SCs |
| | | HATSUKARI | 2 Patrol Boats |
| | | MANAZURU | *HAYO MARU |
| | | TOMOZURU | *KUMAKAWA MARU |

#### FIRST SURPRISE ATTACK FORCE (*Aparri*), Rear Admiral K. Hara

| | | | | |
|---|---|---|---|---|
| CL | NATORI | DD | MINATSUKI | Minesweepers 15, 16, *19 |
| DD | FUMITSUKI | DD | HARUKAZE | 9 Submarine Chasers |
| DD | SATSUKI | DD | HATAKAZE | 6 Transports |
| DD | NAGATSUKI | | | |

* Sunk by U.S. submarines or Army aircraft.

[21] USSBS Interrogation 99; Second Fleet Organization, Dec. 1941, procured by Mr. Salomon (ATIS 160678). This force covered Lingayen landings from off Macclesfield Bank, midway between Luzon and the China coast. Previously it had covered Malaya operations and subsequently was based on Palau until the Java operations got under way.

### SECOND SURPRISE ATTACK FORCE (*Vigan*), Rear Admiral S. Nishimura

| CL | NAKA | DD | SAMIDARE | Minesweepers 7, 8, 9, *10, 17, 18 |
| DD | MURASAME | DD | ASAGUMO | 9 Subchasers |
| DD | YUDACHI | DD | MINEGUMO | 6 Transports |
| DD | HARUSAME | DD | NATSUGUMO | |

### FOURTH SURPRISE ATTACK FORCE (*Legaspi*)
#### Rear Admiral K. Kubo, staged from Palau

| CL | NAGARA | DD | UMIKAZE | Seaplane ∫ CHITOSE [22] |
| DD | YAMAKAZE | DD | YUKIKAZE | Carriers ⎩ MIZUHO |
| DD | SUZUKAZE | DD | TOKITSUKAZE | 7 Transports |
| DD | KAWAKAZE | 2 Minesweepers | | 2 Patrol Craft |
| | | | | 5 Small Ships |

### LEGASPI SUPPORT FORCE
#### Rear Admiral T. Takagi, based on Palau

| CA | NACHI | CL | JINTSU | DD | NATSUSHIO |
| CA | HAGURO | DD | KUROSHIO | DD | HAYASHIO |
| CA | MYOKO | DD | OYASHIO | DD | AMATSUKAZE |
| CV | RYUJO | DD | HATSUKAZE | | |
| DD | SHIOKAZE | | | | |

*Minelaying Force*, Rear Admiral T. Kobayashi, based on Palau

| CM | ITSUKUSHIMA | CM | YAEYAMA | CM | TATSUHARA MARU |

## LINGAYEN FORCE
#### Carrying 48th Infantry Division and attached units.

*First Group*, Rear Admiral Hara, staged from Takao, Formosa
27 Transports escorted by most of Aparri Surprise Force

*Second Group*, Rear Admiral Nishimura, staged from Mako, Pescadores
28 Transports, escorted by most of the Vigan Surprise Force

*Third Group*, Rear Admiral Hirose, staged from Keelung, Formosa
21 Transports, escorted by most of the Batan Island Surprise Force

### LAMON BAY ATTACK GROUP
#### Rear Admiral K. Kubo, staged from Amami O Shima

24 Transports, carrying 16th Infantry Division, 32nd Naval Base Force and attached units. Escort same as that of 4th Surprise Attack Force, plus six converted gunboats including

| KANKO MARU | 6 Subchasers |
| KEIKO MARU | 2 Minesweepers |
| BUSHO MARU | |

* Sunk by U.S. submarines or Army aircraft.

[22] Rear Admiral R. Fujita's flagship. She was in the Lamon Bay Landings.

## SOUTHERN FORCE, staged from Palau

### COVERING GROUP, Rear Admiral T. Takagi
Same as Legaspi Support Force, plus CVS CHITOSE

### DAVAO ATTACK GROUP, Rear Admiral R. Tanaka

| CL | JINTSU | DD | HATSUKAZE | DD | AMATSUKAZE |
|----|--------|----|-----------|----|------------|
| DD | KUROSHIO | DD | NATSUSHIO | CM | SHIRATAKA |
| DD | OYASHIO | DD | HAYASHIO | 5 Transports, 2 PCs | |

### JOLO ATTACK GROUP, Rear Admiral Tanaka
JINTSU, 4 of above DDs, 9 Transports, RYUJO and CHITOSE

## SUPPORTING NAVAL AIR FORCES, based on Formosa
Vice Admiral N. Tsukahara, Commander in Chief 11th Air Fleet

#### *21st Air Flotilla*, Rear Admiral T. Tada [23]

| 30 Type 1 Land Attack Planes | 24 Type 97 Large Model Flying Boats |
|---|---|
| 54 Type 96 Land Attack Planes | |

#### *23rd Air Flotilla*, Rear Admiral R. Takenaka

| 62 Type 1 Land Attack Planes | 13 Type 96 Carrier Fighter Planes |
|---|---|
| 110 Type 0 Carrier Fighter Planes | 15 Type 98 Land Reconnaissance Planes |

#### *Coöperating Army Air Forces*, based on Formosa

| 48 Reconnaissance Planes | 54 Light Bombers |
|---|---|
| 72 Fighter Planes | 27 Heavy Bombers |

#### *4th Naval Air Flotilla*, Rear Admiral K. Kakuta, based on Palaus

| CV | RYUJO and aircraft | DD | SHIOKAZE |
|----|--------------------|----|----------|

[23] USSBS Interrogation 424 lists a total of 190 planes in this. The 21st Air Force was based at Taichu and Tainan, the 23rd at Taichu and Takao.

# CHAPTER VII

# Invasion[1]

## 8–25 December 1941

## 1. The Japanese Plan

WHILE three potential allies were hectically preparing against they knew not what, the Japanese marshaled their vastly superior forces in accordance with a long determined and minutely detailed plan. Few Allied naval officers other than Captain Rooks of U.S.S. *Houston* believed the Japanese capable of more than one offensive operation,[2] but they exceeded even his expectation by attacking the Philippines and Malaya at the same time that they struck the crippling blow on the Pacific Fleet at Pearl Harbor.

Vice Admiral Takahashi's Third Fleet had the mission of taking the Philippines, Borneo and Celebes, while Vice Admiral Kondo's Second Fleet invaded the Malay Peninsula. When these had com-

[1] The main sources of this chapter from the enemy side are: (1) A series of reports prepared by Lt. Cdr. Salomon in Tokyo after the war, based on interrogation of Japanese officers and research in Japanese sources, and translated by ATIS; the most important of these are "On Philippine Landing Operations (Amphibious)" issued as a separate Volume XII; "Operations of the Imperial Navy in the Invasion of the Philippines" 15 May 1946 and "Answers to Matters of Intelligence concerning the Philippines before the Outbreak of War" given by the Japanese Demobilization Ministry in 1945 (ATIS No. 19896–A). (2) The printed *Interrogations of Japanese Officials* by the U.S. Strategic Bombing Survey, and *The Campaigns of the Pacific War* based on these and other enemy sources.

On the American side, the main sources are the Hart reports, narratives and statements heretofore mentioned; Capt. F. D. Wagner "Rough Draft of Patwing 10 Operations" 10 Dec. 1944; Rear Admiral F. W. Rockwell "Narrative of Naval Activities in Luzon Dec. 1, 1941–Mar. 19, 1942" 1 Aug. 1942; printed narratives, of which Allison Ind *Bataan the Judgment Seat* (1944), Lewis H. Brereton *The Brereton Diaries* (1946) and *General Wainwright's Story* (1946) are the most informing.

[2] His "Estimate of the Situation – Far East Area, November 19, 1941."

pleted initial tasks, they would join and, reinforced by the victorious Pearl Harbor Striking Force, slam in for the kill on Java, prize of the Indies. And, in the meantime, Vice Admiral Inouye's Fourth Fleet would capture Guam and Wake.

The Philippines in themselves were of no great importance to the Japanese, except as a source of copper. A democratic and independent commonwealth, trading mainly with the United States, was out of step with "Greater East Asia Co-Prosperity Sphere"; but the primary objectives of the Japanese in the Philippines were strategic rather than economic or ideological. The Philippines in American hands would have been a threat to communications, once the Dutch oil fields were secured. Compared with the attack on Pearl Harbor and the mighty thrust on Malaya, the invasion of the Philippines was merely a sideshow. If the Japanese could make the islands untenable as a fleet and air base, it mattered little to them how long and desperate a defense the United States ground forces put up.

Elimination of General MacArthur's Far Eastern Air Force was a prime concern of the Japanese because they had few fighter planes available to protect their invasion forces.[3] If the threat of United States air power could be removed, the Japanese cruiser force, which lent distant support to the amphibious elements, would always have eyes while American warships would not. Initial opposition from the weak Asiatic Fleet was hardly to be expected. Nevertheless, its three cruisers, over-age destroyers, and considerable number of submarines could not be disregarded until their base of operations was far removed from areas vital to Japan.

Japan depended on amphibious tactics for conquering territory in the Far East. She was the first nation to develop fully the technique of ship-to-shore attack.[4] Japanese landing craft, readily developed by a seagoing nation that depended largely for its living on small boats, were simple but effective adaptations of civilian craft. The most satisfactory, Type A, 49 feet long, 11½ foot beam

[3] Capt. Ishihara, *Inter. Jap. Officials* 1 83. Capt. Fujita, *Inter. Jap. Officials* I 71.
[4] O.N.I. 225-J "Japanese Landing Operations and Equipment" p. 2.

and of very light draft, was fitted with a bow ramp. Armed with one or two .25-cal. machine guns, it could make 8 to 10 knots with a single screw and gasoline or diesel engine, and carried up to 120 men. Somewhat similar in appearance to the later American LCVP, the Type A landing craft was larger and more flimsy in construction, though adequate for the task. There were two smaller types as well, and all three could be carried on the decks and davits of large transports.

The basic concept of the attack on the Philippine Islands was determined by the character of the Archipelago and the distribution of defending forces. Surprise was the keynote. American forces were largely concentrated about the center of Luzon. The size of that island and the large number of small islands in the vicinity made tactical surprise comparatively easy. To avoid giving away the target, Japanese planners eliminated surface bombardment of shore objectives as well as tactical air bombardment. They also delayed their strategical bombing of the sources of our air power until after the convoys were under way.

The attack problem was not too easy. Army fighter planes based on Formosa and Palau could not reach American fields at San Fernando and Manila, and most of the carrier-based air power was engaged in pounding Pearl Harbor. Hence the Japanese were forced to rely on medium Navy bombers, and long-range "Zero" fighters.

To counteract any challenge from the ships of the tiny United States Asiatic Fleet, the Japanese allotted forces of overwhelming strength to cover the amphibious operations. Lacking confidence in their own sound equipment, they were needlessly worried about the submarines of the Asiatic Fleet. Yet, even though the invaders well knew what factors favored the defense, it was unable to profit by them. United States naval officers found the Japanese clever at detecting the presence of submarines, although seldom able to kill.[5]

A many-pronged attack was planned. The initial landings aimed at securing airstrips so that Army fighter planes might render close

[5] Statement of Rear Admiral John Wilkes, then Comsubs Asiatic Fleet.

U.S.S. *Houston*

U.S.S. *Canopus*

*Flagship and a Submarine Tender of the Asiatic Fleet*

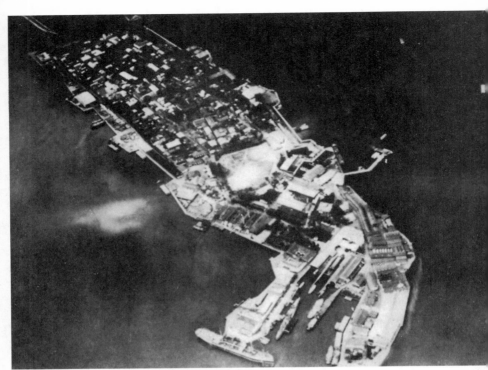

*Cavite, before and after Air Attack of 10 December*

support to ground operations promptly. Three landings, mounted in different parts of Formosa, were scheduled for Luzon; and one, mounted in the Palaus, for Mindanao, where the Japanese had a readymade fifth column. This division and consequent weakening of forces was considered essential in view of the importance of air superiority. The main landing was planned for Lingayen Gulf whence troops would advance toward Manila. The ultimate objective was the capture of Manila and its bay as a naval and military base for more important operations to the southward.

After all the talk about Japanese spies sneaking about vital defenses with candid cameras, it is interesting to note that the enemy completely underestimated the strength of Corregidor. He planned to exploit Manila Bay forty-five days after the landing at Lingayen.

If the postwar interrogations of high Japanese officers from which these details are obtained may be relied upon, the enemy on 8 December 1941 was not the arrogant, war-tested, self-confident foe that the Allies, in the bitterness of those early defeats, imagined him to be. He was full of nervous apprehension over the outcome. Although the Japanese Army had been pushing the Chinese about for several years, it had a wholesome respect for American armed forces — something of the attitude of a bush-league team facing a national champion for the first time. And, in spite of the overwhelming strength it could bring to bear on the forces under Hart and MacArthur, the Japanese high command made a fetish of secrecy. Forces were widely dispersed to escape notice. None but the most exalted generals and admirals knew what was cooking, and they had to fly from one group to another to alert the subordinate commanders, who had no idea of the whole in which they were to play a part. Yet none of their fears were justified. United States cruisers retired to the south without challenging the covering forces. American aircraft were largely destroyed on the ground. That dreaded unknown factor, the powerful submarine force, made only negligible inroads on the amphibious armada. Their invasion of the Philippines, joined with the successes at Pearl Harbor and on the Malay Peninsula, gave these orientals the feeling that they were indeed sons of Heaven. Actually, their victory in the Philippines, as at Pearl, was one of stealth and of strength, rather than skill.

## 2. *Air Preliminaries*

Admiral Hart, who had been working very hard in early December, decided to knock off late in the afternoon of the 7th. He and Admiral Purnell drove to the Manila Golf Club at Caloocan, and played nine holes. It should have been a pleasant game on the winter afternoon, as long shadows from the tropical trees reached over the well-watered fairways. But the Admirals could not keep their minds on the game, the last they were to play of that sort; so they returned to their office in the Marsman Building and worked late. At about 2145 they returned to their apartments in the Manila Hotel where General MacArthur had a penthouse. All top social elements of the city, American and Filipino, professional and business, military, naval and diplomatic, met in that modern hotel. But by this time the wives and families of servicemen had been sent home, and the hotel had become a lonely place for naval officers.

At 0300 December 8, Lieutenant Colonel William T. Clement USMC, duty officer at the Marsman Building, telephoned Admiral Hart: "Admiral, put some cold water on your face. I'm coming over with a message." The Marsman Building is only three hundred yards from the Manila Hotel, and Colonel Clement was soon knocking on the Admiral's door. He came in with an astounding message: AIR RAID ON PEARL HARBOR. THIS IS NO DRILL. It was not an official word but a mere intercept which the Colonel's radio operator had copied. He knew that it was authentic because he recognized the technique of the sender, a Pearl Harbor operator who was an old friend of his. By this informal method word of the Pearl Harbor disaster first reached Commander in Chief Asiatic Fleet.

Sitting on the edge of his bed, Admiral Hart drafted a dispatch for his Fleet: JAPAN STARTED HOSTILITIES. GOVERN YOURSELVES ACCORDINGLY.[6] He then called his chief of staff, dressed, ate a hasty breakfast and arrived at the office at about 0400. Admiral Purnell drove to Army headquarters in the walled city a few minutes away and gave the message to General Sutherland, General MacArthur's chief of staff, who had not yet heard the news.

At dawn, 13 Japanese dive-bombers, escorted by 9 "Zeke" fighters from the carrier *Ryujo*, then east of Davao, opened the campaign of the Philippines by attacking the seaplane tender *William B. Preston* which was anchored in Davao Gulf. One of her three planes was on patrol but the other two were destroyed at their moorings, and an aviator was killed. One enemy dive-bomber was forced down but the crew survived. *Preston* escaped without damage and immediately got under way to seek a safe anchorage where she could resume plane patrols.[7]

At Formosa, dawn broke on 8 December 1941 with ceiling zero. Japanese air operations had to be postponed. If the weather continued bad, the entire operation would be in jeopardy. All hands felt the tension. Surely by now the military in Manila knew of the attack on Pearl Harbor and were taking precautionary measures? Perhaps the American Army planes, target for the bombing raid, had already flown away to safe fields in the southern islands. It was reported that United States bombers were about to attack Formosa, and the Japanese there were actually passing out gas masks when the report was found to be false.

Foul weather, however, did not deter the Japanese Army Air Force: 14 heavy bombers took off from Heito in Formosa shortly after daybreak and at about 0930 struck military installations at Baguio, the summer capital in northern Luzon; while 18 twin-

[6] The original draft reproduced here was written on an old scrap of paper and carried through 3½ years of captivity by a sergeant of the 4th Marines. Admiral Hart, to whom it was returned after the war, remarked that, although he had long before decided what he would say in this situation, he was so nervous as to leave out a letter.
[7] Wagner Report p. 3; *Ryujo* Merit Report.

engined light bombers from Kato in Formosa struck Tugugarao Airfield in the north central part of Luzon.[8]

At 1015, about the time official orders reached Admiral Hart to execute the war plan against Japan, the weather had improved and 192 Japanese naval planes of the Eleventh Air Fleet took off from Formosa to attack Clark and Nichols Fields, while a few Army planes departed for nearer objectives. Some 34 fighters and 54 bombers headed for Clark Field, and 50 fighters escorting 54 bombers aimed at Nichols.[9]

A general alarm at Clark Field about 0830 sent most of the American planes airborne, but by 1000 the All Clear had been sounded. The enemy, winging his way from Formosa, had already struck Baguio but no word of it reached Clark or Manila. The American planes landed, their crews lunched and returned to the field to tune up aircraft while the officers met to plan a reconnaissance over Formosa. At that moment the second flight of Japanese bombers was flying south for Clark Field. No coast watchers or search radar signaled their approach; communications with the only radar in northern Luzon near Aparri failed at this crucial moment.[10] All but two United States planes were still grounded at 1245 when a very strong force of enemy fighters, escorting medium and high-level bombers attacked Clark and the other Army airfields in the vicinity of Manila.[11] This attack put out of action on the first day of the war about one third of our pursuit or fighter strength and over one half of our bomber strength. It was a crippling blow: 12 Flying Fortresses (B–17s) and 30 Curtiss Warhawks (P–40s) were destroyed, and 5 more B–17s severely damaged, at the cost of only 7 planes to the Japanese.

After this crushing blow the enemy had little to worry about in

[8] USSBS Publication "Japanese Air Power" July 1945 p. 7.
[9] *The Campaigns of Pacific War* p. 4.
[10] Allison Ind *Bataan* p. 99.
[11] Capt. F. D. Wagner's "Rough Draft" states that they were attacked at about 1000, but Capt. E. S. Green usa reported 11 Apr. 1942 that the strike on Clark Field took place at 1245, and this is supported by the Takahashi interrogation (USSBS No. 79). Composition of enemy forces is confirmed by USSBS publication on "Japanese Air Power" p. 71. *The Brereton Diaries* (1946) p. 42 give different figures, but the General admits that his sources were incomplete.

Asiatic Fleet              Priority

Japan started hostilities
govern your self
accordingly.

Admiral Hart's order to the Asiatic Fleet

Catalina (PBY) of 1941–42

*The Beginning*

U.S.S. *Peary*

U.S.S. *William B. Preston*

*A Destroyer and a Seaplane Tender of the Asiatic Fleet*

the way of air opposition. United States Army Air Forces Far East were reduced to some 17 bombers and less than 40 fighter planes. Many of these were damaged. Others, newly arrived and assembled on 7 December, had barely been checked over before being called upon for combat duty — and the P–40 was a "hot ship," difficult at best to fly. One large shipment of the fast fighters had recently arrived without coolant.[12] Admiral Hart seized ten crates of Brewster Buffaloes en route to Thailand, and gave them to the Army Air Force to use as trainers; but they were not much use as fighters.[13]

The Japanese planned a similar mission against Manila, but the weather turned bad again and this attack was postponed. Seven planes struck Nichols Field on the 9th but did no damage of consequence. Apart from that, this second day of the war was uneventful. American crews and maintenance men were working frantically to repair damaged planes; everyone else in the armed forces braced himself for the next attack.

At noon 10 December it came. Army Air Force interceptor headquarters received forty-five minutes' notice of enemy planes approaching from the north, and scrambled about 20 P–40s and 15 P–35s to intercept; but they were overwhelmed by the enemy's force of approximately 52 "Zero" fighter planes, escorting somewhat over 80 bombers.[14] The enemy expected to encounter carrier-based air opposition, but of course there was none. North of Manila his air forces divided. Part took care of Nielson and Nichols Fields and Camp Murphy,[15] while over Cavite, for two hours or more, some 54 planes flew back and forth at leisurely tempo and in graceful curves, at 20,000 feet elevation beyond range of the 3-inch anti-aircraft guns, the bombers releasing at will. It was very accurate bombing, too; almost every missile fell within the Navy Yard. From the roof of the Marsman Building Admiral Hart looked on in helpless rage at the destruction of his base. "Direct hits were

---

[12] A cooling agent to carry off frictional heat.
[13] Ind *Bataan* p. 18 and statement by Admiral Hart.
[14] "History of 24th Pursuit Group," A.A.F. Historical Section.
[15] "Operations of Imperial Navy in Invasion of Philippines."

made on the power plant, dispensary, torpedo repair shop, supply office and warehouses, signal station, commissary store, receiving station, barracks and officers' quarters, and several ships, tugs and barges along the waterfront. The entire Yard and about one third of the city of Cavite were ablaze from end to end, but fortunately no direct hit was made on the naval ammunition depot itself, which still contained much powder and ammunition." [16] The wind, constantly changing, whipped the fires to a furious blaze so that it was impossible to save the rest of the yard. Late that night all survivors were assembled in the public school enclosure at San Roque. Admiral Rockwell, who had personally directed salvage, his shirt bloody from helping the wounded, inspected the Navy Yard early next morning (11 December) and reported to Admiral Hart that the fires were completely out of control. The two flag officers decided to salvage as much material as possible, to set up the hospital and the industrial and supply departments, to disperse torpedoes, mines, ammunition and small arms to Corregidor and Mariveles, and to maintain the radio station and fuel depot at Sangley Point as long as possible. [17]

Destruction was not limited to the yard and personnel. Submarine *Sealion*, moored at the dock alongside *Seadragon* and minesweeper *Bittern*, took two direct hits which killed four men. She and the sweeper never again put to sea. *Seadragon* was also damaged. The prudent skipper of tender *Pigeon* had kept steam up for just such an emergency and succeeded in pulling away from the flaming *Sealion*. But the most serious loss the submariners had on that sad day was the destruction of some 230 torpedoes. Destroyer *Peary*, under repair, was towed clear by *Whippoorwill*, but had her foremast broken in two places by a bomb. [18]

The old river gunboat *Mindanao*, with topsides boarded up to make her more seaworthy, chose this hectic day to steam into har-

<hr>

[16] Rockwell Narrative.

[17] Same, and Champlin "One Man's Version" p. 21.

[18] "War Activities Submarines, U.S. Asiatic Fleet, December War Damage Report" 13 Dec. 1941. *Peary* Report 6 Jan. 1942.

bor. She gave the shattered defenders a brief bit of consolation by producing some Japanese prisoners that she had taken at sea, from a radio-equipped trawler.[19]

Disaster followed disaster. For about a week the Catalinas of Captain Wagner's Patrol Wing 10 had been conducting war patrols. The planes wanted routine servicing and the pilots needed rest. Patriotic but ill-advised Filipinos constantly brought in rumors of Japanese ship movements that had to be investigated. Commander Gray of the Catalina squadron stationed at Olongapo sent out all his seven planes searching on the morning of 12 December, when told that a Japanese carrier force was steaming down along the coast of Luzon. As the PBYs returned from their fruitless search, out of fuel and with tired crews, they were shadowed by "Zeros" which struck them at their moorings and destroyed every one. One quarter of our reconnaissance planes, the eyes of the Asiatic Fleet, were gone.

"I am giving thanks that I still have you, and as far as I can learn, most of your people," wrote Admiral Hart to Captain Wagner.[20] Then, bravely and simply, he praised the work done and told the Captain to carry on as best he could in his own way.

Morale was still high, but that was not enough. It was clear that the remaining naval aviators and planes would have to fly south and join Admiral Glassford. Captain Wagner was ordered to embark all his key men in tender *Childs* and weigh anchor after dark the next night. Here was the final admission that the enemy had won complete mastery of the air over and around Luzon. General Brereton now had only 33 fighter planes operational in Luzon, and the fate of the Olongapo patrol proved that to send Catalinas out without fighter protection was suicide.

Commander Asiatic Fleet had always hoped to bring back from the south his striking force of cruisers and destroyers after the air preliminaries were over, to engage the enemy's amphibious forces

[19] "Gunboat Saga" *U.S. Nav. Inst. Proc.* LXX 421.
[20] Most of the PBY crews had gone ashore, and only two men were killed.

approaching Luzon. That was now impossible. By 11 December it was unpleasantly clear that the Navy, without shore-based aircraft, could not control the seas around the Philippines.

## 3. *Initial Landings, 8–17 December*

Long before the results of the air strikes were in, Rear Admiral Hirose's Surprise Attack Group landed about 490 men on Batan Island in Bashi Channel at dawn December 8. This was the first steppingstone in the cautious Japanese push toward Manila. But the success of the attacks on Clark Field made Batan unnecessary, and the projected fields were never developed. Two days later, a part of this attack group occupied Camiguin Island to establish a seaplane base. Vice Admiral Takahashi came in with his powerful task force to cover this minute operation.

The next prong of attack, also to obtain an advanced air base, was aimed at Aparri on the north coast of Luzon. An infantry battalion known as the Tanaka Detachment departed Mako in Formosa on the evening of 7 December. As one of the three advanced detachments, the Aparri Force was given "fast" ships, capable of 12 to 14 knots. During the morning of 8 December, as soon as the ceiling lifted, air cover was furnished to this convoy. At daybreak on 10 December it commenced landing troops at Aparri. Only one company of the 11th Infantry Division was there to oppose the landing, but weather lent a hand; breakers whipped up by the northeast wind had rolled up a heavy surf. Only two companies of the battalion landing team were able to get ashore on the scheduled morning of 10 December. The transports were shifted to a roadstead off Gonzaga, over 20 miles to the eastward, which enjoyed a partial lee from Cape Engaño.

Attacks by two squadrons of P–40s and five B–17s interrupted the landing operations there and hit Minesweeper 19, setting off her depth charges and forcing her ashore, a total loss.[21] The escorting

[21] *General Wainwright's Story* pp. 26–27. On the 12th another B–17 attacked the Aparri force. CL *Natori*, Rear Adm. Hara's flagship, was damaged.

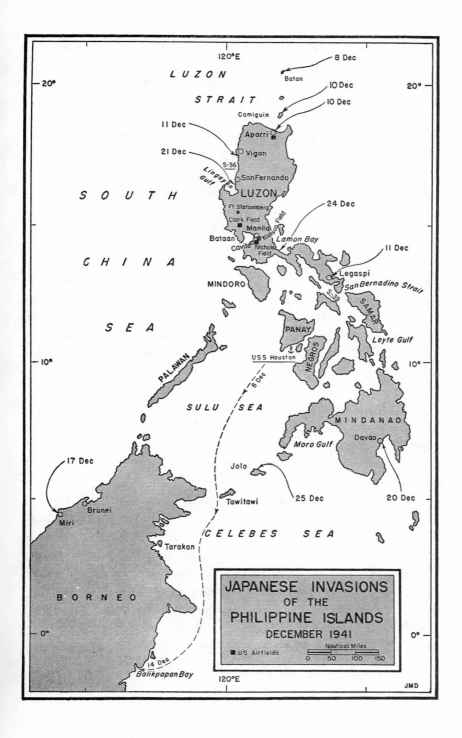

warships, anxious to retire, forced the transports' crews to hasten unloading to the point of tossing drummed oil over the side to drift ashore. Important heavy equipment such as rollers for the airstrip was not unloaded before the retirement. Given a few more planes, the Americans might have defeated the landing completely. As it was, without effective ground defense, the Japanese by 1340 December 10 were in possession of the Aparri airstrip. Both this airfield and the one at Camuluniugan, eight kilometers to the southward, proved to be unusable for Japanese bombers and the entire outfit had to be moved to Tuguegarao, 50 miles south of Aparri, where extensive work had to be undertaken before the airfield was operational. Thus the main purpose of the Aparri landing, to base a sustained air attack to cover subsequent landings of the main force, was brought to naught. Fortunately for the Japanese, no such concentrated air attack was needed after the overwhelming success of the initial strikes. So, contrary to their usual cautious policy, the Japanese field commanders pushed on into the Cagayan Valley,[22] where one battalion of the 11th Infantry Division was deployed to resist them.

Four days after the landing, on 14 December, submarine *Seawolf* missed a good chance to sink *Sanyo Maru*, the converted seaplane tender that had furnished air cover for the landing. Of four torpedoes that *Seawolf* fired only one hit, and that one was a dud.[23]

To protect the rear of the main attack on Lingayen Gulf, and to secure the northern parts of Luzon, the Japanese planned their next landing for Pandan, about three miles southeast of Vigan, the capital of Ilocos Sur Province. This Second Surprise Attack Force, commanded by Rear Admiral Nishimura, had 4400 troops in six transports. On 10 December it attempted a landing at Pandan, only to be beaten off by a combination of weather and the Army Air Force. General Brereton's planes strafed the Japanese admiral's flagship, sank Minesweeper No. 10 and damaged transports

[22] "On Philippine Landing Operations."
[23] Capt. Wilkes Report 14 Mar. 1942.

*Oigawa Maru* and *Takao Maru* so that they had to be beached.[24] Heavy seas caused so much difficulty in debarking men from ships to landing craft that the force withdrew to Santa, a few miles to the south, where they successfully effected a landing the next day.

The Legaspi landing, on the tail end of Luzon, took place on 12 December. The purpose of this operation was to protect the Japanese rear from possible air strikes based in the Visayas, and to control San Bernardino Strait. Although but one infantry regiment was put ashore here, the strategic importance of the operation was such that impressive naval support, in the shape of Rear Admiral Takagi's Legaspi Force, was given. Moreover, Rear Admiral Kobayashi's two large minelayers escorted by two destroyers and light cruiser *Jintsu* on 11 December laid about 300 mines in San Bernardino Strait, and 133 mines in Surigao Strait, without opposition. United States Submarine *S–39* was stationed off Sorsogon Bay near San Bernardino Strait for just such an eventuality, but her efforts to intercept were defeated by a vigorous depth-charge attack by the destroyers.[25]

On 14 December the Army Air Force scraped together five very tired B–17s to attack the enemy ships anchored in Legaspi Harbor. Three got through and one of them, piloted by Captain H. T. Wheless, succeeded in strafing a sweeper but got back by the skin of its teeth. Japanese naval pursuit planes killed the radio operator, wounded two other crewmen, knocked out two of the four engines, broke seven of the eleven control cables, cut off the tail wheel, blew the two other tires and punctured each gas tank in about fifteen places. After a running fight lasting an hour and a quarter, the enemy pilots ran out of ammunition, flew in close to leer at Captain Wheless and then reversed course for home, less six or seven of their number.[26]

By 17 December there were only 14 Flying Fortresses left in

---

[24] "Final Report in Answer to Memorandum No. 11 from USSBS 16 Oct. 1945," 14 Jan. 1946.

[25] Log of *S–39* for 11 Dec. 1941.

[26] "Statement by Capt. H. T. Wheless" 4 Apr. 1942; "Merit Report" of Japanese Desron 2.

the Philippines, and during the next three days they retired to Batchelor Field near Darwin, Australia. Except for one raid, their work in Luzon was over.[27]

## 4. *Line Drive*[28]

The invaders, having now secured the left flank and rear, directed their line drive for Manila into Lingayen Gulf.

The main Lingayen Force sailed in three groups from Takao (Formosa), Mako (Pescadores) and Keelung (Formosa). In all, 76 transports were involved, embarking one infantry division plus all manner of specialist troops and units. The short distance between Formosa and Luzon enabled the Japanese to use for this main invasion the same transports and ships that had escorted and landed the Batan, Aparri and Vigan Surprise Forces. Hara's Aparri Force provided troop float and escort for the first group, Nishimura's Vigan Force for the second, and Hirose's Batan Force for the third. They reached their destination in that order.

Vice Admiral Takahashi's Close or Northern Covering Force departed the Pescadores 19 December to support this amphibious operation from an area about 250 miles west of Luzon. Vice Admiral Kondo's Distant Cover Force of two battleships and two heavy cruisers, just detached from similar coverage off Malaya, joined him there. The Japanese evidently feared surface naval opposition from the southward, which the Allies were completely incapable of offering. General MacArthur estimated that the main stab would be made in Lingayen Gulf, but he did not expect it quite so soon.[29]

On 18 December, Japanese sources state, light bombers and fighters based at Aparri and Vigan softened the already feeble

[27] *Army Air Forces in the War Against Japan, 1941–42* (1945). On that excursion, 23 Dec., four B–17s staged through Del Monte, Mindanao, and attacked enemy ships in Lingayen Gulf.
[28] Except where otherwise noted, data in this section are from Mr. Salomon's "On Philippine Landing Operations."
[29] General MacArthur to Admiral Hart, 21 Dec. 1941.

beach defenses at Lingayen. The convoy, troubled only by foul weather, arrived in the Gulf and proceeded toward the mouth of the Aringai River at midnight 21 December. Owing to failure of lookouts to locate signal fires marking the river mouth, the van did not anchor until opposite St. Thomas, leaving the convoy strung out for twenty miles. Here was an ideal target for submarines, and U.S.S. *Stingray* had been patrolling the Gulf for several days. On the 16th Captain Wilkes, Commander Submarines, ordered her to proceed out to the 100-fathom curve. She sighted the enemy force on 21 December, and her report was the first intimation that the main drive was on. But by that time it had almost hit the beach.

General MacArthur now called on Admiral Hart for all the naval assistance he could render; and the Admiral ordered *Stingray*, *Saury*, *Salmon*, *S–38* and *S–40* to the target. The hoped-for field day proved unproductive because, by the time the submarines entered the Gulf, Japanese ships were in shoal waters where it was difficult for submarines to operate.[30] *S–38* (Lieutenant W. G. Chapple) thrust into the shoals nevertheless and sank the 5500-ton transport *Hayo Maru* at 0900 on 22 December as she was following the third gunboat division. Only by guts and by God did *S–38* escape the severe depth-charge attack that followed. Next day, off Ilocos Sur, *Seal* sank the 850-ton freighter *Hayataka Maru* with two torpedoes.[31] Seaplane tender *Sanuki Maru* was hit twice by shore batteries.[32] These casualties disturbed the enemy less than did the weather.

At daybreak 22 December, as Lingayen landings began, supporting planes made a "neutralizing" strike on Fort Stotsenburg, command post of General Wainwright, and on the near-by Clark Field. Nevertheless a few Army planes managed to take off and strafe a Japanese light cruiser accompanied by destroyers that was delivering a pre-landing bombardment on our shore positions. The assault troops began going over the sides of the transports about 0200,

[30] Wilkes Report pp. 8–9.
[31] Same, Enclosures J and GG; Report of Japanese Desron 4.
[32] Battle Report No. 2 of *Sanuki Maru*.

landed in daylight nearer the American positions than had been intended, and suffered some loss from shore batteries before they hit the beach.

As the sea continued to rise, the convoy had to seek shelter under the lee of San Fernando Point where it completed unloading. A large part of the well trained and equipped 48th Division was now ashore to protect the Japanese right flank from the few American defenders. Throughout the day the landing force, which had no air cover whatever, was annoyed by PBYs and Army planes. *Ashigara*, Admiral Takahashi's flagship, was attacked in company with 2 other heavy cruisers about 100 miles northwest of Lingayen by 5 Catalinas. Shortly after, a message was received ashore (and intercepted by the enemy) from the skipper of one of them stating that he had hit and sunk battleship *Haruna*, for which he had mistaken *Ashigara*. But she was not hit and he was lost. Captain Wagner ordered the PBYs to attack again; the enemy intercepted that message too, and slipped off into a rainsquall.[33]

During the unloading of heavy Japanese equipment, their flimsy landing barges found the surf difficult to take even when carrying men and light gear; artillery and heavy construction materials were too much for them. Anchorages had to be changed several times before the operation was completed and the original plan to leave most of the heavy equipment north of San Fernando had to be abandoned.

At this point the Lingayen Force presented an excellent picture of how not to run an amphibious operation. To avoid one danger, the ships moved into the inner bay, and there encountered another — American coastal batteries. The 48th Division, busy estab-

---

[33] Capt. Ishihara (staff officer then in *Ashigara*) in *Inter. Jap. Off.* I 83. This was the second time in two weeks that *Haruna* had been "sunk." The first and more famous occasion was by Capt. Colin P. Kelly Jr. USA on 10 Dec. He was one of the B–17 pilots who attacked the Aparri Surprise Force that day, reported he had hit a *Kongo* class battleship, later identified as *Haruna*, and left her ablaze. His Flying Fortress was jumped by Japanese pursuit planes on its way back to Clark Field, and Kelly was killed bailing out. See Gilbert Cant *America's Navy in World War II* p. 91. After the war it was ascertained that the Japanese Navy employed no battleships in these Luzon landings, and that *Haruna* was on the other side of the South China Sea. Correction: it now appears *Ashigara* was attacked 10 Dec.

lishing positions in the defile near Rosario and Camp 1 in order to thwart anticipated reinforcements, was unable to detach a sufficient force to silence the guns. Practically no communication existed between elements ashore and those afloat; even ship-to-ship signaling was inadequate. But lack of adequate air opposition, vastly superior force, and good work by the one element of the plan that clicked — the arrival of the advance Infantry detachment from the Vigan Support Force — assured final success.

It would be presumptuous in this, a naval history, to follow the operations of the Japanese troops ashore, when they came to grips with the 11th and 21st Infantry Divisions of General Wainwright's North Luzon Force. We can only remind the reader that the Philippines Campaign of 1941–42 was primarily an Army show, and that the full story of it must be told by Army historians. We must candidly admit that the pitifully few ships and planes of the sadly inadequate Asiatic Fleet were unable to prevent the enemy from landing wherever he chose, or even to delay his efficient timetable of conquest.

Two days after the Lingayen Landing, when advance units of the 48th Division were already moving southward, another group of Japanese ships, floating most of the 16th Infantry Division, effected landings at Lamon Bay on the East Coast of Luzon, practically at the back door of Manila. The 24 transports of this Lamon Attack Group departed Amami O Shima in the Ryukyus on 17 December under escort of six converted gunboats.[34] Rear Admiral Kubo in light cruiser *Nagara* with Destroyer Division 24, which had escorted the Legaspi Landing, steamed north to meet them, and planes of the 11th Seaplane Tender Division provided air cover.[35]

On D-day, the day before Christmas, the gunboats steered a deceptive course to the northward in order to confuse possible defend-

---

[34] 1st Gunboat Division War Diary and Battle Reports.
[35] Desdiv 24 Merit Report and Salomon Report translated as ATIS 1969 2C.

ers ashore — but none there were. The 51st Infantry Division had already been withdrawn from that area. The Legaspi Surprise Force joined the troops and as they marched rapidly over the mountains toward Manila they were subjected to a few rear guard actions which delayed them very little.

With no prospect of naval assistance, air force shot to pieces and the enemy advancing on Manila in strength from two directions, General MacArthur saw that further defense of Manila was hopeless. After declaring it to be an open town in the vain hope that the enemy would respect international law and spare the buildings and the people, he evacuated Manila and on 27 December ordered his army into the ultimate defense area, Bataan.

In the Southern Philippines the enemy was no less active and enterprising than in the north. In his overall strategy Mindanao, as a steppingstone to the North Borneo oil fields, was more important than Luzon. A considerable force was assigned Rear Admiral Tanaka, who in light cruiser *Jintsu* with six destroyers escorted the transports from Kossol Roads in the Palaus, sailing on 17 December. Rear Admiral Takagi in heavy cruiser *Nachi* with two more cruisers and aircraft carrier *Ryujo* and *Chitose* constituted a close covering group.

The amphibious force began landings at Davao in the early hours of 20 December, with carrier-plane cover. As elsewhere, there was little opposition. That very evening a seaplane base was set up at Talomo Bay south of Davao and the security of the invasion was assured. On the afternoon of the 23rd, fighter planes of the Eleventh Air Fleet moved in and relieved the carriers of air cover duty. On the evening of the 22nd, 9 Flying Fortresses struck the anchorage but merely killed two men and wounded three on the destroyers moored there.

Extending their reach still further toward Borneo, nine transports, carrying about 4000 men of the same Japanese force, departed Davao for Jolo on the 22nd. *Jintsu's* destroyer division furnished escort and the carriers flew air support. Early on the 23rd, a lone B–17 attacked the convoy but did no damage. The landing began before dawn Christmas Day. Before noon Jolo was secured, and next day a naval air station was set up there.[36]

Within seventeen days the Japanese had successfully completed nine amphibious operations in the Philippine Islands.

[36] Same, and Desron 2 Merit Report.

# CHAPTER VIII

# Fall of Guam[1]

## 10 December 1941

GUAM, the one American possession in the Marianas which might have been an eastern bastion to the Philippines or a base for submarine and air attack on a southward-pressing enemy, fell into the Japanese bag very easily. Nothing could be done to defend it. The garrison of the island at the time of its capture was composed of 30 naval officers, six warrant officers, five naval nurses, 230 enlisted men; seven Marine officers, one warrant officer, 145 Marine enlisted men, and 246 members of the native Insular Force. Almost all the fighting was done by the Guam Insular Force. There was no weapon on the island larger than .30-caliber machine guns and .45-caliber pistols. Three small patrol craft, U.S.S. *Penguin*, *YP–16* and *YP–17*, and one old decommissioned harbor oiler, *R. L. Barnes*, formed the "Guam Navy." Captain McMillin, the Governor, knew perfectly well the Japanese could take the island whenever they chose and saw to it that all American women and children were evacuated by 17 October 1941.

News of the attack on Pearl Harbor came from Admiral Hart at 0545 December 8. All Japanese on the island were promptly arrested and imprisoned, the Insular Force Guard was assembled at its headquarters on Agaña Plaza, and the Marines, except for a few on patrol stations around the island, took up a field position at the butts of their rifle range on the Orote Peninsula.

---

[1] Report of the Governor of Guam (Capt. G. J. McMillin USN) to Secretary of the Navy 11 Sept. 1945; conversations with Capt. Donald T. Giles (Aide for Civil Affairs and Executive Officer, Naval Station, Guam). Japanese sources give the composition of the escorting and supporting forces as 4 CAs, 4 DDs, 4 AMs, 2 gunboats, 6 SCs and 2 tenders – these landed the special naval landing force and occupation troops.

Enemy planes from Saipan began bombing Marine headquarters at 0827. All that day and the next they flew over the island, bombing installations and strafing native villages at will. Considerable damage was done by glide-bombing attacks on the Marine barracks on Orote Peninsula and to harbor shore installations at Sumay and the little Piti Navy Yard. Also on the morning of the 8th they attacked and sank the *Penguin* off Orote Point. Her skipper, Lieutenant J. W. Haviland, and several members of the crew were wounded but got ashore on life rafts.

The Japanese gave their air force two full days to soften up what was already almost defenseless. On the night of the 8th a dugout landed near the northern cape of the island some natives of Saipan who were sent ahead by the enemy to act as interpreters when they landed. These men when arrested and questioned informed the authorities that the enemy would land next morning (the 9th) on the recreation beach east of Agaña. It was believed that this was a dodge in order to draw the Marines out of their prepared positions; but it turned out to be entirely correct as to the place, though not as to the date.

Vice Admiral Inouye, commander Fourth Fleet, was responsible for the capture of Guam and Wake. He did not personally accompany the Occupation Force but flew his flag ashore at Truk; the officer in tactical command was Rear Admiral A. Goto in heavy cruiser *Aoba*. The invading and supporting forces were in overwhelming strength. An estimated 5000 men landed at various points on 10 December but the one that delivered the punch consisted of about 700 of the Special Naval Landing Force, who came ashore before dawn, as predicted, on the beaches of Agaña. They advanced rapidly on the plaza, where the majority of the Insular Force Guard, composed of about 80 natives, were stationed, together with a few bluejackets and Marines on police duty. Both Americans and Chamorros put up a brave resistance and twice drove the attacking waves back with rifle and machine-gun fire, losing 17 of their men [2] but killing and wounding a much greater

[2] Twelve U.S. servicemen, 3 Insular Force, 2 Chamorro civilians.

number of Japanese. After about twenty to twenty-five minutes of fighting, at 0545, the Governor received reports of other enemy landings. Realizing that further resistance would be suicidal and probably make the lot of the natives harder in the end, he decided to surrender the island. At that time a second force of Japanese that landed south of Orote was approaching the Marines' positions, but they never made contact.

Three blasts of an auto horn sounded the Cease Fire, and a Japanese voice shouted "Send over your captain!" Commander D. T. Giles conducted a parley with Commander Hayashi of the Japanese landing force in sign language and returned with him to Government House where, upon assurance that the civil rights of the native population would be respected and that military personnel would be treated in accordance with the laws of war and of humanity, Captain McMillin signed articles of surrender. The Stars and Stripes were lowered from Government House, where they had flown for forty-two years, and the Rising Sun of Japan — rising indeed at that time — was hoisted.

Military and civilian prisoners were imprisoned for one month in the naval hospital and local buildings, and treated fairly decently; then moved to Japan where treatment was very different. On Guam the Chamorros had all manner of pressure put on them by the Japanese, who intended to keep the island permanently; but the Chamorros fed and protected the few United States bluejackets who had escaped to the hills, and remained thoroughly and touchingly loyal to the United States, never doubting that our forces would eventually return, as return they did in June 1944.

The Japanese completed the airfield on Orote Peninsula that Uncle Sam had felt too poor to build, and made Guam a small naval and air base. In their hands it never became as important as Saipan, but played an important rôle in the Battle of the Philippine Sea.

CHAPTER IX

# Landings in Malaya[1]

## 8–25 December 1941

NOTHING could have been less accurate than the prewar assumption of Allied planners that the Japanese would be able to strike only one objective at a time. They landed almost simultaneously in the Philippines, Hong Kong, Borneo, the Malay Peninsula and Guam.

On the first day of the war, Hong Kong was bombed by Japanese planes from the Chinese mainland and a naval blockade was thrown around the port. The uselessness of Singapore to the Royal Navy was promptly demonstrated by air attacks mounted in Saigon and other airports of Indochina. At Tientsin and Shanghai, already in Japanese possession, United States and British citizens were interned and the river gunboat *Wake* surrendered — the only United States ship to do so during the entire war — after her crew had failed in attempts to scuttle her. A Japanese army invaded Thailand from Indochina and on 9 December occupied Bangkok without striking a blow. But the most serious effort was a three-pronged amphibious invasion of the Malay Peninsula.

Since early November the Japanese had been all set for it. On 2 December D-day had been fixed for the 8th and before sundown on the 4th the ships, including 19 transports, weighed anchor from Samah Bay, Hainan. On the 6th the force safely rounded Cape Kamao and headed up the Gulf of Siam, making a feint toward Bangkok.

---

[1] This brief account of events in which the U.S. Navy had no share, but which had a vital effect on its later operations, is compiled principally from Liaison Commission Tokyo for the Imperial Japanese Demobilization Ministry, "Malaya Landing Operations" 17 Jan. 1946, and from the British Admiralty's Battle Summary No. 14, "Loss of H.M. Ships *Prince of Wales* and *Repulse*" (1943).

With careful timing the force changed course again and headed for Singora where the main body anchored at 2340 December 7. Before dawn on D-day the ship-to-shore movement began, and by 0410 this unopposed beachhead was secured. Almost all the ships were unloaded and steaming back to base by midnight of the 9th. The smallest detachment of three ships made a surprise attack on Kota Bharu early on the 8th, was driven off by British coastal batteries, but landed the troops next day. The remaining five ships landed troops at Patani, between Singora and Kota Bharu, on the 14th. These three points were not on the narrow Kra Isthmus, but halfway from there to Singapore.

Admiral Sir Tom Phillips's battleship *Prince of Wales* and battle cruiser *Repulse* were the core of a strong but unbalanced task force based on Singapore. It should have included H.M. carrier *Indomitable*, but she ran aground and left the capital ships without naval air cover. The Japanese, by striking at three points almost simultaneously, hoped to attract all available land-based fighters of the Royal Air Force and leave Phillips without air cover when they were ready for him; and he steamed right into the trap.

Those who make the decisions in war are constantly weighing certain risks against possible gains. At the outset of hostilities Admiral Hart thought of sending his small striking force north of Luzon to challenge Japanese communications, but decided that the risk to his ships outweighed the possible gain because the enemy had won control of the air. Admiral Phillips had precisely the same problem in Malaya. Should he steam into the Gulf of Siam and expose his ships to air attack from Indochina in the hope of breaking enemy communications with their landing force? He decided to take the chance. With the Royal Air Force and the British Army fighting for their lives, the Royal Navy could not be true to its tradition by remaining idly at anchor.

So *Prince of Wales* and *Repulse*, escorted by destroyers *Electra*, *Express*, *Vampire* and *Tenedos*, sailed from Singapore at 1735 December 8. Admiral Phillips left his chief of staff at the command post ashore and flew his flag in *Prince of Wales*. Shortly after midnight the chief of staff radioed that the Royal Air Force was so pressed by giving ground support to land operations that the Admiral could expect no air cover off Singora; that Japanese heavy bombers were already in southern Indochina; and that General MacArthur had been asked to send Brereton's Flying Fortresses to attack their bases. Little did he know that the United States Army Air Forces of the Far East were in a desperate situation.

The Japanese invasion force was already well established in the peninsular section of Thailand, a country that had promptly surrendered. At Kota Bharu within British Malaya there was bitter fighting in a series of rear guard actions fought desperately by British and native troops. But by the time the British warships arrived, their opportunity had passed; the vulnerable transports were already returning to base. Admiral Phillips did not realize this. He steamed north, leaving the Anambas Islands to port, and at 0629 December 9 received word that destroyer *Vampire* had sighted an enemy plane. Phillips was entering the Japanese air radius without air cover, but he still hoped to surprise a Japanese convoy at Singora. So on he sped to a position some 150 miles south of Indochina and 250 miles east of the Malay Peninsula. At 1830, when the weather cleared and three Japanese naval reconnaissance planes were sighted from the flagship, he realized that his position was precarious and untenable. Reluctantly he reversed course to return to Singapore at high speed. It would have been a happy ending had he persisted in this resolve.

As he steamed south, dispatches from Singapore portrayed impending doom on the shores of Malaya. The British Army was falling back fast. Shortly before midnight 9 December word came through of an enemy landing at Kuantan, halfway between Kota Bharu and Singapore. Admiral Phillips, in view of the imminent danger to Singapore, decided to risk his force in a strike on Kuantan. But the report was false, and his brave reaction to it proved fatal.

At dawn 10 December an unidentified plane was sighted about 60 miles off Kuantan. The Admiral continued on his course but launched a reconnaissance plane from *Prince of Wales*. It found no evidence of the enemy. Destroyer *Express* steamed ahead to reconnoiter the harbor of Kuantan, found it deserted, and closed the flagship again at 0835. Not yet suspecting that his intelligence from Singapore was faulty, the Admiral continued to search for a nonexistent surface enemy, first to the northward and then to the eastward. At about 1020 December 10 an enemy plane was sighted shadowing *Prince of Wales*. The crews immediately assumed anti-aircraft stations. Shortly after 1100 the ships were attacked by 9 enemy bombers. More and more came out, high-level and Navy torpedo-bombers, almost 100 in number, all shore-based. They inflicted lethal wounds on both capital ships. *Repulse* rolled over at 1233; *Prince of Wales* turned turtle and sank within an hour, hitting *Express* as she went down. Many survivors were picked up by the destroyers, but neither Admiral Phillips nor the captain of the *Prince* was among them.

The effect of this action was, literally, terrific. Our battleships sunk at Pearl Harbor had been "sitting ducks," but no free-moving battleship had yet been sunk by air power. The stock of the battle-wagon went down, air power advocates were jubilant, and the half-truth "Capital ships cannot withstand land-based air power" became elevated to the dignity of a tactical principle that none dared take the risk to disprove. And the Japanese had disposed of the only Allied battleship and battle cruiser in the Pacific Ocean west of Hawaii. The Allies lost face throughout the Orient and began to lose confidence in themselves.

Methodically and relentlessly the Japanese forces drove down the Malay Peninsula. British, Australian and native troops fought valiantly but, as at Bataan, with the increasing knowledge that theirs was a lost cause. Frequently their left flank was passed by small shore-to-shore amphibious jumps of troops in barges, and there were no river gunboats or motor torpedo boats as at Bataan to check such movements.

The Allies pitched in to help the British and annoy reinforcement echelons for the Malay invasion. A United States naval

*The Honorable Frank Knox*
Secretary of the Navy

*Admiral Chester W. Nimitz* USN
Commander in Chief United States Pacific Fleet
(Taken in a naval plane, 15 April 1942)

convoy was already on its way around the Cape with British troops for Singapore when war broke.[2] On 8 December an Australian plane sank an enemy transport in the Gulf of Siam. One Dutch submarine attacked four troop-laden transports off Pattani on 11 December and badly damaged them but was herself lost by hitting an enemy mine; another of the same nation sank a small transport off the Malayan beachhead next day. Submarine *Swordfish* of the Asiatic Fleet sank an 8600-ton freighter off Hainan on the 16th. But nothing stopped the Japanese. Their troops moved down the Malay Peninsula and took Penang on the Malacca Strait on 19 December.

To attain their immediate objective of fuel oil, the Japanese, in the second half of December, threw a good-sized force into Sarawak, a native state in northwestern Borneo ruled by a British rajah. Their first landing came on 17 December at Miri, just south of Brunei Bay where the Allies were to return in the last stages of the conflict. Some 2500 men landed from two transports with cover from one battleship, one carrier, three cruisers and four destroyers. The small Anglo-Dutch garrison destroyed what installations they could and retired south to Kuching, the capital of Sarawak. There the enemy struck them again on the 23rd. Netherlands submarine *K-14* penetrated the screen about the anchorage after dusk and torpedoed three transports, sinking two of them. But this was not enough to stall the operation and Kuching was occupied next day.[3]

Hong Kong was wrested from the British by the enemy on Christmas Day. This victory left the Allies only two bases on the Asiatic continent east of Burma — Malacca and Singapore — and their turn, as well as Burma's, would soon come.

These amazing successes of the Japanese in the Indies during the first three weeks of the war were due to surprise, to overwhelming naval and air power, and to a type of defense that was spread

---

[2] Convoy WS–12X; see Volume I of this work pp. 109–13.
[3] "Extracts from log of the heavy cruiser *Kumano*" Dec. 1941–Dec. 1942 and June 1943; A. Kroese *The Dutch Navy at War* p. 41.

too thin. Constantly on the offensive, they were able to achieve local superiority in many places and at astoundingly close intervals. But they ignored the military moral of their prowess and proceeded to spread themselves so thin and so wide that the Allies were eventually able to double back on them in precisely the same fashion.

# CHAPTER X

# Rear Guard in the Philippines

## 10 December 1941–6 May 1942

## 1. *Navy Bombed Out, 10–26 December*

THE Striking Force of the Asiatic Fleet (TF 5), commanded by Rear Admiral Glassford in *Houston*, included light cruiser *Boise*, seaplane tender *Langley* and oilers *Trinity* and *Pecos*. On orders from Admiral Hart this group departed Cavite for Balikpapan on the evening of 8 December 1941. Only the 29 submarines and the inshore patrol were left as naval defense of the Philippines. Great things were expected of these submarines. Eventually the United States underwater fleet proved to be a principal factor in defeating Japan, but performance was disappointing in these early days when everything depended on it. The submarines did not even hamper the Japanese advance.

The enemy's prompt seizure of air control over Manila Bay forced Admiral Hart to abandon his original plan of fighting the submarine war from that base. He sent all boats out promptly to patrol and attack whatever they could find, but three of their tenders, *Otus*, *Holland* and *Isabel*, were dispatched south to join Admiral Glassford. When Captain Walter E. Doyle went with them, Captain John Wilkes relieved him as Commander Submarines Asiatic Fleet, setting up temporary headquarters with Commander James Fife Jr. as chief of staff, in the newly built enlisted men's club at Manila. Luckily this was done before the Japanese attack on Cavite.[1] *Canopus* and submarine rescue vessel *Pigeon*

---

[1] Comsubs AF to Cominch 1 Apr. 1942, "War Activities Submarines U.S. Asiatic Fleet, Dec. 1 1941–Apr. 1 1942."

were now left to service the largest single submarine force in the United States Navy.

On the evening of 10 December, Captain L. J. Hudson (Commander South China Patrol), who had arrived that morning in *Mindanao*, received orders to conduct into safer waters all river gunboats capable of moving. He departed about midnight in *Tulsa* together with *Asheville*, rendezvoused with minesweepers *Lark* and *Whippoorwill*, and proceeded to Tarakan, Makassar Strait and finally Java.[2] *Mindanao* stayed behind.

Submarine operations were further hampered by lack of air reconnaissance. A few damaged PBYs, four of which managed to fly, remained at Mariveles. The rest of Patrol Wing 10 headed south, refueling at Lake Lanao, Mindanao, and on 18 December departed for Menado, on the tail end of Celebes, to join tender *Childs*.[3] This removed the only reliable source of intelligence about enemy movements in Philippine waters and left the submarines to their own devices.

Maintenance of them at headquarters was equally vexing. With enemy planes over Manila most of the daytime, boats that returned from patrol had to submerge by day and close *Canopus* at night. She lay moored to a dock near shore headquarters in Manila, completely covered with camouflage nets. Her spare torpedoes and parts were lightered out to Corregidor, where some of her workshops were set up and her crew worked day and night repairing not only submarines but all other small craft that needed repair; and most of them did.

"This sort of life did not lack for excitement," wrote the skipper of *Canopus*, Commander Earl L. Sackett, "but was far from being the peace and rest which submarine crews must have to prepare them physically and mentally for the strain of their war patrols."[4] She was not hit until Christmas Eve. On the following night she steamed out of the Bay on her last voyage.

[2] "Gunboat Saga" pp. 422–23. *Whippoorwill* proceeded alone to Balikpapan.
[3] Wagner Report p. 4.
[4] "History of U.S.S. *Canopus*," multigraphed by Ships Section Office of Public Information 28 Apr. 1947. This is one of the best ship histories of the entire war.

Many merchant ships sought refuge in Manila Harbor, where they were so many sitting ducks for the Japanese aviators. During the attack of 10 December, one was sunk. On the following day Admiral Hart called a conference of master mariners present and urged them to depart to the southward although he had no escort to offer them. They took his advice and all but one, set afire by air attack, escaped.[5]

On 19 December a high altitude bombing raid on Sangley Point destroyed more gasoline stores. Fortunately Admiral Rockwell had had the bulk of the diesel fuel and gasoline at Cavite dispersed the night before, but the water mains were blown up and the high-power radio station was completely knocked out. This was a most serious loss. To give the Japanese their due, it should be noted that the well-marked naval hospital, although close to military targets, was not hit. Thereafter that part of the bay was virtually abandoned. On 21 December Admiral Rockwell set up his head-quarters in a tunnel on Corregidor, leaving Captain John Dessez at Sangley Point to supervise demolition and final evacuation.

As late as 19 December it was thought that a large and valuable convoy could be brought into Manila Bay from Brisbane, but conditions deteriorated so rapidly that the plan had to be abandoned, and with it went the last hope of reinforcement.[6]

In the confusion General MacArthur neglected to inform Admiral Hart of his intention to evacuate Manila on Christmas Day, and the Admiral learned of it only by chance two days before. This left him little time to evacuate personnel, equipment and the *Canopus*. In a bitter mood he informed the General that loss of submarine matériel and facilities in the metropolis would drastically shorten the period of underwater defense in the Philippine Islands.[7] On 24 December, at a hectic conference with his flag officers in the Marsman Building, which was thrice bombed while they were talking, Admiral Hart decided to let the submarines operate from

---

[5] Hart Report pp. 39–40. S.S. *George G. Henry* stayed, retired with the fleet.
[6] MacArthur to Hart 19 Dec. 1941.
[7] Hart to MacArthur 24 Dec. 1941.

Manila Bay to the limit of possibility.[8] That limit ran out with the old year.

Destroyers *Peary* and *Pillsbury* had been left at Corregidor under Admiral Rockwell's command to assist the offshore patrol. Although damaged in the early attack on Cavite, their underwater sound equipment worked and each carried six torpedoes. Enemy air superiority forced them to maneuver almost to exhaustion until the afternoon of 26 December when, after beating off an attack by about 45 planes, the two destroyers' captains declared that they would have to cut and run or beach themselves, as fuel was running low and crews were exhausted. That night Admiral Rockwell directed them to make their way to Java and join Admiral Glassford's command. *Pillsbury's* voyage via Balikpapan was uneventful but *Peary* had considerable adventure.[9] She departed early in the morning of 27 December for Asia Bay on Negros and anchored there at 1030. Toward evening she weighed and headed for the channel between Pilas and Basilan Islands. A four-engined patrol plane sighted her at 0810 next morning, and, after making one bombing run which *Peary* agilely avoided, continued to shadow throughout the day. *Peary's* skipper, Lieutenant Commander John Bermingham,[10] tried to signal Admiral Glassford that he was in trouble but the radio operator could raise no station on the assigned frequencies. At 1420 three more big bombers joined and attacked the ship in turn for two solid hours. The old four-piper twisted and turned and rang up full speed ahead and astern in a series of seamanlike evasions which foiled the clumsy patrol bombers. After each had dropped two 500-pound bombs, they tried low-strafing runs, but the exhausted anti-aircraft crews beat them back. Just when *Peary* began to hope that she had the best of them, a torpedo plane swooped in off the port bow at 50 feet altitude and dropped two "fish" only 500 yards away. *Peary* backed full on the starboard and the deadly torpedoes passed her bow. About 15 seconds later,

---

[8] Rockwell Report p. 6.
[9] Information from Capt. A. S. McDill and *Peary* Action Report.
[10] He relieved Lt. Cdr. Keith in Cavite Navy Yard when the latter was wounded in the bombing raid of 10 Dec.

a second torpedo-bomber came in on the port quarter and released two more "fish" at about the same altitude and distance off the beleaguered ship. The bridge ordered hard right rudder, the stern swung clear and the torpedoes passed about 10 yards along the destroyer's starboard side. At that moment, when she had little way on, one of the patrol bombers came in from astern. Now Bermingham ordered Full Speed Ahead and, before the plane could release its charge, the twenty-one-year-old engines had the ship moving at 10 knots or more. The bomb fell harmlessly a hundred yards off the fantail, and the planes made off. *Peary* squared away on her course without a scratch. But her luck was running thin.

Shortly after passing through Banka Strait, off Kema in Celebes, *Peary* was sighted by three British Lockheeds. She exchanged recognition signals with one of them but they were not convinced of her friendly character and took her for a Japanese destroyer supporting the landing forces at Menado. One made a glide-bombing run and the anti-aircraft crews naturally fired in self-defense, whereupon the other two joined battle. *Peary* maneuvered so sharply that a man fell overboard. The one bomb dropped, a near miss, damaged the steering gear. There was slight satisfaction in knowing that our allies were better marksmen than our enemies!

The battered ship hid that night by Maitara Island near Ternate where many of the crew contracted a malignant type of malaria. On 30 December she departed for Ambon with only one engine functioning and arrived next day. There she replenished water and fuel and sailed for Darwin where she dropped anchor on 3 January 1942.

Seaplane tender *Heron* made an equally exciting escape and handled herself very creditably, for she had no choice but to travel through enemy-infested waters. She succeeded in shooting down a Japanese patrol bomber en route.[11]

At noon on Christmas Day Admiral Hart turned over all remaining naval forces in the islands to Rear Admiral Rockwell. He had planned to fly down to Java with some of his staff in two of the

[11] *Heron* Action Report, Lt. W. I. Kabler.

three remaining PBYs hidden in the mangroves off Los Banos. One plane left with an advance party on Christmas Eve, but the other two were discovered by the enemy and destroyed. This left only submarine *Shark* to evacuate Commander in Chief Asiatic Fleet and the rest of his staff.[12] They shoved off at 0200 December 26.

## 2. *Navy at Bataan 26 December 1941–11 March 1942*

Such units of the Asiatic Fleet as remained under Admiral Rockwell's command knew that they were expendable. Three river gunboats, three minesweepers, two district tugs, two civilian tugs, two converted yachts, two submarine tenders and six motor torpedo boats were to give the Army what support they could, and fight a losing battle to the end.

The principal task of this naval remnant was to support ground operations on Bataan, primarily by denying water approaches for possible flanking movements. In so doing the Navy somewhat prolonged the defense of Bataan and furnished a sharp contrast to the story of Malaya, where the British apparently had no small naval craft. And the excellent radio station set up by the Navy on Corregidor furnished the only adequate long distance communications in the last stages of the campaign.

A tough spot like this seems to bring out the native ingenuity, initiative and courage of American sailors. There were so many acts of valor during these last days in the Philippines that only a few can be mentioned as examples.

Submarine tender *Canopus*, when she steamed out of Cavite the day of the bombing, tied up at the Mariveles shore of Bataan and covered herself with jungle camouflage. This did not save her from a bad air bombing on 29 December. One armor-piercing bomb went through every deck and exploded on top of the propeller shaft under the magazines, blowing them open and starting fires. Fine work by damage control parties topside and below, who

[12] Hart Report pp. 45–46.

worked for hours extinguishing the fires, prevented the magazines from exploding. She was seaworthy again within a few days; but the retirement of the last submarine on New Year's Eve left her with new duties. *Canopus* became general utility repair ship both to the Army and to the few naval craft left in the Bay. The Japanese bombed her again on 5 January, made one hit with a fragmentation bomb on the stack, and cracked plating with near misses; but she was soon fixed up again in the guise of an abandoned hull. Commander Sackett deliberately provided her with a pathetic list, cargo booms askew and fake fires burning from oily rags in smudge pots. The Japs were fooled into leaving her alone after that, and every night she hummed with activity, making repairs or forging new weapons for the beleaguered forces on Bataan.

After the abandonment of Manila the Philippines campaign resolved itself into a slow retreat on Bataan. On 6 January the American Army formed its line on either side of Mount Natib. Major General Jonathan Wainwright commanded the I Philippines Corps on the left flank. On the right flank was the II Philippines Corps under Major General George M. Parker. But even citadel defense could not long hold out. By 15 January, as a result of repeated enemy attacks, the II Corps had been folded back toward Manila Bay, leaving a gap between which two infantry regiments were unable to close. Increasing pressure was put on the I Corps by a fresh enemy force which landed at Port Binanga on the northwest coast of Bataan on 16 January; and on the 26th what was left of the two corps retired to the reserve battle position, a line running across Bataan from Bagac to Orion.

It has been argued that the last-ditch defense of Bataan was futile and costly, without influence on the Japanese overall strategy. This may or may not be true. The question is one of relative values. Certainly the conquest of Bataan did not progress as rapidly as the invaders had hoped. The Japanese high command, dissatisfied with General Homma's progress, in contrast to earlier successes, shook up his staff, and transferred a considerable number of bomber planes from Burma, to help break United States resistance.[13] The sacrifice of General Wainwright's men and the remaining naval units did deny Manila Bay to the enemy until May 1942, and that was important.

All the Navy could do was to run small-craft and motor torpedo boat patrols to prevent the enemy from turning the American flank. Notwithstanding he succeeded in effecting a landing at Longoskawayan Point near Mariveles, a serious threat so far behind our lines. Commander Francis J. Bridget, a colorful character who had been left in charge of the remnants of naval aviation in the Philippines, had just organized a naval battalion out of his own 150 men (mostly aviation ground crews), 130 bluejackets from U.S.S. *Canopus*, about 100 Marines and a few refugees from the Cavite Navy Yard. Lieutenant "Hap" Goodall of *Canopus* was second in command. After a little drill, this motley battalion sallied forth on 24 January for a "hardening up" hike to the coast. On the way they met an agitated group of soldiers who had just been driven from their signal station by the Japanese landing party. The invaders were working their way inland along the vital communication road. Bridget's men had no trouble driving in the advance patrols, but soon realized that they had a bear by the tail. Five days followed of weird jungle fighting, with all accepted principles violated, and no holds barred. The Japs used their famous infiltration tactics at night, but this did not have the expected result because Bridget's boys, innocent of the military principle that it is fatal to be outflanked, simply held their ground and sent out detachments to mop up the infiltrators. A diary later found on the body of a Japanese, described the strange conduct of the "new type of suicide squads, which thrashed about in the jungle, wearing bright-colored uniforms [14] and making plenty of noise. They would attempt to draw Japanese fire by sitting down, talking loudly and lighting cigarettes."

On the fifth day, the 57th Regiment of Filipino Scouts, trained jungle fighters, relieved Bridget's Battalion. After three days' experience of the deadly marksmanship of the Scouts, and the blasts

---

[13] USSBS Questionnaire No. 6.

[14] The bluejackets had tried to dye their white uniforms khaki but they came out bright yellow.

of huge mortar shells thrown into their main positions from Corregidor, the Japanese landing force had been pushed over the cliffs.

Unfortunately, those cliffs were honeycombed with caves facing the sea, and almost inaccessible from the land; and the enemy had plenty of food and ammunition left. The repair men of *Canopus* rose to the occasion. Her three 40-foot motor launches were each converted into a "Mickey Mouse battleship" with boiler plate for armor, a light fieldpiece and plenty of machine guns. They succeeded in shooting up all caves that were not too deep, and even took a few prisoners.[15]

A second Japanese landing behind American lines at Quinauan Point on 23 January threatened the Bagac-Orion line. To counterattack this force, General Wainwright could spare but one battalion which in twelve days beat back the enemy but itself shrank from 600 to 212 men and at the end was commanded by a second lieutenant. These Japs also took refuge in caves in the cliffs. General Wainwright requested naval gunfire to rout them, and Captain Kenneth M. Hoeffel, Commander Inshore Patrol, sent a gunboat to do it. *Canopus's* "Mickey Mouse battleships" were again called upon to "disinfect" the caves. This they accomplished to the General's taste, but did not come off unscathed; four Japanese dive-bombers attacked the boats on their return trip and, after three men had been killed and one boat riddled with holes, all three boats were beached. Bridget's naval battalion was now detached from Bataan and sent to defend the beaches of Corregidor.

The enemy attempted another flank landing by moonlight 1 February on the southwest point of Bataan. This movement was detected and repulsed by P-40s and Lieutenant John D. Bulkeley's motor torpedo boats. Army planes sank about five barges loaded with men and the PTs accounted for three others besides scaring off a supporting destroyer at which they fired torpedoes.[16]

---

[15] Cdr. E. L. Sackett "History of U.S.S. *Canopus*"; Lt. Cdr. T. C. Parker "The Epic of Corregidor-Bataan," *U.S. Naval Institute Proceedings* Jan. 1943 pp. 9-22.

[16] Rockwell Report p. 15; Lt. J. D. Bulkeley Report 21 May 1942. The PTs did not accomplish much else in this campaign and on every occasion claimed more damage than subsequent investigation substantiates. Of the two cruisers and two large merchant ships that they claimed, none were actually sunk or even damaged.

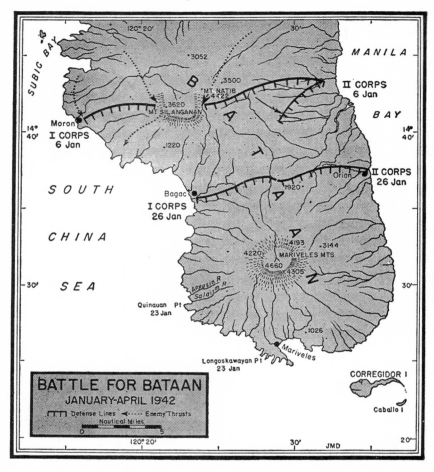

Although some of these small actions stopped a few Japanese for a time, they were but spirited episodes in a brave losing battle. Individual acts of heroism and extraordinary determination enabled the "Battling Bastards of Bataan," as they called themselves, to keep going a few weeks longer.

The most promising attempt to feed Bataan was by small inter-island vessels from the southern part of the Archipelago. President Roosevelt gave General MacArthur *carte blanche* on the expense; he might offer any bonus he chose to island vessels that would run the Japanese blockade. But few would try, and none got through. The only possible means of leaving Manila Bay or Bataan were by submarine or seaplane. U.S.S. *Swordfish* lay on the bottom off Corregidor all day 20 February and surfaced at sunset to take on a distinguished passenger list: President Manuel Quezon and family, Vice President Osmeña, and five high-ranking officers or officials of the Commonwealth. These were landed at San José, Panay. *Swordfish* at once turned back to Manila and carried High Commissioner Sayre, family and staff, to Fremantle, Australia. A similar mission, focused on more material things, fell to submarine *Trout* of the Pacific Fleet. On 3 February she brought ammunition to Corregidor and carried away gold, precious even in this crisis, lest the Japanese use it in neutral countries. On 11 March Admiral Rockwell, General MacArthur and family, and about fifteen others left Luzon by motor torpedo boat, on orders from Washington. Lieutenant Bulkeley took them by devious channels to Macajalar Bay on the north coast of Mindanao, where they were picked up by two Flying Fortresses and flown to Australia.[17]

## 3. *All Gone*

All American forces in the Philippine Islands now came under the command of General Wainwright. Food was pooled between the two services, but the supply was getting low. There was a ship at Cebu with a cargo of food and another with fuel at Iloilo, but no inter-island skipper could be found to run the Japanese blockade. Finally, it was arranged that two United States submarines unload their torpedoes at Cebu and carry about 35 tons of food to Bataan. This amounted to but half a day's rations for the forces.[18]

After a breach in the lines made the situation so confused that further resistance was fruitless, General Wainwright decided on

---

[17] Rockwell Report. An overdramatic account of this episode can be found in W. L. White *They Were Expendable* (1942). Capt. K. M. Hoeffel relieved Rear Admiral Rockwell as Commandant 16th Naval District.
[18] Wainwright pp. 72–73.

8 April to evacuate Bataan. Only the naval personnel at Mariveles and the Philippine Scouts were allowed to be transferred to tiny Corregidor; the rest were taken prisoner. The evacuation had to be completed before dawn brought swarms of enemy bombers. "That wild and horrible, yet weirdly beautiful night must be imprinted forever on the memories of all who lived through its spectacular fury. For miles back on the slopes of the mountain, burning ammunition dumps lighted the sky with showers of rocket-like streamers, while the ground shook with detonations of exploding ammunition. . . . Around the shores of Mariveles Bay, Navy men blew up the *Dewey* floating dry dock which had served the Asiatic Fleet for so many years, and scuttled ships which would be useless in defending Corregidor. *Canopus* backed out under her own power to deep water, where she was regretfully scuttled by the sailors she had served so faithfully."

Corregidor held out for another five weeks. Conditions were frightfully crowded, the tempo of Japanese attacks from the air and from artillery emplaced on Bataan and the opposite shores of the Bay steadily increased; the toll of casualties rose, and the nervous strain was almost unbearable. A certain number of officers and men gave in under the tension. Some saw hallucinations, others became completely ineffectual and could not perform their duties. But the tough and the strong-minded held the team together and inspired the rest. Colonel Howard's 4th Marine Regiment, in which most of the *Canopus* men were incorporated, lived up to the great traditions of their Corps in the last bitter days. The backbone of Corregidor's beach defense, it set an example of courage for those who began to give under the strain. Major Williams was outstanding. He was everywhere, looking after his men and leading rescue parties on dangerous missions when gun emplacements were hit and magazines were in imminent danger of exploding. "But courage alone is never enough." [19]

In one of the early heavy bombardments, naval tug *Keswick* was

[19] Hanson W. Baldwin "The 4th Marines at Corregidor" *Marine Corps Gazette* Dec. 1946.

hit. She broke into flames and lay helpless, taking shell after shell from the implacable enemy. But the old China gunboat *Mindanao* was coming into the game. Lieutenant Commander A. R. Mc-Cracken zigzagged her up to the Bataan shore, holding fire until between *Keswick* and the batteries. Then she opened up, demolished them one by one, maneuvered alongside the stricken tug and took off her crew.[20] That was the last fight in which a naval vessel gave as good as she got. On 11 April *Finch* was at her mooring near the cliff on Caballo Island, and was sunk.[21] On the same day, *Quail* took three hits but was not disabled. Captain Hoeffel then decided to take all spare guns and equipment off the few ships left to him.[22]

In order to evacuate key officers for General MacArthur's staff, and Army nurses, the Navy flew two PBYs up from Darwin to Corregidor 29 April. It so happened that this was Hirohito's birthday, in honor of which the Japs were putting up extra fireworks. *Quail* and *Tanager* set out two lighted buoys and swept a strip of water for the planes, which came in just after dark. Some fifty people were crowded into the two seaplanes, but they were able to take off again before daybreak. At Lake Lanao in Mindanao, where they staged, luck was not so good. One of the two was wrecked and its passengers became prisoners of the Japanese. The other had a hole torn by a log in its bottom. The crew patched her up as best they could, but still she leaked. With true American resourcefulness they placed the plumpest nurse directly over the largest remaining leak and so managed to take off for Australia and liberty.[23]

A number of officers and men were also evacuated from the Rock by submarine. Arrangements for these missions entailed considerable dickering between Army and Navy authorities in Australia. As submarines were the principal United States striking forces in the Southwest Pacific, which could be most profitably

[20] *Mindanao* was hit in the engine room by an air bomb on 2 May and had to be abandoned.
[21] Lt. Cdr. T. W. Davison letter of 23 June 1942.
[22] Lt. Cdr. J. H. Morrill and P. Martin *South From Corregidor* pp. 7–18.
[23] Wainwright p. 101; interview with Rear Admiral Purnell.

employed along the enemy's routes of oil supply, the Navy was reluctant to assign them to ferry duties.[24] Despite the difficulties involved, several rescue voyages were completed. Submarine *Spearfish* of the Pacific Fleet surfaced outside the Corregidor minefield on 3 May and took off twenty-seven passengers — Army, Navy, service nurses and civilians. Except for a few resourceful sailors who got away in small boats, these were the last to escape by sea.[25]

Next morning, 4 May, minesweeper *Tanager* was hit by gunfire from Cavite, burst into flames, exploded and sank. This left *Quail*, *Pigeon*, three river gunboats and two tugs the only naval vessels in Philippine waters. Bombs sank *Mindanao* and *Pigeon* next day; the others were scuttled.

On 6 May General Wainwright surrendered Corregidor and all armed forces in the Philippines to the enemy. The Campaign of the Philippines was over.

Resistance continued — a fascinating story of individual initiative and jerry-built intelligence organizations in the hills. Guerillas, partly supplied by United States submarines from Australia, harassed the enemy in many parts of the islands and kept the flame of Philippine independence alive. Hundreds of American soldiers and sailors who escaped to the jungle rather than surrender were fed and protected by Filipinos at the risk of their lives, and operated with the native guerilla bands. In common suffering a new bond of brotherhood was forged between Americans and Filipinos, to replace the political relation voluntarily broken.

[24] Purnell to Vice Admiral Leary 1 May 1942; Leary to Purnell 5 May 1942.
[25] *South From Corregidor* p. 25; *Nautilus* Patrol Report; Cdr. Hazzard Report on Special Missions. A remarkable 29-day voyage by Lt. Cdr. J. H. Morrill, one other officer and 16 men of the *Quail*, was made in an open 36-ft. motor launch to Darwin, Australia.

# CHAPTER XI

# Pearl Aftermath

## *7–15 December 1941*

### 1. *Balance of Forces*

IN Pearl Harbor it was "a day of trouble, and of treading down, and of perplexity . . . and of crying to the mountains." [1] Both there and at Washington the naval high command for some days was unnerved; and no wonder, for never, since the British "Copenhagened" the Danes, had so devastating a blow been inflicted on men-of-war of a nation supposed to be at peace.

Plenty more bad news came in from across the Pacific, as we have seen. Japan virtually controlled the Pacific Ocean eastward to the 180th meridian, and south to the Line; the doctrines of Mahan had been turned against his own nation. On the other side of the world, Germany and Italy honored the Tripartite Pact by promptly declaring war on the United States, who now had a two-ocean war to wage with a less than one-ocean Navy. It was the most appalling situation America had faced since the preservation of the Union had been assured.

Four years later, when Germany and Japan were utterly defeated and helpless, it became easier to see the alleviating factors. Japan's treacherous attack on Oahu aroused the American people, ended their smug conviction of innate military superiority over orientals, and brought home to everyone in the land the ruthless and dangerous nature of their enemy. Before even the fires burning in battleships were quenched by the waters of Pearl Harbor, the United States had become virtually unanimous in entering the war,

[1] Isaiah xxii 5.

grimly determined to win it, and firmly convinced of a community of interest with the British Commonwealth of Nations and Latin America. And, as Senator Vandenberg, one of the leading isolationists of the prewar era, remarked five years later, Pearl Harbor "drove most of us to the irresistible conclusion that world peace is indivisible. We learned that the oceans are no longer moats around our ramparts. We learned that mass destruction is a progressive science which defies both time and space and reduces human flesh and blood to cruel impotence." [2]

Although the fates decreed that American pride be humbled, they took care that American sea power should not be destroyed. If battleships had to be sunk, it was well for them to receive the blow in Pearl Harbor rather than in the three-thousand fathom deeps off the Mandates or in the Philippine Sea. The loss of brave men and gallant ships on 7 December might in Homeric terms be called a necessary sacrifice to appease the neglected gods of war and of the sea; to dissuade Mars and Neptune from exacting a holocaust later.

There were two bright spots in the situation for the Pacific Fleet. All shore facilities were intact, and the fast carrier forces had escaped because they were out on missions. The following ships under Admiral Kimmel's command were at sea when the Japanese bombers came swooping over the mountains of Oahu: —

1. Carrier *Lexington* (Captain Frederick C. Sherman); heavy cruisers *Chicago*, *Portland* and *Astoria* and five destroyers,[3] temporarily commanded by Rear Admiral J. H. Newton, were at lat. 23°46′ N, long. 170°56′ W, about 420 miles southeast of Midway Island, whither they were bound in order to deliver Marine Scout Bomber Squadron 231. *Lexington* expected to fly them off at noon. This mission could and should have been completed, since Midway was the best base from which to look for the enemy carriers. Admiral Newton, however, turned this task force (then numbered 12) back toward Oahu, and Admiral Kimmel directed it to rendez-

[2] Speech at Cleveland 11 Jan. 1947; *Washington Post* 12 Jan.
[3] *Porter*, *Flusser*, *Drayton*, *Lamson* and *Mahan*.

vous with Admiral Halsey at lat. 22° N, long. 162° W, about 120 miles west of Kauai. *Indianapolis,* the ten-year-old heavy cruiser that fought all through the war only to fall victim to a Japanese torpedo a few days before it ended, was the flagship of this task force, flying the flag of Vice Admiral Wilson Brown.[4] She had been detached a few days earlier to conduct a simulated bombardment and landing exercise, with five newly converted destroyer-minesweepers, on Johnston Island, 700 miles southwest of Oahu. She had just finished the bombardment when Kimmel's message "Air raid on Pearl Harbor" was intercepted. Brown then made best speed to close *Lexington.*

2. Vice Admiral William F. Halsey Jr., destined to become one of the most famous sea fighters of this or of any war,[5] commanded a fast carrier striking force built around carrier *Enterprise.* He had sortied from Pearl Harbor 28 November, delivered Marine Fighter Squadron 221 to Wake Island early on 4 December and then turned back to Pearl. Besides the "Big E" (Captain George D. Murray), this Task Force 8 comprised three heavy cruisers and nine destroyers.[6] Rear Admiral Raymond A. Spruance, who was to acquire a reputation in the war second to none, flew his flag in

[4] Wilson Brown Jr., born Philadelphia 1882, Naval Academy '02, served on Admiral Sims's staff in London and commanded destroyer *Parker* in World War I. He completed the Naval War College course in 1921, and during the next twenty years was successively exec. of U.S.S. *Colorado,* aide to President Coolidge and President Roosevelt, C.O. New London Submarine Base, C.O. *California,* Chief of Staff Naval War College, Commander Training Squadron Scouting Force (the nucleus of the Atlantic Fleet), Superintendent of the Naval Academy. On 1 Feb. 1941 he assumed duty as Commander Scouting Force with rank of Vice Admiral.
[5] William Frederick Halsey Jr., son of a Navy captain, born Elizabeth, N. J., 1882, Naval Academy '04, commanded destroyers *Benham* and *Shaw* in World War I, and five destroyers in succession between 1919 and 1925, during two of which years he was Naval Attaché at Berlin. After tours of duty as exec. of *Wyoming* and Commander Destroyer Squadron 14, Scouting Force, he took the Naval War College and Army War College courses, and qualified as naval aviator in 1935. He served as captain of the carrier *Saratoga,* subsequently Commandant Naval Air Station, Pensacola, Commander Carrier Divisions 2 and 1, and (June 1940) Commander Aircraft Battle Force with rank of Vice Admiral, besides being Comcardiv 2. Upon the detachment of *Yorktown* to the Atlantic Fleet, he hoisted his flag in the other carrier of this division, *Enterprise.* See his and J. Bryan's *Admiral Halsey's Story* (1947). See Vols. IV–VIII and XII–XIV. Ret. 1947; died 1959.
[6] Desron 6, Captain Richard L. Conolly (*Balch, Gridley, Craven, McCall, Maury, Dunlap, Fanning, Benham* and *Ellet*). (Desron 6 War Diary Dec. 1941.)

*Northampton.* At dawn on the 7th, when Halsey was still about 200 miles west of Oahu, he flew off a number of his planes to land on Ford Island. We have already seen what happened to them. When the bad news reached Halsey, he cursed the luck that kept him from the fight; we on the contrary may thank the gods for this little favor. If Nagumo's force had seen *Enterprise* it would certainly have attacked and probably have sunk her, since she had so little anti-aircraft protection. When Halsey entered Pearl Harbor on the afternoon of the second day and witnessed the destruction, he uttered the first of his famous fighting phrases: "Before we're through with 'em, the Japanese language will be spoken only in hell!"

3. Heavy cruiser *Minneapolis* (Captain Frank J. Lowry), flying the flag of Rear Admiral Frank Jack Fletcher,[7] was maneuvering south of Oahu, screened by four destroyer-minesweepers, when the air attack commenced. Light cruisers *Detroit, St. Louis* and *Phoenix,* together with several destroyers and fast minesweepers that sortied during or immediately after the battle, were ordered by Admiral Kimmel to assemble with *Minneapolis* under the command of Rear Admiral Milo F. Draemel[8] and join Admiral Halsey's task force. Unfortunately a scouting plane from *Enterprise* reported them as the enemy carrier force, which encouraged everyone to look for the guilty Japs south of Oahu.

4. Heavy cruiser *Pensacola* (Captain Norman Scott) was passing through the Phoenix Islands, escorting tender *Niagara,* Navy transports *Chaumont* and *Republic,* two Army transports and three freighters. These carried many thousand soldiers, hundreds of aviators and naval replacements, and scores of planes, bound for Manila. Promptly diverted to Suva in the Fijis, the convoy was there joined by an Anzac escort and proceeded through Torres Strait to Darwin, Australia.[9] Heavy cruiser *Louisville* (Captain

[7] Comcrudiv 6. *Astoria* of this division was with Brown; *New Orleans* and *San Francisco* were in Pearl.
[8] Then Commander Destroyers Battle Force and Destroyer Flotilla Two (*Detroit* flagship).
[9] *Pensacola* War Diary; "History of V Army Air Force" (the nucleus of which was on board *Republic*) in Archives Air Historical Office U.S. Army.

Elliott B. Nixon) escorting Army transports *Hugh L. Scott* and *President Coolidge* back from Manila, had reached a point about halfway between the Santa Cruz and the Ellice Islands.[10]

5. On the West Coast of the United States battleship *Colorado* was undergoing overhaul at Bremerton on Puget Sound; six destroyers and five submarines were at Mare Island Navy Yard; and carrier *Saratoga* (Captain Archibald H. Douglas), flying the flag of Rear Admiral Aubrey W. Fitch, was about to enter San Diego, where one light cruiser, three World War I destroyers and four submarines were moored. *Saratoga*, as nucleus of a third fast carrier striking force, was ordered to proceed to Pearl at once, and sailed on the 8th. Submarine *Gar* was sailing along the Mexican coast near Acapulco. The old light cruiser *Trenton* was operating off Panama, and her sister ship *Richmond* off the coast of Peru.

6. The following submarines were already deployed in the Pacific: *Tambor* and *Triton* patrolling off Wake Island; *Trout* off Midway; *Thresher* south of Oahu with destroyer *Litchfield*, and *Plunger*, *Pollack* and *Pompano* northeast of Oahu.

Thus, when we recall that in addition to these ships all but two of the cruisers and all the submarines in Pearl Harbor had survived the attack with no more than light damage, and that all but three of the destroyers were intact,[11] the situation on 8 December was far less serious than it appeared to be at the time. The shock of the surprise and the sinking of the battleships gave an impression of complete disaster that was far from correct. Naval strategists were so accustomed to measure naval power in terms of the Battle Force

[10] *Louisville* War Diary. Convoy arrived Pearl 16 Dec.

[11] Here is the list of Pearl Harbor "survivors," exclusive of auxiliaries, "bird" minesweepers and smaller craft and those heavily damaged though not sunk: —

Heavy Cruisers *New Orleans, San Francisco.*
Light Cruisers *Detroit,* *Honolulu,* *Phoenix, St. Louis.*
Destroyers *Allen, Aylwin,* *Bagley, Blue, Case, Chew, Conyngham,* *Cummings, Dale, Dewey, Farragut, Halbert,* *Helm, Henley, Hull, Macdonough, Monaghan, Patterson, Phelps, Perry, Ralph Talbot, Reid,* *Schley, Selfridge, Tucker, Trever, Wasmuth, Worden, Zane.*
Destroyer Minesweepers *Breese, Gamble, Montgomery,* *Preble,* *Pruitt, Ramsay,* *Tracy,* *Sicard.*
Submarines *Cachalot, Dolphin, Gudgeon, Narwhal, Tautog.*

*indicates lightly damaged or already under repair 7 December.

that they were slow to appreciate how much striking power was left. Of land-based aircraft in the Hawaiian Islands, the Navy had 7 utility planes serviceable on Maui and 3 Catalinas and about a dozen Marine Corps SBDs on Oahu. The Army Air Force, which had suffered even more severely, had 4 Flying Fortresses (B–17s), 11 Bolos (B–18s) and about 75 fighter, reconnaissance and pursuit planes serviceable on Oahu. These, and the patrol squadron on Midway, were the only aircraft available to search for and pursue the enemy.

Steps to reinforce the Pacific Fleet were taken immediately. A few hours after the bad news reached Washington, Admiral Stark ordered Admiral King, Commander in Chief Atlantic Fleet, to assemble carrier *Yorktown* with full plane complement, battleships *New Mexico*, *Mississippi* and *Idaho*, three squadrons of patrol bombers and a destroyer squadron for transfer to the Pacific.

## 2. *The Search*

During the confusion of battle all sorts of theories arose as to where the enemy lay. Since, before the attack, two Japanese carriers had been detected in Kwajalein, it was first assumed that they constituted the enemy striking force. This opinion was strengthened by the fact that many of the attacking planes flew around Oahu and approached Pearl Harbor from the southward. The Opana radar, which had been supposed to secure at 0700, reopened before 0900 and tracked the planes retiring northward; but the Army's central station failed to inform Cincpac headquarters of that important fact. Nevertheless, Admiral Kimmel's first guess was correct. He informed his outlying forces at 0942 December 7 that there was "some indication" of a Japanese fleet northwest of Oahu. In the same dispatch he ordered the *Enterprise* task force to intercept and attack an enemy whose composition and position were completely unknown. Even for Bill Halsey that was too large an order. Shortly after, a false sighting report reached Cincpac headquarters of two Japanese carriers off Barbers Point, only 8 or 10 miles from the mouth of Pearl Harbor. Cruiser *Minneapolis* intercepted this report; and, as she was right on the reported position, her commanding officer tried to radio Cincpac "No carriers in sight." But his radioman sent it as "Two carriers in sight." Fortunately the planes that streaked down there recognized "Minnie" and let her alone.

The next mistake was a false interpretation of a direction-finder bearing on a radio transmission from a Japanese carrier. These instruments record simultaneously reciprocal bearings — both the direction toward and the direction away from the object. One has to estimate which is correct. In this instance the enemy carrier bore 358° or almost due north from Pearl Harbor; but the interpreter made it 178° or almost due south. To add to the confusion, one of Admiral Halsey's aviators identified Rear Admiral Draemel's light cruisers and destroyers, which had sortied from Pearl Harbor to join him, as an enemy force.

As a result of this series of fumbles, Admiral Kimmel concluded that the enemy had attacked from the southward and was now retiring to Jaluit, believed to be his advanced naval base in the Marshalls. Most searches therefore were directed to the southward and westward of Oahu. *Enterprise* launched a torpedo- and dive-bombing mission, which went after but fortunately did not attack Draemel's light forces, then assiduously searching for the enemy they had been mistaken for. The *Lexington* task force turned southward at dusk on the 7th in the lively expectation of intercepting, and the forlorn hope of destroying, the Japanese carrier force en route to Jaluit.

Before the terrible Seventh was over, Admiral Kimmel received word of the first air attacks on Wake Island and Guam, and the shelling of Midway Island by destroyers.

More alarums and excursions followed on 8 December, especially for Vice Admiral Wilson Brown, who at 1000 in *Indianapolis* joined his *Lexington* task force (TF 12) and took over the command from Rear Admiral Newton. Direction-finder bearings had reported strange vessels in the vicinity of Johnston Island the previous night. Cruiser float planes could find nothing there at dawn, but as a precaution a search mission was flown from *Lexington*. The pilot of a patrol plane based on Johnston — said to have been one of the most experienced in the Navy — sent in a report of an encounter with an enemy carrier whose flight deck was "camouflaged to look like a heavy cruiser," and a destroyer "with the rising sun painted on her bows." Fortunately no damage was done, as these turned out to be U.S.S. *Portland*, which naturally did look like a heavy cruiser, and *Porter*, whose bows had been chipped in spots down to the red-lead.[12] Admiral Kimmel recalled the *Lexington* task force to Pearl about noon on the 8th; but en route they received a report that Johnston Island was under attack. The cruisers bent on 25 knots in that direction, *Lexington* following and preparing to launch planes. This proved to be another false alarm, and the course to Oahu was resumed during the night.

By the close of 8 December it was clear that the Japanese attack had come from the north, and that the enemy was retiring in a northwesterly direction. Admiral Draemel's light cruiser force, augmented by *Minneapolis*, searched all that day and the next to the northward of Oahu, well away from the enemy's course — fortunately for them.

*Enterprise*, after her planes had searched fruitlessly to the westward and southward of Oahu, entered Pearl Harbor toward sundown 8 December, and after a quick night fueling sortied before dawn with the mission to hunt submarines to the northward of the islands. Admiral Kimmel knew that it was too late to overtake the Japanese carrier force, but Intelligence correctly estimated that some of the enemy I-boats were proceeding to the West Coast. Halsey spent a very lively five days searching; the lookouts, he said, "were spying periscope feathers in every whitecap and torpedoes in every porpoise." He signaled his task force, "If all the

<hr>

[12] *Lexington* War Diary; conversation with Vice Admiral McMorris. The two ships had been temporarily detached from TF 12 in order to home overdue planes.

torpedo wakes reported are factual, Japanese submarines will soon have to return to base for a reload, and we will have nothing to fear. In addition, we are wasting too many depth charges on neutral fish." [13]

Finally, their eagerness was rewarded. Just before dawn on 10 December, when the formation was steaming about 200 miles northeast of Oahu, an SBD from *Enterprise*, piloted by Lieutenant (jg) Edward L. Anderson, spotted the 2000-ton submarine *I-70*, and made a dive-bombing attack which inflicted such damage on the I-boat that it was unable to submerge. Later in the same day Lieutenant Clarence E. Dickinson, flying another SBD from *Enterprise*, found the submarine surfaced, with men and debris in the water alongside. He dive-bombed and sank it. [14] In the course of the same day *Enterprise* dodged a torpedo and sighted a submarine dead ahead just as she was about to recover planes; destroyers delivered several depth-charge attacks and *Salt Lake City* engaged a submarine with gunfire. On the 11th, *Salt Lake* had another such encounter; a torpedo passed 20 yards astern of *Enterprise*; and numerous depth-charge attacks were delivered by destroyers. Two comparatively quiet days followed, and on 15 December the task force entered Pearl Harbor to fuel.

In the meantime, Admiral Nagumo's Striking Force had made good its escape, without a single contact by plane or ship. At about 1330 on 7 December it made off to the northwestward at speed of 25 knots, dropping to 15 knots next day. At lat. 37° N, long. 172° W, about 550 miles NNE of Midway, it turned west and followed that course until well beyond the range of Midway-based patrol planes. On the 15th (East longitude date) carriers *Soryu* and *Hiryu*, heavy cruisers *Tone* and *Chikuma*, and two or more destroyers were detached to cover the invasion of Wake Island, scheduled for the 22nd. [15] The rest of the Striking Force sighted

[13] *Admiral Halsey's Story* pp. 82–83.
[14] *German, Japanese and Italian Submarine Losses* (published by Opnav, May 1946) p. 22; *Enterprise* log. The position of sinking was lat. 23°45' N, long. 155°35' W.
[15] *The Campaigns of the Pacific War* p. 20.

the Bonins on 20 December, and a few days later arrived at the naval base of Kure on the Inland Sea of Japan. There it was given a tremendous ovation for having delivered a noble and courageous blow for the Emperor.

It may be considered providential that Nagumo did escape. Neither Halsey's nor Brown's striking forces, nor both combined, were any match for the six carriers, the battleships and the heavy cruisers, jubilant with victory and eager to achieve the annihilation of the Pacific Fleet by sinking the carriers that they had missed at Pearl. Admiral Nagumo could put at least 350 planes into the air, as against a total of 131 carried by *Lexington* and *Enterprise*.[16] He would certainly have concentrated on these carriers as soon as they came within range; and the issue of so unequal a battle could hardly have been favorable to the weaker side.

## 3. *The Strategic Situation*

"The World Turned Upside Down," an old tune played at the surrender of Cornwallis in 1781, would have been an appropriate theme song for Pearl Harbor in December 1941. The Japanese attack shattered one illusion, "It can't happen here," only to substitute another, "Anything can happen now."

The Pearl Harbor attack was a hit-and-run raid. For the time being the enemy wanted nothing more in the Central Pacific except Wake Island and the Gilberts; he turned the vast bulk of his forces southwestward to engage in a tempting program of conquest. But at that time no American in a position of military responsibility could afford to assume this. It was not known until months later that Admiral Nagumo's mighty force had gone all the way home; Cincpac had to assume that some or all of his carriers were replenishing in Marshall Islands lagoons, in preparation for a bombing of

---

[16] Figures from Capt. Fuchida's interrogation, USSBS 603 p. 13. U.S.S. *Lexington* had 68 planes on board 14 Dec.; *Enterprise* had approximately 63 on board, although her normal complement would be nine more.

the Pearl Harbor Navy Yard installations which had been neglected on 7 December. Transports escorted by fast battleships and cruisers might be on their way from Truk to land troops on Oahu or some other Hawaiian island. Wake Island was already under attack; and for what would Japan want Wake, unless as a steppingstone to Midway and Hawaii? So, anything might happen. Even strikes on Puget Sound, San Francisco or the Panama Canal were not beyond the range of possibility.

Admiral Stark on 9 December informed Admiral Kimmel that he anticipated Japanese attempts to occupy Midway, Maui and Hawaii before closing in on Oahu. He feared lest Midway would have to be written off, but hoped that Johnston, Palmyra and Samoa might be held. All ships damaged in the battle but able to steam should be sent immediately to West Coast yards; and he advised Admiral Kimmel not to base any ships except submarines and patrol craft at Pearl Harbor until its defenses were greatly improved.

To this far from heartening dispatch, Kimmel stoutly replied that his carriers were untouched, that the workshops at Pearl were intact, and that the morale and determination of the Pacific Fleet remained high. And there was no possible substitute base for Pearl Harbor unless the islands were abandoned to the enemy. As most of the salvageable victims of the blitz were sitting on the harbor bottom, they could not proceed to the West Coast. Hence additional aircraft, maintenance personnel and skilled workmen must be provided promptly for the defense of Oahu and the repair of the Fleet.

On the morning of the 7th, Admiral Stark had ordered by dispatch the execution of the United States basic war plan,[17] which the Chicago *Tribune* had "patriotically" published to the world a few days before as evidence of the "duplicity" and "warmongering" of the Roosevelt Administration. Offensive movements of the

[17] "Rainbow 5" or WPL 46. The parts quoted here are printed in *Pearl Harbor Attack* Part 15 pp. 1425–29.

Pacific Fleet contemplated in this plan were the capture or neutral-ization of the Marshall and Caroline Islands, preparatory to estab-lishing an advanced naval base at Truk; and the support of British naval forces south of the Equator and westward to include the Solomons. Both these tasks being now impossible, Admiral Stark substituted others more in accord with reality.

According to this amended war plan, received at Pearl on the afternoon of 8 December, the primary duties of the Pacific Fleet were now defensive: to support the Army in protecting the Hawaiian Islands, Wake, Johnston and Palmyra; to protect sea communications of the Allies by routing and escorting shipping between American possessions and the 180th meridian, en route to New Zealand and Australia; and to prevent the extension of Jap-anese military power into the Western Hemisphere, including Fiji and Samoa. Submarines and fast carriers were given the tac-tically offensive mission of raiding Japanese sea communications and advanced bases. There was no question of using the depleted Pacific Fleet to defend Guam or the Philippines.

On the basis of this altered war plan, Admiral Kimmel's staff drew up on 10 December an estimate of the situation which was delivered to the Secretary of the Navy on his flying visit to Pearl next day. It opens with this bald statement: —

> With the losses we have sustained, it is necessary to revise com-pletely our strategy of a Pacific war. The loss of battleships commits us to the strategic defensive until our forces can again be built up. However, a very powerful striking force of carriers, cruisers and destroyers survives. These forces must be operated boldly and vigor-ously on the tactical offensive in order to retrieve our initial disaster.

The new tasks assigned by the modified war plan really boiled down to one broad immediate mission — retain what we had as a base for future offensives while securing communications along the lines Panama–Samoa–Fiji–New Zealand, and West Coast–Pearl–Fiji–New Caledonia–Australia. Although American mili-tary potentiality was much greater than the enemy's, Japan had put us on the defensive, "and that is hard for us to take." The Japanese had shown themselves far more daring and skillful in their use of sea and air power than we had anticipated.

The composition of the force that attacked Pearl,[18] and whither it had retired, "are still unknown"; but "we do know that Guam has fallen, Wake is under attack, some of the Gilbert Islands have been occupied, and enemy submarines are operating eastward from Oahu." [19] The possibility of a battleship force penetrating the Hawaiian area or beyond "must be considered, although the logistic requirements render such an operation unlikely." "By 15 December the Army expects to have 42 heavy and 10 medium bombers, and 62 fighter, pursuit and observation planes in Oahu; the Navy will have a maximum of 40 patrol planes operational," together with the 18 Marine Corps scout bombers that never got to Midway. Three 12-plane squadrons "are due shortly from the Coast." Logistic support of the American Pacific islands, difficult enough in peacetime, "will be far more so now"; "present deficiencies" at Oahu in ammunition, ordnance and supplies of every sort "are manifold." Replenishment and buildup "will impose heavy demands on the Fleet for convoy work."

The most probable enemy action in this theater, according to Cincpac, would be raids by fast striking forces on Oahu, Midway and the Aleutians; raids on Wake from shore bases "with possible landing attempts"; submarine and cruiser or converted merchantmen raids on shipping between coast and islands. "Covering or supporting groups of heavy forces including battleships must be anticipated when seeking or pursuing enemy forces outside the range of our shore-based aircraft." All this pointed to the following course of action for the Pacific Fleet: —

[18] The few Japanese prisoners taken (salvaged aviators and one midget submarine sailor) gave very accurate information of its strength, but Cincpac staff was not informed of these interrogations.

[19] U.S.A.T. *Cynthia Olsen* was sunk by a submarine about 1000 miles northeast of Oahu on 7 Dec.; S.S. *Lahaina* was shelled and sunk about 700 miles on the same bearing 11 Dec.; S.S. *Manini* was torpedoed and sunk 17 Dec. not far from Honolulu; S.S. *Prusa* was torpedoed and sunk 19 Dec. 150 miles south of Hawaii; tanker *Agwiworld* was shelled by a submarine 20 Dec. off Santa Cruz, Calif., but escaped; S.S. *Emidio* and *Samoa*, *Larry Doheny* and *Montebello* were attacked off the California coast before Christmas.

1. Employ three search-strike carrier groups, of which two will be constantly at sea and the third replenishing at Pearl, to intercept enemy raids and support menaced bases.

2. Organize battleships and destroyer types in escort groups for coast-to-islands convoy operations. Base the battleships at San Francisco to relieve congestion at Pearl; they will be relieved by Pearl-based cruiser and destroyer escort groups at a mid-ocean meeting point not far from the islands.

3. Strip the West Coast of all but local defense forces, which may be used as escorts for coastal convoys.

4. Employ submarines offensively in Japanese waters, and off Wake and Midway.

5. Organize a thorough offshore search with Army bombers and Navy patrol planes.[20]

6. Keep Australia-bound shipping to the minimum for which escorts are available.

7. Encourage and assist the Army to build up land-based pursuit and bomber strength on Oahu as rapidly as possible, and to establish a proper anti-aircraft defense of Pearl Harbor. A vast augmentation of ship and shore radar installations will be vitally necessary.

This was a sound and sane estimate of the situation that did credit to Admiral Kimmel and his staff. Operation plans based on it were immediately drawn up. News of the most disturbing nature was coming from Wake; there must be quick action to relieve the small Marine garrison of that lonely island.

---

[20] During the three months after their sneak attack, the Japanese reconnoitered Pearl Harbor with planes from the following submarines: *I–7* at dawn 16 Dec.; *I–19* by moonlight 4 Jan.; and *I–9* on night of 23 Feb. 1942. Capt. E. T. Layton "Rendezvous in Reverse" U. S. Naval Institute Proceedings pp. 478–485 (May 1953).

# CHAPTER XII

# Wake[1]

## 8–23 December 1941

Dates of events at Wake Island are East Longitude; times in Zone minus 11.

## 1. *Island Outpost*

WAKE is one of the loneliest atolls in the Pacific. A submerged volcano top, 450 miles from the nearest land, it consists of three low islands (Wilkes, Wake and Peale) disposed like a bony thumb and gnarled forefinger pointing northwestward. From thumbnail (Kuku Point) to finger tip (Toki Point) the land distance is only 13,500 yards by the shortest route, and to sail around the outer reef of the atoll one would have to log less than twenty nautical miles. The lagoon, chock full of nasty coral heads, is difficult of access; the only entrance to it, the 50-yard-wide channel between Wilkes and Wake Islands, would admit only small boats before being dredged. Rain is infrequent, and there are no springs of fresh water, or waving palm trees; only thick scrub such as the desert magnolia and Pisonia, growing to a maximum height of 10 feet. Pacific surges break incessantly on the fringing reef close offshore, and come hissing up the white sand beaches, splashing over big coral boulders and filling the air with a continual roar. Above it may be heard the screaming of boatswain

[1] Lt. Col. R. D. Heinl Jr. USMC *The Defense of Wake* (published 1947 by the Historical Section of the Marine Corps) utilized every available source, American and Japanese, including material obtained for this History in Japan. The best and most comprehensive work on Wake Island history, it was kindly placed at the writer's disposition in advance of publication. Lt. Col. James P. S. Devereux *The Story of Wake Island* (originally published serially in *Sat. Eve. Post* Feb.–March 1946) is a ghost-written book and so not very reliable.

and frigate birds, terns and boobies, which have shared Wake with land crabs and a peculiar breed of rat since time immemorial.

Discovered by Mendaña in 1568, named after the skipper of a British trading schooner that called in 1796, visited by the Wilkes Exploring Expedition in 1841, Wake was claimed and formally annexed by the United States on 17 January 1899. The visiting warship — gunboat *Bennington*, Commander E. D. Taussig — merely sent a boat ashore, hoisted a flag, fired a salute, lowered the flag and departed.

For countless ages this atoll slept and snored in the foam. From time to time a boat put ashore from a becalmed sailing ship to seek food and water in vain. The ubiquitous Jap occasionally called to kill seabirds and collect feathers. Remote from the trade routes of sail or of steam, the island was unwanted and all but forgotten until man had conquered the air.

Then Wake awoke. Here was the ideal fixed aircraft carrier — 1025 miles from Midway, 1300 from Guam; but — and this was ominous — only 764 from Japanese-held Marcus, 450 from Bikini, and 620 from Roi and Namur Islands of Kwajalein Atoll, the principal Japanese air base in the Mandates. Here was the missing and wanted link in the United States east-west axis (San Francisco–Pearl Harbor–Guam–Manila) of American sea and air power; but it would fit equally well into the northwest-southeast axis (Tokyo–Iwo Jima–Marcus–Wotje–Mili) of Japanese power. A presidential order at the end of 1939 placed Wake, like Guam and Midway, under the jurisdiction of the Navy. Officers and bluejackets from U.S.S. *Nitro* had already completed a survey of the atoll.

Before there was any opportunity to begin military installations, Pan American Airways decided to use the little island as a seaplane fueling base and overnight call on its pioneer transpacific route. Peale Island, which made a lee in the lagoon, was chosen for the seaplane station; but ships could only find a partial lee and precarious holding ground off the thumbnail, Wilkes Island. All supplies had to be landed there and lightered through a channel blasted across the lagoon through the coral heads. Dredging the boat chan-

Wake Atoll from the Air

Taken from a Liberator of the VII Army Air Force, 1944

Marine Camp 1, Wake Island, 1941

*Wake*

A Wildcat (F4F–3) of VMF–211

*PC–33* beached on south shore, Wake Island
(Photograph taken after Japanese surrender, 1945)

*Wake*

nel east of Wilkes Island started in May 1935, but even in December 1941 it was only 12 feet deep at high tide and 300 feet wide. A small hotel was built on Peale; rainwater catchments were constructed and a garden set out. Once a week Wake came to life to welcome a passing China Clipper of the Pan American fleet, and then dozed off until the next day of call.

Wake lost half its strategic importance in 1939 when Congress declined to strengthen Guam; for this meant that no attempt would be made to hold Guam when war broke with Japan. But Congress did adopt in 1940 the recommendations of the Hepburn Board to develop both Midway and Wake as air and submarine bases. The contract to build an airfield and facilities for amphibious patrol planes was let to an organization known as Contractors Pacific Naval Air Bases. Captain Ross A. Dierdorff brought out the pioneer work party in U.S.S. *William Ward Burrows* in January 1941.[2] Commander Campbell Keene with a small advanced naval base detachment arrived to combine patrol and air cover. Eventually some 1100 civilians began work there, under a courageous and competent civil engineer, Mr. Nathan Dan Teters. The thick part of Wake Island, where thumb and forefinger join inside of Peacock Point, was selected for the runways; a system of 30-foot-wide coral-surfaced roads was started; dredging of the channel continued, and work began on steel, glass and concrete buildings. The Japanese government, very much interested, sent up an occasional observation plane from the Marshalls. One can imagine the Japanese aviators leering down at this scene of activity, and thinking, "All working for our Emperor!"

Admiral Kimmel, in a letter of 18 April 1941 to the Chief of Naval Operations, pointed out the strategic importance of Wake in the event of hostilities, and urged that defensive measures be adopted at once. His letter was prophetic: —

As an operating patrol plane base, it could prove highly valuable to us in observing the Marshalls, or in covering the advance of our forces

[2] Capt. Dierdorff "Pioneer Party — Wake Island" *U.S. Naval Inst. Proc.* Apr. 1943 pp. 499–508.

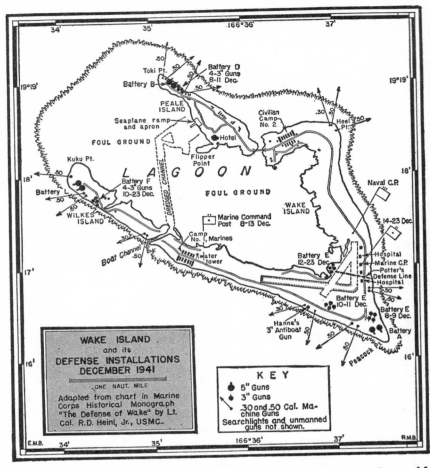

WAKE ISLAND
and its
DEFENSE INSTALLATIONS
DECEMBER 1941

ONE NAUT. MILE

Adapted from chart in Marine
Corps Historical Monograph
"The Defense of Wake" by Lt.
Col. R.D. Heinl, Jr., USMC.

K E Y
5" Guns
3" Guns
.30 and .50 Cal. Ma-
chine Guns
Searchlights and unmanned
guns not shown.

toward the Saipan–Honshu line. In the hands of the Japanese, it would be a serious obstacle to surprise raids in the Northern Marshalls, or on Marcus, Port Lloyd or Saipan, and would be capable of causing serious interference with other secret movements of our forces.

To deny Wake to the enemy, without occupying it ourselves, would be difficult; to recapture it, if the Japanese should seize it in the early period of hostilities, would require operations of some magnitude. Since the Japanese Fourth Fleet includes transports and troops with equipment especially suited for landing operations, it appears not unlikely that *one of the initial operations of the Japanese may be directed against Wake.*

If Wake be defended, then for the Japanese to reduce it would require extended operations of their naval force in an area where we might be able to get at them, *thus offering us an opportunity to get at naval forces with naval forces.*[3]

We have purposely italicized certain phrases of this letter in order to call attention to Admiral Kimmel's foresight and sagacity. Rear Admiral Bloch, who as Commandant Fourteenth Naval District had oversight of the improvements, pointed out the defenseless state of Wake while they were being effected. Until the channel and the lagoon could be dredged to sufficient depth, which he estimated would take two years, ships had to moor in the lee of Wilkes Island and discharge cargo into lighters, the average time of detention being ten days.[4] What a target for an enemy submarine! He and Kimmel therefore urged that substantial components of the 1st Defense Battalion, Fleet Marine Force, then at Pearl Harbor be sent to Wake by 1 June.[5]

It was not done that early — nothing was completed in time in the Pacific that year. The first detachment of the 1st Defense Battalion, 6 officers and 173 enlisted men, disembarked at Wake from U.S.S. *Regulus* on 19 August 1941. Major James P. S. Devereux came out in the same ship two months later, bringing three batteries, each of two 5-inch 51-cal. guns (removed from old battleships but excellent coast defense ordnance), three batteries, each of four 3-inch anti-aircraft guns (only one complete with its fire-control

[3] Cincpac to Opnav 18 Apr. 1941.
[4] Bloch to Stark, 7 May 1941, Navy "Narrative Statement of Evidence" before Hart Committee, I, 199.
[5] The defense battalion was a new development in the Marine Corps since 1939, for the special purpose of placing a ring of defensive fire around a small atoll or island. At the outbreak of war the typical Marine Defense Battalion consisted of a coast-defense group (six 5-inch 51-cal. naval guns, semimobile), an AA group (twelve 3-inch guns with the latest gun-director, computers, etc.), an MG group (48 .50-cal. for AA, 48 .30-cal. for beach defense), a searchlight battery, headquarters and service troops, with a total of 43 officers and 909 men. Only exceptionally, in Samoa, did a defense battalion include an infantry component, and, although air fighter defense might be furnished by a Marine air squadron, that was a separate command.
The deployment of defense battalions Fleet Marine Force on 7 Dec. 1941 was as follows: 1st, divided between Pearl Harbor, Johnston, Wake and Palmyra; 2nd and 7th, on Samoan Islands; 3rd and 4th, at Pearl Harbor; 5th, on Iceland; 6th, on Midway Island; 8th, being formed at San Diego; 9th, in cadre stage at Guantanamo.

equipment), twenty-four .50-cal. machine guns for anti-aircraft work, and a number of .30-cal. machine guns for beach defense. More Marines arrived 2 November, but there were never enough to man the guns. They had to play stevedore and lighterman whenever a supply ship arrived, and service and fuel the B–17s that were staging through Wake to Manila. The contractors' men were dredging, road-making and putting up buildings according to contract; Mr. Teters wished to knock off and help the Marines, but Major Devereux's plea to that effect was answered "negative" by Admiral Bloch.

The individual Marines of the defense battalion were equipped with Springfield rifles, khaki uniforms and the World War I type of steel helmet, together with other light infantry weapons normal for the period.

Eventually Wake was to become a base for Catalinas and other patrol planes. On 28 November 1941 Commander Winfield Scott Cunningham arrived with a few petty officers and bluejackets to take charge of the future naval air station.[6] Pending arrival of the PBYs, which could not be procured for several months, the Marine Corps had to furnish air protection. Major Paul Putnam's Fighter Squadron VMF–211, 12 Grumman Wildcats of an already obsolete type (F4F–3s),[7] was flown off carrier *Enterprise* on 4 December and landed safely. The one air strip then constructed was 5–6000 feet long and 200 feet wide. Underground gasoline storage was not complete; none of the complicated installations needed to operate an air squadron were there; not one revetment or dispersal area for planes had been built. And there was no search radar on the atoll to warn of an approaching enemy. An observation post on top of a water tank, with a seaward horizon of ten miles, was the makeshift substitute.

On 8 December 1941 — the day that the Japanese hit Pearl Harbor — there were on Wake 27 Marine Corps officers and 422

[6] Cdr. Cunningham by virtue of seniority over Maj. Devereux became atoll commander, but he was busy with preparations for the N.A.S. and took little part in defense measures.
[7] They had no armor and no self-sealing tanks.

men (including the aviators), 10 naval officers and 58 enlisted men (including hospital corpsmen), a small Army communications unit of 1 officer and 4 men, 70 Pan American Airways civilians and 1146 contractors' employees.[8] No women, to the eventual astonishment and disappointment of the Japanese. The Marine detachment was undermanned and overworked. All 3-inch and 5-inch guns had been emplaced in three strong points organized on Peale, Wilkes and Peacock Point; some protective sandbagging and camouflage had been set up; but planes had to be parked on the single runway, and ammunition was insufficient for a siege.

Sunday, 7 December, was a day of rest for the Marines on Wake, the first they had had since their arrival; and the last, until they entered the long rest of captivity or the longer one of death. A China Clipper arrived that evening from the eastward and took off at dawn for Guam.

Monday 8 December at 0650,[9] just as the Marines were finishing breakfast, a message came through that Pearl Harbor was under attack. Major Devereux sent for his "music" to come on the double, the bugler sounded Call to Arms, Marines grabbed rifles and spare ammunition, piled into trucks and rushed to their posts; aviators warmed up planes; civilians made for the bush and started digging foxholes; the China Clipper returned. Captain J. H. Hamilton, the Clipper pilot, agreed to fly a patrol 100 miles around the island with Wildcat escort. But before he had completed fueling, 18 Japanese bombers swooped out of a rain cloud onto the island.

## 2. *The First Japanese Attack, 8–11 December*[10]

The Japanese well appreciated the value of Wake Atoll — the "Heaven-gazing Mountain," as one of their war correspondents

[8] All civilians as well as the small Army and Navy detachments were completely unarmed.

[9] Corresponding to 0920 December 7, Hawaiian time.

[10] The Heinl monograph (see first footnote to this chapter) is comprehensive. Cdr. W. S. Cunningham's version is on a sound recording made 9 Jan. 1946 (Film No. 468, Office of Naval Records and Library). Of accounts written during the war, Hanson W. Baldwin "The Saga of Wake" *Virginia Quarterly Review* XVIII 32 (1942) is the best.

called it [11] — Heaven apparently meaning Hawaii, since the highest point on Wake is only 21 feet above sea level. Continued possession by us would be a constant air threat to the Marshalls; capture by them would provide a new link in their "ribbon defense" of the Pacific, a useful base for air reconnaissance, and a leg-up toward Midway, marked out for capture in a few months' time.

The Fourth Fleet, based at Truk, was designated by Admiral Yamamoto to take Wake. An amphibious task force was organized and sent up to Kwajalein in the Marshalls to stand by for X-day; but a preliminary air softening-up began with the Pearl Harbor raid.

The first bombing attack on Wake jumped the gun, as at Pearl, and air bombing continued until the Invasion Force arrived. Thirty-six 2-engined bombers based on Roi and Namur islands of Kwajalein Atoll, 620 miles to the southward, executed the day-bombing missions. The first strike, three 12-plane vees, dove onto the island out of a rain squall at noon 8 December. The surf was roaring so furiously that nobody ashore heard or saw the enemy until fifteen seconds before the first bombs hit. The planes leveled out at 2000 feet altitude and made for the airfield, where 8 Wildcats were being serviced and fueled. Here 4 grounded planes disintegrated under direct hits; fire spread to the rest and destroyed 3; the eighth was hit but later salvaged; 23 Marine officers and men were left dead or dying. The Japanese planes then delivered a heavy bombing and strafing attack on the Pan American air station. Nearly all facilities, including the hotel, were destroyed, and ten civilians killed. The Clipper resting in the lagoon was riddled by a machine-gun burst but not greatly injured, and took off for Midway with a capacity load of civilians in the early afternoon.

Within ten minutes the enemy planes, virtually undamaged by the hastily delivered anti-aircraft fire, pulled out for home. Every pilot was grinning widely and waggling his wings in triumph.

\*    \*    \*

[11] "Hawaii-Malaya Naval Operations," ATIS Enemy Publication No. 6, 27 Mar. 1943 p. 27.

Marines and a few civilian volunteers [12] worked all night 8–9 December repairing damage, building revetments, and mining the runway to frustrate an airborne landing. Next day, the 9th, Lieutenant D. D. Kliewer and Technical Sergeant W. J. Hamilton, flying 2 of the 3 Wildcats then operational, shot down a bomber, while anti-aircraft accounted for a second kill and damaged several more. But the bombing attack destroyed the Navy radio and hit the hospital, killing 4 Marines, several corpsmen and 55 civilians. A new hospital was set up in two underground magazines, a new radio was rigged; and Major Devereux, estimating that the next enemy target would be Battery E, had it displaced to a position 600 yards to the east and north. This proved to be a good guess, for the 27 bombers that came over on the 10th (less 2 shot down by Captain Elrod's Wildcat), first concentrated on Battery E's empty emplacements, while 10 made for Wilkes Island, where the Japanese intended to land. They strafed up, down and crossways and blew up a construction dump of 125 tons of dynamite. This set off all ready ammunition in near-by batteries and damaged the guns of Batteries F and L. To everyone's amazement, only 1 Marine was killed and 4 wounded in this attack.

Shortly after midnight — it was now 11 December — Marine lookouts reported blinking lights to the southward; and, in the light of the waning moon that rose before dawn, ships were visible, closing Peacock Point. The Invasion Force, commanded by Rear Admiral Kajioka in the small light cruiser *Yubari*, was contemptuously weak — 450 special naval landing troops embarked in two old converted destroyers (Patrol Craft *32* and *33*) similar to our APDs, and garrison troops embarked in medium-sized transports, escorted by six destroyers.[13] Two submarines were sent ahead to scout, and two old light cruisers *Tenryu* and *Tatsuta* acted as support force.

[12] A considerable number offered to enlist in the Marines, and 15 volunteers worked incessantly servicing the planes and working one of the guns. Maj. Putnam speaks in high praise of these men, especially of Dr. L. S. Shank, the contractors' physician. But the greater number of the civilian construction workers scattered to the bush and refused to work.

[13] *Yubari* was flagship of Desron 6, comprising *Mutsuki, Yayoi, Oite, Mochizuki, Kisaragi, Hayate.* The last two were sunk.

Rear Admiral Kajioka, faithful to Japanese naval tradition, rode ahead in his flagship. A heavy sea was running before a strong northeast tradewind. At 0500, just as day was breaking, the Japanese ships about 4 miles off Peacock Point swung to port for a run along the southern shore. The three light cruisers commenced firing, but did no damage except to set fire to oil tanks near Camp 1. In the meantime, the other ships deployed and the transports started boating their troops, with very slight success in the heavy sea. Major Devereux withheld fire until 0615, when *Yubari* and three destroyers in column had made another turn and closed to 4500 yards. Then the 5-inch Battery A, at Peacock strong point, commanded by 1st Lieutenant Clarence A. Barninger USMC, opened up. It caught *Yubari* between wind and water in the second salvo; at 5700 yards, nailed her twice more, and she limped over the horizon.

A few minutes later the 5-inch Battery L on Wilkes Island, commanded by 2nd Lieutenant John A. McAlister USMC, engaged several ships with excellent results, despite the previous loss of its rangefinder in the dynamite explosion. Selecting the leading ship of three destroyers, *Hayate*, Battery L delivered three 2-gun salvos so accurately that she blew up, broke in two and sank immediately.[14] The gun crews were so jubilant over this sight that they broke off firing to cheer, but were recalled to their duty by an old China hand, Platoon Sergeant Henry Bedell, who bellowed with a voice like thunder: "Knock it off, you bastards, and get back on the guns. What d'ya think this is, a ball game?" Battery L then took destroyer *Oite* under fire, and scored a hit on her too; next, it trained onto the leading transport. She, after taking one hit, turned seaward with the other *Maru*, retiring behind a destroyer smoke screen, and leaving the survivors of *Hayate* to drown. The same guns scored once on a light cruiser which turned away trailing smoke.

In the meantime the three destroyers not yet engaged had deployed to make a north-and-south run in order to enfilade both Wilkes and Peale Islands. In so doing they ran into the field of fire of Battery B, on Toki Point. First Lieutenant Kessler's 5-inch 51s

---

[14] *Inter. Jap Off.* II 373. The time v as 0652.

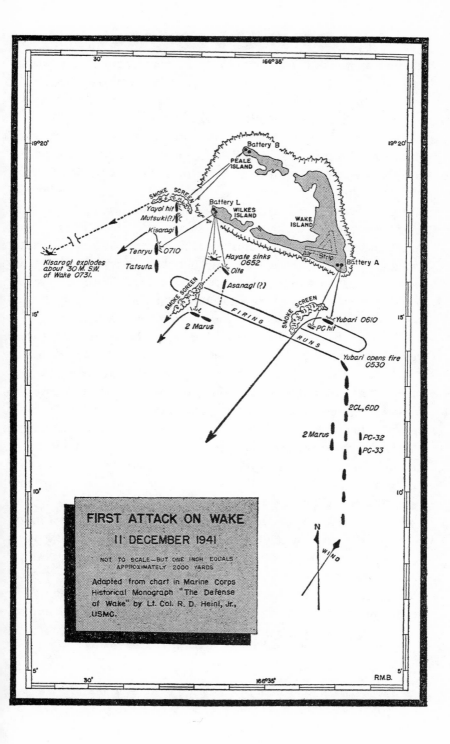

FIRST ATTACK ON WAKE

11 DECEMBER 1941

NOT TO SCALE—BUT ONE INCH EQUALS
APPROXIMATELY 2000 YARDS

Adapted from chart in Marine Corps
Historical Monograph "The Defense
of Wake" by Lt. Col. R. D. Heinl, Jr.,
USMC.

opened on the leading ship, *Yayoi*, scoring one hit. The enemy replied promptly, raking Peale Island, hitting all around the battery, and severing fire-control communications. Battery B shifted fire to another destroyer, and all three retired.

Four Wildcats now got into the battle, strafing the retreating ships and dropping their little 100-pound bombs from an extemporized release, returning to rearm, take off and bomb again. They put the torpedo battery of *Tenryu* out of action, hit the radio shack of *Tatsuta*, and started a severe gasoline fire on a transport. One plane was badly shot up; the pilot, Captain Elrod, just managed to ground it on the beach, burning and broken, but he had already made a lethal pass at the retreating destroyer *Kisaragi*, which carried an extra load of depth charges. A second Wildcat was just pushing over to press home an attack on this destroyer at 0731 when she blew up and sank. There were no survivors.

"Since we had already suffered losses and the defense guns were very accurate," said Captain Koyama, who was on board Kajioka's flagship, "the O.T.C. decided at 0700 to retire to Kwajalein and make another attempt when conditions were more favorable." [15] It was an ignominious retirement. Two destroyers and at least 500 Japanese had been lost; [16] only one American had been killed. To cap this victory for the Marines, their 2 remaining Wildcats ac-counted for 2 of the 18 bombers that made the regular morning "milk run," a third was shot down by anti-aircraft fire, and 4 more flew away smoking.

The eleventh day of December 1941 should always be a proud day in the history of the Corps. Never again, in this Pacific War, did coast defense guns beat off an amphibious landing. Major Devereux and his men were naturally elated. [17] The greater part of their guns, their men and their defenses were intact. But the air squadron was wasting away: only 2 Wildcats were still operational.

[15] *Inter. Jap. Off.* II 371.

[16] Maj. Devereux claims in *Story of Wake Island* p. 90 and in a letter to the writer that the official score was 9 ships and 5350 men, but he is mistaken. Only *Hayate* and *Kisaragi* were sunk; the others returned to Kwajalein and were repaired in time to take part in the second attempt ten days later.

[17] The message SEND US MORE JAPS, attributed to Devereux that day, was never sent by him or anyone else.

They had no illusions about the future and expected the enemy to return in greater force; but they assumed that the Navy would make an earnest attempt to relieve them.

## 3. *The Abortive Relief Expedition, 14–23 December* [18]
### West Longitude dates

It was almost nine months since Admiral Kimmel had written that the defense of Wake would force the Japanese to deploy a part of their Fleet, thus affording us "opportunity to get at naval forces with naval forces. We should try by every possible means to get the Japanese to expose naval units."

His wish was about to be granted. And to make it come true, he conceived a three-pronged expedition, the most formidable United States naval operation of 1941. Organizing and dispatching this force was the last important official act of Admiral Kimmel, and it did him and his staff credit. If pushed through, it might have retrieved his and the Navy's reputation.

Kimmel's plan for relieving Wake was sound, but the execution was attended by many misfortunes. Conceived as early as 9 December, it was doomed to failure by our delays and the enemy's brisk promptitude. All three fast carrier forces Pacific Fleet were to be employed. Wilson Brown's group built around *Lexington* (now designated Task Force 11) was to execute a diversionary raid on Jaluit in the hope of pinning down enemy air and surface forces in the Marshalls, and inflicting destruction. Halsey's *Enterprise* group (Task Force 8) was to fuel in Pearl after the other two had left, operate to the westward of Johnston Island in order to cover Oahu, and if necessary support the main strike.

The actual relief of Wake, the principal mission, was given to an improvised task force which had never sailed as a unit, built around carrier *Saratoga*, then flying the flag of Rear Admiral

[18] Besides the official reports and logs quoted hereinafter, and the message file, there is an excellent article by Lt. Col. R. D. Heinl, Jr. usmc, "We're Headed for Wake" in *Marine Corps Gazette* June 1946. The author was C.O. of one of the batteries loaded in U.S.S. *Tangier*.

Aubrey W. Fitch. It had to be "Sara" rather than "Lady Lex" or the "Big E," because she was then bringing out from San Diego the Marine Corps Fighter Squadron 221 (18 Brewster Buffaloes with full personnel and equipment) to reinforce Squadron 211. Seaplane tender *Tangier*, at Pearl Harbor — promptly loaded with supplies, ammunition and equipment for the beleaguered Marine defense battalion at Wake — awaited arrival of *Saratoga* to proceed.

In view of the great significance of this Wake expedition, and the necessity for prompt, decisive execution of the plan, the choice of a commander for the whole Task Force became exceptionally important. In retrospect, it appears that Admiral Kimmel may have doomed his own project by a perfunctory handling of the command assignment. Circumstances dictated that *Saratoga* be the one carrier of the expedition, and Rear Admiral Fitch was in her. The only heavy cruisers available to operate with *Saratoga* were the three remaining of Cruiser Division 6, *Astoria*, *Minneapolis* and *San Francisco*, commanded by Rear Admiral Frank Jack Fletcher.[19] He and Fitch had been classmates at the Naval Academy, but Fletcher graduated well up in the first half and Fitch very near the anchor. Fletcher had shown outstanding merit in the lower ranks. Salty, genial and popular, he became a flag officer earlier than Fitch; but he had had no carrier experience. "Jakey" Fitch, on the other hand, was probably the most experienced carrier admiral in the Navy. An aviator since 1930, he had commanded patrol wings, naval air stations and three flat-tops in succession. For the past year he had been commander of a carrier division. There was nothing in Navy regulations that compelled Kimmel to give Fletcher the command. He could, after asking Fletcher's permission as a matter of courtesy, have appointed Fitch to command the Task Force; or he could have ordered Fletcher to stay ashore during the operation. But he did the conventional thing, and ap-

[19] Frank Jack Fletcher, nephew of Capt. Frank "Pat" Fletcher and of Rear Admiral Frank Friday Fletcher, famous characters in the old Navy. Born Marshalltown, Iowa, 1885, one of the Medal of Honor men at Vera Cruz in 1914, he commanded a destroyer in World War I. Subsequently took the Naval and Army War College courses, served as chief of staff Asiatic Fleet, aide to Secretary Swanson, and C.O. *New Mexico*. Became Comcrudiv 3 with rank of Rear Admiral in 1939.

pointed the senior flag officer task force commander, without, apparently, making any serious effort to determine whether or not Fletcher's conception of the operation was such that he could be relied upon to overcome unforeseen difficulties and accomplish the mission. In advance, with a plan involving carrier operations which might have to be executed in the face of an enemy assault on Wake, logic would seem to have indicated Fitch for the command. Today, with the record before us, it is evident that the failure to relieve Wake resulted from Admiral Pye's decision not to risk the loss of any of his three precious carriers, and not from any lack of aviation knowledge.

Fletcher's cruiser division entered Pearl 10 December, but he could not assemble his task force and get going until *Saratoga* arrived and refueled.

One delay after another slowed up the relief expedition, while the sands were running out on Wake. The initial one — subsequently blamed by Admiral Pye for all the rest — was the inability of *Lexington* to fuel at sea, owing to rough weather. Admiral Brown's force finally completed fueling at Pearl on the afternoon of the 14th. It included heavy cruisers *Indianapolis*, *Chicago* and *Portland*, Destroyer Squadron 1 (Captain A. R. Early) and fleet oiler *Neosho*. Brown's orders were to support Fletcher's relief of Wake by a diversionary air bombing attack on Jaluit on or before 22 December.

This objective was based on faulty intelligence. Owing to the tight secrecy Japan had maintained in the Mandates, nobody in the United States knew what really went on there. It was estimated that Jaluit would prove to be the most important center of enemy power to the east of Truk; but all the Japanese had done was to start work on a seaplane base. This was more than half complete by 1 November 1941, but no seaplanes had yet been flown in.[20]

Admiral Brown felt uneasy about this mission from the first; and at his request, just before sailing, Admiral Kimmel gave him the

[20] Maj. Robert E. Hatton usmcr "Survey of Jaluit Atoll, Overall Military Effects of Air Attack, etc.," USSBS Guam–Marshalls–Gilberts–New Britain Party 24 Oct. 1945 p. 2.

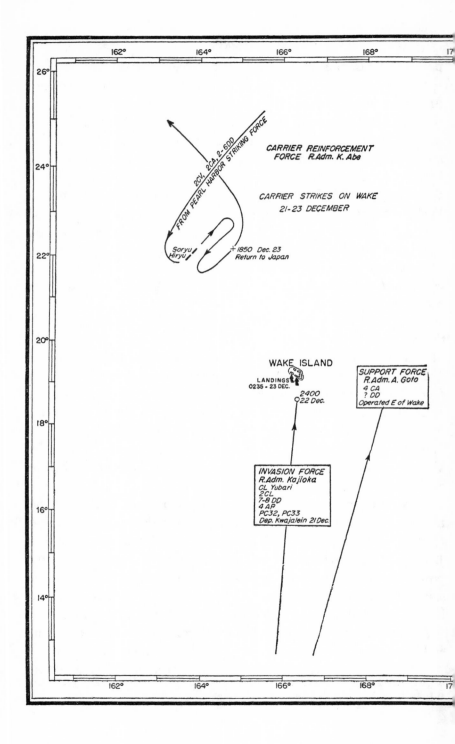

162°     164°     166°     168°

26°

CARRIER REINFORCEMENT
FORCE R.Adm. K. Abe

24°        CARRIER STRIKES ON WAKE
21-23 DECEMBER

2CV, 2CA, 2-6DD

FROM PEARL HARBOR STRIKING FORCE

Soryu
Hiryu        +1850 Dec. 23
22°                Return to Japan

20°

WAKE ISLAND                    SUPPORT FORCE
LANDINGS                       R.Adm. A. Goto
0235 - 23 DEC.                 4 CA
                2400           ? DD
             22 Dec.           Operated E of Wake
18°

INVASION FORCE
R.Adm. Kajioka
CL Yubari
2CL
16°                        7-8 DD
                           4 AP
                           PC32, PC33
                           Dep. Kwajalein 21 Dec.

14°

162°     164°     166°     168°

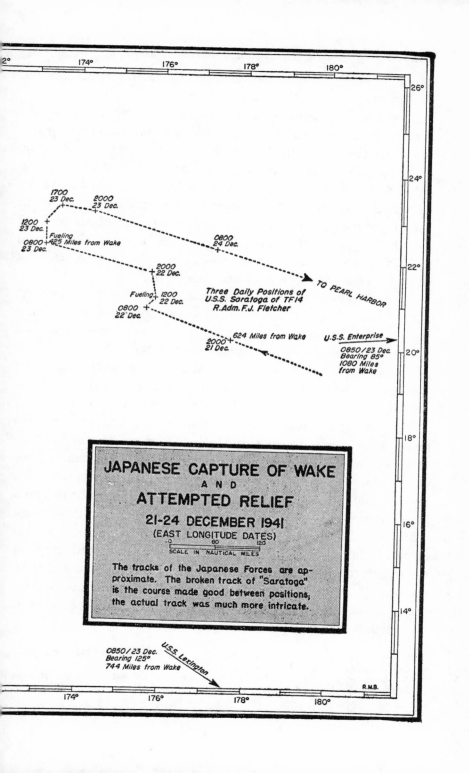

174° 176° 178° 180°

26°

24°

1700
23 Dec.
2000
23 Dec.

1200
23 Dec.
Fueling
0800 425 Miles from Wake
23 Dec.

0800
24 Dec.

22°

2000
22 Dec.

Fueling 1200
22 Dec.

Three Daily Positions of
U.S.S. Saratoga of TF14
R.Adm.F.J. Fletcher

0800
22 Dec.

624 Miles from Wake

2000
21 Dec.

TO PEARL HARBOR

U.S.S. Enterprise

0850/23 Dec.
Bearing 85°
1080 Miles
from Wake

20°

18°

## JAPANESE CAPTURE OF WAKE
### A N D
## ATTEMPTED RELIEF
### 21-24 DECEMBER 1941
(EAST LONGITUDE DATES)

0        60       120

SCALE IN NAUTICAL MILES

The tracks of the Japanese Forces are approximate. The broken track of "Saratoga"
is the course made good between positions,
the actual track was much more intricate.

16°

14°

0850/23 Dec.
Bearing 125°
744 Miles from Wake

U.S.S. Lexington

R.M.B.

174° 176° 178° 180°

option to shift his objective or to retire, as circumstances and his best judgment might dictate.

This task force departed Pearl on the afternoon of 14 December. On the morning of the 16th, three of *Lexington's* scout planes reported an enemy carrier "of the *Ryuzyo* class," with no planes on deck, 95 miles to the southward; they dropped bombs but missed. Admiral Brown ordered *Lexington* to launch an attack, and detached oiler *Neosho* to the westward, lest enemy carrier planes hit her. An attack group of 29 bombers and 7 fighter planes took off from *Lexington* for the target. The Japanese "carrier," alas, proved to be a derelict dynamite barge which a naval tugboat had cast adrift off Oahu during the 7 December battle.[21]

On 17 December this *Lexington* group held anti-aircraft practice, but the ammunition on board the cruisers completely failed to function; not reassuring to a force that expected to engage land-based planes, and possibly carrier-based planes as well. Next day there arrived from Pearl a greatly exaggerated Intelligence report of the Japanese occupation of the Gilbert Islands on 9–10 December. Actually, the enemy had placed only a token force on Tarawa and a small base-construction unit for setting up a seaplane base, together with a few seaplanes, at Makin. Cincpac's staff intelligence officer, however, believed that the redoubtable Yokohama Corps of the Japanese Air Fleet, comprising from 40 to 200 planes with a big seaplane tender,[22] had already reached Makin, ready to bomb any United States ship that came within range. In order to reach Jaluit, Admiral Brown's force would have to pass about 100 miles north of Makin, with Mili Atoll, of unknown air potentialities, on the starboard hand. Cincpac, moreover, informed Brown that to the best of his belief the Japanese overall submarine commander was at Jaluit, which suggested that a large submarine force had been deployed in the vicinity.

[21] This was the barge that *Antares* was towing when trailed by the midget submarine subsequently sunk by *Ward*.
[22] This vessel was actually the 4400-ton minelayer *Okinoshima*. The Japanese also visited Nonuti and Beru in the Gilberts to gather up British officials, but withdrew.

Accordingly, it is not surprising that Admiral Brown concluded that he was steaming into a trap, running a grave risk of losing *Lexington* to air or submarine attack. On the afternoon of the 20th he had just decided to exercise his option, and to attack Makin instead of Jaluit, when he received new orders from Admiral Pye, who had relieved Admiral Kimmel as Commander in Chief Pacific Fleet. The *Lexington* force was ordered to turn northward and render support to Admiral Fletcher, then slowly closing Wake.[23] That was a wise move, on the assumption that Fletcher would be allowed to execute his mission; for any damage that the *Lexington* could have inflicted on Makin at that early stage of its development was not to be balanced against the possible risk, or the aid she might render to *Saratoga* off Wake.

Admiral Halsey's *Enterprise* group was unfortunately doomed by circumstances to play a purely passive rôle in this sad drama — that of covering the Hawaiian Islands within support distance of a possible sea fight. His Task Force 8 entered Pearl for fuel and replenishment on 16 December, after *Saratoga* had departed, and sailed at 1000 December 20. Halsey steamed westerly to a position about 230 miles south by east of Midway [24] by noon of the 23rd, passed about 100 miles to the westward of Midway, hovered about that area for a couple of days, and entered Pearl at noon on the last day of 1941, after an uneventful cruise in which not even a firm submarine contact was made.

Two submarines of the Pacific Fleet, *Tambor* and *Triton*, had been patrolling the waters around Wake without rendering any assistance to the defenders. *Triton* fired four torpedoes at an enemy ship on 10 December, but missed; neither submarine took part in the fight on the 11th. *Tambor* developed a bad leak and pulled out for Pearl on the 16th; *Triton* was recalled by Cincpac on the 21st lest she mistake the approaching Task Force 14 for the enemy.[25]

[23] CTF 11 to Cincpac, Report on Operations 14–27 Dec. 1941, 26 Dec. 1941; *Lexington* War Diary.
[24] Lat. 24°32'15" N, long. 176°25'15" W.
[25] Statement by Vice Admiral McMorris Jan. 1947.

So much for the supporting forces. The mission for the direct relief of Wake was entrusted to Admiral Fletcher's force, built around *Saratoga,* beloved "old Sara" who fought her way across the Pacific and back again and again, giving and receiving blows until she was sacrificed to the atomic gods at Bikini. News of the Pearl Harbor attack found her rounding Point Loma, San Diego. She made a quick turnaround, passed Point Loma outbound at 1019 December 8, escorted by three old destroyers, and made good a speed of 20 to 21 knots, all that the four-pipers could stand even in a moderate sea. She was routed to the southward of Hawaii in order to avoid an enemy submarine. That detour would not have prevented her from making Pearl by sundown 14 December, but a midget-sub scare in Pearl did; she was diverted when some 90 miles off the harbor entrance and finally entered Pearl at 0900 December 15, with barely enough fuel left to coast into her berth.[26]

The Marine defense reinforcements had been loaded in *Tangier,* which swung idly around the hook for two days waiting for the carrier to appear. Time was running so short that Admiral Kimmel sent *Tangier* and fleet oiler *Neches* ahead on the 15th, escorted by a destroyer division, while *Saratoga* finished fueling. The carrier finally got under way at 1115 December 16, in company with cruisers *Minneapolis, Astoria* and *San Francisco,* and Destroyer Squadron 4 (Captain J. H. S. Dessez).

So many rumors, alarms and dire predictions were in circulation while "Sara" and her consorts were in port that they set forth into an ocean that seemed full of Japanese; Columbus's men could hardly have found the Atlantic more inscrutable and less friendly.[27] Submarines were popping up around the islands; Midway and Johnston had been shelled; nobody knew whither the "bastards" who blitzed Pearl had retired. Most of the sailors and aviators expected

[26] *Saratoga* log; conversations with Vice Admirals Fitch and McMorris in 1947. Some careless engineer had been using her reserve fuel tanks for water ballast. Her log shows that until this discovery forced a reduction to 15 knots, or when fueling the DDs, the disposition maintained a speed of 20–21 knots from San Diego, whence it sailed on the 18th. It could not have done much better for that distance without refueling.
[27] Lt. Col. Heinl in *Marine Corps Gazette* June 1946 p. 37.

to engage a major fleet of the Japanese Navy, and regarded themselves as expendable; but all were grimly determined to put up a
good fight. Not a man jumped ship at Pearl.

Admiral Fletcher caught up with the *Tangier-Neches* convoy
during the forenoon watch of the 17th, and sent their destroyer
escort back to Pearl. Owing to the sluggishness of the oiler — and
none faster was available — the maximum speed of advance was only
12¾ knots.[28] Fair days with a light ENE tradewind and calm sea
passed uneventfully, the Date Line was crossed on 20/21 December,
and fueling of the destroyers commenced at daylight on the 22nd,
just when wind and sea were making up.

No naval commander likes to risk battle with half-empty destroyers. Fletcher's orders were to fuel at discretion; but this was no time
to do it. He was receiving dispatches from Wake that indicated
clearly enough the desperate plight of the defenders. At 1000 on the
21st (local time, East Longitude date) Commander Cunningham
sent out from Wake an "urgent" that he had just been attacked by
carrier-borne dive-bombers, and at noon he stated that 17 heavy
bombers had followed this up, inflicting heavy damage on the
meager island defenses; all the Marine Corps planes were already
shot up. If Fletcher felt that he could not risk a battle without fueling, he should have commenced fueling then and there, when he
had an exceptionally good chance, with a 5 to 8 knot northwest
wind and smooth sea; having missed that chance, he should have
pressed on to execute his mission, regardless of the destroyers.[29]

[28] CTF 14 (Rear Admiral Fletcher) "Report of Operations 16–29 Dec. 1941."
[29] Since my last edition appeared, I have been convinced that Admiral Fletcher
was ordered by disptach from Cincpac to fuel when and where he did, because it
was then hoped to have Admiral Brown's task force join him, and Brown had to
know where to find him. The logs of the four destroyers with least amount of
fuel oil on hand at 0000 Dec. 22 (E. Long. date), state the following:

|  | On hand |
|---|---|
| *Mugford* | 94,188 |
| *Jarvis* | 90,918 |
| *Patterson* | 89,923 |
| *Blue* | 96,000 |

Although consumption might easily surpass 15,000 gallons per diem in a running
fight, it is clear that there was no immediate danger of the DDs going dry unless

The cause of this marked contrast to the aggressiveness of the Japanese Pearl Harbor Striking Force which had been ordered to press home its attack without destroyers was the risk of losing more than could be won by keeping on.

At 2000 on the 21st (East Longitude date) *Saratoga* was just 600 miles from Wake; that was the time for a run-in at 20 knots, which would have encountered the Japanese Invasion Force just before dawn on the 23rd. But Admiral Fletcher elected to fuel next day, and, on the 22nd, although the wind was not excessive (16 to 24 knots), a long cross-swell made fueling difficult. Several towlines parted, seven oil hoses were ruptured, and only four destroyers were filled during a ten-hour fueling period, during which the speed of advance slowed to 6 or 8 knots.[30] Actually, several of the ships even increased their distance from Wake while the fueling continued, owing to the necessity of heading up into the brisk tradewind. At the end of the morning watch on the 23rd, *Saratoga* was less than a hundred miles nearer Wake than she had been twenty-four hours before.[31] And the Admiral still had four more destroyers to be fueled on that day, whose dawn saw the last of the Star-Spangled Banner on Wake for almost four years.

## 4. *The Second Japanese Attack, 20–23 December*

After the failure of its first attempt on 11 December, Admiral Inouye's Fourth Fleet mounted a second and more formidable invasion force with an alacrity that the United States Navy could not then have approached.

---

the force tanker was sunk. The disposition was about 750 miles ENE of Wake at 0800 that day. And the cruisers had oil to spare for the destroyers. At 0000 Dec. 23 (E. Long. date) *San Francisco* had 422,646 gals. or 70.38 per cent capacity, and *Minneapolis* 462,070, or 77 per cent capacity.

[30] CTF 14 Report and *Saratoga* log.

[31] *Saratoga*'s positions: —

| | | | |
|---|---|---|---|
| 21 Dec. 2000 | 20°16′ N | 177°38′ E | 625 miles to go |
| 22 Dec. 0800 | 21°02′ N | 175°27′ E | 515 miles to go |
| 1200 | 21°17′ N | 175°52′ E | |
| 2000 | 21°50′ N | 175°44′ E | |
| 23 Dec. 0800 | 22°39′ N | 173°15′ E | 425 miles to go |

The original Invasion Force, less the two destroyers sunk by the
Marines, retired to Kwajalein Lagoon, arriving on 13 December.
Other destroyers were substituted for those lost, and a third was
added. Besides the two transports and two large patrol craft that
took part in the 11 December fiasco, Kajioka now had a transport,
a minelayer and a seaplane tender loaded with Special Naval Landing Force troops, some of whom had already taken part in the
occupation of Guam. Probably there were about 2000 of these
tough, seasoned and well-practiced "Jap Marines" to oppose some
500 United States Marines on Wake.[32]

Rear Admiral Kajioka was given a chance to regain face by re-
taining command of the actual Striking Force, and his light cruiser
*Yubari*, which the Marines believed they had sunk, was patched up
in time to serve again as flagship. The two old light cruisers,
*Tenryu* and *Tatsuta*, again tagged along. Vice Admiral Inouye sent
Kajioka a strong support force from Truk, commanded by Rear
Admiral A. Goto, comprising heavy cruisers *Aoba*, *Kinugasa*,
*Furutaka* and *Kako* and destroyers which had supported the invasion of Guam. Coöperating air forces were enlarged by flying into
the Marshalls, seaplane carrier *Chitose's* air group of 28 flying boats.
But the most formidable increment of air and surface support, detached from Admiral Nagumo's Pearl Harbor Striking Force on
its homeward passage, comprised carriers *Soryu* and *Hiryu*, each
with 54 planes, heavy cruisers *Tone* and *Chikuma* and two or more
destroyers. This force, commanded by Rear Admiral Hiroaki Abe,
maneuvered in an area about 200 miles northwest of Wake, and
launched its first bomber strike on the 21st.

Kajioka departed Kwajalein 20 December for a pre-dawn landing on Wake on the 23rd. Meantime, the defenders were being
worn down by repeated air strikes. On 12, 14, 15, 16, 17 and 19 De-

[32] Capt. Koyama's account in *Inter. Jap. Off.* II 372 says "We embarked about
250 troops on each of the 800-ton transports," and leaves it to be inferred that they
took the island; but the information obtained by Lt. Cdr. Salomon shows that the
Invasion Force was constituted as above with four APs and two large PCs, and our
Marines were certain that at least 1200 troops landed early on the 23rd. The rest
went ashore after the surrender.

cember the island was bombed at noontime by planes from Kwajalein, the largest flight numbering 51 bombers; and at dawn or dusk
by four-engined flying boats [33] which terrified the civilian personnel
and took several brave men out of the defense picture. Every day
one or two planes, the valiant remnant of Squadron 211, took the
air to patrol and intercept; and a third, destroyed on the ground,
was replaced by cannibalizing others. All above-ground installations were being systematically demolished. Long hours of hard
work, day and night bombings, insufficient food and rest, were
wearing the Marines down. A Catalina flew in from Pearl on the
20th with official mail, and particulars of the relief expedition that
had sailed three days earlier; this was a great help to morale. By
return mail, Major Devereux begged to have the civilians evacuated,
and asked his commanding officer at Pearl "to try to stop the
ridiculous and exasperating dispatches we were getting." [34]

Two hours after the PBY departed, at 0850 December 21, the
island received its first attack by carrier-borne planes: 29 "Vals"
covered by 18 "Zekes" lashed down through the overcast on all
battery positions, ineffectively. Repeated strafing runs failed to hit
one grounded Wildcat; the other was promptly flown off by
Major Putnam to search for the carriers, but he had not enough gas
to follow the planes back to their ships. At noon the same day, land-
based bombers knocked out the fire director of Battery D. Next day
a second carrier-borne raid by 39 planes shot down the last two
Wildcats — together with Captain Freuler, who crash-landed after
accounting for two "Zekes," and Lieutenant Davidson, who was
killed when alone trying to break up a group of bombers. Major

[33] There were 15 of these, based at Majuro until 13 Dec. and thereafter at Wotje
in the Marshalls. They also flew bombing missions against Nauru and Ocean
Islands.
[34] *Sat. Eve. Post* 23 Feb. 1946 p. 90. For instance, on the 17th, Commandant 14th
Naval District radioed that dredging of the channel should continue; "Give estimated date of completion." To which Cdr. Cunningham replied, "We are concerned only with preserving life and defending the island. No night work possible
without lights; daytime work interrupted by air raids and we have no radar. Our
equipment is greatly reduced and we have no repair facilities. . . . Civilian workers' morale extremely low. . . . No estimate of date of completion can be made.
This outlook would be improved by relief."

Putnam and the pitiful remnant of VMF–211, twenty officers and men, now joined the Marine Defense Battalion as infantrymen.

That evening the Japanese Invasion Force took positions for the landing. The Support Force, of four heavy and two light cruisers, maneuvered about 150 to 200 miles to the eastward of Wake,[35] as if tempting Admiral Fletcher to come in; but that day his task force was fueling at a safe distance to the ENE. The two Japanese carriers with their attendant cruisers and destroyers were operating 200 to 250 miles northwestward of Wake. Shortly after midnight Marine lookouts on Wake observed gunfire flashes over the horizon. Probably this was anti-aircraft fire at imaginary Wildcats, for the enemy was too smart this time to alert the Marine batteries by bombardment.

It was now 0235 December 23. The Japanese made simultaneous pre-dawn assaults with four to six landing barges containing about 50 men each, and the two patrol craft, on Wilkes Island and the southern shore of Wake. These carried about 1000 men of the Maizuru 2nd Special Naval Landing Force, the Japanese equivalent of a Marine Battalion Landing Team. The weather was rough and squally. The detachment that hit Wilkes, 100 picked men, was met at the water's edge by Captain W. M. Platt's unit of 70 Marines, armed with rifles and hand grenades, and, after a bitter struggle lasting all of four hours, was almost wiped out.

The Marines' 5-inch guns were unable to bear either on this landing or the next one to the eastward, which was effected by landing barges and the patrol craft, which were run ashore on the south coast of Wake Island. These were immediately taken under fire by one 3-inch anti-boat gun emplaced to the southward of the diagonal runway, manned by 2nd Lieutenant R. M. Hanna USMC and a scratch crew of twelve. They scored some 15 hits on the grounded patrol craft, killing the captain and causing the ship to burst into flames; but most of the troops got ashore. One company attacked Hanna's gun, around which Major Putnam and Captain

[35] Capt. Koyama *Inter. Jap. Off.* II 372. The Marines, however, insist that they sighted the heavy cruisers from the island on the morning of the 23rd.

Elrod, with the remnant of VMF–211 and a few civilians, had formed a defense line. These brave fighting men resisted several hundred Japanese for six hours, when all but one of them were killed or wounded. The rest of the enemy forces on Wake Island fanned out, engulfing small knots of defenders.

There were now between 1000 and 1500 troops ashore, opposed by fewer than 80 Marines, as most of the defenders were still on Peale or on the northern limb of Wilkes Island.

The invaders were held up in front of Camp 1, whose flagstaff was shot away; but the Stars and Stripes was hoisted on the near-by water tower. The enemy captured the hospital, killed a civilian and trussed up the wounded Marines with wire; but Major Potter and 40 men resisted them from a defense line that crossed the airfield. Then, at 0700, carrier-based dive-bombers appeared and attacked all positions incessantly. Over 20 ships were counted off shore, and some of them were firing too.

Commander Cunningham from his command post had already sent this dispatch to Pearl at 0250 on the 23rd: —

ENEMY APPARENTLY LANDING.

And a little over two hours later, at 0500: —

THE ENEMY IS ON THE ISLAND. THE ISSUE IS IN DOUBT.

His last dispatch, sent about 0630, reported that the island was ringed with ships, which prudently kept beyond range of the Marines' 5-inch guns.

Communications had been broken between Major Devereux's command post and the Wilkes Island strong point, as between various knots of defenders on Wake Island. Although Captain Platt's unit had the situation on Wilkes well in hand, the Japanese had established a command post on that island and surrounded it with a ring of flags so that the fire support ships would spare it. Marines on Peale and Wake Islands, looking across the lagoon, saw numerous Rising Sun flags fluttering in the tradewind and assumed that Platt had been overcome. Platt eventually mopped up the flag-waving detachment by a skillfully executed counterattack which killed every Japanese but one (who played dead); but this action came too late to affect the outcome.

Commander Cunningham, who had no knowledge of the movements of the relief force, was trying to direct *Triton* to attack the Japanese ships ringing Wake. His dispatch to the submarine was intercepted by Cincpac, who informed him by radio dispatch at 0319 Wake time [36] that the two United States submarines were already returning to Pearl Harbor, and that no friendly ships would be in the vicinity of Wake during the next 24 hours. It was easy to infer from the last clause that no assistance was to be expected from Fletcher's carrier force.

By 0500, half an hour before first dawn, the Japanese, in strength capable of overwhelming the defenders at any point, had secured a firm beachhead and were steadily exploiting their initial gains. Everywhere they had been checked and suffered losses, including Lieutenant Uchida, who led the attack against the Marine position about the 3-inch anti-boat gun; but nowhere except on Wilkes were they stopped. And there was still a strong floating reserve on board the ships.

## 5. *Recall and Surrender*

"A victory is very essential to England at this moment," said Admiral Sir John Jervis one morning long ago, when sighting a Spanish fleet of almost twice his strength. He promptly closed and won the Battle of Cape St. Vincent.[37] God knows, America needed a victory before Christmas 1941. Admiral Kimmel had done all that he could do to provide the set-up, and the enemy's eagerness to capture Wake had brought important units of the Japanese Fleet within reach, just as he had hoped. Yet there was not even an engagement.

If Admiral Kimmel had been allowed to retain the Pacific Fleet

[36] Cincpac file; letter of Capt. W. S. Cunningham to the writer 7 Feb. 1947.
[37] W. V. Anson *Life of John Jervis Admiral Lord St. Vincent* p. 157.

command a few days longer, Wake might have been relieved, and there would certainly have been a battle. But President Roosevelt, on the advice of Secretary Knox, relieved Kimmel from active service in the Navy on 17 December, the day after *Saratoga* sailed from Pearl. His successor, Admiral Chester W. Nimitz, was an admirable and fortunate choice; but Nimitz was then in Washington and could not reach Pearl Harbor for several days; someone on the spot had to be designated Commander in Chief Pacific Fleet *pro tem*. The man chosen was Vice Admiral W. S. Pye, Commander Battle Force, who had lost his flagship *California* in the Battle of Pearl Harbor.

Admiral Pye [38] was one of the most respected senior officers of the Navy, especially for his knowledge of strategy. His mental attitude toward an immediate problem was the opposite to that of his predecessor. Kimmel was inclined to make up his mind what the enemy would do, and act accordingly; Pye, on the contrary, could apprehend everything that the enemy might do, but was inclined to wait and see what developed before doing anything himself. By the time Pye took command, his fleet intelligence officer had worked out, from plans found in a Japanese bomber that crashed in an Oahu canefield, that there had been six carriers, two battleships and two heavy cruisers in the force that attacked Pearl Harbor. Where were they now? Nobody knew; but it was conjectured that some ships, including at least one carrier, had peeled off from the Japanese force on its homeward passage, and in the direction of Wake.

On 20 December, as we have seen, Admiral Pye diverted Admiral Brown's *Lexington* force northward to support Fletcher. In so informing Washington he observed that maintenance of the Pacific

[38] William Satterlee Pye, born Minneapolis 1880, Naval Academy '01, Fleet Intelligence, Tactical, and War Plans officer on the staff of Commander in Chief Atlantic Fleet in World War I. Between the two wars he served as exec. of *Pennsylvania*, C.O. of *Nevada*, member of War Plans Division, Office of Naval Operations (in which capacity he drafted the Basic War Plan for the Pacific), assistant to President Naval War College, Commander Destroyers Battle Force, Commander Battleships, and from 31 Jan. 1941 Commander Battle Force with rank of Vice Admiral.

Fleet's strength was absolutely essential to defend Hawaii. Admiral Stark replied with the discouraging remark that both he and Admiral King considered Wake Island to be a liability, and authorized Admiral Pye at his discretion to evacuate the forces there rather than strengthen them.

That left the decision squarely up to Admiral Pye. As a stopgap commander, he did not wish to make Admiral Nimitz a Christmas present of more casualties. During 21/22 December, the day that Fletcher was fueling destroyers and increasing rather than closing his distance from Wake, Pye sent him several conflicting dispatches. *Saratoga* was to proceed up to a distance of 200 miles from Wake and there launch her planes to search out and attack the enemy. That was countermanded. *Tangier* was to be sent ahead unescorted to evacuate Marines and civilians from Wake. That was countermanded. The general impression was one of irresolution at Pacific Fleet headquarters, which was correct. But that was the more reason why Fletcher should have pressed forward to meet the enemy. By the evening of 21/22 December, Fleet Intelligence at Pearl Harbor estimated that at least two Japanese carriers, two battleships and two heavy cruisers were operating near Wake. Admiral Pye began to feel very anxious about the safety of *Saratoga*. If she were sunk or damaged, the enemy might be encouraged to make another pass at Oahu, or even attempt a landing on the Hawaiian Islands. He doubted whether he should risk a carrier against battleships; but "Sara" could outrun any battleship.

During the morning watch of 22 December (the 23rd at Wake) Captain C. H. McMorris, operations officer on Cincpac staff, was presented with Commander Cunningham's dispatch, "Enemy . . . landing." He at once called Admiral Pye and his chief of staff, Admiral Draemel. The three met promptly and for hours discussed what they should do. Shortly after 0730, Cunningham's second dispatch — "Enemy on island, issue in doubt" — came through. All three officers concluded that it was too late to evacuate Wake or to relieve Wake. It was. But should they allow or encourage Fletcher to press on and accept an engagement with enemy supporting forces of unknown strength? Our need of a naval victory was recognized. The chances of obtaining it seemed good. Brown's *Lexington* force was already closing from the south, and Halsey's *Enterprise* force could be sent down from its position near Midway to assist Fletcher or cover his retirement. Withdrawal without a fight would impair fleet morale and public confidence. But, in view of the weakened state of the Pacific Fleet, could the chance of battle be risked? Admiral Pye decided not. At 0911 on 22 December, before receiving news of the surrender, Admiral Pye ordered Fletcher and Brown to return to Pearl.

On board *Saratoga* and in the task force generally this order was received with dismay and indignation. Some of Admiral Fletcher's staff wished him to disregard the order and press on. One cruiser captain afterwards said, "Frank Jack should have placed the telescope to his blind eye, like Nelson." Captain Douglas of *Saratoga* begged his division commander to intercede with Fletcher for permission to make a fast run-in with the destroyers that had the most fuel, launch search missions, and attack whatever enemy ships were encountered. Marine aviators, all set to fly to the rescue of their fellows, cursed and even wept with vexation and disappointment. Admiral Fitch afterwards said that the talk was so mutinous that he had to retire from the bridge — especially as he felt that way himself.

The surrender of Wake followed hard on Pye's order to Fletcher to retire. Commander Cunningham had no knowledge of that order, but inferred it from the dispatch he had already received, to the effect that no friendly vessels would be near Wake in the next twenty-four hours. Shortly after 0700, Major Devereux notified the atoll commander that organized resistance could not long be continued, and inquired whether relief was to be expected. Commander Cunningham's negative reply ended all hope. The obvious conclusion was to surrender Wake in order to prevent further loss of life — especially among the civilians, who were becoming increasingly difficult to handle. Commander Cunningham so decided at about 0730 December 23, and notified Major

Devereux. The major ordered every unit that he could reach by telephone to destroy its records and weapons. He hoisted a bed sheet over his command post, and, with a sergeant carrying a rag lashed to a swab handle, walked forth to meet the nearest Japanese officer. Commander Cunningham drove down in a car to arrange the terms — unconditional, of course — after which Devereux had to visit every position in order to persuade his Marines to stop shooting. The fighting actually continued, in one place or another, for hours; Marines surrender hard, and the sad process was not completed by the intrepid detachment on Wilkes Island until the afternoon.

Altogether 470 officers and men of the armed forces and 1146 civilians became prisoners of the Japanese. The bodies of 49 Marines, 3 sailors and about 70 civilians were left on the atoll, or in the surrounding sea.[39] A conservative estimate of enemy casualties is 820 killed, 333 wounded.

Admiral Pye's decision was an honest one, natural in view of the circumstances. "The use of offensive action to relieve Wake had been my intention and desire," he said in a dispatch to the Chief of Naval Operations. "But when the enemy had once landed on the island, the general strategic situation took precedence, and the conservation of our naval forces became the first consideration. I ordered the retirement with extreme regret."

By the time Fletcher received the recall, around 0700, it was probably too late for him to catch the Japanese supporting forces. According to the best information available from enemy sources, Admiral Goto's four heavy cruisers, which operated between him and Wake, departed the area at 1400 on the 23rd. Admiral Abe's carrier division was detached at 1850 the same day, and started for Japan.[40] Fletcher had little chance of catching either, even if Pye had ordered him to belay fueling and run in at full speed; for at

---

[39] Heinl *Defense of Wake* p. 67 gives the final official figures. An aftermath of the surrender was the suit of twelve of the civilian workers against the construction firm for $500,000 back wages and damages during the entire period of captivity. (Washington *Daily News* 17 Jan. 1947.)
[40] Information secured by Lt. Cdr. Salomon in Japan.

0800 he was still 425 miles from Wake, a good eight hours' steaming from a launching position; only by pressing forward earlier could a dawn search by his fighter planes have discovered the carriers or the cruisers in time to direct a bomber strike on them. He could, however, have wreaked vengeance on the Japanese transports and light forces which were anchored off the island or steaming about in a state of unreadiness for combat, according to observant Marines. Up to 12 January 1942, when the American prisoners were removed from Wake, they were hoping and praying for a counterattack, which would have caught the Japanese garrison, the anchored transports, and other ships close to the atoll in a state of complete relaxation.[41]

No word of this fiasco was given to the public, or to the armed forces at large. When Admiral Joseph M. Reeves, former Commander in Chief of the United States Fleet, learned the full story, as a member of the Justice Roberts inquiry, he regarded it as a disgrace to the United States Navy.

"By Gad!" he remarked soon after his return from Pearl, "I used to say a man had to be both a fighter and know how to fight. Now all I want is a man who fights."

Admiral Kajioka, in whites, medals and dress sword, took formal possession of Wake on the afternoon of 23 December for his Emperor, who renamed it Otori Shima, or Bird Island.

By that evening all Japanese troops were ashore and all American prisoners had been rounded up. Wake was blacked out, and nothing could be heard but the thunder of the surf.

[41] Letter of Capt. W. S. Cunningham, 7 Feb. 1947.

# CHAPTER XIII

# Communications and Carrier Strikes

*January–March 1942*

West Longitude dates, Hawaiian time (Zone plus 10½ until 9 February 1942, when it went into Zone plus 9½ for the duration). East Longitude dates in operations west of the 180th meridian.

## 1. *Enter Nimitz*

THE CLOSE of the disastrous year 1941 saw a change in the high command that promised better things for 1942. Admiral Ernest J. King, formerly Commander in Chief Atlantic Fleet, was appointed Commander in Chief United States Fleet on 20 December, and on Christmas Eve issued his first statement as "Cominch." [1]

The way to victory is long.
The going will be hard.
We will do the best we can with what we've got.
We must have more planes and ships — at once.
Then it will be our turn to strike.
We will win through — in time.

Rear Admiral Chester W. Nimitz,[2] designated Commander in Chief Pacific Fleet (Cincpac) on 17 December with the rank of

---

[1] The former abbreviation of this command, *Cincus,* seemed unfortunate after Pearl Harbor; Admiral King substituted *Cominch* on 12 March 1942, and as Cominch he will always be remembered.

[2] Chester William Nimitz, grandson of a master merchant mariner, b. Fredericksburg, Texas, 1885, Naval Academy '05, graduating 7th. From 1909 through World War I he was on submarine duty, rising to be chief of staff to Commander Submarine Force Atlantic Fleet. Exec. of *South Carolina* 1919, C.O. *Chicago* 1920, Naval War College course 1922–23, and assistant chief of staff to Admiral S. S. Robison when Commander in Chief of the Fleet. Captain 1927; Comsubdiv 20, 1929; C.O. *Augusta* 1933; assistant chief Bunav 1935; Comcrudiv 2 with rank of Rear Admiral 1938; Combatdiv 1 later that year; Chief Bunav 15 June 1939.

Admiral, arrived at Pearl Harbor on Christmas Day, and took over the command on the last day of the year, the same day that Admiral King assumed his.

Nimitz, chosen by the President and Secretary from many possible candidates for this highly important post, accepted it with reluctance. What he wanted was a seagoing command, which Cincpac could never be by reason of the communications problem in time of war. Instead of making a clean sweep of Kimmel's staff and substituting officers of his own choice, Nimitz brought only a flag secretary with him to Pearl. And at his first meeting with the Cincpac staff he assured them of his confidence and declared that he intended to make no changes. He encouraged Admiral Pye to remain as his unofficial adviser. Morale at Pearl Harbor, which had reached an all-time low with the recall of the Wake relief expedition, now rose several hundred per cent.

These initial acts of Nimitz were typical of the man whose knowledge of human nature and whose humility had made the most accessible, considerate and beloved of fleet commanders. A man "of cheerful yesterdays and confident tomorrows," as described in his Academy class yearbook, he was no facile optimist but a realist of long views. He had an immense capacity for work, an equal talent at obtaining the best work from others, an almost impeccable judgment of men, and a genius for making prompt, firm decisions. Chester Nimitz was one of those rare men who grow as their responsibilities increase; but even at the end of the war, when his staff had expanded to 636 officers and he had almost 5000 ships and over 16,000 planes under his command, he retained the simplicity of his Texas upbringing. Ever calm and gentle in demeanor and courteous in speech, he had tow-colored hair turning white, blue eyes and a pink complexion which gave him somewhat the look of a friendly small boy, so that war correspondents, who expected admirals to pound the table and bellow as in the movies, were apt to wonder "Is this the man?" He was the man. No more fortunate appointment to this vital command could have been made. He restored confidence to the defeated Fleet. He had the patience to wait through the lean period of the war, the capacity to organize both a fleet and a vast theater, the tact to deal with sister services and Allied commands, the leadership to weld his own subordinates into a great fighting team, the courage to take necessary risks, and the wisdom to select, from a welter of intelligence and opinion, the strategy that defeated Japan.

It is said that the first thing Admiral King did on taking command of the United States Fleet was to draw a line on a chart from Midway to Samoa, Fiji and Brisbane, and to order Admiral Nimitz to hold it "at all costs." [3] His initial dispatch to Nimitz said just about that. The Pacific Fleet had two primary tasks of almost equal importance: to protect the Midway–Johnston–Hawaii triangle and to maintain communications between the United States, Australia and New Zealand along the route through the Line Islands, Samoa and Fiji. There was considerable evidence that the enemy intended to break into that route from his new bases in the Gilberts where he appeared to be building up air forces; Japanese bombers had already hit Ocean and Nauru Islands and submarines had shelled Johnston and Palmyra. He had an estimated 15 submarines between Hawaii and the West Coast, an area where several merchant ships had already been sunk. Although carrier *Yorktown* was en route Panama to San Diego, she must cover the reinforcement of Samoa, lest the Japs lunge in that direction before the Marines could construct an adequate defense. The other three carrier forces, with cruiser and destroyer components reduced to strengthen the escorts of merchant convoys, must cover Midway and the Johnston–Palmyra line. And the air defenses of Oahu were dangerously weak, now that Navy Patrol Squadron 22 had been sent out to help Admiral Hart, and most of the Army heavy bombers had left for Australia.[4]

Nothing could now be done about Wake. To recapture it would require a strong amphibious force, and there was not yet a landing craft or a trained amphibious unit in the Pacific. The 2nd Marine

[3] Forrest Davis in *Sat. Eve. Post* 9 Dec. 1944 p. 10.
[4] Cincpac to Cominch 5 Jan. 1942.

Division (less the 6th Regiment), then under amphibious training at San Diego, must be saved for a more important objective. Enemy exploitation of Wake as an observation post and base for bombing missions against Midway must be accepted for the present.[5] Midway appeared to be fairly safe, protected as it was by two Marine air squadrons and a defense battalion, with a small infantry component about to arrive shortly. Enemy submarines, however, adopted the unpleasant routine of shelling Midway under cover of darkness during their outward and homeward passages. On 27 January United States submarine *Gudgeon* caught one, the 1700-ton *I–73*, and sank it.

Indeed, the most cheerful picture in the war album during the dark month of January 1942, when the Axis seemed to be on the march the world over, was that of Submarines Pacific Fleet. Between 5 and 18 January 1942, U.S.S. *Pollack, Gudgeon, Pompano, Tautog* and *Plunger*, on a war patrol that took them to the coast of Japan, claimed to have sunk five freighters of 5000 to 7000 tons each, one minelayer, one 16,500-tonner "of the *Yawata* class." [6] But this picture was out of focus. The total score of that patrol was one 4700-ton freighter sunk by *Plunger*, and two, totaling 7600 tons, by *Pollack*.[7]

Admiral King made every effort to build up strength in the Pacific Fleet and on the Pacific bases, as American production slowly gathered momentum. Since all ships from the Atlantic bound for Samoa, New Zealand or Australia must come through the Panama Canal, he decided as early as 1 January 1942 to establish a naval fuel station at Bora Bora in the Society Islands, well out of any possible combat zone.

<hr/>

[5] Cincpac Appreciation of the Situation 1 Jan. 1942.

[6] Comsubspac to Cincpac 26 Mar. 1942.

[7] Joint Army-Navy Assessment Committee *Japanese Naval and Merchant Losses World War II by U.S. Submarines* (1947).

## 2. *Strikes and Counterstrikes* [8]

Admiral King hoped that Admiral Nimitz could see his way to taking a crack at one of the Japanese-held islands at earliest opportunity. But Japan still retained the initiative. On 6 January planes from Truk started pounding the advanced Australian air base at Rabaul in the Bismarcks.

Canton Island, an important port of call on the Oahu–Samoa–Fiji route, only 960 miles from enemy-held Makin, gave the Navy considerable anxiety since it was even less defensible than Wake. A 5000-foot airstrip was ready for Flying Fortresses but no planes were yet stationed there, and the garrison on 8 January consisted of 78 Army engineers with no guns, no radar, no direction-finder, "no nothing."

On 11 January a Japanese submarine shelled the United States naval station at Pago Pago, Samoa, suggesting that a lunge in that direction was imminent; but Australia reported that the enemy was massing ships at Truk and suggested that Suva rather than Rabaul was his objective. The British had only one airfield in the Fijis, at Nandi, where 22 planes were stationed. Fewer than 8000 British and native troops were available to defend the entire Fiji group. They begged for help from the United States, but we had none to spare until Samoa had been taken care of.

The Marine reinforcements for Samoa, loaded in four transports and one fleet cargo vessel, accompanied by an ammunition ship and a fleet oiler, departed San Diego on 6 January. They were covered by Admiral Halsey's *Enterprise* force, near Samoa. A new fast carrier force commanded by Rear Admiral Frank Jack Fletcher formed around *Yorktown*, which had just come through the Canal, had met and escorted them on the ocean passage, and the Marines were all ashore at Samoa on 23 January.

That very day an amphibious force under the Japanese Fourth

[8] O.N.I. Combat Narratives *Early Raids in the Pacific Ocean, Feb. 1 to Mar. 10, 1942; Admiral Halsey's Story* pp. 85–97.

Fleet, with much the same composition as the one that had taken Wake, but covered and supported by Admiral Nagumo's Carrier Striking Force, landed at Rabaul. No Allied ships were there to oppose, and the slender Australian garrison was overwhelmed. Few realized at the time the strategic significance of this event. The Japanese soon expanded their power along the coasts of New Britain and New Ireland, and presently into the northern coast of Papua and the northern Solomons, which gave them complete air and naval control of the Bismarck Archipelago. They began transforming Rabaul into a powerful naval, air and military base that effectively checked any Allied advance in that quarter until 1944.

Admiral Nimitz saw at once that the capture of Rabaul brought the Coral Sea within range of Japanese bomber planes and, on 23 January, ordered that all ships entering the Anzac area be escorted.

Now that Samoa was properly reinforced, carrier raids on Wake and the Marshalls, which Admiral King had been demanding with increasing urgency, could be carried out.

Vice Admiral Wilson Brown, still in command of the *Lexington* group, was to have inaugurated these operations by delivering a bombing attack on Wake. When steaming about 135 miles west of Oahu during the mid-watch on 23 January, his force oiler *Neches* was torpedoed and sunk by a Japanese submarine. As the force could not proceed without fueling at sea, and Cincpac had no other tanker to spare, the Wake strike had to be called off.

When Rear Admiral Fletcher was sent to the new *Yorktown* group, Vice Admiral Herbert F. Leary relieved him in command of the *Saratoga* force. But the change of command did not alter the luck of Task Force 14. On 11 January a deep-running torpedo from a Japanese submarine struck *Saratoga* 500 miles southwest of Oahu. Six men were killed and three firerooms flooded, but the carrier managed to reach Oahu under her own power. Thence she proceeded to Bremerton for permanent repairs and modernization, such as improved watertight integrity and additional anti-aircraft armament. Her air group was distributed among the other carriers or sent to training centers; Task Force 14 was broken up. Admiral Leary flew out to Wellington early in February to take command of the Australia-New Zealand (or Anzac) Force that had just been set up, on recommendation of the Combined Chiefs of Staff.

This Anzac Force, which was under the immediate strategic direction of Admiral King, comprised the Australian heavy cruisers *Australia* and *Canberra*, Australian light cruiser *Hobart*, two destroyers and a few corvettes. It was soon to be reinforced by U.S.S. *Chicago* and two United States destroyers. This force was responsible for protecting the eastern approaches to Australia and New Zealand, in case the enemy lunged in that direction from Rabaul.

A more likely lunge, so it then appeared, would be an amphibious expedition mounted in the Marshall Islands or Truk, to take Samoa. The early Japanese occupation of Makin in the Gilberts seemed to point that way. The best insurance against anything of that sort would be a devastating raid on the Marshalls, where the earlier attacks on Wake had been mounted. Accordingly, Halsey's *Enterprise* group, which had covered Fletcher's *Yorktown* group in escorting the reinforcement convoy to Samoa, received orders to depart thence 25 January and deliver a carrier-plane strike and bombardment on Wotje and Maloelap, the two enemy seaplane bases in the eastern Marshalls, while Fletcher hit Makin, Mili and Jaluit. Submarine *Dolphin* made a careful reconnaissance of the Marshalls and reported on 27 January that the entire group was very lightly defended, and that the greatest concentration of planes and shipping was at Kwajalein Atoll, right in the center of that archipelago. So Halsey decided to take on Kwajalein too. He divided Task Force 8 into three groups: *Enterprise* accompanied by three destroyers to launch plane strikes on Wotje, Maloelap and Kwajalein; Rear Admiral Raymond A. Spruance in heavy cruiser *Northampton* with *Salt Lake City* and one destroyer to bombard Wotje; and Captain Thomas M. Shock in *Chester* with two destroyers to bombard Maloelap. Rear Admiral Fletcher in *Yorktown* had an independent command (TF 17) comprising light cruisers *Louisville*, *St. Louis* and four destroyers to take care of the three southern islands. Each force had a fleet oiler for fueling at sea.

At last "Bill" Halsey was in the money. He had chafed at conducting fruitless covering patrols and longed for aggressive action. His assignment to conduct a raid deep into the Japanese Mandates was a guarantee that it would be carried out with the utmost energy and skill. This was by all odds the most hazardous operation yet undertaken by the Pacific Fleet. His plan required *Enterprise* to steam to lat. 10° N, long. 170° E, between Wotje and Ailuk Atolls, and thence launch fighter-plane strikes on Wotje and Maloelap and a dive- and torpedo-bomber strike on Kwajalein, while the cruisers bombarded enemy installations and ships at Wotje and at Taroa Island, Maloelap Atoll. Fletcher's *Yorktown* group in the meantime was to steam to lat. 5° N, long. 171°50′ E, and launch carrier strikes on Jaluit, Mili and Makin, all on 1 February (East Longitude date).

The forces proceeded in company from Samoa until 1830 January 31 when they parted for fast run-ins from the eastward. Halsey pressed on at 30 knots during the night and commenced launching at 0443 February 1, with a full moon lighting a perfect scene of calm tropic seas. The carrier was then 36 miles from Wotje, 106 from Maloelap, 155 from Kwajalein, the principal objective.[9] Commander Howard L. Young of the *Enterprise* air group led off 9 torpedo-bombers and 37 dive-bombers. At 0658, fifteen minutes before sunrise, the formation divided, the SBDs heading for the Roi air base on the northern end of the atoll, the torpedo-bombers for Kwajalein Island 44 miles distant across the lagoon.

The Roi attack was not a success. Mist obscured the atoll so that the dive-bombers, whose charts were of Wilkes Exploring Expedition vintage, could not identify Roi until 0705. In the meantime they had been sighted, and had given the enemy plenty of time to alert his anti-aircraft batteries and get fighter planes into the air. Lieutenant Commander H. L. Hopping, the squadron commander, had barely released the first bomb when his plane was shot down by anti-aircraft fire. Three more SBDs were lost by

[9] *Early Raids in the Pacific Ocean* p. 8.

the same means, or shot down by fighter planes. The Kwajalein Island attack, in which ten SBDs helped the torpedo-bombers, was an unqualified success. Transport *Bordeaux Maru* (6500 tons), and a subchaser were sunk; a second subchaser, net tender *Kashima Maru* and gunboat *Hoyo Maru* were badly damaged; minelayer *Tokiwa* (9240 tons), transport *Nagata Maru,* light cruiser *Katori, Kanto Maru* (8600 tons), an ammunition supply ship and a submarine tender were damaged. In addition 18 planes were destroyed or badly damaged, and about 90 men, including the area commander Rear Admiral Yashiro, were killed.

The strike of 5 Wildcats on Taroa airfield, Maloelap Atoll, shot down 2 Japanese planes and returned safely. Nine SBDs that returned from Roi were launched against the same target at 0935, and had the satisfaction of hitting some brand-new airfield installations. There were other fighter strikes on Wotje, coördinated with shore bombardment by Admiral Spruance's cruisers and destroyers. That pounding opened at 0715 with full salvos from *Northampton* and *Salt Lake City,* aimed at warships alleged to be cruisers that were making a fast getaway from the lagoon. Again, it does not appear that anything afloat was sunk, although some hits may have been scored; and the damage to buildings was not severe. Japanese coast defense batteries replied, but their shooting was very bad.

U.S.S. *Chester,* flagship of the bombardment group that took Taroa Island under fire, was not so lucky. Eight twin-engined bombers managed to take off from the airfield in the midst of the bombardment and concentrated on "Tommy" Shock's cruiser. She did some fancy dodging but took one light bomb that penetrated her main deck, killed 8 men and wounded 11.

Admiral Halsey had all the luck there was. For nine hours he maneuvered his *Enterprise* group in a rectangle only five by twenty miles, mostly within sight of Wotje. Surely some kind angel was guarding them from submarines and air bombers. Around 1300 the Admiral decided he had been riding his luck hard enough and

"Haul out with Halsey!" became the word. Some almost failed to make it; at 1340 a "Betty" twin-engined bomber tried a suicide crash on the flight deck of *Enterprise*. She would have done it, too, if a young aviation mechanic, Bruno P. Gaida, had not had the presence of mind to jump into the rear seat of the plane spotted farthest aft and open fire with its machine gun. That, and a quick "hard right" order by the officer of the deck, caused the would-be kamikaze to strike the port edge of the flight deck and topple harmlessly over the side.

Two more bombers with nonretractable landing gear under streamlined cowls attacked *Enterprise* unsuccessfully on her retirement, and were shot down.

While all these things were going on in the northern Marshalls, Rear Admiral Frank Jack Fletcher was leading *Yorktown*, heavy cruiser *Louisville*, light cruiser *St. Louis* and four destroyers against the southern islands. Jaluit was the first target, of 11 torpedo and 17 dive-bombers under the air group commander, Commander Curtis S. Smiley. Their luck was bad: thunderstorms concealed Jaluit at dawn. Only two ships off Jabor Town were hit — but not sunk — and a minimum amount of destruction was done ashore, at the heavy cost of six planes that failed to return. At Makin Island, attacked by 9 SBDs before sunrise, the only target was a minelayer which may have been hit but certainly was not sunk. The attack on Mili was equally inconclusive.

Task Force 17 did not have to contend with counterattacks, as did Halsey's force, except from one four-engined bomber which attacked the destroyers unsuccessfully and then approached *Yorktown*, whose combat air patrol shot it down.

The first strike on Jaluit was so costly, the weather so bad, and the planes took so long to return, that Admiral Fletcher, estimating that a second strike on this atoll would entail a night recovery, retired that afternoon.

It would not be fair to judge this raid by the meager material results. The two carrier air groups had valuable combat practice. The over-optimistic accounts of damage inflicted on the enemy

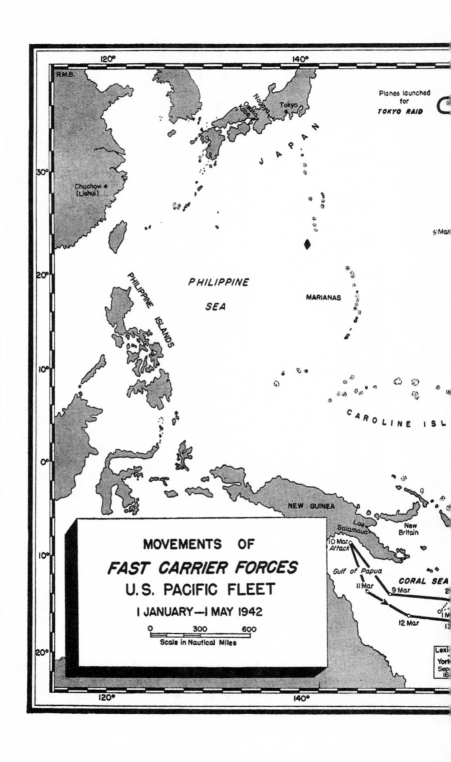

MOVEMENTS OF
*FAST CARRIER FORCES*
U.S. PACIFIC FLEET
I JANUARY—I MAY 1942

0      300      600
Scale in Nautical Miles

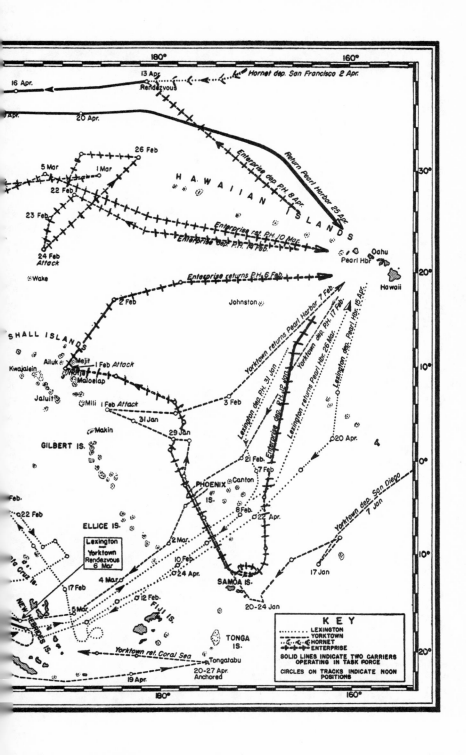

16 Apr.

180°

13 Apr.
Rendezvous

Hornet dep. San Francisco 2 Apr.

160°

7 Apr.

20 Apr.

H A W A I I A N

Return Pearl Harbor

Enterprise dep. P.H. 8 Apr.

30°

26 Feb

5 Mar

1 Mar

22 Feb

23 Feb

24 Feb
Attack

Wake

2 Feb

I S L A N D S

Enterprise ret. P.H. 10 Mar.

Enterprise dep. P.H. 16 Feb.

Enterprise returns P.H. 6 Feb.

Oahu

Pearl Hbr.

Enterprise ret. P.H. 25 Apr.

20°

Hawaii

Johnston

SHALL ISLANDS

Ailuk    Mejit    1 Feb Attack

Kwajalein    Wotje

Maloelap

Jaluit

Mili    I Feb Attack

Makin

GILBERT IS.

31 Jan

29 Jan

PHOENIX
IS.

Canton

3 Feb

Yorktown returns Pearl Harbor 7 Feb.

Yorktown dep. P.H. 17 Feb.

Lexington dep. P.H. 31 Jan.

Enterprise dep. P.H. 12 Apr.

Yorktown dep. Pearl Hbr. 26 Mar.

Lexington returns Pearl Harbor P.H.

Lexington dep. Pearl Hbr. 15 Apr.

10°

20 Apr.

21 Feb

7 Feb

0°

8 Feb

22 Apr.

Feb.

22 Feb

ELLICE IS.

Lexington
—
Yorktown
Rendezvous
6 Mar

2 Mar.

10 Feb

24 Feb

SAMOA IS.

Yorktown dep. San Diego
7 Jan

10°

Cruis ls.

17 Feb

4 Mar.

12 Feb

17 Jan

NEW HEBRIDES IS.

5 Mar.

FIJI IS.

20-24 Jan

KEY

20°

Yorktown ret. Coral Sea

TONGA
IS.

Tongatabu

20-27 Apr.
Anchored

19 Apr.

LEXINGTON
YORKTOWN
HORNET
ENTERPRISE

SOLID LINES INDICATE TWO CARRIERS
OPERATING IN TASK FORCE
CIRCLES ON TRACKS INDICATE NOON
POSITIONS

180°

160°

were a help to low morale, and the audacity of Halsey in striking into the heart of the Mandates gave his country its first naval hero of the war.

In the meantime the Pacific Fleet was strained to the limit to provide proper escorts between Hawaii and the coast, and to other island bases and Australia. Two large convoys came through the Canal at the end of January, one consisting of six ships carrying 4500 men and equipment to construct the new naval fuel station at Bora Bora. This, fortunately, could be escorted by Rear Admiral Jack Shafroth's Southeastern Pacific Force consisting of the old light cruisers *Trenton* and *Concord* and two destroyers. Cincpac had to take care of a much larger convoy carrying 20,000 troops in eight transports, two for garrisoning Christmas Island, two for Canton Island and the other four for Nouméa, New Caledonia. Wilson Brown's *Lexington* force covered the advance of both these convoys into the Central Pacific, and all reinforcement missions were completed satisfactorily, except that transport *President Taylor* dragged ashore at Canton Island.

The Australian government, alarmed over the progress of Japanese power in the Bismarcks and New Guinea, warned Admiral Nimitz on 27 January that the enemy might well take Nouméa before United States troops already en route could occupy it. They were anxious about Port Moresby, too. Our own Intelligence believed that, as soon as the enemy was well established at Rabaul, he would have two carriers, several cruisers and possibly battleships available for an invasion of the New Hebrides and New Caledonia. Admiral King therefore ordered Cincpac to send Wilson Brown's *Lexington* force, and all Navy patrol planes and Army bombers that could be spared, into the Fiji-New Caledonia area to operate under the direction of Admiral Leary of the Anzac force. In the meantime the Pacific Fleet would pull a diversionary raid on Wake or the northern Marshalls in order to relieve pressure in the southwest.

Unfortunately no carrier raid within range of the Pacific Fleet and its oilers could possibly divert the enemy from his plans of conquest to the southwestward. In early February, as we have seen, the sands were running out at Malaya, Bataan and the Netherlands East Indies. Admiral Nimitz alerted Halsey's *Enterprise* and Fletcher's *Yorktown* groups to raid Wake and one of the Marshalls, because King so ordered; but he had little faith in their accomplishing more than giving the air groups more exercise. In the end, Halsey was sent against Wake in preference to the Marshalls, and he made the raid alone as Fletcher was covering the waters around Canton Island.

Before that took place, there had been a notable air fight deep in Japanese-controlled waters, some 300 miles east of Rabaul. Admiral Leary, jubilant over the temporary addition of Wilson Brown's *Lexington* group [10] to his Anzac Force, gladly accepted Brown's suggestion of a heavy air strike on Rabaul. As a preliminary, Rear Admiral Crace RN [11] with four cruisers and two destroyers patrolled the Suva–Nouméa line, while Australian planes searched from Port Moresby and American Army planes from Nouméa.

This was a very risky operation for that stage of the war. It meant sending one of our precious carriers 3000 miles from the nearest base, Pearl Harbor. At that time there was no nearer port where fuel could be obtained, and no place nearer than Sydney where temporary repairs could be effected; carriers could not be sent into Nouméa for security reasons. And, as Admiral Brown observed, his Admiralty charts of the Bismarcks and Solomons were based on the imperfect surveys by Bougainville, D'Entrecasteaux and other navigators of the eighteenth century. A tanker had to be sent out to a designated rendezvous so that the force could fuel after the first strike. Admiral Crace, after protesting that he was out there to "shoot Japs" and not to "chaperon a blooming oiler," accepted the assignment and did it well. The task force kept the strictest radio silence, delivering necessary messages by plane to Brisbane.

[10] Then comprising heavy cruisers *Minneapolis, Indianapolis, Pensacola* and *San Francisco*, and 10 destroyers (*Phelps* flag). Principal sources for this operation: *Early Raids in the Pacific Ocean* pp. 35–40; conversations with Admiral Brown.
[11] Pronounced "Crayse."

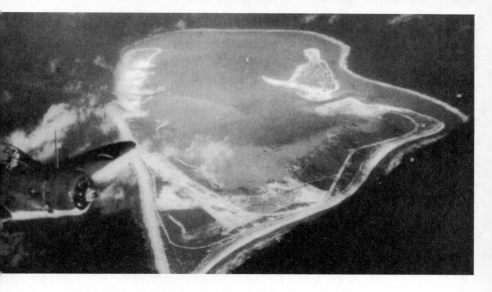

Wake Island during the air attack of 24 February
(TBD torpedo-bomber at left)

U.S.S. *Enterprise*
hoto taken January 1944. The parked planes are of a later type than those
used in the strike of 1942)

*February 1942*

Wotje, after bombardment of 1 February
(Cruiser float plane at left)

U.S.S. *Indianapolis*

*February 1942*

The Japanese 25th Air Flotilla, based on the two airfields at Rabaul, was not a force to be easily surprised. It conducted regular air searches on sectors 45° to 165° six hundred miles out from Simpson Harbor.[12] Admiral Brown suspected this, and so made the shortest possible approach, from the eastward, intending to launch planes 125 miles from the objective at 0400 February 21.[13] At 1015 on the 20th, when his force was north of the Solomons and 350 miles east of Rabaul, the radar on *Lexington* showed a "bandit" (unknown plane). Lieutenant Commander John S. Thach sliced off 6 Wildcats, which located a four-engined flying boat 43 miles out and shot it down. Lieutenant (jg) O. B. Stanley, with 2 more planes, inflicted the same fate on a second snooper. A third got away.

That afternoon at 1542, *Lexington's* radar picked up a flock of "bandits" 76 miles to the westward, and an additional combat air patrol of 6 Wildcats joined the others already in the air, just as the enemy closed.

This first fight between Japanese and American carrier type planes was conducted in great part right over the task force, in full view of *Lexington* and the other ships, amid scenes of wildest enthusiasm — everybody topside waving and yelling encouragement to the pilots. "I even had to remind some members of my staff that this was not a football game," said Admiral Brown. The action went on intermittently from 1620 to after 1800, as two waves of 9 planes each attacked; and it is believed that few escaped. Lieutenant Edward H. ("Butch") O'Hare especially distinguished himself by shooting down 5 "Kates," one of which attempted to crash *Lexington* in its fall. Only two of our planes and one pilot (Ensign J. Woodrow Wilson) were lost.

This air action made "Lady Lex" the proudest carrier in the United States Navy, and enhanced the morale of all carrier plane pilots in the Fleet. It was they and they alone who had defeated a heavy bombing attack; the anti-aircraft fire was wildly inaccurate

---

[12] War Diary 25th Air Flotilla (Bismarck Area Base Air Force), translation from Washington Document Center, No. 161725.
[13] East longitude dates and local times are used on this operation.

and only got in the pilots' way. Nevertheless, Admiral Brown felt obliged to call off the attack on Rabaul, since surprise had been lost.

On 23 February came the bad news of the destructive Japanese air raid on Port Darwin, Australia, facing Timor across the Arafura Sea. Next day, the 24th (East Longitude date), Admiral Halsey's task force raided Wake Island. Two heavy cruisers and two destroyers bombarded for 30 minutes from a range of 14,000 to 16,000 yards, just outside that of the Japanese shore batteries. A few buildings were destroyed, but the shore batteries were not silenced and only one small patrol craft was sunk. *Enterprise* closed the island that night and launched 36 bombers and 6 fighters at dawn. This was good practice, but only 3 flying boats were seen on the atoll and the total destruction effected was hardly worth the loss of a dive-bomber with its crew.

The next raid, also by Admiral Halsey's group, was a bold one. Little Marcus Island, less than a thousand miles southeast of Tokyo, was the objective. The attack was arranged to take place before sunrise on 4 March (East Longitude date) in full moonlight; the planes were coached in for a large part of their 175-mile run by the radar in *Enterprise*, which kept the group commander posted as to his course and position. No enemy planes were seen or encountered, but anti-aircraft fire was fairly heavy and one scout bomber was shot down.[14]

Both the Wake and the Marcus raids were planned as diversions (in the military, not the moral sense); but there is no evidence that they pulled any forces of the enemy up from the southwestward, as had been hoped. As one officer remarked, "the Japs didn't mind them any more than a dog minds a flea."

[14] On the following night two long-range Japanese "Emily" flying boats staged a strike on Pearl Harbor. Departing Wotje, each with a ton of bombs, they refueled from three I-boats at French Frigate Shoals and thence took off for Pearl. Army radar stations detected them but poor visibility over Oahu prevented interceptor planes, anti-aircraft gunfire, or searchlights from spotting the Japanese in light rain and overcast. One dropped its bombs on a barren hillside six miles east of Pearl, the other pilot's four bombs were released too far off shore to be noticed. Both returned safely. The three I-boats, homeward bound from this mission, searched for Halsey's Marcus Island force, in vain. Capt. E. T. Layton "Rendezvous in Reverse" U. S. N. Inst. Proc. (May 1953).

*PART IV*

# Defense of the Malay Barrier[1]

*January–March 1942*

[1] To the general sources mentioned under the first footnote to Part II, add Admiral Hart's "Events and Circumstances Concerning the Striking Force," 24 May 1944.

# CHAPTER XIV

# The Abda Command

## 1. *Composition of Allied Forces*
## *15 January–23 February 1942*

### ABDA COMMAND

Field Marshal Sir Archibald Wavell, Supreme Commander (Abdacom)
  General Sir Henry R. Pownall, Chief of Staff
  Lieutenant General G. H. Brett usa, Deputy Commander [1]
  Admiral Thomas C. Hart usn, Commander Naval Forces (Abdafloat) [2]
    Rear Admiral A. F. E. Palliser rn, Chief of Staff
    Rear Admiral K. W. F. M. Doorman rnn, Commander Combined Striking
      Force (from 2 February)
  Lieutenant General Hein ter Poorten, Netherlands East Indies Army, Com-
    mander Ground Forces (Abdaarm)
  Air Chief Marshal Sir Richard E. C. Peirse raf, Commander Air Forces
    (Abdaair) [3]

### ALLIED NATIONAL COMMANDS

*United States:* Admiral Hart, Navy; Maj. Gen. J. F. Barnes, Army; General
  Brereton,[4] Air
*Great Britain:* Commodore John Collins, Navy; Lieutenant General Percival,
  Army; Air Chief Marshal Peirse, Air
*Netherlands:* Admiral Helfrich, Navy; General ter Poorten, Army; General van
  Oyen, Air

### UNITED STATES ASIATIC FLEET
#### Admiral Hart [5]

### TF 5 STRIKING FORCE
#### Rear Admiral W. A. Glassford

| CA | *houston | CL | boise | CL | marblehead |
|---|---|---|---|---|---|

[1] Commander U.S. Army Forces in Australia 1 Jan. 1942, relinquished when he became
Wavell's deputy but resumed when Abda was dissolved.
[2] Relieved 12 Feb. as to actual direction by Admiral Helfrich.
[3] Maj. Gen. L. H. Brereton usa acting Abdaair until Peirse's arrival in late January.
[4] On 15 Jan. a directive from the War Department made Brereton also American ground
force commander to 27 Jan., when General Barnes took command of U.S. troops in Australia, where the only U.S. ground forces other than MacArthur's were located.
[5] Relieved 4 Feb. by Vice Admiral W. A. Glassford, Commander U.S. Naval Forces
Southwest Pacific. Squadron, division and commanding officers same as at the opening of

## STRIKING FORCE (*Continued*)

### Destroyer Squadron 29

DD        PAUL JONES

| *Desdiv 57* | *Desdiv 58* | *Desdiv 59* |
|---|---|---|
| WHIPPLE | BULMER | * POPE |
| ALDEN | BARKER | * PEARY |
| JOHN D. EDWARDS | PARROTT | * PILLSBURY |
| * EDSALL | * STEWART | JOHN D. FORD |

## TF 4 PATROL AIRCRAFT
### Captain F. D. Wagner

Tenders    CHILDS, WILLIAM B. PRESTON, HERON
28 Catalinas of Patrol Wing 10, of which 25 were expended

## TF 3 SUBMARINE FORCE
### Captain J. Wilkes

This was the same as at the opening of hostilities (see above p. 158), less *S-41* and *Sealion*. The only personnel changes were that Lt. Cdr. R. J. Moore now commanded *Stingray* and Lt. Cdr. R. C. Voge, *Sailfish*.

## TF 2 SERVICE FORCE
### Captain W. E. Doyle, based on Darwin

| | | |
|---|---|---|
| AG | GOLD STAR | Cdr. J. W. Lademan, Jr. |
| AV | * LANGLEY | Cdr. R. P. McConnell |
| AO | * PECOS | Lt. Cdr. E. P. Abernathy |
| AO | TRINITY | Cdr. W. Hibbs |
| AD | BLACK HAWK | Cdr. G. L. Harriss |
| Merchant | S.S. *George G. Henry* | J. G. Olsen, USNR Master |

#### *Miscellaneous*

| | | |
|---|---|---|
| PG | * ASHEVILLE | Lt. Cdr. J. W. Britt |
| PY | ISABEL | Lt. (jg) F. W. Payne, Jr. |

## BRITISH NAVAL FORCES
### Admiral Sir Geoffrey Layton RN

| | | | | |
|---|---|---|---|---|
| CA | * EXETER | DD | * ELECTRA |
| CL | HOBART | DD | * ENCOUNTER |
| CL | * PERTH | DD | * JUPITER |

* Lost in or as a result of action with the enemy during these operations.

hostilities (see Part II Chapter VI of this volume), with following exceptions: On 29 Jan. Lt. Cdr. E. N. Parker relieved Cdr. P. H. Talbot as Comdesdiv 59 and was relieved by Lt. J. N. Hughes as C.O. *Parrott;* on 28 Jan. Lt. D. A. Harris relieved Cdr. L. J. Manees as C.O. *Bulmer;* Lt. Cdr. J. M. Bermingham relieved Cdr. H. H. Keith as C.O. *Peary* when Cdr. Keith was wounded on 10 December.

## NETHERLANDS NAVAL FORCES [6]

Vice Admiral C. E. L. Helfrich RNN

| | | | |
|---|---|---|---|
| CL | * JAVA | DD | * KORTENAER |
| CL | * DE RUYTER | DD | * WITTE DE WITH |
| CL | TROMP | DD | * VAN GHENT |
| DD | * VAN NES | DD | * PIET HEIN |
| DD | * EVERTSEN | DD | * BANCKERT |

### Submarines

| | | | |
|---|---|---|---|
| * K–7 | K–13 | *K–17 | O–19 |
| K–10 | K–14 | *K–18 | *O–20 |
| K–11 | K–15 | *O–16 | K–8 |
| K–12 | *K–16 | *O–17 | K–9 |

U.S.S. LARK and WHIPPOORWILL (p. 159) operated under R.N.N. till 1 March.

## 2. *Japanese Naval Forces in Southwest Pacific Operations January–March 1942* [7]

Vice Admiral Nobutake Kondo, Commander in Chief Second Fleet, was officially responsible for all naval and amphibious operations in the Philippines, Malaya and the Netherlands East Indies. The area was split vertically into two areas of responsibility, as follows: —

### Eastern Area

Philippines, Makassar Strait, Java Sea and waters to the eastward, for which Vice Admiral I. Takahashi, Commander in Chief Third Fleet, was responsible.

### Western Area

South China Sea, Malay Peninsula and Sumatra, for which Vice Admiral J. Ozawa, Commander in Chief Southern Expeditionary Fleet, was responsible.

[6] Much of the information in this Part on the R.N.N. is from Lt. Cdr. A. Kroese *The Dutch Navy at War* (London 1945). The author was C.O. of *Kortenaer* in this campaign.
[7] Data for this section, largely obtained by Mr. Salomon in Tokyo, includes Cdr. Chihaya "Outline of Battle of Makassar Strait" (ATIS Doc. 15685); ATIS Doc. 19692 B (WDI–112); Reports of Japanese Desrons 2 and 4.
Data are confessedly incomplete, owing to the constant shifting of ships from one group to another in the rapid Japanese advance, but it is believed that this composition is reasonably accurate. Menado, Kendari and Makassar Town were occupied initially by Special Naval Landing Force units. Ambon, Timor, Tarakan, Balikpapan, Palembang, Bandjermasin and Bali were occupied by 16th Army.

## EASTERN FORCE
### Vice Admiral I. Takahashi

### (*a*) Menado, Kendari and Ambon Occupations

### COVERING GROUP, Rear Admiral T. Takagi

| | | | |
|---|---|---|---|
| CA | NACHI | DD | IKAZUCHI |
| CA | HAGURO | DD | INAZUMA |
| CA | MYOKO | | |

### ESCORT GROUP, Rear Admiral R. Tanaka (Comdesron 2) in CL JINTSU

#### Desron 2

| *Desdiv 16* | | *Desdiv 15* | | *Desdiv 8, 1st section* | |
|---|---|---|---|---|---|
| DD | YUKIKAZE | DD | KUROSHIO | DD | OSHIO |
| DD | TOKITSUKAZE | DD | OYASHIO | DD | ARASHIO |
| DD | AMATSUKAZE | DD | NATSUSHIO | | |
| DD | HATSUKAZE | DD | HAYASHIO | | |

Patrol Boats 1, 2 and 34; 2 PCs; 1 subchaser; Minesweepers 7 and 8.

### ATTACK GROUP

10 Transports (of which 2 were sunk by B–17s) carrying Kure 1st Special Naval Landing Force; other transports carrying units of 16th Army.

### AIR GROUP (11th Carrier Division), Rear Admiral R. Fujita

| CVS | CHITOSE | CVL | ZUIHO | Patrol Boat No. 39 |
|---|---|---|---|---|

### BASE GROUP, Rear Admiral K. Kubo [8]

| CL | NAGARA | AK | TSUKUSHI MARU | CM | AOTAKA |
|---|---|---|---|---|---|

### (*b*) Makassar Town Occupation

### COVERING GROUP, Admiral Takagi

(Same as Menado, etc., Cover Group, less MYOKO, and AKEBONO replacing INAZUMA.)

### ESCORT GROUP, Admiral Kubo in NAGARA

(Destroyers same as Menado Escort Group, except that Desdiv 16 was replaced by Desdiv 21.)

| DD | ARASHIO | DD | MICHISHIO | DD | HATSUHARU |
|---|---|---|---|---|---|
| DD | HATSUSHIMO | DD | NENOHI | DD | WAKABA |

### TRANSPORT GROUP

6 Transports

[8] In the Kendari Operation Kubo relieved Tanaka as Escort Commander, and *Jintsu Oshio* and *Asashio* did not participate.

## CLOSE COVER GROUP

| | | | | | |
|---|---|---|---|---|---|
| DD | UMIKAZE | DD | KAWAKAZE | DD | ASAGUMO |
| DD | MINEGUMO | DD | NATSUGUMO | 4 Minesweepers | |

AIR GROUP (11th Carrier Division), Rear Admiral Fujita

| | | | |
|---|---|---|---|
| CVS | CHITOSE | 3 Patrol Boats | |
| CVL | ZUIHO | 1 Subchaser | |

(*c*) Timor Occupation

COVERING GROUP, Rear Admiral Takagi

| | | | |
|---|---|---|---|
| CA | NACHI | DD | AKEBONO |
| CA | HAGURO | DD | YAMAKAZE |
| DD | INAZUMA | DD | KAWAKAZE |

ESCORT GROUP, Rear Admiral Tanaka

(Same as Eastern Force Escort Group, plus 3 YPs and AM–7.)

## CENTRAL FORCE [9]

(*a*) Tarakan Occupation, Admiral Hirose

Same as Reinforcement Echelons and Support Air Group for Timor, plus: —

Desron 4, Rear Admiral Nishimura

| | | | | | |
|---|---|---|---|---|---|
| CL | NAKA | DD | HARUSAME | DD | SAMIDARE |
| DD | YUDACHI | DD | NATSUGUMO | DD | MURASAME |
| DD | ASAGUMO | DD | MINEGUMO | | |

*Advance Echelon*, Admiral Hirose [10]

Minelayers *Itsukushima, Wakataka, Imizu Maru,* carrying 2nd Base Unit
Several torpedo boats and patrol craft

*Support Air Group,* 21st Air Flotilla

Seaplane tenders *Sanyo Maru* [11] and *Sanuki Maru.*

*Minesweeping and Anti-Submarine Group*

4 Minesweepers (* *13* and * *14* sunk) and SC–12.

(*b*) Balikpapan and Bandjermasin Occupations, Rear Admiral Nishimura in *Naka*

About 15 Transports, including * *Nana Maru,* * *Jukka Maru,* *Kuretake Maru,* * *Tsuruga Maru,* * *Tatsukami Maru,* * *Sumanoura Maru,* carrying units of the Sixteenth Army.

* Lost as a result of enemy action.

*Advance Echelon*

| | | | | |
|---|---|---|---|---|
| One Transport | DD | KAWAKAZE | DD | UMIKAZE |

[9] It is not clear to the writer whether this force was commanded by Vice Admiral Takahashi or Vice Admiral Hirose; probably the latter.

[10] Advance echelon at Tarakan and reinforcement at Balikpapan, 26 Jan.

[11] Departed Tarakan 24 Jan.; arrived Balikpapan 25 Jan.

ESCORT GROUP, Rear Admiral S. Hashimoto

| CL | YURA | DD | SHIRAYUKI [12] | DD | AMAGIRI |
|----|------|----|------|----|------|
| CL | KASHII | DD | HATSUYUKI [12] | DD | YUGIRI |
| DD | FUBUKI | CL | SENDAI | DD | ASAGIRI |

5 Minesweepers and 3 Subchasers, 3 Minelayers and Frigate SHIMUSHU.

AIR GROUP (3rd Air Force), Rear Admiral K. Kakuta

| CV | RYUJO | DD | SHIKINAMI |
|----|------|----|------|

## WESTERN FORCE
Vice Admiral J. Ozawa

Palembang Occupation

### COVERING GROUP, Admiral Ozawa

| CA | CHOKAI | CA | MOGAMI | CA | MIKUMA |
|----|------|----|------|----|------|
| CA | SUZUYA | CA | KUMANO | DD | SHIRAKUMO |
| DD | MURAKUMO | DD | ISONAMI | DD | AYANAMI |
| DD | URANAMI | DD | SHIRAYUKI | DD | HATSUYUKI |

### ATTACK GROUP

9 Transports, carrying units of 16th Army; Minesweepers 7 and 8.

## BALI FORCE
Rear Admiral K. Kubo

| CL | NAGARA | DD | WAKABA |
|----|------|----|------|
| DD | HATSUSHIMO | DD | NENOHI |
| DD | OSHIO | DD | ARASHIO |
| DD | ASASHIO | DD | MICHISHIO |

Transports *Sagami Maru* and *Sasago Maru* carrying units of 16th Army.

## MISCELLANEOUS FORCES

These occasionally coöperated, as at Ambon and Darwin.

### SOUTHERN FORCE, Vice Admiral N. Kondo in *Takao*

| BB | KONGO | CA | ATAGO | CA | MAYA |
|----|------|----|------|----|------|
| BB | HARUNA | CA | TAKAO (D) [13] | | |

Desdiv 4 and Desdiv 6, first section.

### CARRIER STRIKING FORCE, Vice Admiral C. Nagumo

| CV | AKAGI | CV | HIRYU (D) | CA | TONE (D) |
|----|------|----|------|----|------|
| CV | KAGA | CV | SORYU (D) | CA | CHIKUMA (D) |

8 Destroyers of Desron 1; 8 Tankers and Supply Ships.

[12] Subsequently detached to Western Force for Palembang.
[13] Those marked (D) according to Airdiv 8 Merit Report participated in Darwin strike.

## 3. *Consolidation in Java*

On the afternoon of New Year's Day, 1942, the picket boat of Her Netherlands Majesty's Navy that guarded the outer roadstead of Surabaya beheld an unusual sight: a submarine fully surfaced and flying the four-starred flag of an Admiral of the United States Navy. Admirals seldom travel in submarines, and Thomas C. Hart would have preferred any other means of conveyance from Manila than U.S.S. *Shark;* but the successful application of Mahan's doctrine by the Japanese left him no other choice.

The Commander in Chief of the Asiatic Fleet was no longer young, and he arrived tired and worn. But he quickly recovered his normal determination and optimism. He had come south to continue the fight from a new base, in combination with our Dutch and British allies. Rear Admiral Glassford had already set up an advanced command post at Surabaya for Task Force 5, the Striking Force. But the service base was established at far-off Port Darwin, Australia, by the Chief of Naval Operations at Washington.

During the better part of January there was much confusion among the three national commands which had fallen back on Java.

This new command, activated 15 January by order of the Combined Chiefs of Staff, was named "Abda" for the American, British, Dutch and Australian elements. Its theater included the Dutch East Indies, Burma, the Philippines, the South China Sea and the northeastern part of the Indian Ocean. Adjoining it to the southeastward was the "Anzac" Area, commanded by Vice Admiral Leary, which comprised the waters of Eastern Australia, New Zealand, British New Guinea, the Solomons, Loyalties and Fijis.

The Abda was the first attempt at a combined command in the Pacific. The Supreme Commander, Field Marshal Sir Archibald Wavell, was responsible for the coördination of all services and nationalities in his area. Lieutenant General Brett USA of the American Army Air Force was designated deputy commander, and the British General Pownall chief of staff. Under this supreme authority there was a naval commander (Admiral Hart), a ground forces operational commander (Lieutenant General Hein ter Poorten) and an air commander (Air Chief Marshal Sir Richard E. C. Peirse RAF). Tasks were to be assigned to forces of a single nationality whenever possible — which seldom happened.

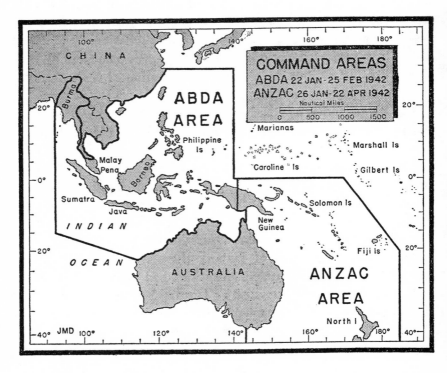

Under this arrangement the United States Navy still maintained the Asiatic Fleet with Hart in command. Owing to his preoccupation with the duties of Abda naval commander, he delegated most of his national and administrative responsibilities to his own chief of staff, Rear Admiral Purnell. This arrangement was changed on 30 January 1942 when Secretary Knox promoted Glassford to the rank of Vice Admiral and ordered him to assume command of United States Naval Forces in the Southwest Pacific.[14] Five days

[14] Secretary Knox to Admiral Hart, 29 Jan. 1942.

later Admiral Hart was relieved of his duties as Commander in Chief Asiatic Fleet, an organization which thereupon ceased to exist although never formally abolished. These rapid and sometimes overlapping changes in command relations are confusing indeed; even the admirals themselves hardly knew what their status really was.

To further the interests of a closely coördinated command, Admiral Hart spent most of his time at General Wavell's headquarters at Lembang near Bandoeng in the interior of western Java. Communications, extemporized by radio and wire, were always slow and unreliable. The Asiatic Fleet had to be based at Surabaya, where logistic support was available. Port Darwin, 1200 miles to the eastward, was an unfortunate choice for a service base; but the tenders and tankers of the Asiatic Fleet had been sent there in December at the cost of considerable time and effort, and the Navy Department did not wish to make a change. Thus Admiral Hart experienced unusual difficulty in carrying out his command functions over forces afloat.

# CHAPTER XV

# Balikpapan

## *6–24 January 1942*

East Longitude dates. Javanese (Zone minus 7½) time.

### 1. *Moves and Countermoves*

GIVEN free access to the oil and rubber of the Indies, the Greater East Asia Co-Prosperity Sphere could live on its own. Japan proposed to take these regions that yielded products vital to her economy, consolidate her position with a perimeter of steel and then repel any counterattacks offered by the enemy.

With the threat of the United States Pacific Fleet temporarily removed and the Philippines eliminated as a menace to their flank, the Japanese could proceed with this primary task. The landing at Miri in December had driven the British from northern Sarawak, leaving little opposition to the next movement in that direction. On 15 December 1941 a small amphibious force took possession of Brunei Bay to the north of Miri and on 11 January one of the same kind landed at Jesselton, northwest of Brunei.

To cover their eastern flank, and to reach the richest oil fields in Borneo, the invaders also entered the Celebes Sea. On 11 January paratroop and amphibious forces landed on the Menado Peninsula of Celebes, and on the same day a large amphibious force secured Tarakan Island off the east coast of Borneo.

The Menado Force departed Davao 9 January 1942 in six transports under the comand of Rear Admiral Tanaka. It was supported by Rear Admiral Fujita's seaplane carriers and Rear Admiral Takagi's three heavy cruisers. From the newly captured airdrome near Davao, 28 planes carrying 324 naval paratroops took off at dawn 11 January. At 0800 the assault teams from the amphibious force started moving ashore. The Dutch defenders were so few at this important point that they were able to offer only token resistance, and the Japanese soon had control of the area. Fearing a Dutch air attack they landed troops and equipment in record time and pulled the transports out as rapidly as possible.[1]

The Tarakan force — 16 transports, four minesweepers, two seaplane tenders, and a suitable escort — weighed anchor at Davao on the same day as the Menado force, arrived off the important oil center of Tarakan on 11 January and effected a landing promptly. A Dutch coast defense battery sank two minesweepers,[2] but there was only one infantry battalion to contest the landing. The United States Army Air Force, however, lent a hand. Seven Flying Fortresses which had been based at Malang Field, inland from Surabaya, since the first of the year, were flown up to bomb the transports. Foul weather caused four of them to turn back; the other three released bombs from 29,000 feet elevation in very poor visibility, and naturally hit nothing.[3]

Now that the Japanese controlled the northern approaches to Makassar Strait, they were ready to enter with a large force and seize their principal objective, the region around Balikpapan.

Sumatra, Borneo, Java, Celebes and Timor were not only bastions in the Malay Barrier but links in the sagging chain that connected American, British and Dutch sea power. The Abda command, established to protect the chain, never could see but a few links at a time. For the British, the protection of Singapore and of the eastern entrances to the Indian Ocean was paramount. For the United States and Australia, the ultimate danger was an enemy penetration of the Southwest Pacific to an extent that would deny them the bases necessary for reconquest. For the Dutch, the im-

[1] "Summary of Japanese Fleet Movements in the Dutch East Indies Invasion Operations," obtained by Mr. Salomon.
[2] Third Fleet Merit Report.
[3] Information from Journal of 19th Bombardment Group (H), communicated by Capt. Bernhardt Mortensen usa, Air Historical Office, U.S.A.F.

mediate threat to their choicest possessions loomed largest. Java
and Sumatra meant far more to the Netherlands than did the Philippines to America; they were a second homeland where the Dutch
had been trading and living for over three centuries, and where
there was a Netherlands population of over half a million, in addition to the many millions of Indonesians.

Under the supreme command of Marshal Wavell it was inevitable that emphasis should be placed on guarding Singapore. Nobody expected to be able to hold the center — Borneo and Java —
as well as both flanks. But, as Marshal Wavell firmly believed that
the safety of the center depended on the left flank, he made every
effort to deploy the major strength of the Allied navies on escort-
of-convoy duty, covering reinforcements to Singapore. At the
Inter-Allied Conference at Singapore on 18 December, Sir Robert
Brooke-Popham stressed the importance of overseas communications in the Indian Ocean for the British war effort and declared
that it would be a great mistake to retire Rear Admiral Glassford's
Task Force 5 to Darwin.[4] Admiral Hart agreed (although for a
different reason) that Darwin was unsuitable as a base; but he insisted that the unity of his Striking Force be maintained.

On 7 January Admiral Hart divided his fleet into four task
forces: Glassford's Striking Force, based at Surabaya; patrol aircraft (largely the relics of Patwing 10); submarines; and the Service
Force, based at Darwin. He took responsibility for the flank east of
Bali, the British for the western one and the Dutch for the center.

Rear Admiral Glassford readied his Striking Force to break up
any hostile landing reported, hoping to hit the enemy in the darkness before dawn. The first planned strike, on Kema, Celebes, was
called off 17 January when reconnaissance showed that the enemy
had already departed. The Striking Force then retired for fueling
to Kupang, Timor, a convenient place to meet the Darwin-based
oilers, but unduly far from the next Japanese objective, the nature
of which was soon learned.

---

[4] "Report on Inter-Allied Conference at Singapore, Dec. 18th and 20th" 25 Dec.
1941.

## 2. *Landing at Balikpapan*

Six of Captain Wilkes's submarines, newly based at Surabaya, were sent out to patrol the Strait. U.S.S. *Saury*, off Balikpapan Harbor, on 19 January 1942 exchanged recognition signals with a Netherlands submarine of the "K" class, and lay-to within hailing distance while Lieutenant Commander John L. Burnside swapped news with the Dutch skipper. *Pickerel* at the same time sighted a destroyer in the middle of Makassar Strait, heading southwest at high speed — a clear sign that the enemy was on the move.[5]

In ten days' time the Japanese had been able to consolidate their positions on both coasts of northern Borneo and use them as jumping-off places for new invasions. Admiral Takahashi was so pleased with the easy conquest of Tarakan that he signaled Admiral Nishimura on 17 January to expedite the next operation.[6] This was the capture of Balikpapan, the important oil center about halfway down Makassar Strait, unconnected by land with the rest of Borneo. Accordingly, on the afternoon of the 21st, 16 transports escorted by three patrol boats put out from Tarakan. An advance echelon, consisting of two transports with labor troops embarked, steamed ahead of the main body, escorted by two destroyers. Either this echelon or the main force was picked up by *Sturgeon* on the night of 22–23 January. She made a sound approach on one target and fired a spread of her forward torpedoes. Two or three of them exploded with a great flash and bang. The skipper, Lieutenant Commander W. L. Wright, sent in a laconic report that provided one of the few laughs of this grim campaign: "*Sturgeon* no longer virgin."[7]

Catalinas of Patrol Wing 10 made several sighting reports of enemy shipping moving in the direction of Balikpapan. Nether-

---

[5] Captain Wilkes's Report of 14 Mar. 1942.
[6] Japanese Desron 4 Report.
[7] The Joint Army-Navy Assessment Committee credits *Sturgeon* with no sinking on that day. She may have damaged an enemy destroyer, but there is no record of it. I am afraid the explosions were "prematures."

lands aircraft sighted the convoy, made several attacks, and on the evening of 23 January set on fire transport *Nana Maru,* which became a total loss.[8]

At 2000, half an hour after this air attack, the enemy minesweeping group entered the designated transport area four miles off the Borneo coast; at 2130 the transports came to an anchor and commenced debarking the occupation force. They were well screened by Admiral Nishimura's flagship *Naka,* nine destroyers of Squadron 4, the minesweepers, and a subchaser. Shortly before midnight, when the landing of troops was proceeding according to plan, the Admiral made new patrol dispositions for close cover, and steamed eastward with some of the destroyers to ensure against a sudden strike by the Allies.

Admiral Glassford's Striking Force was anchored at Kupang Bay in the Dutch end of Timor on the morning of 20 January when word came of this enemy movement. As soon as his four destroyers (*Ford, Pope, Parrott, Paul Jones*) could be refueled out of *Marblehead,* they and the two cruisers[9] departed. *Marblehead,* with one turbine out could make only 15 knots. *Boise,* when passing through Sape Strait on 21 January, hit an uncharted pinnacle rock which left her in no condition for offensive action. Captain Robinson was not to blame for this accident; Netherlands East Indies waters are as tricky as any in the world, and the charts then available to the United States Navy were based on incomplete surveys.

Admiral Glassford now ordered both cruisers to double back and rendezvous at Warorada Bay, Sumbawa. That evening he shifted his flag to *Marblehead,* and filled her fuel tanks from *Boise.* The latter proceeded to the southern coast of Java to have her bottom inspected.

[8] Comair Asiatic Fleet (Gen. Brereton) War Diary 20–24 Jan. 1942; Chihaya "Outline."

[9] *Houston* and two DDs were on escort duty Darwin to Singapore, and the rest of the Striking Force was under repair or escorting.

U.S.S. *John D. Ford*

U.S.S. *John D. Edwards*

*"Four-pipers" of the Asiatic Fleet*

*Photo by Royal Netherlands Department Van Marine*

Admiral Helfrich inspecting Royal Netherlands Marines aboard
H.N.M.S. *Tromp*

Wounded being removed from *Marblehead* at Tjilatjap
(*Houston* in background)

*East Indies Defenders*

## 3. *Night Action off Balikpapan, 24 January* [10]

Commander Paul Talbot in *John D. Ford* continued with the three other four-pipers through Sape Strait toward the Postillon Islands in the Flores Sea, en route to Makassar Strait. Since *Marblehead* could not possibly catch up with them, she made for Lombok Strait east of Bali, whence she would head directly north to a rendezvous some 90 miles below Balikpapan and furnish cover for the destroyers' withdrawal. Talbot passed the Postillon Islands and headed for Cape Mandar, which marks the Celebes side of the entrance to Makassar Strait. By 1632 January 23 he had passed Makassar Town well to starboard and had the Spermonde Archipelago abeam. Talbot then altered course to the eastward so that enemy air patrols might think he was heading for the Gulf of Mandar. At 1930, about an hour after sunset, the column turned left to the course for Balikpapan Bay, leaving Cape Mandar 6 miles to starboard. As it headed for the coast of Borneo, *Ford's* coding officer decrypted Admiral Hart's latest order — "Attack!" The four old "cans" were on their own. Commander Talbot conveyed tactical instructions to his skippers over voice telephone: "Torpedo attack; hold gunfire until the 'fish' are gone; use initiative and prosecute the strike to your utmost."

The column now bent on 27 knots. At 0047 January 24, a searchlight appeared on the flagship's starboard bow and a Japanese ship, probably a destroyer, challenged with blue blinkers. To avoid detection, the destroyers made several slight changes of course during the next two hours, but all in the general direction of Balikpapan.

The Dutch had laid waste their oil facilities at Balikpapan before

[10] Frequently called the Battle of Makassar Strait in war literature; but Balikpapan, the more accurate name, is preferred by participants. Principal American source is Admiral Hart's Report "Naval Engagement off Balikpapan" 29 Jan. 1942, including Action Reports of the four destroyers and that of the O.T.C., Cdr. P. H. Talbot (Comdesdiv 59). Cdr. R. N. Antrim, exec. of *Pope* in this fight, helped me to reconstruct the scene. Principal Japanese source is a report prepared for this work after the war by Cdr. M. Chihaya, "Outline of the Battle of Makassar Strait" ATIS 15685.

retiring and, for good measure, had bombed them from the air that very afternoon. Those old Hudsons and Brewsters flown by Dutch pilots did a good job; besides sinking *Nana Maru*, they set fires ashore which provided an infernal backdrop for the destroyers' devilish work and silhouetted the enemy's transports very accept-

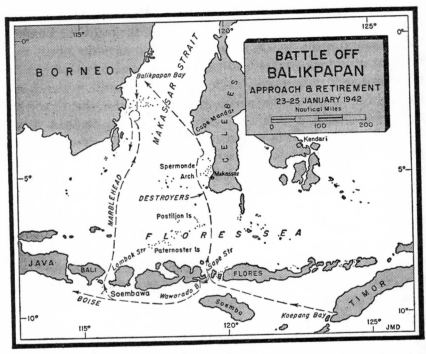

ably.[11] This was the moment every destroyer man dreamed of — launching torpedoes at "sitting ducks." It was not easy to distinguish the number and disposition of the transports. Momentarily they would be silhouetted by the fires, then obscured in the murk of petroleum smoke. Talbot's four destroyers piled in.

Ten minutes' steaming after the first sighting brought them

[11] O.N.I. Combat Narratives "Java Sea Campaign" p. 18. The fact that the fires appeared to port led the destroyer sailors to believe that they came from burning ships. In the rapid action that follows, times and other data differ considerably in the various reports. Facts have been reconciled as much as possible between the American and Japanese sources.

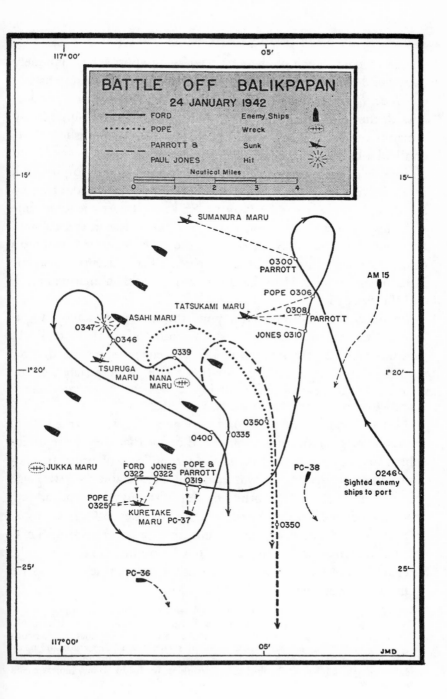

BATTLE OFF BALIKPAPAN
24 JANUARY 1942

FORD
POPE
PARROTT &
PAUL JONES

Enemy Ships
Wreck
Sunk
Hit

Nautical Miles
0    1    2    3    4

SUMANURA MARU

0300
PARROTT

AM 15

POPE 0306

TATSUKAMI MARU

0308
ASAHI MARU
0347
0346
0339
TSURUGA
MARU
NANA
MARU

PARROTT

JONES 0310

0350
0400    0335

JUKKA MARU

FORD    JONES    POPE &
0322    0322    PARROTT
0319

PC-38

0246
Sighted enemy
ships to port

POPE
0325

KURETAKE
MARU    PC-37

0350

PC-36

JMD

within torpedo range of their targets. They approached obliquely the second line of transports, anchored about 5 miles off the harbor entrance. *Parrott* was the first to launch. All three of her torpedoes missed; the close range and high speed made marksmanship largely a matter of luck. They would probably have accomplished more, and had a better chance of escaping detection, with less speed and a more deliberate torpedo fire. *Parrott* veered slightly to port and, two minutes later, fired five more torpedoes to starboard, at a ship she thought to be 1000 yards away. Still no hits. At the same time *Ford* fired one astern, and at 0257 *Paul Jones*, last in the column, fired one to starboard. Some thought the target a destroyer, some a cruiser. Actually the vessel that received all this attention was the little minesweeper *AM–15* heading south on anti-submarine patrol, and she escaped.

Since *Ford* had now passed beyond the anchored convoy, Commander Talbot at 0300 led his ships south for another crack. At that moment *Parrott*, still parallel to the enemy ships, fired three torpedoes at a target on her port bow. Two minutes later, as she rounded the turn, she heard a mighty explosion. *Sumanoura Maru*, a 3500-ton transport, went up like a powder keg.[12]

The transports and their escorts were now thrown into confusion. Some Japanese commanding officers thought that they were under submarine attack and so ordered the wrong kind of protective action. Others grasped what was going on, but, unable to distinguish friend from foe, fired at both. Admiral Nishimura — who, judging from his actions here and at the Battle for Leyte Gulf in 1944, must have been one of the least competent Japanese flag officers — led his destroyer squadron right out into the strait, where he circled aimlessly searching for nonexistent submarines, leaving his transports to the mercy of the Americans.[13]

---

[12] Hart Report; Japanese Desron 4 Report agrees precisely on the time.

[13] Dutch submarine *K–14* had been lurking in the background and probably sank transport *Jukka Maru* at 2300 Jan. 23; but now, observing that her "friends were doing very well," she withdrew from the scene. "Java Sea Campaign" p. 23. "Brief Summary Netherlands Submarines" says *K–18* had a grandstand seat but made no attack. Chihaya "Outline" admits sinking of *Jukka Maru*, but *Japanese Naval and Merchant Shipping Losses* does not mention it.

On her reverse course *Pope* at 0306 fired a spread of her last five torpedoes at a transport. A minute or two later her three consorts straightened out on their southerly course, and began launching a succession of "fish." One hit *Tatsukami Maru*, which blew up and sank. Two transports were now accounted for, but the destroyers had few torpedoes left.

Commander Talbot at 0314, ascertaining that he was opening range on the anchored ships, ordered his column to execute a 90-degree turn and head for the southern end of the anchorage. Five minutes later, when well along on the new course, *Pope* and *Parrott* fired two and three torpedoes respectively at PC-37, patrolling on their port beam, believing it to be a destroyer. It was, in fact, a converted 750-ton torpedo boat. Three of the torpedoes hit and PC-37 went down. A transport appeared to port, silhouetted in the weird light. *Ford* and *Paul Jones*, the only destroyers with torpedoes left, each fired one. This transport, already under way, turned and avoided both; *Paul Jones* got her with a third, making a neat hit on her starboard bow. The 5000-ton *Kuretake Maru* blew up and sank.

The destroyers now made a wide turn to port. As the column doubled back upon itself all ships opened gunfire and the few remaining torpedoes were launched at targets which offered themselves on both sides. By this time the enemy was shooting very wild. It was now 0335. The many violent turns made by the leader had so far been closely followed by the other three; but now they became separated. Commander Talbot in *Ford* turned northwestward; *Pope* followed for a space, but *Parrott*, with *Paul Jones* close behind, lost sight of the others and retired independently to the southward. That took them out of the fight, and *Pope* soon followed.

*Ford* continued the fight alone. As no fresh targets immediately presented themselves, Commander Talbot turned again toward the burning shore. At 0346 he fired his last torpedo at a transport that appeared close aboard and to port. The explosion was heard, a flash was seen and the ship was observed listing rapidly; but apparently it floated, as the Japanese have no record of a sinking at that stage of the battle. At that moment, when *Ford* was about to double back in order to avoid running aground, she received her only battle damage, from a shell hit that wounded four men and started a fire which was quickly extinguished. The destroyer turned southwesterly and fired at several targets. According to Commander Talbot, every shot found its mark. Several transports, including *Asahi Maru*,[14] received superficial damage at this juncture. The 7000-ton *Tsuruga Maru* had already been eliminated, by Netherlands submarine *K–18* before midnight.

With torpedoes expended there was not much more that Talbot and his flag captain, Lieutenant Commander Cooper, could do. So *Ford* turned up 28 knots and set a course for the planned rendezvous with *Marblehead*. At break of day the other three destroyers found their division commander, formed column on him, and a few minutes after the end of the morning watch they raised the *Marblehead*.

In the cold light of day, six years later, that mad night seems somewhat less glamorous than it did at the time. Three four-pipers had run amuck through an anchored and silhouetted convoy, choosing their own range and time to fire torpedoes; yet even the over-optimistic "score" of the morning after was disappointing. Only 4 transports out of a possible 12, and 1 patrol craft out of 3, were sunk, and a few more damaged.[15] Reasons for the numerous misses of torpedoes can only be guessed. Probably a large proportion of them were duds, for that was so in other actions at this stage of the war. Shoal water may have deflected many "fish" from running true. The darkness of the night, combined with the high speed of the attacking ships, the close range and the general confusion of a night action were largely responsible for the failure to bring down more game. Commander Talbot and the junior officers who commanded

[14] Chihaya "Outline" states that this ship was hit as early as 0315, but the destroyers did not open fire that early.

[15] Japanese Desron 4 Report states that the aircraft tender *Sanuki Maru* was severely damaged by 5 four-engined bombers at 1130 Jan. 27. She was the most valuable ship hit off Balikpapan, but this happened three days after the battle.

his ships showed the utmost gallantry and skill at maneuvering under very difficult conditions. They deserved every bit of the praise they received from a nation hungry for news of action and for victory. The "leather medal" goes to the Japanese admiral who led his combat ships out to sea just when the transports needed his protection.

The Battle off Balikpapan, neglected in the press of events, should always be remembered as our first surface action in the Pacific War; indeed, the first undertaken by the United States Navy since 1898. It was a tactical victory without a doubt; but from the broad strategic viewpoint the Japanese claim that it failed to halt their advance by so much as a day was correct.

# CHAPTER XVI

# The Octopus

*January–February 1942*

## 1. *Clutching Tentacles*

A T the end of January 1942 it seemed that nothing the Allies could muster would be able to stop the Japanese advance. The enemy was obviously converging on Sumatra and Java. By the last week of January he was firmly entrenched at various points on both sides of the South China Sea, in Makassar Strait, and on the Celebes side of the Molucca Sea. At most of them he was building or improving airfields and staging forces for a further advance. Already he had control of the three principal air-sea approaches to the Java Sea.

The manner of the Japanese advance resembled the insidious yet irresistible clutching of multiple tentacles. Like some vast octopus it relied on strangling many small points rather than concentrating on a vital organ. No one arm attempted to meet the entire strength of the Abda fleet. Each fastened on a small portion of the enemy and, by crippling him locally, finished by killing the entire animal.

This strategy was easy to effect on a loose-jointed organization such as the Abda command. Owing to diverse interests the three Allied powers dissipated their forces in various directions and on sundry missions. That was why Admiral Hart had been able to collect only two cruisers and four old destroyers to execute the opportunity of a lifetime, the strike on Balikpapan. A gloomy afterthought of that fight was the prediction that never again could the enemy so be taken by surprise.

The Japanese spread their tentacles cautiously, never extending beyond the range of land-based aircraft unless they had carrier support. The distance of each advance was determined by the radius of fighter planes from airfields under their control. This range was generally less than 400 miles, but the Japanese made these short hops in surprisingly rapid succession. Amphibious operations, preceded by air strikes and covered by air power, developed with terrifying regularity. Before the Allies had consolidated a new position, they were confronted with a system of air bases from which enemy aircraft operated on their front, flanks and even rear.[1]

During the afternoon of 24 January, the day of the action off Balikpapan, Lieutenant (jg) Campbell in a PBY spotted a large enemy surface force in the vicinity of that oil port and led Army B–17s to the attack.[2] They probably inflicted some damage, but stopped nothing. The Japanese Eastern Force that had taken Menado had embarked on 21 January to capture Kendari in southeastern Celebes.[3] The six transports allotted, and their escort, were staged from an anchorage on the northeastern extremity of Celebes; while the cruiser and carrier groups, for reasons best known to Rear Admiral Takagi, at first took a northeasterly course.[4]

Seaplane tender *Childs*, flagship of Asiatic Fleet aircraft, was getting under way from her anchorage in Kendari Bay at 0532 January 24. To the amazement and consternation of the ship's company, enemy vessels were sighted approaching. By the good fortune that sometimes attends sailors, this unpleasant apparition was covered by a sudden rain squall into which *Childs* promptly steamed. Twenty minutes later more Japanese destroyers appeared, and they too were avoided. Two hours passed, and *Childs*, making her best speed, was attacked by 6 "Zeros," but they scored no hits and the valuable ship escaped safely. But the Invasion Force came to anchor, disembarked, and promptly took possession of Kendari.

---

[1] "Technique of Japanese Amphibious Operations in 1941–42" 12 June 1946, Japanese answers to inquiries by Mr. Salomon. (ATIS Doc. 19692 D.)
[2] Asiatic Fleet Air Command War Diary 24 Jan. 1942.
[3] See Composition of Forces above.
[4] "Summary of Japanese Fleet Movements in the Dutch East Indies Invasion Operations."

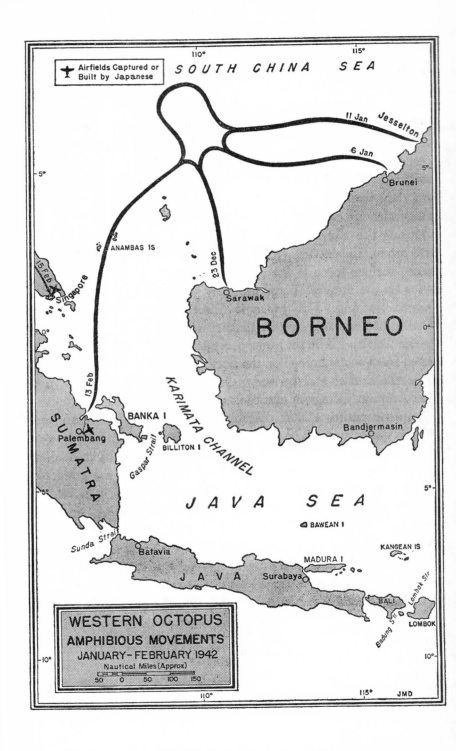

Airfields Captured or
Built by Japanese

SOUTH CHINA SEA

110°                                                    115°

11 Jan    Jesselton
6 Jan
Brunei                    5°

ANAMBAS IS

23 Dec

Sarawak

BORNEO

Bandjermasin

Singapore    15 Feb

13 Feb

SUMATRA    BANKA I
Palembang    BILLITON I
Gaspar Strait

KARIMATA CHANNEL

JAVA    SEA

BAWEAN I

KANGEAN IS

Sunda Strait

Batavia
MADURA I

JAVA    Surabaya

BALI

LOMBOK

WESTERN OCTOPUS
AMPHIBIOUS MOVEMENTS
JANUARY–FEBRUARY 1942
Nautical Miles (Approx)
50    0    50    100    150

JMD

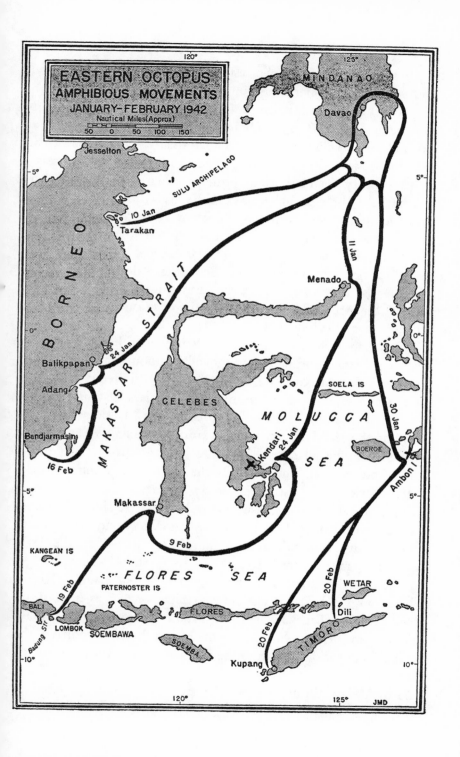

EASTERN OCTOPUS
AMPHIBIOUS MOVEMENTS
JANUARY-FEBRUARY 1942
Nautical Miles (Approx)
50    0    50    100    150

MINDANAO

Davao

Jesselton

SULU ARCHIPELAGO

10 Jan
Tarakan

B O R N E O

M A K A S S A R   S T R A I T

11 Jan

Menado

24 Jan

Balikpapan

Adang

C E L E B E S

SOELA IS

M O L U C C A

Bandjarmasin

16 Feb

Kendari
24 Jan

S E A

BOEROE

30 Jan

Ambon I

Makassar

9 Feb

KANGEAN IS

F L O R E S        S E A

PATERNOSTER IS

19 Feb

BALI

Badung Str

LOMBOK   SOEMBAWA

SOEMBA

FLORES

WETAR

Dili

20 Feb

20 Feb

T I M O R

20 Feb

Kupang

JMD

Japan now controlled the shortest route between Java and Australia and was within air-bombing range of Surabaya.

Admiral Hart expected an invasion of Kendari to be followed by a move against Ambon (Amboina or Amboyna), the small island 350 miles east of Kendari, whose spices had been a bone of contention between English, Portuguese, and Dutch in the seventeenth century. Kendari, as the principal town in southeast Celebes and base for the next jump toward the Malay Barrier or Ambon, was the most logical enemy objective after Menado; but the Dutch guessed wrong and sent some of their best troops, reinforced by an Australian battalion, to Ambon. Here there were also a few tired aircraft of both nationalities. Admiral Hart recommended that these elements be withdrawn immediately. But Field Marshal Sir Archibald Wavell made the decision to let them stay and fight it out as best they could.

The Japanese high command evidently considered Ambon of great importance, and wished to move in without waiting for land-based aircraft from Kendari. Accordingly they allotted two seaplane carriers and several destroyers plus two carriers that had participated in the Pearl Harbor strike to cover the Invasion Force and soften up the island defenses. Planes from carriers *Soryu* and *Hiryu* began striking installations there on 24 January, the very day of the Kendari occupation. This was only the beginning. Admiral Tanaka in *Jintsu* with four destroyers, on 27 January sailed from Davao with the first echelon of transports for Ambon. Crossing the Celebes Sea they were covered by heavy cruisers *Nachi* and *Haguro* and three destroyers, to which four more were joined on the 28th, when they entered the dangerous waters of the Molucca Passage. On the 29th another transport group departed Bangka Roads, Celebes, with two destroyers and two minesweepers as escorts, and joined Admiral Tanaka at sea. Two more destroyers, three minesweepers and two subchasers, which had been supporting the Kendari occupation, departed thence, and on the 30th also joined Tanaka.

As the Allies still had a few old planes on Ambon, the Japanese dispatched seaplane carriers *Chitose* and *Mizuho* with a patrol craft escort from Bangka on 30 January. Their planes were launched from near Kelang Island, west of Ambon, to provide air cover for the landing operations.

Thus, the Japanese approached Ambon with the overwhelming and irresistible air-surface and amphibious forces that the United States Navy was unable to provide in Pacific Ocean operations before the close of 1943. They could not lose. First assault was made on Ambon Town on 31 January, and by 3 February the valuable airfield was in their hands and all Dutch and Australian survivors were taken prisoner.

So much for the Eastern or Celebes Octopus. Now let us turn to the South China Sea monster, and linger for a moment at dying Singapore.

On the first day of the war, 8 December 1941, carrier planes flying from Indochina attacked this mighty naval base, and the quick seizure of Kota Bharu was followed by a rapid advance down the Malay Peninsula. The British felt reasonably secure in Singapore despite the loss of their two capital ships, enemy command of the air, and the relentless advance of ground forces. Marshal Wavell told Admiral Hart as late as 31 January that the island of Singapore could hold out indefinitely, although he admitted that it could no longer serve as a fleet base, and the order had already been given to evacuate ground forces from the peninsula.[5]

At that time Admiral Hart's international team (Helfrich, Glassford and Collins) had been working under Wavell for two weeks. The change in the defense plans for Singapore released considerable striking power for offensive naval operations. At a conference on 1 February, Hart formed on paper the first Abda Combined Striking Force with teeth enough to warrant the name; yet only a few of the ships were immediately available. The Dutch cruisers and destroyers had been sent on a wild-goose chase to Karimata Strait between Borneo and Sumatra, where a Japanese surface force was

[5] Hart Report pp. 69–70.

rumored to be. That rumor was false, as Admiral Hart happened to know; but Helfrich had not asked his opinion before sending the ships out.

Even in those most difficult days the Netherlander was not entirely frank with his American superior in command; but Admiral Hart, appreciating the ambiguous nature of Helfrich's position, bore him no grudge. Helfrich was not only local naval commander but Minister of Marine of the Netherlands East Indies, which involved civil duties as well. The Governor insisted on receiving a play-by-play report every morning and, as this information was soon circulating in the town where there were numerous enemy spies, Admiral Hart had to be reticent, too.

As Darwin had proved to be too distant from Surabaya as a service force base, Admiral Hart ordered up several of his larger auxiliaries to Java. They had not yet arrived when, on 3 February, the Japanese air force made its first raid on Surabaya, destroying a number of Dutch planes. This meant that their airdrome at Kendari was already in operation, and that more of the same could be expected. Perhaps it was already too late to fight the war from Java; from Surabaya, in any case. So tenders *Holland* and *Otus* were diverted to Tjilatjap on the south coast of Java, where the old China gunboats *Asheville* and *Tulsa* had been based for some time.[6]

Tjilatjap was by no means ideal — most American bluejackets referred to it as "that lousy dump" — but no other berth remained. After threading a very hazardous pass one entered a long, narrow bay with more shoals than deeps. Ships had to moor in line in the middle of the harbor, interfering with traffic and furnishing neat targets for enemy aircraft.

## 2. *The Ordeal of* Marblehead [7]

*Marblehead* and destroyers *Stewart*, *Edwards*, *Barker* and *Bulmer* had retired to Bunda Roads at Madura Island which separates Sura-

[6] W. B. Porter "Gunboat Saga" *U.S. Nav. Inst. Proceedings* LXX 424–27.
[7] *Marblehead* "Report of Action with Japanese Planes North of Lombok Strait, Feb. 4, 1942"; information from Cdr. N. B. Van Bergen, her Executive Officer; Doorman's Operation Order of 3 Feb.

baya from the Java Sea. Cruiser *Houston* and destroyers *Paul Jones*, *Pillsbury* and *Whipple*, oiler *Pecos* and Admiral Doorman's Dutch force were already there.

Rear Admiral Doorman, who had already assumed active command of the Combined Striking Force, had plans for a try at Makassar Strait. Three enemy cruisers, several destroyers and about 20 transports had been seen by our planes steaming about the southern entrance to the strait, evidently about to "go places" — probably Makassar Town or Bandjermasin. If he were to strike, he must do so quickly. Hazardous, no doubt, since the enemy controlled the air over the Java Sea; but now or never. So the Dutch Admiral in light cruiser *De Ruyter* led the Combined Striking Force out of Bunda Roads at 0000 February 4. At a rendezvous 5 miles north of Meyndertssdroogte Light, cruising formation was assumed and a course set for the Japanese concentration. *De Ruyter* led the cruisers (*Houston*, *Marblehead* and *Tromp*) spaced 700 to 800 yards; the four American destroyers guarded the flanks and the four Dutch destroyers the rear.

At 0935, when they had reached lat. 7°28′ S, long. 115°37′ E, Admiral Doorman relayed word to his ships by radio that 37 enemy bombers were known to be on their way to Surabaya. These were twin-engined "Nells," naval bombers of the Eleventh Air Fleet based on the newly conditioned field at Kendari.[8] The higher peaks on Bali and Lombok could be seen from the deck of *Marblehead* between scudding clouds to the southward, and in the other direction Kangean Island was visible at 0949 when 4 formations of 9 bombers each appeared from the east at an elevation of 17,000 feet.

Captain Robinson of *Marblehead* at once ordered General Quarters and Condition Zed (the maximum of watertight integrity), dumped more than 4000 gallons of aviation gasoline over the side, and squared his ship around for action. Although she already had enough steam to make over 25 knots, the remaining six boilers were lighted off so that in twenty minutes full power would be available. All Allied ships scattered. In those days, before we had learned to double and treble the number of anti-aircraft guns in fighting ships,

[8] Capt. C. Takahashi *Inter. Jap. Off.* I 74.

which made a fairly close concentration of fire desirable, it was every ship for herself during an air attack. This gave them a chance to maneuver quickly and tempted the enemy force to split up into small groups. But, with no radar mounted and consequently only a brief warning, there was no time for effective dispersal. The only air cover over the force consisted of 4 clumsy but valiant Catalinas which stayed on the job until shot down.

At 0954, nine bombers peeled off from the enemy formation and headed for the two leading cruisers, ignoring *Tromp* and the destroyers. In a shallow V formation, almost abreast, they came down to about 14,000 feet and then leveled off, making about 150 knots. When he guessed that they were nearing the point of bomb release, Captain Robinson ordered full left rudder in order to swing his ship a split second after it was too late for the enemy bombardiers to meet the ship's change of course, and increased his speed. But he was a little too early and the attackers flew over the ship without dropping a bomb. A second attack was equally futile. On a third, at 1019, a stick of about seven bombs fell 50 to 100 yards from the port bow. They sounded "like gravel thrown against a ship" to the men below, but caused no damage, and one bomber was disintegrated by a 3-inch shell. Immediately after this run a plane started spiraling towards *Marblehead*. It was hit, and the aviator had evidently decided to be a 1942-style kamikaze. As he approached, the gunners let him have all the .50-caliber machine-gun fire that they could dish out, and the plane turned away and splashed. Just then, 7 attacking bombers appeared on the port quarter and at 1027 straddled *Marblehead* with a half-dozen thin-walled and highly explosive bombs. One crashed through the starboard motor launch, pierced the deck and exploded below, wiping out the sick bay, demolishing the wardroom and near-by cabins, and blowing a 6-foot hole in the deck. Fires broke out all over the stricken section. A near miss close aboard started a number of bow plates which the high speed of the vessel bent in still more, and soon she was appreciably down by the head. A third landed square on the fantail, piercing the main deck and exploding in the hand-steering compartment. Happily the explosion folded back a big section of the main deck against the after gun turret, which let out the chlorine gases escaping from damaged batteries and saved many lives. All living quarters in that part of the ship were gutted and leaks started, big enough to let in green water. Suddenly the after part of the ship burst into flame. Here the fire mains were ruptured and hand brigades were the only means of combatting the fire. The rudder jammed hard left and the ship started steaming in circles with a 10-degree list to starboard. Casualties were light in comparison to the severe damage to the ship — 15 killed or mortally wounded, and 34, including the executive officer, unable to continue at their stations. Most of the severe injuries were burns on exposed parts of the body; it was largely as a result of this experience that the United States Navy forbade shorts or sleeveless shirts to be worn at sea, no matter how hot the climate.

Captain Robinson kept the ship steaming at 25 knots as the best defense against further attack, although he could not steer her and she continued to make small circles.

The damage control officer at once set to work trying to right the rudder and control the fires. Tons of loose water on the main deck accentuated the list, and, with compartments flooding both fore and aft, there was danger of the ship's breaking in half.

Still she had to fight; the enemy gave no respite. Another flight of planes approached; the captain ordered both engines ahead full speed but these planes did not attack. Two more groups of planes appeared at 1111. *Marblehead* repeated her previous maneuver and opened fire; but this time they dropped their bombs close aboard *De Ruyter*. This was the fourth attack received by Admiral Doorman's flagship. She was straddled and her anti-aircraft fire control knocked out.

*Houston* fared as ill as *Marblehead*, although her anti-aircraft gunners did better and shot down several attacking planes. Her sister ships had time to admire her twisting and turning, through the geysers of near misses, like a great animal at bay. A heavy bomb, dropped in the last of four attacks, exploded on her main deck, killed some fifty men and knocked out the after gun turret. "The shrapnel pierced the turret in a hundred places and set fire to the powder in the gun chamber. The crew on the electric deck, powder circle and shell deck and the crew of turret 3, except for two men,

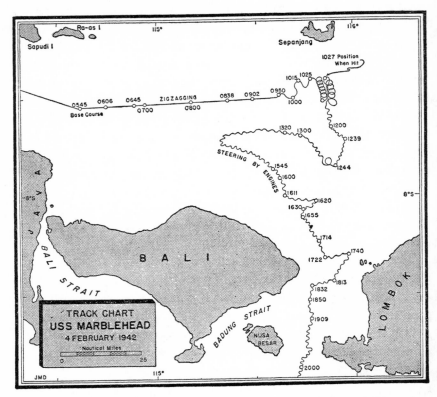

were all burned to death," reported Coxswain Madson. "The after repair party was also wiped out with the exception of Eddy and Collins. . . . One of the repair party trained a hose inside the turret and shorted the firing circuit causing the center gun to fire. There was no confusion or shouting. All was well organized. After our hit it was every dog for himself and no fooling. We started away and noticed the *Marblehead* was going in circles. We offered to help but her skipper said he was O.K. so we headed for Bali Strait. Luckily there were quite a few rainstorms right on our course so we ran from one to the other without being attacked again." [9]

At last the planes disappeared in the clouds. They reported they had sunk two cruisers and damaged two more.[10]

By noon *Marblehead* was able to steer a wavering course by keeping one engine going steadily and starting and stopping the other at intervals. The task force headed for Lombok Strait, and Captain Robinson sent a plea for fighter planes to Admiral Glassford. *De Ruyter* and the United States destroyers steamed around her in a protecting circle as *Marblehead*, following Glassford's instructions, made her painful way toward Tjilatjap. At midnight 4–5 February, when Admiral Doorman was assured that *Marblehead* could take care of herself, he steamed on ahead.

## 3. *Submarines at Surabaya* [11]

The small submarine repair base at Surabaya, although in many ways a model of efficiency, was inadequate to take care of the United States submarines that based there after evacuating Philippine waters at the year's end. No American spare parts were available nor were the technicians familiar with American machinery. For about three weeks it seemed to the submariners in Surabaya that they had left the war behind them; when they came in from a patrol they could enjoy a real rest. But from the first Japanese air attack on Surabaya, 3 February 1942, there was no more of that. As in Manila Bay, they had to clear the docks at dawn and sit all

[9] *Houston* Survivors' Report, Enclosure B. Compare Hanson W. Baldwin "Saga of a Stout Ship" *N.Y. Times Magazine* 3 Mar. 1946; and Fletcher Pratt "Campaign in the Java Sea" *Harper's Magazine* Nov. 1942.

[10] Japanese War Diary.

[11] Captain John Wilkes, Commander Submarines Asiatic Fleet, arrived at Surabaya in *Swordfish* 7 Jan. 1942. His chief of staff (Commander James Fife) accompanied tenders *Holland* and *Otus* to Darwin, where the logistics base was established 2 Jan. Until the end of the Java Sea campaign, Capt. Wilkes directed submarine operations from Surabaya, but his logistics base remained at Darwin until 4 Feb., when *Holland* and *Otus* were moved up to Tjilatjap in anticipation of air attacks. On 19 Feb. *Holland* again moved, to Fremantle; and on 15 Mar. to Albany, Australia. Comsubsaf (Capt. Wilkes) to Cominch 1 Apr. 1942 "War Activities Submarines U.S. Asiatic Fleet, Dec. 1, 1941 to Apr. 1, 1942."

day on the bottom of the outer harbor, then surface at dusk, steam back to the docks and work all night on maintenance and repairs. The Dutch submarine *K–7* took two direct hits and was destroyed on 17 February while lying on the bottom.[12]

During January, February and March, United States submarines continued to molest enemy supply lines from Davao down through the Molucca and Makassar Straits and from the Sulu Sea to Hainan and Indochina. On 10 January *Stingray* sank a 5000-ton transport south of Hainan; and on the same day *Pickerel* sank 3000-ton *Kanko Maru* at the mouth of Davao Gulf. On the 24th, Lieutenant C. C. Smith's *Swordfish*, by far the most successful boat of the Asiatic Fleet, sank a 4000-ton freighter off Menado. *Seadragon* at the end of January extended her patrol to Lingayen Gulf and there sank a 6500-ton *Maru*. On the 8th, *S–37* scored the only submarine's kill of a destroyer in this campaign when she torpedoed *Natsushio* off Makassar Town; and on 2 March *Sailfish* sank a 6500-ton aircraft ferry off Bali. On 4 March *S–39* sank a 6500-ton tanker in the western part of the Java Sea. *Sturgeon* finally did lose her virginity on 30 March, but not too nobly; the agent was only an 850-ton freighter.[13]

Captain Wilkes's boats accounted for only 12 Japanese ships aggregating a little over 50,000 tons; their own losses were considerable. Besides *Sealion*, bombed at Cavite, *Perch* was lost in the Java Sea, *Shark* disappeared somewhere off Celebes and *S–36* grounded. But only a small portion of Wilkes's nominal strength was available. The boats were constantly harassed from the air in Surabaya; they were running low on torpedoes and fuel; and Admirals Hart and Helfrich had to make use of them as a defensive screen for Java.

---

[12] "Brief Summary of Activities of H.N.M. Submarines in the Southwest Pacific for Period Dec. 1941–Mar. 1942." Document lent to the writer by Netherlands Naval Attaché at Washington.

[13] These sinkings, checked in the Joint Army-Navy Assessment Committee's *Japanese Naval and Merchant Losses World War II by U.S. Submarines* (1947), are the only ones made by Asiatic Fleet submarines at this period. There were others in the North Pacific by submarines of the Pacific Fleet, and in the Southwest by Dutch submarines.

After the Battle of the Java Sea, Surabaya was no longer tenable even as an advanced base, and the last United States submarine departed on 1 March. Captain Wilkes shifted both headquarters and base to Fremantle, whence the veterans of the Asiatic Fleet, reinforced by new boats and new blood from home, waged a successful war of attrition against the Greater East Asia Co-Prosperity Sphere.

## 4. *Courage and Caution*

Admiral Doorman was increasingly apprehensive of enemy air attack; and well he might be. The 36 Army P–40 fighter planes brought in to Java from Australia at great cost [14] were rapidly expended, owing largely to poor warning facilities which allowed them to be caught on the ground or at altitudes too low for effective interception. And, as the Allies had no carriers in this area, there was practically nothing with which to intercept a Japanese bombing attack on his ships.

So, to keep out of harm's way, the Dutch admiral in his flagship *De Ruyter* continued westward along the south coast of Java after he had dropped *Marblehead* astern at 0000 February 5, and through Sunda Strait to Batavia. Admiral Hart, indignant over the retirement, thought seriously of relieving this cautious commander but decided not to do so because the Netherlanders, fighting for their own soil, would feel slighted if not represented in the high command. He ordered Doorman to return to Tjilatjap, and met him there on 8 February.

Allied Intelligence considered the next objective of the enemy to be Bandjermasin in southeast Boreno. While the admirals were in conference, word came in that an enemy task force was rounding the southeast point of Celebes. Admiral Hart decided that a

[14] Of 120 to 124 Army P–40s sent forward from Australia, 11 were destroyed in the raid on Darwin, 14 were lost in transit, including those at Timor, 32 were sunk with U.S.S. *Langley* and there was no time to assemble the 27 crated in *Sea Witch* (see below), and only 36 reached Java. "History of V Army Air Force" Pt. I chap. ii, at Army Air Historical Office.

night attack on it should be attempted. He directed Doorman to make plans and proceed as soon as possible.

After the conference was over, Admiral Hart inspected the damage that *Houston* and *Marblehead* had received in Flores Sea. Although the heavy cruiser was defenseless aft, since her after turret was completely knocked out, she still had fire power equivalent to that of the British cruiser *Exeter* and the Admiral decided to keep her until relief could be obtained. For the time being she was assigned convoy duty to protect an important troop movement from Darwin to Timor.

*Marblehead* was out of the picture as far as the Java campaign was concerned. It was even questionable whether she could be made seaworthy enough to go home. A skillful Dutch naval architect succeeded in hoisting her bow into the small floating dry dock in Tjilatjap. In this awkward position it was possible to place a rough patch over the hole in her bottom. But they dared not hoist the heavy stern into the little dock and consequently were unable to repair the rudder. A few days later, steering with her engines alone, she sailed for Ceylon with tender *Otus* as escort. Here further temporary repairs were effected and she continued westward to the Brooklyn Navy Yard, arriving on 4 May. Her officers and crew showed superb seamanship, infinite resource and unfailing good humor amid the many hardships of this difficult voyage.[15]

Admiral Doorman's plan for his strike involved a fueling rendezvous some 300 miles south of the Malay Barrier, directly away from the enemy and in waters known to be too rough for fueling at sea. Admiral Hart found himself in the embarrassing position of ordering the Striking Force commander to fuel elsewhere.

The Japanese force which the Catalinas had reported rounding Celebes was actually headed for Makassar Town on the same island; Bandjermasin, their estimated target, had been taken care of by troops conveyed in barges and small craft to a point on the south-

---

[15] Hart Report, pp. 74–76. For details of *Marblehead's* voyage see her official report and G. S. Perry and I. Leighton *Where Away.*

east coast of Borneo. Thence they marched overland and took Bandjermasin on 9 February.[16]

The Makassar Town Occupation Force, commanded by Rear Admiral Kubo in *Nagara*, had sailed from Kendari in six transports, with three destroyer divisions on 6 February. On the very day that Hart and Doorman at Tjilatjap were discussing what to do about it, the Japanese landed at Makassar Town. As elsewhere there was only token resistance on shore, but the United States submarine *S-37* (Lieutenant J. C. Dempsey), as we have seen, torpedoed and sank destroyer *Natsushio*.

That was something, but far from enough to stop the enemy.

The Allies hardly knew where to turn. Singapore no longer served as a delaying factor in the Japanese advance. The enemy landed on the island on 8 February, and made rapid advances against the equivalent of three fully equipped British divisions. Already, most of the Japanese forces allocated to the conquest of the British fortress could be diverted to Sumatra and the Java Sea.

While his left flank was threatened by these newly available forces, Admiral Hart well knew that trouble could also be expected on the right. The landing at Makassar Town was probably a mere consolidation of the various attacks on Celebes which brought the radius of air power still closer to Java. Any move they might make now would directly jeopardize the Dutch stronghold.

While Abda high command discussed how best to meet the mounting crisis, American ships in Tjilatjap were at last being serviced by the auxiliaries recalled from Darwin. Even the few undamaged warships were in great need of attention. Destroyers and submarines, which had been working overtime, required torpedoes, ammunition, provisions and upkeep. Tjilatjap was to be their last bomber-free haven in Java.

The port was jammed with combat ships and auxiliaries. Other harbors in Java, particularly Priok, the port of Batavia, were glutted with merchant shipping seeking refuge from Singapore and other untenable anchorages. But all except Tjilatjap were now within

[16] "Summary of Japanese Fleet Movements"; Intelligence Report 99-42.

Japanese bomber range. Indonesian longshoremen, terrified at the first sign of bombardment, streaked off for the interior, leaving common labor to be done by ships' crews.

Although Allied prospects in Java were bleak, Admiral Doorman's Striking Force was fairly strong on 13 February. He still had H.N.M. cruisers *De Ruyter*, *Java* and *Tromp*, H.M. heavy cruiser *Exeter*, H.M.A.S. *Hobart* (a light cruiser), four Dutch destroyers and six American destroyers.

The two main arms of the Octopus were closing in on the defenders of Java. Whence should the Allies expect the next thrust? For several days foul weather made air reconnaissance impossible. Intelligence reported two Japanese convoys containing 22 ships in the South China Sea, steaming south and southeast. Was their destination Sumatra? And the Eastern (or Celebes) Force must be getting ready to attack either Madura Island or Bali in the near future.

The Japanese convoys moving through the South China Sea were covered by the most powerful task force yet to appear in the Southwest Pacific. On 9 February Vice Admiral Ozawa, Commander First Detachment (or Southern Expeditionary) Fleet, in *Chokai*, carrier *Ryujo*, with cruisers *Kumano*, *Suzuya*, *Mikuma*, *Mogami* and *Yura* and six destroyers, steamed out of Camranh Bay. An advanced echelon of eight transports with five destroyers, five minesweepers and two submarine chasers departed the ninth under Rear Admiral Hashimoto, followed on the eleventh by 14 more transports under Captain Kojima, with a screen. These were the two convoys which Allied planes had sighted moving through the South China Sea. The advanced echelon was joined at sea on 12 February by a large number of shoal-draft vessels and three transports, carrying troops no longer needed for the reduction of Singapore.[17]

Admiral Doorman fueled his ships from a Dutch oiler in Pigi

[17] These were staged through the Anambas Islands off the Malay Peninsula. "Summary of Japanese Fleet Movements"; *Hatsuyuki* War Diary; Desron 3 Report.

Bay, southern Java, and shoved off for Sumatra on 13 February. Next day, 700 paratroops were dropped from 100 Japanese planes on Palembang, the capital of Sumatra. One of the seven Dutch battalions in Sumatra was on hand to greet them, and soon there were no paratroops left; but all hands knew that this was merely an introduction, and that the big enemy Expeditionary Force was coming that way.

The approach of the Combined Striking Force of the Allies, meager as it was, and the hearty rebuff to the paratroops, made the Japanese hesitate in their onward march. At dawn 15 February their advanced echelon, including shoal-draft river vessels, arrived at the mouth of the Musi River, which leads up to Palembang. But at 1000, when Admiral Ozawa had received word that Allied fighting ships were coming, he turned most of his transports northward to avoid Doorman's threat.

The Dutch commander, after threading Sunda Strait successfully, lost destroyer *Van Ghent*, which hit a reef in Stolze Strait during the night of 14 February. *Banckert* was detached to take off her crew. Next morning, the Striking Force arrived northeast of Banka Island. Admiral Doorman intended to round the island, double back into Banka Strait and attack the convoy anchored off Musi River. But the enemy was not asleep. Soon after dawn Japanese reconnaissance planes appeared near the Allied force, horsing about beyond range of the anti-aircraft guns, but sending in reports of the force's movements. The worried sailors knew that bombers could be expected at any moment, and that they could hope for no help from friendly fighter planes; there were none to send.

Admiral Ozawa planned to annihilate this small force that dared to challenge his advance, by first attacking with carrier planes from *Ryujo* and following them with gunfire from his powerful cruisers.[18]

From 1030 to 1830 February 15, the Striking Force was attacked by successive waves of Japanese high-level bombers. Owing to

---

[18] "Summary of Japanese Fleet Movements."

experience gained in previous air-surface actions, the ships were maneuvered cleverly and succeeded in evading every attack. Approaching planes were observed with the closest attention so that timely warning could be given the particular ship that appeared to be the target. Then the anti-aircraft fire of all ships within range would concentrate to protect her. The Japanese were so regular in their dropping altitudes and angles that sextants could be used to determine the moment of bomb release. At that moment the attacked ship would make a radical change of course. When the scream of falling bombs was heard the rudder would be laid amidships in order to avoid the danger of a hit or near miss jamming steering gear in its extreme position. Near misses raised huge columns of water, rendering the ship invisible to her consorts who, though rapidly maneuvering themselves, watched eagerly to see in what condition she would reappear from the slowly subsiding Niagara. Shouts of "Missed again!" rose from friendly decks as the ship seemed to shake off the mass of white water and reappeared unharmed.[19]

Admiral Doorman felt that, without fighter protection, he could not risk an encounter between his now scattered formation and an enemy surface force. He did not know how much fuel his ships still had, or how badly they were damaged by the encounter. The American destroyers *Barker* and *Bulmer* actually were badly shaken up. So, at 1300, he decided to abandon his projected thrust into Banka Strait, and to return through Gaspar Strait to the Java Sea. He later remarked to Admiral Hart that he expected history would condemn him for the retirement. This History, at least, will not; but it must be observed that some of the Netherlands naval commanders in the Indies had not learned the basic lesson that defense is impracticable without an offensive posture. Admiral Helfrich was an accomplished seaman and aggressive in command; but others were unwilling to take "commensurate risks." This does not, however, apply to the Netherlands submariners. They showed a fine

---

[19] Kroese *Dutch Navy At War* p. 57. Mr. Kroese commanded *Kortenaer* in this fight.

offensive spirit but were unfortunate in that their boats were over-age, and spare parts were wanting.

The disappointed captains steered their ships to Priok and to Oosthaven on Sunda Strait for refueling. On their arrival the Americans found that the Dutch were burning their installations. The Striking Force then retired south of the Barrier.[20]

With the Allied threat wholly removed, the Japanese invading force changed course again for the anchorage in Banka Strait and anchored on 16 February off the Musi River mouth. There an infantry division was embarked in small boats and proceeded fifty miles upstream to Palembang. Remnants of New Zealand and Australian outfits strafed them en route with everything they had, but there were too many Japanese and not enough planes.[21] In eastern Sumatra there were not enough Dutch troops to stop them, and Palembang was soon in their possession, together with half the petroleum reserves of the East Indies.

## 5. *Reorganized upon the Floor*

On 15 February, the day of the air-surface battle off Banka, Singapore surrendered.

"Operational reverses," the official euphemism for a series of beatings by the Japanese, increased tensions in the Abda command. When everything goes ill, it is a national as well as a human trait to see the mote in your neighbor's eye rather than the beam in your own.

The Netherlands government in exile, which had not been consulted about setting up the Abda Command, disliked having anyone but a Dutchman as Abdafloat. Admiral Helfrich's semi-military, semi-political position placed him in an ambiguous relationship with Admiral Hart and Doorman's caution nullified Hart's efforts to hit the enemy hard at the right time. The Dutch, in turn, pointed

[20] Glassford Report p. 58.
[21] Flight Lt. R. D. Millar RNZAF "Narrative of Prisoner of War Experiences in the Far East," 13 Apr. 1946, Historical Records Section New Zealand Air Force.

to *Marblehead* and *Prince of Wales* as object lessons in the futility of surface attack when the enemy controlled the air. When Hart urged an offensive strike the Dutch were apt to reply, "All right, if your country will send us more planes." To Hart, the only real problem was how to do best with what he had. Perhaps it would be better for the Allies to abandon defense of the Malay Barrier and retreat to Australia, but that was for the Combined Chiefs of Staff to decide. As long as orders were to stay and fight, he would stay and fight. Nothing could be accomplished by staying and not fighting.

The Japanese did not wait for the Allies to make up their minds on these matters. Every few days they mounted a new air or sea offensive. With each new attack they aggravated the Allied tensions. Tempers rose at Lembang headquarters. The Dutch complained louder and more often of the slight control they had over the defense of their own islands.

The deciding battlefield for these staff squabbles was Washington. There the Netherlands Ambassador argued long and stubbornly to have Hart relieved by a Dutchman as Abdafloat. The influence of Winston Churchill was enlisted, too. Finally President Roosevelt, Secretary Knox and Admiral King, on the ground that Java could not be held much longer anyway, decided it would be better to let a Dutch commander take the rap. On 12 February Marshal Wavell received a directive from the Combined Chiefs of Staff to let Hart maintain the nominal title of Abdafloat but delegate his operational duties to Admiral Helfrich.[22] This left the Abda naval command without any United States flag officer.

So, on 16 February 1942, Admiral Hart left Java. The publicly announced reason was ill health. This was regarded as a poor joke in the Asiatic Fleet, since a few days before, when inspecting the damage to *Marblehead* and *Houston*, "Tommy" Hart had swarmed all over the ships "like a midshipman." All hands hated to lose this good skipper in a bad storm. He had fought with determination, patience and circumspection. He could make prompt decisions in

[22] Hart Supplementary Report; reasons for the decision from other sources.

the midst of confusion and defeat and get the best out of his men.

Admiral Helfrich on assuming the Abdafloat operational command was beset by the same problems which had troubled his predecessor. Abda never succeeded in becoming a truly unified command. In addition to the national divergencies it was difficult to obtain joint action between ground, sea and air forces of a single nation. Commanders of the three services were not in the habit of clearing their plans through the high command before acting. Marshal Wavell never ordered air support in a surface operation; he left it to the naval commander to request assistance "as practicable." Coöperation was achieved by informal collaboration, rather than through the proper chain of command.

# CHAPTER XVII

# Prelude to Invasion of Java

### 15–27 February 1942

## 1. Timor Lost, Darwin Bombed, Bali Occupied

TO defend the precarious line of communications between Java and Australia, Washington decided to reinforce the airfield at Timor with American and Australian troops. Accordingly, on 15 February 1942, U.S.S. *Houston* steamed out of Darwin Harbor in charge of a convoy carrying the 148th Field Artillery Regiment in United States Army transports *Mauna Loa* and *Meigs*, as well as a few thousand "Aussies" in two small transports. United States destroyer *Peary* screened ahead of *Houston*, the transports followed, and Australian sloops *Swan* and *Warrego* protected the flanks.

The convoy departed in darkness but it had not long been under way when an enemy four-motored flying boat appeared. Believing this to be an advance scout for the enemy's bombers at Kendari, Captain Rooks of *Houston* sent a message to Darwin asking for air cover. He was presently rewarded by the appearance of a single P–40, just as the enemy seaplane was beginning a bombing run on *Houston*. The cruiser's anti-aircraft fire appeared to rattle the Japanese, who dropped their bombs at a safe distance and disappeared over the horizon.[1] The P–40 left, too, possibly for lack of gas, or engine trouble.

Captain Rooks knew well enough that more would follow; as the convoy approached Timor next morning, 16 February, his fears

---

[1] *Houston* Senior Survivor's Report; two reconstructed logs in Enclosures A-10 and B, which differ in several particulars.

were realized. As soon as the Japanese obtained word of the north-bound convoy, they dispatched 36 land-based bombers and 10 sea-planes to intercept. At 1100 *Houston* sighted the bombers in the clouds. She fired rapidly and drove back wave after wave, while one of the merchant ships in the convoy laid a smoke screen. *Houston* twisted in and out of the transport columns, firing over 900 rounds in the 45-minute action, and appearing to the merchant sailors like a sheet of flame. Naval Reservist F. S. Link, master of Army transport *Meigs*, stood beside a naval quartermaster on liaison duty, saying over and over again, "Look at that bastard go! Look at that bastard go! I thought she'd leave us."

It was the enemy bombers who left. Only the last wave of them got near enough to drop bombs on the convoy and the only damage was two men in *Mauna Loa* wounded by a near miss. But this effort to reinforce Timor was too late. Abda headquarters, realizing that the convoy was in a precarious situation owing to the enemy carrier force operating to the north, ordered the convoy back to Darwin. It arrived there 18 February.

The Japanese believed it important to deny Timor to the Allies. The airfield there was the only possible staging point for short-range fighter planes en route to Java; and, as Marshal Wavell said, the Malay Barrier could not be held without fighter planes.

On 17 February the seaplane carrier *Mizuho* cruised off Kendari with but one subchaser as escort and launched her planes over the Banda Sea. Admiral Tanaka in his flagship *Jintsu*, with eight or ten destroyers, sailed from Ambon at 0800 February 17, escorting nine transports to the objective. He was joined by two others en route. This force was followed next day by a second echelon of about five transports escorted by two destroyers. The approach was uncontested except by U.S.S. *Pike*, who launched a torpedo at Minesweeper No. 7 at 0243 February 20 after the convoy had passed Alor Island. But the torpedo missed ahead.[2] Later in the morning the first echelon anchored off Kupang on the southwestern extremity of Timor and the second off Dili, the capital of the Por-

[2] *Pike* Report of Third War Patrol.

tuguese part of the island. On 20 and 21 February, split into two groups, the naval landing force closed in on the airfield. By the 24th it had the whole island so well under control that the naval task force returned to Makassar Town for the next operation.[3]

Prior to invading Java, the Japanese determined to cut down Allied will and power to resist by their usual squeeze methods. In the west, the same arm of the Octopus which had seized the rich oil center of Palembang prepared landing strips in Sumatra, whence Batavia and Allied shipping in Sunda Strait could be bombed. The eastern arm, in possession of Timor, put the squeeze on Java from that side. Traffic thither from Australia now became exceedingly hazardous.

When *Houston* arrived in Darwin 18 February, after the attempt to reinforce Timor had been given up, she promptly fueled and weighed anchor for Tjilatjap. It was a good thing she did.

Paramount in the Japanese plan for the attack on Java was the severance of the island's communications with Australia, especially with the Allied base at Darwin. The enemy brought up his powerful carrier striking force to render that base untenable.

Vice Admiral Kondo with two battleships and three heavy cruisers, and Vice Admiral Nagumo with four carriers, steamed past the Moluccas into the Banda Sea. This was the most powerful striking force that Japan had sent on a single mission since the attack on Pearl Harbor.[4] The Allies had nothing capable of stopping it, even for a moment.

Kondo planned his approach to arrive in the southern part of Timor Sea at dawn 19 February. The fast night approach through the dangerous waters of Banda Sea was safely effected without detection by Allied search planes or submarines. At first light the carriers swung into the wind and launched their planes. In coöperation with them, 54 land-based bombers took off for Kendari and Ambon. The three forces, 242 planes strong, joined and streaked for Darwin.

[3] "Summary of Japanese Fleet Movements"; Desron 2 Action Summary Timor Operation (Wash. Doc. Center 160702).
[4] Cdr. Isawa interrogation of 12 Oct. 1945 USSBS 94 (Navy 19); "Japanese Air Power" USSBS release of July 1946.

In the bleak outpost of the Australian subcontinent, ships of several Allied nations jammed the harbor. The anchorage was unusually crowded on the morning of 19 February because *Houston's* convoy had just made its unscheduled return. The two Australian

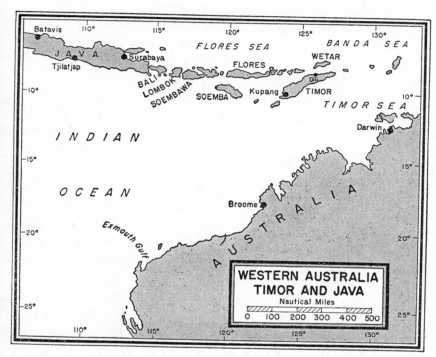

transports were at anchor; the two American Army transports had also anchored after disembarking troops. Destroyer *Peary*, which departed the previous day with *Houston*, tangled with an enemy submarine and expended so much fuel that she, too, had returned. Aircraft tender *William B. Preston* swung on her hook in the eastern arm of the harbor. An Australian hospital ship, *Manunda*, two Australian sloops, tanker *Benjamin Franklin*, an Australian troopship, and a freighter of the same registry, lay near by. It was a clear morning with a light westerly breeze — a bombardier's dream of a day.

Presumably there was no search radar at Darwin, and so no warn-

ing. At 0930 some 70 planes were sighted over the horizon. The first wave, 18 four-motored bombers painted a light silver, headed for the docks. There was little opposition to their approach. Ten P–40s, under the command of Major F. S. Pell usa, returning to Darwin after an unsuccessful attempt to reach Kupang, intercepted. One P–40 shot down an enemy plane, but was promptly jumped by four others and went down in flames.[5] An Australian troopship and a freighter discharging ammunition near an oil barge at the docks were demolished in a terrifying explosion. A second wave of 18 heavy high-level bombers attacked the airport before any more planes were able to leave the ground. The Japanese pilots, after discharging their bomb loads, flew in low over the town of Darwin, strafing it and starting numerous fires among the flimsy wooden buildings.

Next came the dark green dive-bombers that concentrated on shipping. Lieutenant Lester A. Wood, executive officer of *Preston*, had steam up for just such an emergency and got under way at once; destroyer *Peary* followed. Both ships maneuvered as radically as they could in the restricted waters. As *Preston* turned hard-a-starboard making better than 20 knots, she and the destroyer were attacked by 4 dive-bombers at 1010.[6] Rapid fire by *Preston's* .50-caliber machine guns, which the foresighted skipper had obtained from some destroyed planes, dissuaded two of the attackers, but the other two dove low onto the twisting ships.

A dive-bomber is a tough customer. If he can weather the anti-aircraft fire, he stands a good chance of scoring, which cannot be said of his high-altitude cousins. This time, 3 out of 4 bombs hit, and the fourth was a near miss close aboard *Preston*. One struck her on the main deck aft, exploded on contact and sent splinters throughout that part of the ship, killing eleven men and blowing the skipper overboard; but this bomb was not fatal to the ship.[7]

---

[5] *Army Air Forces in the War Against Japan, 1941–42.*

[6] *Wm. B. Preston* Damage Report 1 May 1942; Lt. W. J. Catlett letter 6 Mar. 1942, "Action in Port Darwin."

[7] Patwing 10 War Diary 19 Feb. 1942. This mentions destruction of 3 PBYs, but they must have been ashore or moored.

*Peary* did not fare so well. One bomb exploded on the fantail and competely demolished the steering gear; the second, an incendiary, hit the galley deckhouse and quickly enveloped the ship in flames. Then more planes dove at her repeatedly for an agonizing 45 minutes. The anti-aircraft gunners, working under frightful conditions, kept dishing it out after two more bomb hits, but a fifth was too much for the old four-piper. At about 1300 she broke up and went down. An Australian reported that as *Peary* sank he saw a bluejacket on the after deckhouse continue to fire his .50-caliber machine gun until the deck collapsed under him in flames.[8] Lieutenant Commander Bermingham and about 80 of the crew went down with her; only one officer survived.

The bombers also gave plenty of attention to the merchantmen, none of which were armed. *Mauna Loa* sank quickly when two bombs landed in an open hatch, but none of her crew were killed. Shrapnel from a near miss perforated the sides of *Portmar* and she beached in shoal water. Tanker *British Motorist* and S.S. *Admiral Halstead,* loaded with 14,000 drums of valuable high-octane gasoline, escaped. An Australian hospital ship narrowly escaped disaster when struck by a dud. The two corvettes, and a Norwegian tanker, *Benjamin Franklin,* were hit.[9]

United States Army transport *Meigs* was anchored not far from the fated *Mauna Loa.* Planes came in only 25 feet off the water and circled some 75 feet from the ship. She took about twenty bomb hits, and probably an aërial torpedo, which caused her to begin settling. Flames were licking dangerously close to the ammunition stores; and the master, wounded in the throat, chest, back and thigh, ordered Abandon Ship. When all men were clear she sank in 18 fathoms.[10]

After the dive-bombers had expended all their bombs, they came in low over the many small boats in which men were escaping from burning or sinking ships, and strafed them unmercifully.

[8] Information from Capt. McDill.
[9] Records of the Naval Transport Service; Lt. H. A. Burch Memorandum for file with CNO, 22 Apr. 1942.
[10] Master F. S. Link to Superintendent U.S.A.T.S. 16 Apr. 1942.

This air attack of 19 February dealt the Darwin base a severe blow. Besides 8 ships lost and 9 damaged, 18 aircraft were destroyed; valuable stores and the airport were demolished. The town itself was abandoned temporarily in fear of a return visit, and there was not much left to abandon. An important link in the lifeline had been broken.

With the enemy entrenched in southern Sumatra on the west flank and in Timor and Bali on the east, Admiral Glassford felt that there was no longer much security, even at Tjilatjap. He decided to begin retiring his tenders and auxiliaries to Exmouth Gulf. *Holland* and *Black Hawk,* accompanied by two submarines that needed servicing and the much shaken-up *Barker* and *Bulmer,* sailed for Exmouth on 19–20 February.

Simultaneously with the invasion of Timor and the strike on Darwin, Rear Admiral Kubo reorganized his Makassar Town occupation group to capture Bali. That island, famous among tourists for exotic dances and bare-breasted girls, almost touches the eastern point of Java, and its western portion is but a little more than a hundred miles by air from Surabaya. Intelligence knew about the preparations as early as 9 February, but Admiral Doorman's Striking Force was too distant and too scattered to do anything to break them up. Consequently, the occupation proceeded according to plan. Units of the Sixteenth Army embarked at Makassar Town in two transports and sailed thence 18 February, escorted by Admiral Kubo in *Nagara* together with seven or eight destroyers that had already figured in several operations of the sort. Late the same night they arrived off the designated landing place, Sanur Roads in Badung Strait on the southeast coast of Bali, facing the island of Nusa Besar.[11] The transports were unloaded in great haste, since an enemy reaction was expected.

Next day (19 February) the Japanese force was disturbed only by a few B–17s and U.S.S. *Seawolf.* That submarine was on patrol

---

[11] Cdr. Chihaya "Engagement of Badung Strait 20 Feb. 1942" (ATIS trans. 5 May 1946), prepared for this work; "Japanese Fleet Movements."

off the southern approaches to Badung Strait. Shortly after midnight her skipper, Commander Warder, received word from Captain Wilkes to close in on the hourly expected enemy landing. Turning up 18 knots, she headed for the most likely spot and made a good guess, at Sanur. But the Japanese destroyer screen picked her up on their sound gear, and put her on the defensive for a time. *Seawolf* was maneuvered with great skill in the shallow waters, twice running aground but getting off, and in the early afternoon of 19 February came within range of the 2 anchored transports. But Commander Warder's torpedo attack failed to connect with them.[12]

During the day the few B–17s still available at Malang and Madiun attacked the transports of the Bali force in sporadic raids. *Sagami Maru* received a direct hit in her engine room, which disabled one engine completely. The pilot of a PBY saw her burning while on a scouting mission that afternoon; a "nice show," he thought.[13] But she was able to depart that afternoon for Makassar, escorted by two destroyers. The landings were successfully completed on the 19th and around 2225 the second transport got under way escorted by *Asashio*. At that very moment, a really powerful Allied force put in its appearance.

## 2. *Strike on Badung Strait, 18–20 February* [14]

Although, as we have seen, the Allies had ten days' warning of what was cooking, and although Admiral Doorman's Combined Striking Force was perfectly capable of meeting Kubo's Bali Occupation Force at sea with superior strength, he was unable to collect his ships in time to strike until the landing was completed.

[12] *Seawolf* Report of 4th War Patrol, 7 Apr. 1942.

[13] Patwing 10 War Diary.

[14] The principal enemy sources are Cdr. Chihaya's "Engagement of Badung Strait" prepared for this work by a participant, and *Inter. Jap. Off.* I 27, 84. The principal American ones are Admiral Glassford's "Report of Action with Japanese Forces in Badung Strait 20 Feb. 1942" 12 Mar. 1942; Comdesdiv 59 (Lt. Cdr. E. N. Parker) "Preliminary Report on Night Attack on Japanese forces in Badung Strait Night of 19 Feb. 1942" 24 Feb.; Comdesdiv 58 (Cdr. Binford) "Report of Naval Engagement Night of 20 Feb. 1942"; Action Reports of individual destroyers, especially *Parrott*; A. Kroese *The Dutch Navy at War*. Capt. H. E. Eccles, who commanded *Edwards* in this fight, has been over it carefully with the writer.

When word came 17 February that the enemy was about to get under way, Doorman's flagship *De Ruyter*, cruiser *Java*, five Dutch and two American destroyers (*John D. Ford* and *Pope*) were at Tjilatjap. Dutch light cruiser *Tromp* was at Surabaya, and the other four American four-pipers (Commander T. H. Binford's division) [15] were fueling at Ratai Bay, Sumatra, after the Banka Strait operation. The British ships had been detached to escort convoys through Sunda Strait.

This unfortunate division of forces did not altogether preclude a rendezvous before battle in the southern part of Bali Strait, but it would have been difficult to arrange in the face of the enemy. So Admiral Doorman decided to attack the enemy concentration at Sanur Roads in three successive echelons. He, in command of the first group, including all combat ships at Tjilatjap, would deliver a gun-fire and torpedo attack and retire promptly through Lombok Strait. Commander J. B. de Meester RNN in *Tromp*, with the four United States four-pipers, would come in two or three hours later and hit the Japanese again. Finally, five Dutch motor torpedo boats were supposed to arrive in the midst of the confusion, raise as much hell as possible, and dispose of cripples. [16]

Admiral Glassford and the other United States naval officers who knew about the plan did not like it but had no choice. [17] Accordingly, at 2200 February 18, *Ford* and *Pope* got under way from the narrow harbor at Tjilatjap. They negotiated the narrow entrance all right, but the Dutch destroyer *Kortenaer* ran aground. One less fist with which to jolt the enemy! The rest of the first wave formed up clear of the mine fields and headed eastward through a moderate swell. *Pope* and *Ford* formed a sound screen ahead of the cruisers. As evening approached the ships took attack stations: *Java* astern of *De Ruyter* and, at the extreme limit of visibility, *Piet Hein* leading the destroyer column. Before 2200 Febru-

---

[15] *Stewart, Parrott, J. D. Edwards, Pillsbury.* Cdr. E. N. Parker was in *Ford*.

[16] Glassford Report pp. 19–20.

[17] The plan sacrificed the value of a surprise torpedo attack and depended too much on gunfire, which could hardly be very effective at night, especially from lightly armed four-pipers after surprise had been lost.

ary 19 the column rounded Cape Tafel into Badung Strait, the narrow pass between Bali and Nusa Besar Island. The cruisers steamed about three miles off the Bali shore, in the direction of the Japanese

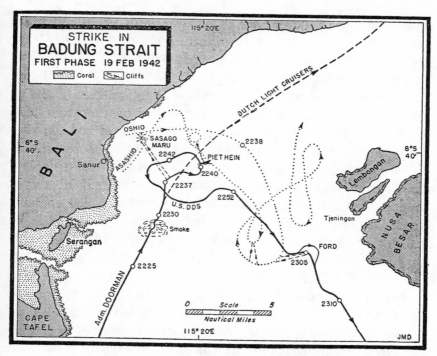

anchorage, and the leading destroyer was about three miles behind them.

Actually the force to receive them in Badung Strait was very weak. The landings had been completed; transport *Sasago Maru* was just getting under way with destroyer *Asashio* as escort; destroyer *Oshio* was standing by. Nothing else, except possibly small craft, was present. The strike should have been a pushover.

*Java's* lookouts were the first to see dark shapes of ships ahead, and at 2225 *Java* opened fire. The Japanese immediately illuminated with searchlight and star shell and returned fire. As the destroyers came within range, a little after 2225, *Piet Hein* zigged left and right, opened gunfire and launched a torpedo at a target invisible to *Ford*. She then commenced laying a smoke screen, for what purpose the Americans could not make out, leaving *Ford* and *Pope* considerably astern when they slowed on a tight turn. They bent on 28 knots and cut through the smoke heading east, picked up their leader again and followed her about 1000 yards astern. At about 2230, when this destroyer column turned left, *Ford* sighted transport *Sasago Maru* bearing north by west, and what she believed to be a cruiser bearing northeast by north. The latter was destroyer *Oshio* who had unknowingly crossed the Dutch cruisers' T and at the last minute exchanged fire with *Java*. Although these two ships were at point-blank range, their speed was so great and the visibility so poor that neither scored. The transport, however, was hit by Dutch gunfire, and at 2237 both *Ford* and *Pope* launched torpedoes at her, at least one of which hit. Destroyer *Asashio* now dropped the transport, turned south toward the Allied column, struck *Piet Hein* a fatal blow by either torpedo or gunfire at 2340, and doubled back in a tight circle, exchanging torpedo fire with *Ford* and *Pope*, who were following in a ragged column behind *Piet Hein*. The Dutch destroyer went down.[18]

*Asashio* next trained her guns on *Ford*, who laid a smoke screen and turned quickly to the right and then hard left. To get clear of this straight-shooting ship the American destroyers swung around in a circle, headed south and then made for the northern entrance of Badung Strait, as Admiral Doorman had ordered. Both *Oshio* and *Asashio* were bearing down on them so hard that *Ford* and *Pope* at 2252 turned south again, roughly parallel to the enemy, with whom they exchanged gunfire for a space of about six minutes. This was a bad spot for the Americans, since they were low on torpedoes on their engaged side. Commander Parker now tried to close the Nusa Besar shore where he would be less visible and where his port side would be covered. As he turned hard left to accomplish this, he crossed the bows of *Oshio*, who fired rapidly. *Pope*,

---

[18] About 19 of her survivors got into a whaleboat which *Parrott* later jettisoned. Lt. Cdr. Eccles adds that they fueled her with gasoline from a drum that floated by, and reached Java in safety.

following *Ford*, launched five torpedoes to starboard at the enemy and was neatly covered by *Ford*, who swung under her stern and made heavy smoke to protect her from the answering fire. At a little after 2305 the two Americans were back in column, making high speed on course 135°, *Ford* astern of *Pope*. As they retired southward, they heard the sounds of battle raging in the north.

It is a pity they did not know what was happening up there, for it would have afforded them a good laugh. *Oshio*, swinging away from the United States destroyers, sighted another ship that she took to be enemy and opened fire. *Asashio* promptly replied and the two indulged in a duel. After a few minutes, they recognized each other; then *Oshio* fell in astern of her temporary adversary and steamed north.

It was now time for the appearance of the second wave of the Striking Force, Commander de Meester in *Tromp* with Commander T. H. Binford's Destroyer Division 58, U.S.S. *Stewart, Parrott, J. D. Edwards* and *Pillsbury*. As they approached Cape Tafel, lookouts saw searchlights and the flares of explosions in the distance. How had the first echelon fared? Binford tried to make radio contact with Parker but without success. A few chance intercepts of messages between *Ford* and *Pope* were all they could get.

Around midnight *Tromp* dropped astern of the American destroyer column and took her designated position as the "heavy" (5.9-inch) caliber follow-up of the destroyer torpedo attack. *Stewart* led the column past the cape and roughly parallel to the shore. At 0114 lights were visible on the port bow, and by 0126 the destroyers were passing them broad on the port beam. The lights were probably made by Japanese troops who had gone ashore the previous afternoon. By 0135 the column, passing Serangan Island and making 25 knots, was only four or five miles from the Japanese anchorage off Sanur.

Commander Binford, as he raced up the strait at 25 knots, felt that his ships were at some disadvantage. There was a haze along the shore-line where Japanese ships were dimly seen, while his column was out in the clear under the brilliant southern starlight. Enemy

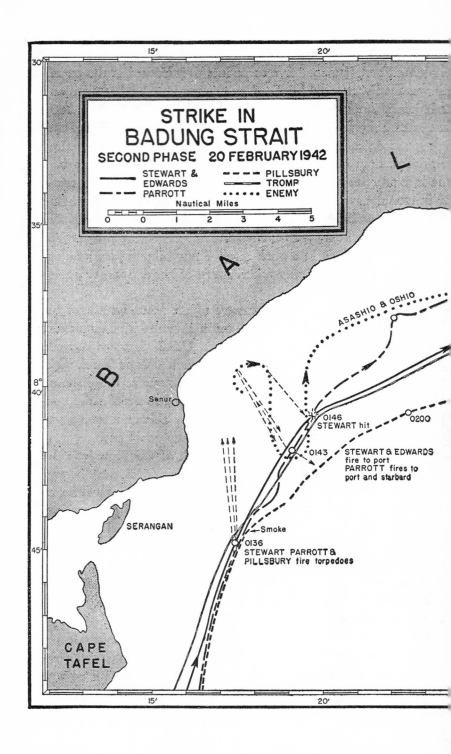

STRIKE IN
BADUNG STRAIT
SECOND PHASE   20 FEBRUARY 1942

STEWART & EDWARDS ——— PILLSBURY — — — —
PARROTT — · — · — TROMP ▭▭▭ ENEMY · · · · · ·

Nautical Miles
0   0   1   2   3   4   5

L

A

B

Sanur

SERANGAN

CAPE TAFEL

ASASHIO & OSHIO

0200

0146
STEWART hit

0143   STEWART & EDWARDS
fire to port
PARROTT fires to
port and starbard

Smoke

0136
STEWART PARROTT &
PILLSBURY fire torpedoes

15'   20'
30'
35'
8° 40'
45'

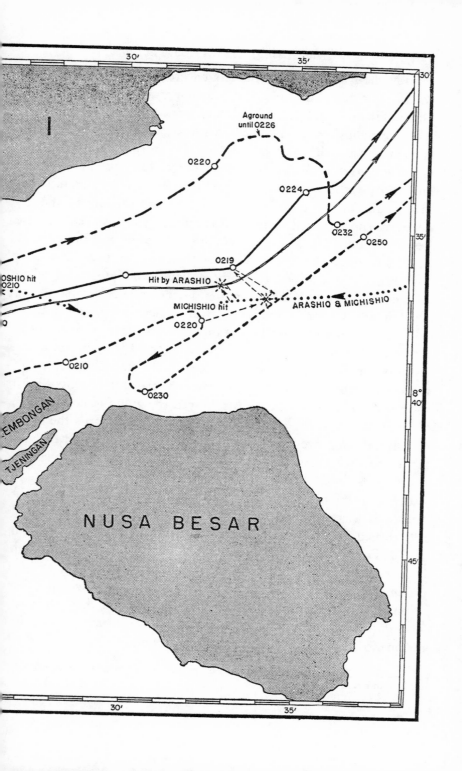

30'                                    35'

I

Aground
until 0226

0220

0224

0232
0250

0219

OSHIO hit
0210

Hit by ARASHIO

MICHISHIO hit

ARASHIO & MICHISHIO

0220

0210

0230

LEMBONGAN

TJENINGAN

NUSA BESAR

35'

8°
40'

45'

30'                                    35'

ships in the narrow part of the strait were signaling to each other with bright greenish blinkers. It was important to get in the first punch. He ordered his division to fire torpedoes to port.

*Stewart* and *Parrott* launched six torpedoes apiece and *Pillsbury* launched three, all at a vague target. The torpedoes ran clear of *Oshio* and *Asashio* circling in the anchorage. They promptly swung around to starboard and headed toward the Allied column. Commander Binford temporarily lost contact with the enemy and ordered his ships to hold their gunfire. Suddenly *Stewart* sighted the destroyers on the port hand, making great speed. She illuminated, fired torpedoes at 0136 and opened gunfire at 0143. *Edwards* launched two torpedoes; two others would not leave their tubes. The enemy answered with rapid and accurate fire that straddled the United States destroyers. At 0146 a ricochet hit on *Stewart* killed one man and severely wounded the executive officer, while a direct hit flooded the steering-engine room. *Pillsbury* fell hopelessly out of formation, owing to a near collision with *Parrott*, but the other three continued to steam north, exchanging salvos with the enemy destroyers. *Edwards* followed the guide's example. The three four-pipers, still in column, were heading towards the shore of Bali and things were getting too hot; *Oshio* and *Asashio* were giving more than they were getting. Commander Binford changed course to 65°.

Behind the United States ships steamed *Tromp*, the Dutch light cruiser. It was her job to deliver the decisive punch, but her actual rôle turned out to be rear guard. On board *Pillsbury*, men could see the Dutchman exchanging fire with *Oshio* and *Asashio* which had reversed course and were steaming roughly parallel to her. *Oshio* took a hit forward of the bridge at about 0210 which killed seven men,[19] but she was still able to score more than once on *Tromp*, whose bright blue searchlight made her an easy target. The opponents steamed on and eventually lost contact.

---

[19] Desron 2 Merit Report. *Asashio* was hit at some time during the action, losing 4 killed and 11 wounded.

As the five Allied ships raced north of Nusa Besar, more Nips were tearing in to meet them head-on from the northeast. Admiral Kubo in *Nagara*, warned of the first attack at 2230, at once turned south from his supporting position in the Bali Sea, with destroyers *Wakaba*, *Hatsushimo* and *Nenohi*. He was too far away to reach the scene of action in time, but he ordered destroyers *Arashio* and *Michishio*, then escorting *Sagami Maru* back to Makassar, to leave the transport and pile in. As the Allied ships pressed on to the north of Nusa Besar, these enemy destroyers raced in from Lombok Strait and at 0219 opened up on *Stewart* and *Edwards*.[20] Both sides launched torpedoes and fired guns in rapid succession. *Pillsbury*, coming up on the other side of the enemy, fired at *Michishio*, hitting her so hard she swerved to starboard; then swung hard right to avoid searchlights — and a shell from *Edwards*, whose course her skipper followed lovingly with his eye, exploded brightly on the enemy's superstructure. After all this punishment at the hands of *Pillsbury* and *Edwards*, unfortunate *Michishio*, all propulsion lost, lay dead in the water with 96 killed and wounded lying about the decks,[21] but she survived this punishment and was not finally put away until the Battle of Surigao Strait two and a half years later.

Having passed this hazard, *Stewart* and *Edwards* made best speed to Lombok Strait, followed by *Pillsbury*. *Parrott* touched ground on the shoals off Bali at 0220 but churned herself free and followed the rest. By 0300 all ships were clear of Bali. Commander Binford gathered his scattered vessels and retired to Surabaya.

The planned third phase, by the five Dutch motor torpedo boats, was rather curious. They claimed to have steamed right through the strait but to have seen nothing.[22]

The result of this battle was exactly what one might have expected from the faulty plan. A wonderful opportunity to smash up a transport protected only by two destroyers was sacrificed by di-

---

[20] Capt. Eccles is positive that there were four ships in this column, but three independent Japanese authorities say not.

[21] Desron 2 Merit Report.

[22] Told by Admiral Doorman to Lt. Cdr. Eccles after the battle.

viding the superior Striking Force into two echelons. Admiral
Doorman merely disabled one of the enemy ships in exchange for
the loss of a destroyer.

## 3. *The Logistics of Retreat*

The strike in Badung Strait in no way improved the Allied position. Singapore had surrendered 15 February, and Darwin was
abandoned as a naval base on the 20th. Southern Sumatra, Borneo,
Celebes, Ambon and Timor were all in enemy hands. The Octopus
was ready for its final squeeze on Java. Admiral Helfrich no longer
expected reinforcements, and the ships under his command were
not enough to parry a powerful threat at Java itself. But he was
determined to resist to the end.

Admiral Glassford, as we have seen, had already begun sending
such fleet auxiliaries as were in Tjilatjap to Exmouth Gulf, behind
the Northwest Cape of Australia. This port was actually nearer to
Java than Darwin, and most of the route thither was not yet controlled by enemy air power. Nevertheless the logistics situation was
becoming desperate.

Most of all, in oil. It is paradoxical that United States ships operating in the midst of one of the world's great oil producing centers
should have suffered from fuel shortage; but such was the case.
Java itself was not an oil-producing island comparable to Borneo
and Sumatra, both of which were now in Japanese hands. It had
ample storage facilities, but these were mostly in the interior and
not readily accessible, while those in the seaports were inadequate.
Moreover, as soon as the Japanese air raids began on Javanese ports,
most of the native employees of the Dutch oil companies vanished,
so that ships' crews had to operate the pumps, a slow process at
best. Around 5 February Admiral Glassford had proposed to fill
U.S.S. *Pecos* to capacity from the storage tanks near Surabaya and
have her proceed to the south shore and fuel the ships at sea, out
of enemy air range. But Admiral Helfrich would have none of that.

In desperation, Glassford on 17 February dispatched Navy oiler *Trinity* to the Persian Gulf for fuel, and on the 19th sent a chartered tanker on a similar mission to Ceylon.[23]

For long-term planning this was very well. But by 20 February the fuel shortage in Java was so acute that something had to be provided for the immediate future. Admiral Glassford virtually abandoned all hope of obtaining any of the vast Dutch oil stores on the island. With the approval of Admiral Helfrich he ordered the chartered tanker *George G. Henry* to proceed to Exmouth Gulf from Fremantle where she was standing by loaded. But it was too late even for that to help.

Even more pressing was the need for upkeep and repair of the fighting ships. They were worked far beyond their capacity, and the limited facilities available in the shipyards at Surabaya were still more limited by the frequent visits of Japanese bombers. *Tromp* and *Stewart* urgently needed repairs after the strike in Badung Strait. The American destroyer was immediately placed in the 15,000-ton floating dry dock at a private shipyard in Surabaya. Under the hectic working conditions that prevailed, she was badly braced on the keel blocks, none were placed along her bilge, and the shores to the dock wall were ineffective, so that when the dock began to lift she rolled over on her port side. This seriously damaged the only available dock and eliminated one more fighting ship that could ill be spared. Abda sea power was being whittled away. On 17 February the Dutch destroyer *Van Nes*, on escort duty in the western Java Sea, was hit and sunk by enemy bombers. Her sister ship *Banckert* was knocked out by a bombing attack on Surabaya on the 24th.[24]

Cruiser *Houston* and destroyers *Paul Jones* and *Alden*, released from escort-of-convoy duties by the fall of Singapore, arrived at Tjilatjap 22 February, fueled, and on the same day departed for Surabaya westabout, via Sunda Strait. Although *Houston's* after turret was inoperative, she still represented no small proportion of

[23] Glassford Report pp. 12–17.
[24] Admiralty Battle Summary No. 23 "Battle of the Java Sea" p. 13.

Abda fire power and Helfrich could not afford to send her home for repairs.

The United States destroyer force was being whittled away. *Peary* and *Stewart* were gone, *Whipple* was temporarily out of action from a collision with *De Ruyter*, and *Edsall's* stern was damaged by a depth charge dropped too close aboard. Admiral Glassford on 21 February sent *Ford* and *Pope* to pick up the last reserve of seventeen torpedoes from *Black Hawk* at Exmouth and next day had to withdraw *Pillsbury* and *Parrott* from the Abda Striking Force, since they had practically no torpedoes left and were sadly in need of overhaul. *Bulmer* and *Barker*, in the same condition, were escorting *Black Hawk* to Australia. *Pope* had developed feed-water leaks at Badung Strait and was laid up temporarily in Surabaya, along with *Stewart*. This left only four United States destroyers, *Ford*, *Edwards*, *Alden* and *Paul Jones*, in the Striking Force.[25]

These desperate conditions of readiness and supply were not alleviated by action on the political front. When close coöperation between the Allies was most needed, the Abda Combined Command practically fell apart.

## 4. *Composition of Forces*

The enormous disparity between the Japanese naval forces marshaled for the invasion of Java and the Abda naval force available to defend it is evident from the bare list of ships on the eve of the decisive Battle of Java Sea.

### ABDA COMBINED STRIKING FORCE
#### Rear Admiral K. W. F. M. Doorman RNN in *Java*

##### Heavy Cruisers

| | |
|---|---|
| U.S.S. HOUSTON | Capt. A. H. Rooks |
| H.M.S. EXETER | Capt. O. L. Gordon RN |

[25] The Australian cruiser *Hobart*, though still untouched by battle or accident, was too low on fuel to be used when the Japanese force was reported approaching Java.

## Light Cruisers

| | |
|---|---|
| H.N.M.S. JAVA | Capt. P. B. M. Van Straelen RNN |
| H.N.M.S. DE RUYTER | Capt. E. E. B. Labomble RNN |
| H.M.A.S. PERTH | Capt. H. M. L. Waller RAN |

### United States Destroyers
#### Division 58, Cdr. T. H. Binford [26]

| | |
|---|---|
| JOHN D. EDWARDS | Lt. Cdr. H. E. Eccles |
| PAUL JONES | Lt. Cdr. J. J. Hourihan |

#### Division 59, Cdr. E. N. Parker

| | |
|---|---|
| JOHN D. FORD | Cdr. E. N. Parker |
| ALDEN | Lt. J. E. Cooper |
| POPE | Lt. Cdr. W. C. Blinn |

### British Destroyers

| | |
|---|---|
| ELECTRA | Cdr. C. W. May RN |
| JUPITER | Lt. Cdr. N. V. J. T. Thew RN |
| ENCOUNTER | Lt. Cdr. E. V. St. J. Morgan RN |

### Netherlands Destroyers

| | |
|---|---|
| EVERTSEN | Lt. Cdr. W. M. de Vries RNN |
| WITTE DE WITH | Lt. Cdr. P. Schotel RNN |
| KORTENAER | Lt. Cdr. A. Kroese RNN |

# JAPANESE JAVA INVASION FORCES [27]

Ships that actually participated in the Battle of Java Sea are designated (J).
General H. Imamura (Commanding General 16th Army), Supreme Commander
Vice Admiral N. Kondo (Commander in Chief Second Fleet), Naval Commander

## SOUTHERN STRIKING FORCE
### Admiral Kondo

### SURFACE GROUP

| | | | | |
|---|---|---|---|---|
| CA | ATAGO | | CA | TAKAO |
| CA | MAYA | | | |

Destroyers NOWAKI, HAGIKAZE, MAIKAZE, ARASHI.

[26] By this time the entire organization of U.S. DDs was disrupted. *Whipple* and *Edsall* (Desdiv 57) were on the south coast of Java.
[27] Merit Reports *Akagi, Kaga, Soryu, Hiryu, Mizuho;* War Diaries *Tokitsukaze, Hatsukaze, Harusame, Hatsuyuki;* Logs of *Kumano* and *Ryujo;* Reports of Crudiv 7, Desron 1, Desron 3, Desron 5; Japanese Torpedo School Report; Chihaya "Outline Battle of the Java Sea"; *Nachi* Document No. 2; Cdr. Y. Isawa Interrogation; USSBS *Inter. Jap Officials,* I, p. 90.

CARRIER GROUP, Vice Admiral C. Nagumo

| CV | AKAGI | CV | SORYU |
|----|-------|----|-------|
| CV | KAGA | CV | HIRYU |
| CV | SHOKAKU | CV | ZUIKAKU |

1 BB, 2 CAs, 1 CL, 9 DDs.

## ATTACK FORCES

Vice Admiral I. Takahashi (Commander in Chief Third Fleet)

### SUPPORTING GROUP, Admiral Takahashi

| CA | ASHIGARA | DD | AKEBONO |
|----|----------|----|---------|
| CA | MYOKO | DD | IKAZUCHI |

### EASTERN ATTACK GROUP, Rear Admiral S. Nishimura in *Naka*

*Transport Unit*

41 Transports

*Destroyer Squadron 4*

| CL | (J) NAKA | DD | (J) MURASAME |
|----|----------|----|--------------|
| DD | (J) YUDACHI | DD | (J) HARUSAME |
| DD | (J) SAMIDARE | DD | (J) ASAGUMO |
| DD | (J) MINEGUMO | | |

4 more DDs, PCs *4, 5, 6, 16, 17, 18*; Minelayer WAKATAKA; Minesweepers *15, 16*.

### EASTERN COVERING GROUP, Rear Admiral T. Takagi

| CA | (J) NACHI | CA | (J) HAGURO |
|----|-----------|----|------------|

*Destroyer Squadron 2*, Rear Admiral R. Tanaka

| CL | (J) JINTSU | DD | (J) KAWAKAZE |
|----|------------|----|--------------|
| DD | (J) HATSUKAZE | DD | (J) YUKIKAZE |
| DD | (J) YAMAKAZE | DD | (J) TOKITSUKAZE |
| DD | (J) USHIO | DD | (J) SAZANAMI |

### WESTERN ATTACK GROUP, Vice Admiral J. Ozawa in CA CHOKAI

*Transport Unit*

56 Transports and Freighters
*Desron 3:* CL   SENDAI and 14 Destroyers
*Desron 5:* CLs   NATORI, YURA and 9 Destroyers
CV      RYUJO, 2 Destroyers, 1 Seaplane Carrier, 1 Seaplane Tender

### WESTERN COVERING GROUP, Rear Admiral Kurita

| CA | MOGAMI | CA | KUMANO |
|----|--------|----|--------|
| CA | MIKUMA | CA | SUZUYA |

## 5. *Japanese Movements, 18–25 February*

While Admiral Doorman's force was making futile strikes on the arms of the Octopus, the head of the beast was getting ready to fasten its beak on the jugular vein of Java. The largest amphibious operation yet attempted in World War II was under way. Japan now had enough combatant and auxiliary ships in the Southwest Pacific to divert the enemy with the one and slam in troops with the other.

On 18 February Vice Admiral J. Ozawa led the main or Western Attack Group out of Camranh Bay, Indochina. Three cruisers, six destroyers and a large minesweeper escorted and covered some 56 transports and cargo vessels. The force headed south to the Anambas Islands, where it awaited the approach of D-day, 28 February. On the 19th the Eastern Attack Force under Rear Admiral Nishimura in light cruiser *Naka* weighed anchor from Jolo in the Sulu Archipelago. With six destroyers he escorted 41 transports to Balikpapan, and departed 23 February from this last stop before Java. Rear Admiral T. Takagi's Eastern Covering Group of three cruisers and seven destroyers formed in Makassar Strait off southeastern Borneo on 26 February. This force steamed ahead of the convoy at considerable distance, to meet whatever challenge the Allies might offer.

The Japanese commanders could hardly expect their movements to remain unnoticed. On 25 February a small advance force landed on Bawean Island about 150 miles north of Surabaya and set up a radio station which was promptly bombarded by U.S. submarine *S–38*. It was obvious that this site was useful only as an advanced combat information center and that Java was the objective. Other submarines and the few remaining PBYs of Patrol Wing 10 relayed fragments of information. The Japanese force was apparently approaching in three prongs aimed at eastern, central and western Java.

## 6. *Abda Disintegrating, 20–26 February*

At this juncture Field Marshal Wavell decided that the defense of Java was no longer possible and that a last-ditch struggle would cost more than the results could justify. He recommended to his own government that Java be evacuated as soon as there were no more fighter aircraft to support Allied operations on land and sea. This situation, calculated on the basis of current supply and daily losses, was expected to occur in the very near future. The Marshal on 20 February requested authority to evacuate British forces from the Abda area. He did not so inform his subordinate commanders of the other nationalities, but it leaked out in Abda headquarters at Bandoeng on that or the next day. General ter Poorten, Commander in Chief of the Netherlands East Indies Army, was naturally worried. He had determined to fight to the finish, even if the Dutch had to do it alone; but he could make no battle plans without knowing what forces were available and which would retire overnight. He asked Admiral Glassford what the American plans were. Glassford replied that his orders were to defend the Netherlands East Indies. Ter Poorten expressed his gratitude, observing that although he was shocked by Wavell's action he would fight to the last.

The British staff was not the only one contemplating withdrawal. On 19 February General Brereton had already decided to withdraw the United States Army Air Force with Wavell to India,[28] and had received the approval of Wavell, Brett and Peirse. On the 20th, Brereton cabled General "Hap" Arnold at Washington to this effect; and on the 24th he flew to India. General Brett had already left for Australia. Brereton hoped to evacuate all his planes to India; only some of the B–17s and a few transport planes, heavily loaded with air personnel, were able to get away.[29]

Field Marshal Wavell flew to Colombo on 25 February. There was no more Abda command.

[28] Glassford Report p. 26.
[29] Brereton Report pp. 95–96 and information from Capt. B. Mortensen USA.

Netherlands officers now assumed full control of operations in the Java campaign. Under the theoretical coördination of the Governor General, Vice Admiral Helfrich commanded the Navy, Lieutenant General ter Poorten the Army, and Major General Van Oyen the Air Forces. All armed forces in Java were now Dutch; excepting a few American and British ships, and a few American and Australian planes that flew and fought until they could no longer leave the ground.[30] There were also 7000 British or Australian and 541 American soldiers. On 22 February Doorman signaled the ships under his command: —

In accordance with a message I received from Abdafloat I inform all officers and ships' companies that the situation is very serious. I wish to impress upon all of you the necessity for every effort against the enemy to prevent his landing on Java. Every opportunity for offensive action must be seized and sacrifices must be made to this end. This will be the general line of our conduct in the next days.

Owing to the experiences during several engagements with the enemy during the last three weeks I fully trust that every man shall understand the earnestness of this message and will realize that we will have to do our duty until the last moment.[31]

On 25 February Admiral Purnell flew to Broome, Australia, where he picked up tender *Childs* and in her sailed for the new logistics base in Exmouth Gulf. The remainder of his staff left Tjilatjap in submarines *Sturgeon* and *Seawolf* on their way to Sydney, Australia, for overhaul. The naval port office was now virtually the only American administrative activity remaining in Java. Captain Hudson, one of the outstanding logistics officers in the Southwest Pacific, took charge of this outfit and helped in the evacuation of wounded in the last bitter days.[32]

The psychological situation in Admiral Glassford's force was

[30] Under the command of Col. Eugene L. Eubank USA, there remained in Java 26 Feb. 1942, 13 P-40s (some flown by Dutch pilots), 6 F2As, 6 Australian Hurricanes and 3 A-24s. Also 7000 Empire and 541 U.S. ground troops. The last mission flown, of 9 P-40s, was on 29 Feb. Every remaining plane was badly shot up by strafing. "History of V Army Air Force" I chap. ii, Reports of 27th Bomber Group, Journal of 19th Bomber Group (H), communicated by Capt. Mortensen.
[31] Fleet Order, Doorman to Striking Force 22 Feb. 1942.
[32] Glassford Report pp. 28–29.

not nearly so good as in the remnants of the Asiatic Fleet that were in an equally desperate situation up north. For one thing, the men had no heartening feeling that they were fighting for American soil; and the Javanese, unlike the loyal Filipinos, were apathetic in their own defense. Japanese propaganda such as the cooing threats of "Tokyo Rose" aroused only ridicule in American bluejackets; but a broadcast from Secretary Knox in Washington declaring that Germany was our first enemy, and that the main American effort for some time would be directed toward Europe, raised the devil with morale. There had been too many abortive missions, recalled after steaming most of the night at top speed; ships were fast wearing out for want of proper upkeep. Mighty Singapore had fallen, building up a myth of Japanese invincibility. And American naval officers lacked confidence in Admiral Doorman's tactical ability.

## 7. *Searching for Invasion Forces, 25–27 February*

Admiral Kurita's Western Attack Group, augmented at Anambas Islands to four heavy cruisers, three light cruisers, carrier *Ryujo*, seaplane tender *Kamikawa Maru*, about 25 destroyers and 50 to 60 transports and auxiliaries, sailed from that South China Sea anchorage at 1630 February 24. Planes of Patrol Wing 10 were still on the job, and a PBY sighted them in Karimata Strait at 0925 on the 26th. Submarines *Seal* and *S–38* sighted Admiral Nishimura's Eastern Attack Group near Bawean at 0830 February 24, and on the same day *Saury* noted a convoy escorted by at least six destroyers off Sepandjang in the Kangean Islands.[33] Thus the Allied command was fairly well informed of what to expect, and Admiral Helfrich estimated that the three convoys would reach Javanese waters at about daybreak on the 27th. At 1125 February 24 he ordered the British ships which had been engaged in convoy duty to reinforce Rear Admiral Doorman's Combined Force; and the same day Commodore Collins RN dispatched cruisers *Exeter* and *Perth* and de-

[33] *Kumano* log; Crudiv 7 track charts; *Seal* and *Saury* Reports.

stroyers *Electra, Jupiter* and *Encounter* from Tanjong Priok to Surabaya where Doorman still based his force. Without waiting for these British reinforcements to arrive, Admiral Doorman at dusk 25 February led out his available ships (three cruisers and seven destroyers) to sweep the Javanese coast from Surabaya to Bawean Island.[34] He was too early to encounter the enemy, and returned to Surabaya to refuel on the 26th, just in time to receive, at 1615, an urgent dispatch from Helfrich in Bandoeng. The first part of it informed him that 30 transports and two cruisers and four destroyers were reported 25 miles northwest of Arends Island (about one third of the way from Borneo to Java) heading west by south at 10 knots. The second part ordered Doorman to "weigh anchor and attack at night, then head for Tanjong Priok." This was followed by a second order, at 2045: "Pursue attack until you have demolished the Japanese force."

All that afternoon Doorman worked feverishly on plans. At 2200 February 26, with his entire force except *Evertsen*, he cleared Surabaya Strait, the narrow waterway between western Madura Island and Java. For the rest of the night the Combined Striking Force steamed north, east and west in search of the enemy, tense and straining, but failed to make contact. At dawn of the 27th, tired eyes searched the betraying light above for planes, hoping to see their own; but only four Brewster Buffaloes of the Netherlands Air Force were available at Surabaya and they were too short-ranged to be of any service to the Allied ships. At 0855 the ominous throbbing of Japanese motors was heard, and isolated attacks began as individual planes made sporadic runs on the task force. The British destroyer *Jupiter*, curiously enough, received most of their attention, but *Houston's* anti-aircraft crews, who had proved themselves before, kept most of the planes out of range and the seven bombs dropped at *Jupiter* missed.

Worried by this unhappy augury, lack of fighter protection, dwindling fuel tanks and the fatigue of his people, Rear Admiral

[34] Admiralty Battle Summary No. 28 "Battle of the Java Sea"; Comdesdiv 58 (Cdr. Binford) Action Report 4 Mar. 1942.

Doorman turned the Striking Force south toward Surabaya Strait at 0930 February 27. Half an hour later, Vice Admiral Helfrich, apprised of this change of course, signaled Doorman: "Notwithstanding air attack you are to proceed eastwards to search for and attack enemy." That old sea dog could not understand Doorman's caution. "Air attacks had been expected and this attack should not have been a reason for withdrawing from the area of action," he said in his report. Doorman disregarded the order and continued to retire.

As the Striking Force passed the outer entrance of Surabaya Harbor at 1427 February 27, Doorman received from Admiral Helfrich definite word of the enemy's whereabouts. About forty minutes earlier, patrol planes had sighted three enemy groups: (1) two cruisers, six destroyers and 25 transports 20 miles west of Bawean Island; (2) more transports and destroyers about 65 miles northwest of the island; and (3) a lone cruiser about 70 miles astern of the second. The group nearest Bawean was the advanced echelon of Admiral Nishimura's Eastern Attack Group. It had known of Doorman's whereabouts some hours earlier; at about noon Nishimura had ordered the transports diverted to the westward with two destroyers, while he in *Naka* with the ten destroyers of Squadron 4, together with Admiral Takagi's powerful Eastern Covering Group of two heavy cruisers and part of Destroyer Squadron 2 (*Jintsu* flag), steamed ahead to seek contact.[35] Obviously this was the target for Admiral Doorman and his tired force. They had no choice but to turn and fight.

Another Allied force, which might have reinforced Doorman, proved wanting. This was the Western Striking Force, formed 21 February, consisting of H.M.A.S. *Hobart*, H.M. light cruisers *Danaë* and *Dragon* and destroyers *Scout* and *Tenedos*, which had been released from escort-of-convoy duty. Admiral Helfrich kept it near Batavia, in order to meet a possible Japanese strike from the South China Sea. When the enemy threat developed in that direction on 26 February, this force swept up to Banka Strait

[35] Chihaya Report on Java Sea.

without making contact; but planes of the large Japanese Western Attack Group sighted it, and Admiral Kurita detached two heavy and two light cruisers and three destroyer divisions to intercept.[36] Again, no contact. The five British ships returned to Tanjong Priok at noon on the 27th, refueled, and were then ordered to Tjilat-jap, apparently because dwindling fuel supplies and constant air raids on the port of Batavia rendered further stay there inadvisable. After passing through Sunda Strait on the 28th this force retired to Ceylon. Whether this was done on Admiralty orders or on Helfrich's orders as a result of British pressure is not certain; the result was the same. One third of available Allied sea power was not present for the showdown.[37]

[36] Japanese Desron 5 War Diary.

[37] Admiral Helfrich "Chronological Report of Operations of Royal Dutch Navy in Netherlands Indies, 8 Dec. 1941–1 Mar. 1942" (translation made for this work from the original); Glassford Report pp. 37–38; Battle Summary No. 28. Later information makes it certain that Admiral Helfrich gave the orders.

## CHAPTER XVIII

# The Battle of the Java Sea[1]

## 27 February 1942

### 1. The Enemy Encountered, 1525–1612

A DMIRAL DOORMAN did not even have time to enter Surabaya Harbor that fateful afternoon of 27 February. At 1500, when just inside the outer entrance, he received an order from Admiral Helfrich to attack the enemy force "east of Bawean." The cruisers formed in column at 1525, *De Ruyter* leading *Exeter, Houston, Perth* and *Java* in that order on course 315° at 20 knots. British destroyers screened ahead, and the Dutch and American destroyers were on the port flank and rear.[2]

In the quick turnaround at Surabaya, Admiral Doorman had no time to get out an operation plan, much less distribute it; and, as Abda command never had worked out a common code of tactical signals, Doorman's signals had to be translated by a United States liaison officer in *De Ruyter* and transmitted to *Houston*, who passed

[1] *Enemy sources:* "Lessons Learned in Battle in the Greater East Asia War" (referred to as Torpedo School Report), Jicpoa Item 355; Desron 4 Warfare Report No. 9, WDC 161512; Records of Desron 2, WDC 161711; Cdr. Chihaya "The Battle of the Java Sea" and track charts enclosed; ATIS "Japanese Navy Plans and Orders 1941–44 in 12 Volumes" (*Nachi* Documents). *Allied sources:* Admiral Helfrich "Report of Naval Operations of Striking Forces in Southwest Pacific During the Last Week of February and First Days of March 1942"; Admiralty Battle Summary "The Battle of the Java Sea"; *Houston* Senior Survivor's Report 16 Nov. 1945; O.N.I. Combat Narratives *The Java Sea Campaign*; O.N.I. Intelligence Report 42–42 March 27, 1942, "The Battle of Java," based on a report made by H.M.A.S. *Perth*; A. Kroese *The Dutch Navy at War* Chap. v. See also pp. 333–4 above.

[2] U.S. destroyer *Pope* in Surabaya, which was to have joined the Striking Force, steamed toward it but had to be left behind because she still had several miles of narrow, twisting channel to steam through at low speed and Admiral Doorman realized she could not possibly catch up.

them on over her voice circuit.[3] As the signals did not reach him in their correct order, Commander Binford in *Edwards* never knew how to reconcile conflicting instructions.

After one Japanese air attack, which fortunately did no damage, Admiral Doorman radioed ashore a final plea for air cover, at 1600. But the Netherlands Air Force commander at Surabaya decided to use his 8 Brewsters to cover a few remaining dive-bombers in a last futile strike against the Japanese transports. Doorman could not even profit by gun spot from his own cruiser planes; for *Java* had no catapult and the others' planes had been left on the beach because a night engagement had been expected when they sailed on the 26th.[4]

About ten minutes after Doorman's last appeal, 3 float planes, spotters from cruisers *Nachi* and *Haguro*,[5] appeared to the northward. And at 1612, when the Striking Force had reached a point about 30 miles northwest of Surabaya, lookouts in *Electra* sighted "one cruiser, unknown number large destroyers bearing 330°, speed 18, course 220°." They were crossing the formation's bows from starboard to port. Doorman immediately called for flank speed — 26 knots — from his cruisers, which gradually left the Dutch destroyers behind. Every moment more enemy masts appeared over the horizon. *Perth* ran up her big white battle ensigns on the fore and main, and to old-timers on board *Houston* the "meteor flag of England" looked good.

## 2. *The First Hour of Battle, 1616–1715*

At 1616 Admiral Takagi's heavy cruisers *Haguro* and *Nachi* commenced firing at their opposite numbers, *Exeter* and *Houston*,

---

[3] *Edwards* Report, and information from her former C.O., Capt. H. E. Eccles. After *Houston's* TBS went out, all communications were by plain language searchlight. What few radio messages Binford received were relayed to him through headquarters at Bandoeng.

[4] *Houston* Senior Survivor's Report 16 Nov. 1945. H.M.S. *Exeter* carried one old plane, which for some reason was not used.

[5] Chihaya and Crudiv 5 Reports.

from an extreme range of 28,000 yards.[6] Almost immediately after, Admiral Tanaka in light cruiser *Jintsu* led his destroyer squadron in column up to 18,000 yards from the British destroyers and straddled *Electra* with his first two salvos. She and *Jupiter* replied when the range closed to 15,700 yards, but even then they could

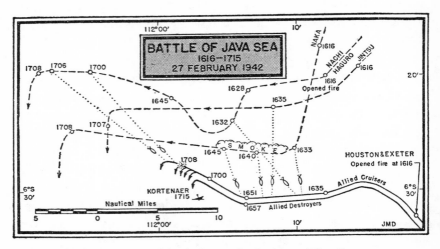

not reach the enemy with their 4.7-inch guns. The Japanese practice of using a small light cruiser as flagship for a destroyer squadron paid off in the Java Sea, and on many other occasions as well.

If Doorman continued on his present course, the Japanese would cross his T — the classic maneuver which would enable them to rake his column fore and aft. In such a position *Nachi* and *Haguro* could bring twenty 8-inch guns to bear; *Exeter* and *Houston* only ten.[7] But even if Doorman turned to parallel the enemy's course, he would still be fighting an unequal battle. He must get his three light cruisers within range, for in that category the Allies had superior fire power.

[6] Admiralty Report, Chihaya's Report, *Nachi* Diary, Desdiv 58 Report, Helfrich's Report, Jap Desron 2 and 4 Reports, are all in fairly close agreement about time and range of first contact. Unfortunately, agreement ceases at that point; I have simply done my best to reconcile conflicting statements. Since Admiral Doorman and most of his key officers were lost, many facts of this important battle will never be known, and one can only surmise from information he is known to have had, what considerations led the Admiral to act as he did.

[7] *Houston's* after turret was permanently out of commission; with *Exeter* it was a matter of gun train limits.

In this tactical dilemma Admiral Doorman compromised, and at 1621 swung his column 20 degrees left to course 295°. The range continued to close until *Exeter's* after guns could bear. She opened promptly and *Houston* followed a minute later. The United States cruiser used crimson dye in her shells to identify her own salvos, and the huge blood-red geysers from her near misses terrified some of the junior officers in *Nachi*.[8] *Exeter* and *De Ruyter* were straddled but not hit.

The United States destroyers, after remaining on the disengaged quarter of *Java* in order to comply with Doorman's order "Do not pass Dutch destroyers," finally took assigned positions on the disengaged beam of *De Ruyter*. To maintain a favorable maneuvering position on the flagship, the destroyers hung as close as they dared alongside the cruiser column, some 700 to 1000 yards.

After closing the enemy for eight minutes, Doorman at 1629 turned his column left to course 248°, west southwest. Now both columns were almost parallel and the light cruisers were within maximum 6-inch gunfire range, 26,000 yards, of *Naka*. Since the enemy had three spotting planes in the air and the Allies none, his fire at this great range was much more accurate than theirs. *De Ruyter* and *Exeter* were continuously straddled and the other ships received their share of near misses as the shells dropped almost vertically close aboard. The Japanese, as was their practice throughout the war, fired salvos in small tight patterns of about 150 yards' diameter.

This phase of the action had continued only two minutes when, at 1631, flagship *De Ruyter* was hit in the auxiliary engine room by an 8-inch shell which failed to explode. Four minutes later the Admiral turned his column right to course 267°, almost due west, in order to close range for more accurate shooting. Takagi saw what was in his enemy's mind and ordered a torpedo attack.[9] Torpedoes were carried by all Japanese cruisers, heavy as well as

---

[8] *Nachi* Diary. *Houston* thought she made several hits, but apparently did not.
[9] The Japanese Torpedo School Report says he gave this order "about 18 minutes after the beginning of the engagement," which would be about 1634-37. Chihaya Report does not mention this attack. *Nachi* Documents, Diary No. 1, mentions opening fire about this time, as does Desron 4 Report.

light. *Naka* led her seven destroyers south across the heavy cruisers' bows at 35 knots, while *Jintsu* and her destroyer column on their engaged flank also prepared to launch fast, powerful and long-range torpedoes. Allied sailors were to learn respect for those deadly warheads but, on this occasion, the distance was too great for them to be effective. During the next quarter-hour, the 16 light ships and *Haguro* launched forty-three torpedoes, not one of which hit.[10]

As the Japanese destroyers completed torpedo runs, they dashed between the opposing cruiser columns and laid a smoke screen. This increased their advantage, for their spotting planes continued to give accurate information while the Allied ships lost visual contact, their only means of directing gunfire. None of them had radar.

The Japanese convoy could now be seen to the northwestward from light cruiser *Jintsu*, flagship of Rear Admiral Tanaka, who determined to reach a decision promptly, before the Allied column could take transports under fire. Shortly after 1700 he turned his column toward the enemy for a short-range torpedo and gunfire attack. At 1707 his squadron launched torpedoes. Shooting as they were at the thin frontal silhouette of Admiral Doorman's column, there was little chance to score. But a sudden and disastrous mishap to the Allies, one minute after the torpedoes were launched, spread their force in a confused pattern right through the torpedo water.

While Tanaka was closing, Admiral Takagi continued to the westward at high speed with *Nachi* and *Haguro*. After almost an hour's constant firing with every advantage — more guns than *Exeter* and *Houston*, three spot planes, smoke protection and a numerous destroyer screen — he had been unable to score. Since Doorman by failing to close had foregone his unique advantage of superior light cruiser fire, it was to be expected that sooner or later Takagi would cash in on Japanese superiority at long range. At 1708 an armor-piercing shell from *Haguro* fell almost vertically

---

[10] During the torpedo attack, the Dutch light bombers and Brewsters, sent out to attack the transports, tried to bomb Takagi's ships instead, but did no damage. They could more usefully have attacked the spotting planes.

on *Exeter,* crashed through an anti-aircraft mount and exploded in the powder chamber below. The British cruiser, severely damaged, slowed immediately to half her former speed. This severe blow to the Striking Force was magnified many-fold by the ensuing confusion.

Now the lack of combined doctrine, combined communications and combined planning brought disaster. *Exeter,* next behind the flagship in the cruiser column, swung hard left to avoid a collision with *Houston,* third in the column. Captain Rooks assumed, lacking any signal to the contrary, that Admiral Doorman had ordered a turn movement.[11] So he turned *Houston* to port and *Perth* and *Java,* interpreting *Exeter's* move in the same way, did likewise. At 1715 destroyer *Kortenaer* exploded, jackknifed and sank almost at once, probably from a torpedo launched by *Jintsu* before the Allies broke column.

The Combined Striking Force was now in disorder. *De Ruyter* steamed on alone for a few minutes and then, seeing what had happened, turned outside the British destroyers, which were to port. By this time every Allied ship except the United States destroyers had turned south, and they soon followed to get out of the others' way.

## 3. *The Second Hour of Battle, 1715–1808*

Admiral Takagi, seeing the Allied force fanning out in a way to make ideal torpedo targets, ordered his entire force to strike in for the kill. His two heavy cruisers and Nishimura's Destroyer Squadron 4 (*Naka,* flag) turned hard left and launched torpedoes.

Almost every Allied ship now offered a beautiful target for stray "fish." Confusion was heightened by torpedo wakes suddenly appearing in the midst of them. Fired from extreme range, these torpedoes surfaced at the end of their runs and exploded automatically.

[11] In naval language a "turn" is a simultaneous turn of all ships, whereas a "column movement" is follow-the-leader, each ship turns in the wake of the column leader.

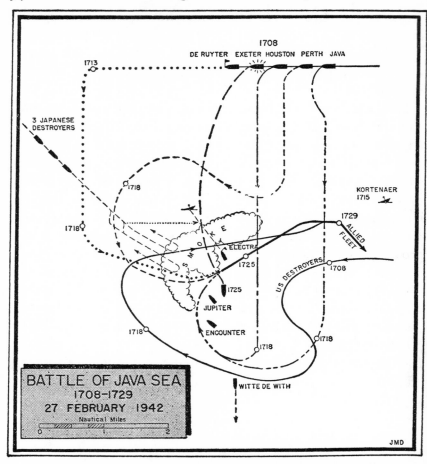

Several commanding officers believed they were fired by submarines, a notion which increased the tactical confusion.[12]

Admiral Doorman, swinging in a wide arc, vainly endeavored to
gather his force around *De Ruyter*. *Exeter* resumed headway at
about 15 knots, exuding clouds of smoke from her wounds. *Perth*
veered away to screen her with smoke from the enemy destroyers,

[12] All Allied reports state that there were submarines in the engagement area,
but none were there. Until mid-1943, when after much bitter experience the
Pacific Fleet realized the speed, range and tactical skill of Japanese destroyers' torpedo fire, it was a common delusion that submarines were responsible for torpedo
hits that were really made by destroyers.

but Doorman signaled the Australian to follow him, and ordered the British destroyers to cover *Exeter* and counterattack. The senior British destroyer officer in *Electra* ordered an attack through the smoke to the northwestward, toward which direction *Jintsu* and her seven destroyers were steaming. By this time smoke laid intentionally, together with that resulting from explosions and shell-fire, had reduced visibility to less than a mile in the gathering dusk; the entire battle area was wreathed or shrouded in smoke, through which only occasional visual signals from Admiral Doorman could reach his ships.

*Electra*, after receiving the Admiral's order to counterattack at 1725, headed northwest into the smoke. *Jupiter* and *Encounter*, too far away to fall in behind her, turned independently in the same direction. *Electra* and *Encounter* penetrated the smoke and came clear north of it just as *Jintsu* and three Japanese destroyers were about to enter it. *Encounter*, hopelessly outnumbered, fired a quick salvo and retired into the protecting smoke. *Electra* poured rapid fire into the oncoming enemy, hit *Jintsu*, killing one man and wounding four, but in unequal exchange took a shell in No. 2 boiler room which stopped her dead. One enemy destroyer closed and drilled her unmercifully at point-blank range. *Electra's* bridge communications were out and she could only answer with locally controlled fire.

Meanwhile *Jintsu* and two destroyers drove into the smoke screen toward crippled *Exeter*. Here *Jupiter* and *Witte de With* frustrated their attempted torpedo attack, and with prudent *Encounter* ran an improvised covering patrol ahead of the cruiser. None of the three were damaged by the enemy in this particular brawl, although *Witte de With* was badly shaken by the explosion of one of her own depth charges, swept overboard during the radical maneuvers.

The enemy destroyers, foiled in their attempts to finish off *Exeter*, swung back through the smoke and joined their sister ships who had silenced *Electra's* guns one by one. When none were left, Commander May RN reluctantly ordered Abandon Ship. He saw

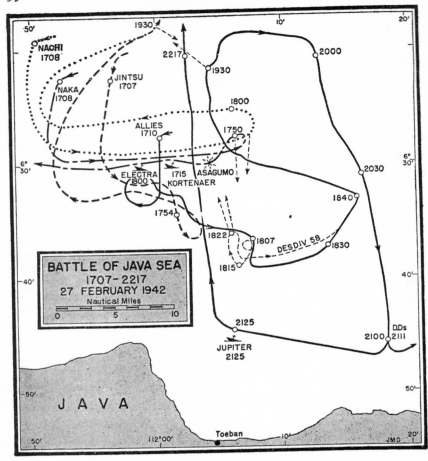

all survivors clear, waved at the men in the water "who cheered lustily"; he was still on board at 1800 when *Electra* fulfilled her destiny.[18]

While the British destroyers fought their own fight separate from the main force, Admiral Doorman gathered his remaining ships and radioed Admiral Glassford at Bandoeng to send submarines north of central Java to get after the Japanese convoy. He evidently still hoped to check Takagi's force and then attack the transports. By

[18] Admiralty Report quoting senior survivor. *S–38* picked up the 54 survivors at 0315 Feb. 28.

1729 Doorman's column was reformed. *De Ruyter* now led *Perth*, *Houston* and *Java* on a generally southeasterly course. Off and on through the smoke they sighted *Nachi* and *Haguro* and exchanged fire with them, *Houston* zigzagging constantly so that her forward turrets would bear. Firing in this awkward manner she failed to score, but a dud from one of the Japanese cruisers struck her and ruptured fuel tanks. A moment later she was hit again by a dud which went clear through the bow and let in water. By this time *Houston* had expended her ammunition for her two forward turrets. The crew had to move the heavy 8-inch shells from the disabled after turret up to the magazines of turrets 1 and 2, an arduous task in the excessive temperature below decks as the cruiser made high speed, constantly changed course, and received hits.

Admiral Takagi, confident that he had routed the Striking Force, now ordered his force to close and advised the convoy that it could safely steer for the beaches of Java. At the same time *Naka* and the destroyers of Squadron 4 bore down on the Allies in a wide arc. Around 1745 the advancing column could be seen by the after port lookouts of Doorman's force, occasionally emerging from the smoke. *Exeter* fired intermittently and *Naka* answered. The Japanese light cruiser reversed course at 1750, her six destroyers following, and each of them fired four torpedoes as they rounded the turn or immediately after. Although the range was only a matter of 4400 yards, all twenty-four torpedoes ran wild.

## 4. *Desdiv 58 Attacks, 1809–1830*

Admiral Doorman now swung his force south to course 190° away from the torpedoes and ordered the four United States destroyers to counterattack.

Commander Binford in *John D. Edwards* at once led his division away from *Java's* wake, turning right to a northerly course. Almost immediately Doorman cancelled his order and at sunset, 1809, directed the destroyers to make smoke. By this time Binford's fourstackers were between the opposing cruiser columns. Here also was crippled *Exeter* steaming slowly south escorted by *Witte de With*. At 1815 Doorman signaled "Cover my retirement." What did the Admiral want? Commander Binford quickly figured out that the proper way to cover the cruisers' retirement was to attack. On the bridge of *Alden* a bluejacket observed: "I always knew these old four-pipers would have to go in and save the day." That was the right spirit, but the day was too far gone to save.

Some eleven miles to the northwestward two large ships steaming west were sighted from the bridge of *Edwards*. These were probably *Nachi* and *Haguro*, which, after looping down on the engagement area, were retiring toward their convoys. Admiral Takagi, who was close enough to the shore to sight Surabaya lighthouse, believed the explosions he had seen in the engaged area to be enemy mines (and indeed there were mines on the coast off Tuban) but actually these explosions were from his own torpedoes going off at the end of their runs. He was also afraid of a submarine trap, mindful of his primary task as close cover to the amphibious force.

Most unfortunately the torpedoes on the four American destroyers were set for broadside attack, which requires that the full silhouette of the destroyer be exposed to the enemy before launching. If Commander Binford pressed his attack close enough to ensure accurate torpedo fire his ships would almost certainly be sunk by the cruisers before they had a chance to launch. So, at 1822, he ordered starboard torpedoes to be fired at a range of 10,000 yards, then reversed course and fired the port torpedoes. At that range Takagi had plenty of time to turn his column north after sighting the torpedo wakes and the attack was a complete fiasco.[14]

Although Binford's torpedoes missed, his 4-inch guns possibly had a little luck. As the United States destroyers got ready to launch

---

[14] Curved fire ahead with the destroyers on a division front would have been the logical attack method but, since Doorman had announced that a night attack was expected, torpedoes had been set for broadside fire.

fish, they got occasional glimpses through the smoky scene to the northwest, of destroyers *Minegumo* and *Asagumo* lagging behind *Naka* and the rest of Destroyer Squadron 4. Commander Binford believed that he scored a hit or two. Anyway, someone holed *Asagumo* above the waterline and stopped her engines temporarily.

The four United States destroyers now struggled to catch up with their friends. Voice transmitters on the flagship and *Houston* had been knocked out, it was too dark for flag signals, searchlight and blinker were the only means of communication left. At 1831 Commander Binford received a blinker message from Admiral Doorman, "Follow me." He complied, wondering what the Admiral had in mind.

What Doorman wanted was to get at the Japanese transports. During the engagement he had received news of Japanese convoys northwest of Bawean and north of Kangean Island; obviously the former was the one which Admiral Takagi had been defending. Perhaps it was even now approaching the coast of Java; possibly it was lying-to, awaiting the outcome of the battle. Doorman never learned. At 1830 he radioed to Helfrich, "Enemy retreating west. Where is convoy?"

## 5. *Defeat, 1830–2400*

Admiral Takagi, to play safe, ordered the convoy at 1830 to reverse course to the northward. It was already 30 miles to the northwest of him. Destroyer Squadron 4, except *Asagumo* lying dead in the water, was sent to protect the southern flank of the convoy. All destroyers were very low on fuel.

The Japanese commander speculated as to what Doorman would do next. Would he have to return to Surabaya to fuel? Had Admiral Takahashi's force to the east of Madura Island been reported to him? When his lookouts had last spotted the Allied cruiser line, at 1830, it was heading northeasterly. Would it double back and again try to intercept the convoy? Takagi had to assume the last, which was the greatest threat. He summoned *Jintsu* and Destroyer Squadron 2 to close and described a great loop which brought him some 20 miles southeast of his convoy. Thus the transports were protected in the two directions from which the Allies could approach. During the next hour both *Jintsu* and *Naka* launched planes to reconnoiter enemy movements.

Admiral Doorman, on the other hand, had to play a fatal game of blindman's buff. He had no planes of his own, and intelligence relayed through the cumbersome chain of command in Surabaya never reached him in time. The convoy, which had been last reported some 20 miles west of Bawean Island, had steamed to a point about 50 miles west and slightly south of that island, although it was now retiring northward; but Doorman never knew how closely he had approached it. At 1840, ten minutes after Takagi sighted him last steaming northeast, he swung northwesterly. The American destroyers, having completed their abortive torpedo attack, swung in astern of the cruiser column and strained all engines to catch up. The tired old four-pipers were soon logging 28 to 29 knots, but had difficulty closing the gap. All communications had broken down and Commander Binford was as much in the dark as to Doorman's intentions as he was of the enemy's movements.

Actually the Netherlands commander was steering almost directly toward the enemy convoy. If only he had had air reconnaissance he might have evaded Takagi and struck the fatal blow. But the dice were loaded against him.

At about 1927 the converging cruisers sighted each other again in the gathering darkness. *Nachi* led *Haguro*, *Jintsu* and several destroyers; only 13,000 yards to the southeastward was *De Ruyter* followed by *Perth*, *Houston*, *Java* and the four American destroyers. H.M. destroyer *Jupiter* steamed about a mile from *De Ruyter* on her port bow. One of *Jintsu's* planes dropped flares to illuminate the target. At 1933 *Perth* and *Houston* opened fire, but their shells fell short. The enemy continued to fire star shell, and at 1936, when the captain of *Perth* saw a row of flashes in the enemy column, he suspected that they meant torpedo launchings and swung hard right to course 60°. Fortunately the other ships followed his cue and turned at the same moment or shortly thereafter.

*De Ruyter* was back at the head of the column by 1938, steering east. Doorman did not know where the Japanese convoy was, nor did he know how much enemy gun power lay between him and that target; but he may well have suspected that there was more than met the eye, and that a running duel with the force encountered ten minutes earlier would be just what the enemy wanted, letting the transports head south for Java. At all events he decided to reverse course, in order to avoid further contact with Takagi's Covering Group. By thrusting close along the coast of Java he hoped to intercept the convoy.

At 1955, therefore, he swung his column south and at flank speed steamed toward the coast which soon loomed up in the moonlight. There was little chance that he could outflank the enemy, for he was constantly shadowed by Japanese float planes dropping flares. At 2023 and again twenty minutes later, exhausted and nervous lookouts on the Allied ships thought they saw Japanese destroyers first to port and then to starboard, approaching as if to attack with torpedoes. But these were products of their imaginations; the Japanese were then some 25 miles to the northwestward.

When the cruiser column reached shoal water, at 2100, Admiral Doorman swung to starboard to parallel the coast. The United States destroyers here [15] left the formation and turned east for Surabaya. Doorman had instructed Binford before the battle to retire to Tanjong Priok when his torpedoes were expended, as now they were; but Binford decided to fuel at Surabaya before proceeding to the Batavian port.

As Doorman's force continued westward along the Java coast, it skirted a newly laid Dutch minefield whose exact position had been broadcast at frequent intervals. At high speed the cruisers, followed by the first destroyer, cleared the mined area safely;

---

[15] *Edwards's* fix at this point is the only certain position in this phase of the operation. All times and courses in my track chart are worked forward and backward from it, reconciling as far as possible the reports and charts of the Allied and Japanese commands.

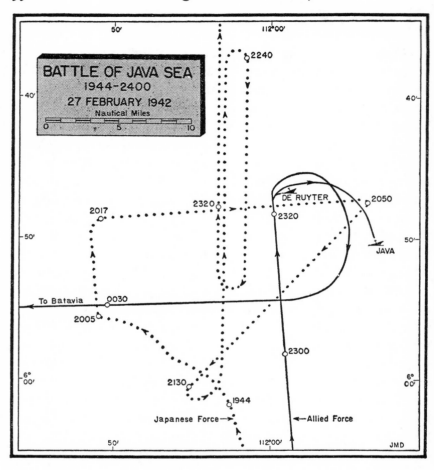

BATTLE OF JAVA SEA
1944-2400
27 FEBRUARY 1942
Nautical Miles
0        5        10

2240

DE RUYTER    2050

2320

2320

2017

JAVA

To Batavia    0030

2005

2300

2130

1944

Japanese Force→

←Allied Force

JMD

but at 2125 an explosion tore apart the last ship in the column, H.M. destroyer *Jupiter*. There is still doubt whether she was the victim of these mines, or, as she then signaled, "I am torpedoed." [16] Only 78 of her crew reached the coast of Java; a few others were picked up by the Japanese.

Shortly after *Jupiter* went down, Admiral Doorman led his cruisers north. Possibly he thought he had passed the enemy pickets but actually he was running up the same meridian as on his north-

[16] Japanese sources state categorically that there were no submarines or destroyers in this vicinity. But the Dutch are positive that their mines did not do it.

ward lunge two hours earlier. Every time that he changed course to deceive the enemy, aircraft overhead dropped calcium flares that illuminated him brightly. At 2217 the column steamed through water strewn with life rafts bearing survivors of *Kortenaer*. *Perth* ordered *Encounter* to drop out and help them.[17]

The four Allied cruisers were now without destroyer support. Vulnerable as was their situation, Admiral Doorman determined to make a last desperate thrust to thwart the invasion of Java. Zigzagging slightly, the column steamed on northward, hoping to bypass the enemy. By 2300 Doorman must have realized that he had failed in this attempt when *Nachi* and *Haguro* were sighted in the bright moonlight on the port beam, steering south. The two columns exchanged fire at extreme range. The salvos were slower now, since both sides were low on ammunition and their crews near exhaustion. The Japanese reversed course to the northward and the two columns exchanged attrition fire for the next twenty minutes, hoping for a lucky hit. At 2320, when the two columns were almost parallel, 8000 yards apart, the Japanese launched torpedoes and this time luck was with them. Both *De Ruyter* and *Java*, caught by the wide spread, were immediately enveloped in flames and stopped dead. On board the flagship the crew were driven forward by the fire, and when the 40-mm. ammunition began to explode the order was given to abandon ship. *Java*, also beyond saving, was abandoned shortly after; and both cruisers soon went down.

Brave Doorman, before he lost contact with *Perth* and *Houston*, ordered them not to stand by but to retire to Batavia. They separated, hoping to shake off the tracking enemy planes, rejoined at midnight and headed for Tanjong Priok, where they signaled to Admiral Helfrich the tragic results of the Battle of the Java Sea.

In one afternoon and evening, half the ships of Admiral Doorman's Striking Force had been destroyed; and the Admiral had gone

---

[17] This destroyer, which had fallen behind the formation, headed westward after rescuing 113 men, but subsequently reversed course when she heard that the enemy was concentrated in that direction.

down with his flagship. The Japanese had not lost a single ship, and only one destroyer was badly damaged. The convoy was untouched.

It is unnecessary to point out the lessons of this battle in any detail, for they stand out on the record. Admiral Doorman's Striking Force was not greatly outnumbered or outweighed in ships and gunfire, and on the whole his shooting was better than that of the enemy. The main factors, any one of which doomed him to defeat, were his almost complete lack of air power whether for protection, scouting or spotting, bad communications, and the enemy's vast superiority in torpedo matériel and tactics. It must be admitted that the United States Navy component did nothing to raise the Allied average, although it had the good luck to lose not one ship.

The most surprising thing about the battle was its length. Before World War II, most strategists thought that gun and torpedo fire had been developed to such a point that naval battles would be decided in a few minutes, at the end of which one side would either be annihilated or so crippled that it could fight no more. Several battles in this war — notably Savo Island — were of that description. But in the Battle of the Java Sea the two opponents slugged each other intermittently over a period of some seven hours before the Allied survivors had to break off and admit defeat. That it lasted so long was due to Admiral Doorman's stubborn determination and the admirable manner in which men of the three Allied Navies under his command fought and fought until they could fight no more.

# CHAPTER XIX

# Bloody Sequel

## 27 February–9 March 1942

### 1. *Loss of* LANGLEY, *27 February*[1]

ALTHOUGH Marshal Wavell had given up the fight for Java on 25 February, basing his decision on the lack of fighter protection, there was still a desperate chance that aircraft could be brought in to hold the line. Even before the loss of Timor, very few planes had succeeded in making the hazardous flight from Australia to Java. Poorly trained pilots, rushed to the front in the first frantic days of hostilities, lost more aircraft landing or taking off from the little staging strip in Timor than in combat. After the Japanese took that island, fighter planes could be brought into Java only by sea.

United States aircraft tender *Langley* was ideal for a ferry job of that sort. This thirty-year-old ship, built as a collier, converted to a carrier in 1922 but long since relegated to the humdrum rôle of an auxiliary, was now given a chance at the spotlight.

U.S.S. *Langley*, carrying 33 Army Air Force pilots and 32 P–40 planes all ready to fly, and freighter *Sea Witch* with 27 more P–40s crated in her hold, departed Fremantle, Australia, on 22 February as part of a convoy headed for Bombay. Light cruiser *Phoenix*, detached from the Anzac Force, joined. The three American ships were to peel off near Cocos Island, several hundred miles southwest of Sunda Strait, and thence backtrack to Tjilatjap.[2] But Admiral

---

[1] Action Report "Operations, Actions and Sinking of U.S.S. *Langley* 22 Feb.–5 Mar. 1942" written on board *Mount Vernon* 9 Mar. 1942; Glassford Report.
[2] *Phoenix* War Diary.

Helfrich ordered *Langley* and *Sea Witch* to be detached en route, at a point much nearer Tjilatjap, and proceed thither alone. He had to have planes quickly if at all; and, in the confusion of the time, he failed to consult or promptly to inform Admiral Glassford at Tjilatjap.

That was the only remaining Javanese port where *Langley* and *Sea Witch* could possibly deliver planes without enemy interference. There were no airfields near by, and only partially cleared space from which to stage the planes northward across Java. All hands pitched in to widen the roadway down which the planes would have to be towed to this improvised strip. Many huts and trees had to be taken down so that the wings of the P–40s could pass; and the scarcity of native laborers, most of whom had fled to the hills, thrust almost the whole of this humid task on Dutch and American sailors.

The planes crated in *Sea Witch* could not be utilized at once but those in *Langley* might mean the difference between defeat and victory. Admiral Helfrich had originally planned to route both ships so that they would make port in the early morning of 28 February after an unescorted night run. This was the safer way to do it; but time was precious when the Japanese invasion forces approached Java. So the Dutch Admiral, assuming full responsibility, ordered *Langley* early on 23 February to make best speed for Tjilatjap in order to arrive on the afternoon of the 27th. It was a rash but brave decision, which Admiral Glassford approved, and for the consequences of which he gallantly insisted on sharing the blame. As yet no Japanese forces had been sighted south of Java and the tender's daylight approach might not be detected. It was a long chance but worth the try.

*Langley* proceeded as ordered without incident until the afternoon of 26 February, when two Dutch Catalinas flew out to report that *Willem Van der Zaan*, a 1300-ton Netherlands minesweeper, was about 20 miles to the westward, coming to escort her into Tjilatjap. This was a surprise to Commander R. P. McConnell, skipper of *Langley*. He had already been informed that United

States destroyers *Edsall* and *Whipple*[3] would come out from Tjilatjap to escort him over the last leg of the voyage. And, as he had heard nothing to the contrary, he still counted on them.

Consequently he decided to leave the slow sweeper astern, and steamed ahead, zigzagging. Since his fuel burners were not adapted to the use of thin Borneo oil, his maximum speed was 10 knots. After dark came a radio message from Admiral Glassford confirming the Dutch Catalinas' statement that they and *Van der Zaan* were to be his escorts. *Langley* reversed course, losing valuable time, and eventually sighted the Catalinas hovering not over the sweeper but over *Edsall* and *Whipple!* It was now 0720 February 27. More time was lost while the destroyers ran down a submarine contact that failed to develop, but eventually the three ships resumed course for Tjilatjap.

February 27 was a fair day with a good breeze and scattered high clouds — ideal weather for carrier-based aircraft. At 0900, sight of an unidentified plane flying high caused Commander McConnell to request air cover from Admiral Glassford. As usual none was available. At 1140 more planes were sighted; the captain went to general quarters and signaled his plight to Java.

Admiral Kondo's battleship and carrier force was already operating south of the Malay Barrier, precisely to prevent the Allies' receiving reinforcement from that quarter. It had departed Kendari on the 25th, steamed through Lombok Strait into the Indian Ocean, and then headed west.[4] When *Langley* left the convoy, Japanese carriers, judging from their postwar track chart, must have been fairly close behind her, within striking distance. But it was not carrier-based aircraft that struck her.

The Eleventh Air Fleet, a shore-based naval command, coöperated closely with Admiral Takahashi's invasion forces. Planes of the

[3] *Whipple* was recently out of dock at Tjilatjap with a soft bow and stem as a result of her collision with *De Ruyter* and had to be employed on light duty only thenceforth. *Edsall*, leaking badly as a result of damage from one of her own depth charges dropped at slow speed, could not be relied upon for duty with the Striking Force. (Glassford Report p. 38.)

[4] *Soryu* and *Ryujo* Merit Reports; chart of track of Japanese carriers, here reproduced.

21st and 23rd Air Flotillas flew patrols from Kendari and Bandjer-masin into the Java Sea and Indian Ocean to keep a close watch on Allied movements. It was one of these which first sighted *Langley* and called for reinforcements.[5]

Next, 9 two-engined bombers approached the formation at 15,000 feet altitude. *Langley* opened fire as soon as the Japanese planes came within range. As they glided in on an 80-degree angle from the ship, Commander McConnell ordered hard right rudder, and the bombs landed some 100 feet to port. The same maneuver foiled the Japanese again; but on the third round *Langley* took five hits and two near misses.

She was now badly damaged. Planes topside broke into flames, one after the other. The bridge steering mechanism and gyro compass were destroyed and she listed ten degrees to port. Six fighter planes came in strafing but soon made off.

Commander McConnell maneuvered his stricken vessel to reduce the windage as much as possible. He hoped to control the fire, but in a 20-to-25-knot breeze it could not be done. He caused burning planes to be jettisoned, and counterflooded to reduce the list. Realizing that in his present condition he could not hope to negotiate the narrow mouth of Tjilatjap Harbor, he laid a direct course to the Java coast, planning to beach her if necessary. The order to "make ready boats and rafts for lowering" in case it were necessary to abandon ship was misinterpreted by many of the crew, who jumped overboard. A short time after, inrushing water flooded both main motors, and she went dead in the water. At 1332 Commander McConnell decided to abandon ship while there was still an escort to pick up the crew.[6]

In the transmitting room the chief radioman, who had kept up an informal chatter to maintain contact with the outside world, tapped

[5] *Inter. Jap. Off.* II 379. The 22nd Air Flotilla also took part.

[6] Admiral Glassford's endorsement on the *Langley* Report 4 Apr. 1942 gives the impression that in his opinion the ship might have been saved. If so, this was not the only premature abandonment of a U.S. ship in the first eight months of the war; but it must be remembered that *Langley* did not have the damage control equipment that was later installed in U.S. fighting ships. Her pumps could not cope with the flooding.

on his keys: "Mamma said there would be days like this. She must have known!"

All but 16 of the crew and aviation personnel were rescued by the two destroyers, which then scuttled the old tender with torpedo and shellfire. *Langley* went down about 75 miles south of Tjilatjap. With better luck she could have got through.[7] Lieutenant Commander J. M. Hatfield, master of the luckier *Sea Witch*, made Tjilatjap, discharged his planes, took on 40 refugee soldiers and returned to Australia undetected.

## 2. *The Battle of Sunda Strait, 28 February–1 March*[8]

Admirals Palliser and Glassford knew that the jig was up; but if Admiral Helfrich was aware of his grave position he did not reveal it to his allies.

What course of action he could take was not clear. His forces were split between Surabaya and Batavia with a powerful enemy between. The Japanese had postponed their invasion,[9] but only for a couple of days. Little fuel remained at Tanjong Priok and skippers were reluctant to fly the Baker flag at Surabaya under almost constant air attack. It was imperative to retire all fighting ships from the enemy-controlled Java Sea into the Indian Ocean. Once they had passed the Malay Barrier it would be most precarious to venture through any of the narrow passages and straits to challenge the Japanese Navy. Yet the Abdafloat commander attempted to reassemble his forces in Tjilatjap and fight again from there.

[7] *Langley* Report; Comdesdiv 57 (Cdr. Crouch in *Whipple*) Report. Survivors were transferred to oiler *Pecos* in the lee of Christmas Island; some lost in her, others picked up by U.S. transport *Mount Vernon* on her way home from Singapore.

[8] For this action the main Allied sources are the *Houston* and *Perth* Survivors' Reports, thought out in Japanese prison camps and written after the war was over; and on the enemy side, the Chihaya "Outline," Reports of Desrons 3, 4 and 5, and Crudiv 7 Track Chart. It is a difficult action to reconstruct, at best. The chart we have used, by the C. O. of *Mogami*, Capt. (later Rear Admiral) Soji in *Inter. Jap. Off.* II 438, will be found to conflict with several statements in our text, but for consistency's sake we have left it pretty much as is.

[9] Desron 4 Report; Chihaya "Outline."

Haste to do now what must be done anon
Or some mad hope of selling triumph dear
Drove the ships forth: . . .

The four American destroyers who had participated in the
Battle of Java Sea were at Surabaya, almost out of torpedoes and
in no condition to fight. Admiral Helfrich authorized Admiral
Glassford to send them to Australia for rearming. *Pope*, the only
American destroyer left with a full load of torpedoes, remained to
help H.M.S. *Encounter* escort the wounded *Exeter* to the Indian
Ocean.

Which passage would be the less dangerous? Glassford recommended Lombok Strait, since Bali Strait was too shoal and narrow
for the cruiser; but Admiral Palliser, believing that the enemy had
occupied eastern Bali in great strength, directed the *Exeter* group
to seek Sunda Strait — ignorant, for want of air intelligence, that
the enemy had already closed it.

Tjilatjap via Sunda Strait was also the destination of the two
cruisers that had put in at Tanjong Priok after Java Sea. During
the afternoon of 28 February Admiral Glassford talked with Captain Rooks of *Houston*, for the last time, over the telephone; and
at 1930 she sortied from Tanjong Priok, in company with H.M.S.
*Perth*. "Scuttlebutt," the gossip of bluejackets on board the United
States cruiser, eagerly discussed her rumored destination, an overhaul in California. It was high time. She had been in the Far East
for 17 months. *Houston* was a proud and a happy ship, but her
men had reached the limit of endurance. Twice on 25 February
and twice on the 26th they had been under air attack in Surabaya.
The intervening night and the following were spent sweeping along
the coast of Madura, everyone at General Quarters. And then came
the Battle of the Java Sea. A few hours' rest in the port of Batavia,
and now they must move along. H.N.M.S. *Evertsen* was to have
escorted the two cruisers, but she was delayed in starting and never
caught up.

Thus, on the last night of February 1942, two of the three surviving groups of the Combined Striking Force — *Houston, Perth*

and *Evertsen* out of Batavia, and *Exeter*, *Pope* and *Encounter* out of Surabaya — started towards Sunda Strait, which a powerful Japanese force had already closed in order to effect the largest landing yet attempted in the Southwest Pacific.

*Perth* and *Houston*, steaming along the northern coast of Java without surface or air escort, expected trouble. They could hardly hope to avoid the Japanese Western Attack Force which H.M.A.S. *Hobart* had sighted the day before near Banka Island. It was a clear, calm night and the moon was full.

Rear Admiral Kurita, pleasantly surprised at the flight of British ships from Tanjong Priok that morning, brought his Western Attack Force down from Banka Island to land on St. Nicolas Point, the northwestern extremity of Java which makes the eastern entrance to Sunda Strait. There are good anchorages in Banten Bay and excellent road communication with Batavia, some fifty miles distant. A strong task force built around four heavy cruisers and the aircraft carrier *Ryujo* maneuvered twenty miles north of Banten Bay, to protect the landing force from any attack from that quarter. *Mogami* and *Mikuma* were near enough to close if necessary, and light cruiser *Natori* with a whole destroyer squadron covered the transports as they disembarked troops on the shores of the bay.

Between 2240 and 2255 February 28, while the ship-to-shore movement of troops was under way, destroyer *Fubuki*, patrolling off shore, sighted *Perth* and *Houston* approaching Banten Bay. A little later, the cruisers sighted anchored Japanese transports broad on the port bow, and opened fire on them. Although *Houston* and *Perth* were only trying to escape, they had accidentally fulfilled the long-felt desire of Hart and Helfrich; they had run into an enemy amphibious force at its most vulnerable moment. But, alas, they were so few and the time was so late.

*Fubuki's* presence was not detected by the weary lookouts in *Perth* and *Houston* for about half an hour, as she shadowed them zigzagging toward the convoy.[10] At 2315 *Perth* sighted the destroyer and challenged, hoping it was a friendly ship sent to see

[10] Chihaya "Outline"; Desron 5 Report.

the cruisers through the Strait. Hope vanished when the Japanese answered with a flare and fired nine torpedoes from the short distance of 2500–3000 yards.[11] The cruiser column swung hard right and opened fire. The torpedoes missed *Perth* and *Houston* but hit some of the Japanese transports on their port hand.

As they swung north through the narrow passage between Panjang Island and St. Nicolas Point, *Perth* and *Houston* escaped from one trap only to enter another. A light cruiser and ten destroyers lay between them and Sunda Strait; heavy cruisers *Mogami* and *Mikuma* and another destroyer or two were hastening to intercept, in response to frantic signals from *Fubuki*. Yet even in their flight the Allied cruisers raised hell with the anchored transports. Between them, *Perth* and *Houston* had accounted for four loaded transports out of the 56-ship convoy. One of them, the 7000-ton *Sakura Maru*, sank outright; the other three were able to beach themselves. Two of these were headquarters ships and one bore General Imamura himself. This important character leaped over the side and clung to a piece of driftwood for twenty minutes before a passing boat picked him up. Shortly thereafter the ship that he had abandoned listed still more and dumped tons of mechanized equipment into the sea "with a dreadful sound." Once ashore the soggy General sat down on a bamboo pile and his aide "limped over to him and congratulated him on his successful landing."[12] Unfortunately the crew of *Houston* knew nothing of this diverting incident.

As the senior surviving officer of *Houston* remembered the scene when his ship debouched from Banten Bay: —

The disposition of the enemy vessels was such as to completely encircle the *Houston* on all offshore bearings. Light patrol and torpedo boats operated with the transports in Banten Bay. Enemy planes were

[11] Japanese Torpedo School Report; Desron 5 Report gives 2314 as time of torpedo firing.

[12] Desron 5 Report and an "Account of the Netherlands East Indies Operations" written by an officer of Gen. Imamura's staff (ATIS enemy publication No. 32, 11 Sept. 1943). The official *Japanese Naval and Merchant Shipping Losses* mentions only *Sakura* and *Horai* sunk at this point; the other two must eventually have been salvaged.

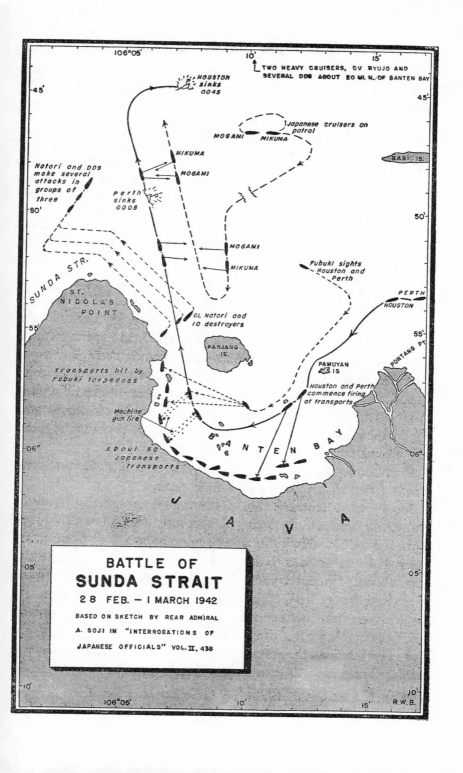

TWO HEAVY CRUISERS, CV RYUJO AND
SEVERAL DDS ABOUT 20 MI. N. OF BANTEN BAY

HOUSTON
sinks
0045

Japanese cruisers on
patrol

MOGAMI   MIKUMA

MIKUMA

MOGAMI

BABI IS.

Natori and DDS
make several
attacks in
groups of
three

Perth
sinks
0005

MOGAMI

MIKUMA

Fubuki sights
Houston and
Perth

PERTH

HOUSTON

SUNDA STR.

ST.
NICOLAS
POINT

CL Natori and
10 destroyers

PANJANG
IS.

PAMUYAN
IS

PONTANG PT.

Transports hit by
Fubuki torpedoes

Houston and Perth
commence firing
at transports

Machine
gun fire

About 50
Japanese
transports

B A N T E N   B A Y

J

A   V   A

# BATTLE OF
# SUNDA STRAIT
## 28 FEB. — I MARCH 1942

BASED ON SKETCH BY REAR ADMIRAL

A. SOJI IN "INTERROGATIONS OF

JAPANESE OFFICIALS" VOL. II, 438

R.W.B.

overhead. Enemy ships believed to be cruisers or carriers were firing at the *Houston* from about 12,000 yards to seaward. Having established hitting range they were pouring fire into the ships and causing considerable damage. Destroyers operating in formations of three or four were making repeated attacks on the bows and quarters of the *Houston*, using both guns and torpedoes. The proximity of the ship to shoal water and the strong current running were additional hazards to maneuvering. Since control of the whole area was rapidly passing over to the enemy, grounding of the ship would inevitably lead to capture. All communication systems which were still operative were hopelessly overloaded with reports of damage received, of approaching torpedoes, of new enemy attacks begun, or changes in targets engaged.[13]

Around 2340 (it was still 28 February) the Japanese fighting ships that had been summoned to the spot converged on the two intrepid cruisers. In the mad mêlée that followed, both sides fought under the full moon with everything they had, and at ranges from 5000 down to 500 yards. Four torpedoes struck *Perth*. Destroyer *Harukaze* took a shell on her rudder but was shortly able to come in with *Hatakaze* to launch six more torpedoes at the British cruiser. A hit by *Houston* at 2355 damaged *Mikuma's* electric power supply, but it was quickly restored and she resumed shooting, registering several hits.

Five minutes after midnight, at 0005 March 1, H.M.S. *Perth* went down, holed by torpedoes and 8-inch gunfire.

Now every Japanese ship concentrated on putting *Houston* away. She was already listing dangerously to starboard. Around 0010 she took a salvo in her after engine-room which burst all the steam lines and scalded to death the entire engine-room force. Live steam hissing through breaches in the deck forced gun crews to retreat temporarily from their battle stations. A torpedo hit forward smashed up main battery plot, whose crew was wiped out by a shellburst as they came topside. Turrets went to local control, and for a few moments the gunners profited by a mistake that the enemy made, illuminating his own ships, and put a couple of shells where

[13] Cdr. A. L. Maher's official *Houston* Action Report, 13 Nov. 1945.

they did good; one of them may have sunk minesweeper *AM-2*.[14] Then, around 0020, an enemy shell hit No. 2 turret just as powder bags were being loaded, starting a fire which forced Captain Rooks to have both magazines flooded. Now the two 8-inch turrets had no ammunition except what was already in the hoists. Three torpedoes hit the ship on her starboard side and shrapnel from small-caliber fire ricocheted about her superstructure.

The decks were already strewn with the dead and the dying, and water was pouring fast into the hull when, at 0025, Captain Rooks ordered Abandon Ship. A few moments later, when standing near a machine gun mount, he and the entire gun crew were killed by a shrapnel burst. As the ship still had too much way on for safe abandonment, Commander David Roberts, the executive officer, cancelled the order before the word had gone very far. The men stood by their guns and fired every bit of ammunition they had, even starshell, until all was expended. Then, and as the ship lost headway, Japanese destroyers swarmed about her, machine-gunning the quarterdeck and the port hangar where many of the survivors from below had congregated.[15]

Commander Roberts ordered Abandon Ship, and seaman Stafford, standing on the careening fantail, sounded the call a second time on his bugle, at 0033. Within twelve minutes at most, this great fighting ship rolled over and sank.[16]

Illumination from a Japanese destroyer enabled her men in the water to see their ensign still flying until it dipped below the waters of Sunda Strait.

[14] Sunk, according to Desron 5 Report, at 0007; other Japanese sources say only damaged, but they admit that *Houston* hit three different destroyers in the last phase.

[15] Many of these details are from "Partial Log" in *Houston* Survivors' Reports, Enc. A–9. Cdr. Maher says that in the hour's battle she took 4 to 6 torpedo hits, 3 whole salvos and 11 individual shell hits, and 5 others that may have been from shells or torpedoes. The Japanese Torpedo School Report says that 87 torpedoes were expended on *Perth* and *Houston*.

[16] Time 0045 in Maher's official Report; Japanese Desron 4 Report gives 0036; Soji, allowing for difference in time, says 0030. Maher states that *Houston's* position at 0025 was about 12 miles NW of Nicolas Pt. and 5 miles from Babi Island, which bore 135°. None of the Japanese statements about her sinking agree as to the position.

Over a thousand men were on board when *Houston* began her last fight. All survivors, 368 in number, were recovered by the Japanese and imprisoned. They and the survivors of *Perth* had over three years of starvation and brutality ahead of them, during which they often wished that they had gone down with their shipmates off Sunda Strait.[17]

They were soon to be joined by officers and men from the destroyer *Evertsen*, which was to have escorted them through to safety. By extraordinary luck she slipped past the Japanese beachhead and penetrated Sunda Strait, only to be attacked shortly before dawn by two destroyers and forced to ground in a sinking condition on the island of Sabuku at the entrance to the Indian Ocean.[18]

*Houston's* great fight, the last half hour of it waged singly against overwhelming odds, is one of the most gallant in American naval annals. Unfortunately no word of it, except the mere fact of her loss, was revealed until after the war was over.

The Japanese Western Attack Group had now crushed all naval opposition, and could proceed at leisure to consolidate and expand the beachhead.

## 3. *Finis the Striking Force*

The Eastern Attack Group lingered about 100 miles northwest of Bawean Island during 28 February, waiting for word from Admiral Takahashi to commence landing operations. Commander Third Fleet had left his position northeast of Java and was now some thirty miles northwest of the Fifth Cruiser Division. That night the screening cruisers led the convoy up the beachhead at Karanganjan, 100 miles west of Surabaya.[19] They were challenged en route by three submarines and the attacking destroyers claimed that they sank all three; but the submarines escaped.[20]

---

[17] Some 292 were repatriated after the war or escaped from prison camp, out of a total of 1064 sailors and Marines in the ship's company at the time of the sinking. The other 76 survivors died in prison camps.

[18] Helfrich Report; Kroese *Dutch Navy at War*.

[19] Chihaya "Outline."

[20] Desron 2 Report; *Tokitsukaze* and *Hatsukaze* War Diaries.

About ten light bombers and fifteen fighter planes, from remnants of the U.S. Army, Netherlands, New Zealand and Australian air forces, also attacked the convoy. They managed to kill about 150 Japanese soldiers in the transports and caused one of the ships to beach herself; but the landing was completed without serious loss.[21] The enemy now had two beachheads on Java, fast expanding.

While these things were going on, Captain O. L. Gordon RN in H.M. cruiser *Exeter* led *Encounter* and *Pope* through the Surabaya mine fields on their last voyage, hoping to make Ceylon.[22] *Exeter's* engineering department worked frantically to repair her damaged boilers and managed to boost her speed to 23 knots. The force was ordered to pass eastward of Bawean Island, thence to Sunda Strait. Shortly before 0400 March 1, one small and two large ships were sighted to the westward in the light of the setting moon. Captain Gordon interpreted his instructions as an evacuation rather than an attack order, and therefore reversed course to avoid what appeared to be two merchant ships escorted by a destroyer. Apparently the enemy did not sight him for they failed to close and the Japanese make no mention of contact at this time. At 0750, after day had broken with high visibility, the crow's nest reported two heavy ships steaming toward the Allied force from the SSW.[23] *Exeter* hoped again to avoid, but the enemy ships changed course and launched aircraft. The British cruiser worked southwestward, zigzagging occasionally.

Back on a westerly course at 0935 she sighted the masts of two heavy cruisers steaming to the southward. This was Admiral Takagi with *Nachi* and *Haguro*. Immediately Captain Gordon turned his force northwest, again to avoid battle, but Takagi turned too and further trouble developed ahead. Admiral Takahashi's flagship group, *Ashigara* leading *Myoko* and two destroyers, appeared to the northwest. Four heavy cruisers were closing in on *Exeter*,

[21] Chihaya "Outline"; Desron 4 Report; Flight Lieutenant R. D. Millar RNZAF "Narrative of Personal Experiences of War in the Far East."

[22] *Witte de With* was also directed to join this small force at the last minute but, since her skipper had granted shore leave, she was unable to comply. She was hit and sunk in drydock 2 March.

[23] *Exeter* Report corroborated by Chihaya Track Chart, and former C.O. *Pope* Action Report of U.S.S. *Pope* 1 March 1942.

*Encounter* and *Pope*. At 1020 they opened fire and *Nachi* followed suit.

The three beleaguered ships swung hard right and made best speed — 25 to 26 knots — to the eastward. *Pope* and *Encounter* laid smoke to protect *Exeter* as a heavy gun duel ensued, at a range which closed to 18,000 and then 14,000 yards. A failure in the fire control on board *Exeter* multiplied her disadvantage. All her salvos fell wide of their mark, while the Japanese cruisers with the aid of a spotting plane became more and more accurate.

It was a race with death. By 1100 the situation seemed hopeless. One or two slight rain squalls to eastward offered a thin hope of concealment, but *Exeter* did not live long enough to seek even such temporary shelter. She launched her torpedoes at *Myoko* and *Ashigara*, but at too great a range to obtain hits. Enemy destroyers closed on her starboard hand and were hotly engaged by *Encounter* and *Pope* as well as by *Exeter's* secondary battery; but it was clear to all that the end was near.

At about 1120 *Exeter* received her first serious hit, in a boiler room. Soon all power was lost, so that main and secondary gun controls could not function, and the ship slowed down. *Encounter* and *Pope*, unable to help her, sped on. The cruiser was already silent and making only 4 knots. The Japanese cruisers, choosing their own range, straddled her continually. Captain Gordon ordered Abandon Ship. A few minutes after all hands had gone over the side, one of eighteen torpedoes fired by destroyers of Admiral Takahashi's force finished her off. *Exeter* rolled over and sank.

*Encounter* too was fatally hit and abandoned. *Pope*, a World War I destroyer alone in a narrow sea where prowled a dozen Japanese cruisers and scores of destroyers, and over which flew hundreds of hostile aircraft, could not hope to live much longer. At about 1145 a heavy rain squall appeared ahead. Commander W. C. Blinn ordered every ounce of speed the old engines could provide and made smoke until his ship reached the temporary shelter of the rain. All hands took full advantage of the lull to assess damage and effect emergency repairs and redistribute ammunition. The brick walls of No. 3 boiler had caved in from repeated concussions. All ammunition was exhausted forward. Blinn hoped to dodge eastward along the southern coast of Borneo and then, under cover of darkness, dash for Lombok Strait.

Death came from the skies. Shortly after noon, as she emerged from a second rain squall, the lone destroyer was sighted and trailed by a cruiser-borne plane. At about 1230, 6 dive-bombers from *Ryujo* came in.[24] The after 3-inch gun opened up as they came within range, but after the 75th round it failed to return to battery and had to be abandoned. Then the planes began individual dive-bombing runs on *Pope*. On the eleventh of these attacks a close miss abreast of No. 4 torpedo tube exploded under water and blew a large hole in the ship's plating, threw the port shaft out of line and flooded many compartments. The port engine immediately started to vibrate seriously and had to be secured. Despite frantic efforts by the damage control party, water levels rose rapidly.

After their twelfth run the dive-bombers were relieved by 6 high-level "Kates," also from *Ryujo*, which made four bombing runs from about 3000 feet altitude. *Pope* twisted and turned as best she could.

While she was maneuvering to avoid a second high-level attack the captain noticed that his ship was settling aft. Lieutenant Antrim, damage control officer, reported that flooding was beyond control and it was obvious that *Pope* would have to be abandoned. During the next ten minutes all classified material was destroyed, watertight doors opened and demolition charges set. It was now about 1250 and word was passed for all hands to stand clear. A charge was set off to explode the secret sound gear. The motor whaleboat was lowered and the men commenced abandoning ship. Last to go except the skipper was a special demolition team under command of the gunnery officer, which set off a charge in the engine room. When all were clear splashes from cruiser gunfire appeared all about the *Pope*. On about the sixth salvo, the last Allied ship in the Java Sea was hit, and sank stern-first in fifteen seconds.

[24] *Pope* Report; *Ryujo* Merit Report.

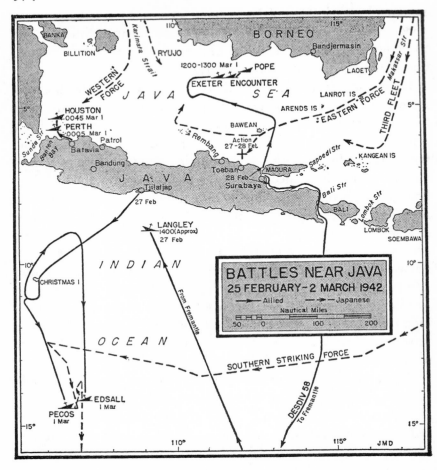

The survivors who had obtained a place in the ship's one whaleboat were examined by a seaplane which flew low over them. The
lads were still so fighting mad that they opened up on the plane
with two Browning automatics. This was unfortunate, for more
aircraft now appeared and for half an hour enjoyed strafing the
boat and survivors in the water. Commander Blinn then rounded
up all the life rafts he could find and lay-to, awaiting developments. During the battle he had sent many messages to Java and
hoped to be rescued; but it was a Japanese destroyer that picked

up the exhausted survivors of *Pope*, on their third night out.[25]

Of all American fighting ships that sailed from Javanese ports on 28 February, our old four-piper friends *Ford, Paul Jones, Edwards* and *Alden* were the only ones to escape. They got under way from Surabaya after dark 28 February. All precautions were taken to slip through Bali Strait undetected.[26] Bright surfaces were carefully covered to prevent telltale reflections from the moonlight. When the narrows were entered at 0020 March 1 the four destroyers hugged the western bank so that the moon, now hanging on their starboard beam, would not silhouette the ship. Many small sailing craft were passed, but no warship until at 0205, immediately after threading the narrows, a slowly patrolling Japanese destroyer was seen. About five minutes later she sighted the Americans and took a course parallel to them, in which she was shortly joined by two more destroyers. At 0222 they opened fire. The American column replied from a range of about 6000 yards but Commander Binford was primarily interested in escaping, as his ships were low on ammunition and had no torpedoes. He concentrated on opening range, and when that was done the enemy ceased fire. Division 58 continued without further incident to Australia. These four destroyers, with *Parrott* and *Whipple* which made good their escape from Tjilatjap, cruiser *Marblehead* and two gunboats, were the only surface fighting ships of the old Asiatic Fleet to survive the Java campaign.

## 4. *Abda Falls Apart*

While *Perth* and *Houston* were fighting their last battle off Sunda Strait, Admirals Palliser and Glassford argued at Allied headquarters in Bandoeng. Both were convinced that the fight for Java had been lost and that nothing could be gained by a last-ditch stand. At midnight, as they were talking, a report came in that a

[25] *Pope* Report and lecture by Cdr. R. H. Antrim at Naval War College, Newport.
[26] *John D. Ford* Report, 13 Mar. 1942; *Edwards* Report, 4 Mar.

B–17, flying from Java to Australia, had sighted two strong groups of enemy ships some 150 miles southeast of Tjilatjap, heading northwest. These were Kondo's Southern Force with Nagumo's Carrier Force, on the warpath again. They had departed Kendari 25 February and debouched into the Indian Ocean through the Straits of Ombai, then steamed westward in the direction of Christmas Island with the mission of destroying the remnants of Allied shipping and, at the same time, discouraging any attempt to reinforce Java from India or Australia.[27]

Although Palliser and Glassford lacked the information to identify this force, they expected the worst. The next bad news they expected was the bombing of Tjilatjap. Four destroyers, two gunboats and four other American vessels were still based there; and submarine tender *Otus* and several small British vessels were bound thither.

Early in the morning of 1 March they called on Vice Admiral Helfrich to request him to cancel his order to fight to the last. As Admiral Glassford remembered the conversation, it went as follows: —

HELFRICH: I must decline to accept your recommendation. I must continue resistance as long as I have ships that can fight. I have already ordered a greater concentration of submarines against the enemy in the Java Sea. The enemy will make another attempt to land tonight near Rembang. He may succeed tonight but I shall attack the next wave of transports.

PALLISER: Then I must say to you as the Senior British Naval Officer in this area, that my instructions from the Admiralty are to withdraw His Majesty's ships from Java when resistance will serve no further useful purpose. That time, in my judgment, has come. Therefore, I feel it my duty to order His Majesty's ships to India at once, and this I propose to do.

HELFRICH: You realize that you are under my orders?

PALLISER: I do of course. But in this vital matter I cannot do other than my duty as I see it.

HELFRICH: You know that I lent to the British when Malaya was

[27] Isawa Interrogation. Lt. LaRocque's answer to Mr. Salomon 8 Oct. 1946; Track of Japanese Aircraft Carriers.

threatened, all of my fighting fleet — my cruisers, my destroyers, my submarines, my air — all of it was placed at your disposal for operation as you saw fit. In doing so we suffered grave losses. Furthermore, you did not hold Malaya. Singapore now is in the hands of the enemy. You failed. I think the wisest course now is to let me continue to handle this situation and save Java.

PALLISER: I cannot alter my decision.

HELFRICH: Will you delay one hour until I see the Governor General and inform him what you intend to do?

PALLISER: I cannot delay longer. Every minute counts now.

HELFRICH: And you, Admiral Glassford, what do you intend to do?

GLASSFORD: My instructions are to report to you for duty. Any order you give me will be obeyed at once. I wish to say to you, however, that I concur without reservation in the advice given you by your Chief of Staff. I am to retire on Australia by order of my Commander in Chief if necessary to abandon Java, but that is for you to decide.

HELFRICH: Very well then, Admiral Palliser, you may give any orders you wish to His Majesty's ships. Admiral Glassford, you will *order* your ships to Australia.[28]

Around 1000 March 1, about an hour after this conversation, Admiral Helfrich advised his naval colleagues that the Governor General had dissolved the Abda naval command in the Netherlands East Indies.

Admiral Glassford had already ordered all of his ships to Exmouth Gulf, Australia; and Admiral Palliser directed the British ships to the same port, rather than to India.

## 5. *Evacuation and Surrender*

At about 1030 Helfrich sent for Admiral Glassford, thanked him for his naval support and told him that, if he wished to leave Java, he better do so at once. Helfrich intimated that he too was about to leave; and leave he did next day by air for Colombo. Glassford set out from Bandoeng by car and arrived Tjilatjap late that evening. There he assembled the American officers and men to give orders for evacuation. The two remaining Catalinas at Sura-

[28] Glassford Report, pp. 58–60.

baya were ordered to fly in, and two were summoned from Broome, Australia. They arrived that afternoon, but one developed engine trouble, so only three were available as evacuation ferryboats. A large submarine came into Tjilatjap and took as many men on board as she could hold. Admiral Palliser — who had also moved to Tjilat-jap — and Admiral Glassford dispatched all remaining ships to Australia. Old China gunboats and British corvettes furnished escort for the merchant ships, where quarters were found for American citizens and consular staffs. The two admirals took off in a PBY about midnight and arrived at Exmouth Gulf in the early morning of 2 March.

Not every ship could be evacuated. Destroyer *Stewart*, which had capsized in dry dock, was wrecked by a demolition charge on 2 March. The Japanese managed to salvage her nevertheless.[29]

The tale of the rest can be told briefly.

Naval oiler *Pecos* was bound from Tjilatjap towards India on 27 February when she was ordered to take *Langley* survivors off destroyers *Whipple* and *Edsall*. When about to make the transfer next morning off Christmas Island, she and the destroyers were attacked unsuccessfully by land-based bombers from Borneo or Kendari. Commander Crouch, the division commander in *Whipple*, headed the three ships southward until they were out of range, when the transfer was completed on 1 March and the ships parted. But Kondo's battleships and Nagumo's carrier planes were looking for just such evacuees. *Edsall* was dispatched by battleships *Hiei* and *Kirishima* that very afternoon.[30] *Pecos* was jumped by planes from carrier *Soryu* at noontime, again an hour later, and finally at 1500. That finished her. *Whipple* intercepted her distress signal, picked up 232 men from the water and life rafts that evening, and delivered them safely at Fremantle. The rest perished.

---

[29] *All Hands* April 1946. U.S. fliers were often bewildered to see an American ship deep in enemy-held waters. They recognized her lines even though the two forward stacks had been combined into one characteristically raked stack and a tripod substituted for the pole foremast. Recovered after the war, she was nicknamed "Ramp," for "Recovered Allied Military Personnel."

[30] Japanese Batdiv 3 War Diary (WDC 160998).

Destroyer *Pillsbury*, gunboat *Asheville* and Australian gunboat *Yarra* were sunk one after the other by Admiral Kondo's ships during the first five days of March. *Lark*, *Whippoorwill*, gunboat *Tulsa* and *Isabel* got through to Fremantle.

The Japanese landings on Java were only slightly embarrassed by such naval demonstrations as the Allies had been able to make against them, and the Netherlands ground forces were confused by the many-pronged nature of the attack. The Japanese Western Force, whose landing *Houston* had disputed, had possession of an important airfield by dusk of D-day, 1 March, and captured Batavia and Bandoeng on the 5th. The Eastern Force took Kragan and Surabaya and swept diagonally across the island to Tjilatjap, preceded by refugees and sailors who had been stranded in the northern ports. At Tjilatjap Captain L. J. Hudson, senior United States officer after the departure of Admiral Glassford, and Lieutenant Commander Corydon M. Wassell USNR of the Navy Medical Corps, did wonders in evacuating the wounded and the able-bodied by submarine or small Dutch merchantman. The Japanese overran Java as swiftly as Sennacherib advanced on Jerusalem: —

> He is come to Aiath — he is passed to Migron —
> At Michmash he hath laid up his carriages —
> They are gone over the passage —
> They have taken up their lodging at Geba —
> Ramah is afraid — Gibeah of Saul is fled.
> Lift up thy voice, O daughter of Gallim! [31]

Tjilatjap was occupied on 8 March, and next day General Ter Poorten surrendered Java unconditionally to the Japanese.

The Malay Barrier was completely broken. Except for small pockets of resistance like Corregidor, the colonial empires of the United States, the Netherlands and Great Britain, as far west as India and as far south as Australia, were in Japanese hands. Greater East Asia Co-Prosperity Sphere was achieved — like *Mitteleuropa*.

Was, then, all this gallantry and grief in vain? Were our efforts to defend the Barrier a waste of men and matériel? The answer

[31] Isaiah x:28–30.

depends largely on moral factors such as national pride and oriental "face," which in the last analysis are imponderable. Admiral King is reported to have characterized the whole Southwest Pacific Campaign as "a magnificent display of very bad strategy." True enough; but the strategy was imposed by the enemy's initiative, by the failure of the three principal victims of his lust for conquest to concert defensive measures before he was ready to strike, and by the inability of the Allies to deploy sufficient force to stop him. The Dutch believe that the Abda forces held up the enemy for a month or more, and so saved Australia from invasion; but, so far as could be ascertained from the Japanese after the war, their time-table of conquest was not seriously delayed, and they had no plan to invade Australia. Be that as it may, the Allies did well to fight for the Malay Barrier although their fighting could not save it. They had a recent and horrible example of the moral disaster in too easy and complacent a capitulation — that of France. Another Vichy régime in the Southwest might have been too much for the Allies to bear.[32]

So, while we may mourn *Houston* and the other ships of three navies that went down with most of their officers and men, after fighting so bravely and so well, we must not regard their efforts as vain. The United States Asiatic Fleet seldom tasted victory. It drank the cup of defeat to the bitter dregs. Nevertheless, the fortitude of that Fleet in the face of almost certain disaster inspired the rest of the Navy in the forty months of war that followed, and its exploits will always be held in proud and affectionate remembrance.

[32] Capt. Ohmae states that the Japanese Navy proposed a plan for the invasion of Australia but the Army rejected it because they estimated that it would require more divisions than they could spare.

# CHAPTER XX

# Events in the Indian Ocean[1]

## 25 March–8 April 1942

THE tale of defeat and disaster in the Far East is not yet complete. Although the United States Navy was not involved, we must mention the Japanese conquest of Burma and briefly describe the Japanese naval raid on Ceylon, because of the effect that both had on the general situation.

The Kingdom of Thailand, which surrendered to the Japanese the very first day of the war, served the enemy not only as a corridor for the invasion of the Malay States but as a base for his invasion of Burma. Rangoon, capital and chief seaport of Burma, was occupied by the Japanese 8 March 1942, the day before Java surrendered. The army then pushed up the valley of the Irawaddy and on 1 May occupied Mandalay, anchor of the Burma Road. China was now cut off from outside aid by land or by sea; northeastern India and even Calcutta were threatened.

The Andaman Islands — lying about 250 miles southwest of Rangoon and a little farther from the western entrance to the Strait of Malacca — would, if properly developed, have been an excellent air and naval base for an Allied counterattack on Burma, the Malay Peninsula or Sumatra. Japan realized this perfectly well and occupied them on 23 March. The southern flank of their westernmost advance was now effectively covered against anything but a carrier-based air attack. The commercial port of Colombo, facing west, and Trincomalee, facing east, were the two principal British naval and air bases in the Indian Ocean. Forces for a counterattack on the newly won Japanese positions would have to be assembled

[1] Based largely on Battle Summary No. 15, "Naval Operations Off Ceylon," prepared by the Historical Section, British Admiralty.

at one or the other, or both. So the enemy decided to give Ceylon a taste of Pearl Harbor.

All Royal Navy vessels that escaped from the Java Sea rendez-voused at these Cingalese bases and joined the British Eastern Fleet, over which Admiral Sir James Somerville RN assumed command on 24 March at Colombo. By this time the Eastern Fleet had become a powerful force, comprising five battleships (*Warspite, Resolution, Ramillies, Royal Sovereign* and *Revenge*), three aircraft carriers (*Hermes, Indomitable, Formidable*), eight cruisers, 15 destroyers and five submarines.[2]

On 28 March, only two days after he had hoisted his flag in H.M.S. *Warspite* at Trincomalee, Admiral Somerville received intelligence that a Japanese carrier force would make an air strike on Ceylon about 1 April. That was correct. Essentially it was the same Striking Force under Vice Admiral Nagumo that had pounded Pearl Harbor and Darwin and covered the occupations of Rabaul and Ambon. It consisted of carriers *Akagi, Zuikaku, Shokaku, Soryu* and *Hiryu*; battleships *Kirishima, Hiei, Haruna* and *Kongo*; heavy cruisers *Tone* and *Chikuma*, light cruiser *Abukuma* and eight destroyers.[3] Nagumo had retired to Kendari in Celebes to refuel and reorganize on completing his mop-up south of Java. He departed Kendari 26 March, two days before Admiral Somerville got the word.

Unfortunately, that was the only word that the British did get. Somerville correctly estimated that the enemy would approach Ceylon from the southeastward and made excellent dispositions for searching in that direction, but his ships searched for only three days and two nights, which was not enough. On the evening of 2 April they gave it up and headed for Addu Atoll in the Maldive Islands, for after such high-speed steaming the battleships ran low on fresh water, their condensers being inadequate.

The Eastern Fleet was watering and fueling at Addu on the

[2] Two of the cruisers, one destroyer and three of the submarines were Dutch.
[3] Also, a Supply Group of 6 tankers escorted by 3 destroyers. Information from the G–2 Historical Section of General MacArthur's Command.

afternoon of 4 April when word came that a search plane had sighted the Japanese carrier force at lat. 0°40′ N, long. 83°10′ E, steaming hellbent for Ceylon. Admiral Somerville sortied promptly with all ships that had been refueled, leaving the rest to oil up at best speed from the few tankers available.

Vice Admiral Sir Geoffrey Arbuthnot flew his flag ashore at Colombo, 600 miles from the Maldives. On the last day of March he began clearing out merchant ships from that crowded harbor; but by midnight 4 April it still contained 21 merchantmen, eight fleet auxiliaries and five combat ships which for one reason or another could not sortie. All planes on near-by airfields were airborne or dispersed by 0800 Easter Sunday, 5 April, when about 70 Japanese carrier-based fighters and bombers struck Colombo. Profiting by what they failed to do at Pearl Harbor, Admiral Nagumo's bombers paid special attention to naval workshops and shore installations, seriously damaging them; in the harbor they did not do so well, sinking only one destroyer and an armed merchant cruiser that were immobilized; the merchant vessels had steam up and successfully evaded the rain of bombs. Of 32 R.A.F. planes that rose to intercept, 24 were lost; but they probably accounted for an equal number of the enemy's carrier-based aircraft.

Colombo afforded but slender pickings for Admiral Nagumo's boys, compared with the big game they had enjoyed since 7 December. But a ripe quarry was awaiting them at sea.

At noon on the same Easter Sunday heavy cruisers *Dorsetshire* and *Cornwall* were steaming at 27½ knots en route from Colombo to rendezvous with Admiral Somerville, when they were seen by Japanese search planes. At 1340 a carrier air group attacked. *Dorsetshire* promptly up-ended and plunged by the stern; *Cornwall* went down at 1359 after absorbing eight bombs. Fortunately over 1100 survivors were recovered, but 425 officers and men went down with these ships.

Admiral Somerville now played an understandably cautious game in the face of this enemy force, greatly his superior in strength, battle practice, morale and technique. He withdrew from the Japanese air range by day and closed at night in the hope of making a gunfire attack, but in two days never made contact; and at noon 8 April he returned to Addu for fuel and water. After consulting his staff and commanding officers, the Admiral wisely decided to keep away from Ceylon.

In the meantime, a second Japanese force under command of Vice Admiral J. Ozawa, consisting of carrier *Ryujo* and five heavy cruisers with their screening destroyers, had been raising havoc with merchant shipping in the Bay of Bengal. Japanese submarines, moreover, were taking their toll of Allied merchant shipping off the West Coast of India. And Nagumo was making ready to strike the other important Cingalese base, Trincomalee.

Admiral Arbuthnot ordered that harbor to be cleared on the afternoon of 8 April, when he received word that a reconnaissance plane had sighted the carriers approaching a launching position. Most of the combat and merchant ships were outside, although not beyond the range of the carrier planes, by 0725 next morning when the Japanese attacked with some 91 bombers and 38 fighters. Again the enemy concentrated on shore installations, and only one merchant vessel was sunk. Nine Blenheim bombers of the R.A.F. counterattacked carrier *Akagi* on its retirement, but they were just too late to catch it recovering planes, and made no hits. Five of them were shot down by anti-aircraft fire, and the other four were damaged. Of 11 Hurricanes (the only fighter aircraft available) which intercepted the attacking planes off Trincomalee, 9 were lost; but of the enemy's only 1 "Kate" and 3 "Zekes" were shot down.

Once more the Japanese did most of their damage at sea. That afternoon their search planes picked up H.M. carrier *Hermes* escorted by destroyer *Vampire*, which had sortied from Trincomalee before the attack and were now endeavoring to return. At 1035, when steaming at 24 knots off Batticaloa and not far from their destination, they were set upon from all directions by a carrier air group. *Hermes*, with no planes aboard, was hit by at least forty bombs, and sank within twenty minutes. Then 15 or 20 of the Japanese bombers proceeded to polish off the escorting destroyer

*Vampire.* A near-by hospital ship made prompt recovery of survivors, but 315 officers and men were lost. And before 1300 the Japanese carrier planes had also disposed of a near-by corvette, a fleet auxiliary and a merchant ship, which were trying to return to Trincomalee.

Admiral Nagumo, now short of fuel, retired to the Strait of Malacca and thence to Kure. His and Ozawa's Northern Force had

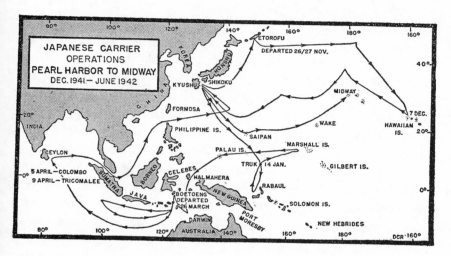

sunk 23 merchantmen [4] and crippled the British Eastern Fleet, which was forced to retire to the western half of the Indian Ocean and to East African bases. It could safely be disregarded by the enemy in his later operations to the eastward.

Admiral Nagumo had good reason to feel proud. In four months he had operated across 120° of longitude — one third of the way around the world — between Hawaii and Ceylon. He had conducted strikes against ships and shore installations at Pearl Harbor, Rabaul, Ambon, Darwin, off Java, Colombo, and Trincomalee. He

[4] The 23 merchant ships were sunk in the Bay of Bengal between 5 and 9 April and totaled 98,413 tons. Of these, 15 were sunk by aircraft and 8 by surface ships. In the period 2–9 April 5 merchant ships were sunk and one damaged by submarines off the west coast of India, making another 37,276 tons. In short, the Allies lost a grand total of 135,689 tons of merchant shipping around India during this unhappy Holy Week of 1942. Admiralty Report p. 24.

had sunk 5 battleships, 1 aircraft carrier, 2 cruisers and 7 destroyers; damaged several more capital ships, and disposed of thousands of tons of fleet auxiliaries and merchant ships. Hundreds of Allied aircraft and important shore installations had been destroyed. Yet *not one ship* of his Striking Force had been sunk or even damaged by Allied action. "Indeed the force was seldom sighted and never effectively attacked." [5]

Nevertheless, and in spite of the heavy bill paid by the Royal Navy, it would have been better for Nagumo had he stayed at home this time. For the destruction of Japanese carrier planes by the R.A.F. paid handsome dividends to the United Nations.[6] Only two of the five participating carriers were able to get into the Coral Sea battle a month later; the other three had to return to Japan and train new planes and pilots to replace depleted air groups. According to Japanese postwar testimony, the caliber of the replacements — who took part in the Battle of Midway on June 4 — was inferior to that of the veterans. Thus, if Yamamoto had canceled the Indian Ocean raid, or if the R.A.F. at Ceylon had been less enterprising, the Japanese Carrier Group might have had enough margin to reverse the score, both at Coral Sea and Midway.

[5] *The Campaigns of the Pacific War* p. 31.
[6] Capt. Stam RNN, who was at Colombo at the time, informed me that the British authorities collected 36 or 37 Japanese planes that had been shot down over Ceylon, and displayed the wreckage in a public park at Colombo to impress the natives. And at least as many more were shot down over the sea.

# CHAPTER XXI

# First Light

## 10 March–18 April 1942

### 1. *Wilson Brown's Transmontane Raid*

10 March, East Longitude date.

A FTER his first attempt at Rabaul, Admiral Brown advised Cincpac that any future attack on an air base of similar strength should be delivered by two carriers at least, and he wanted two tankers as well, since carrier operations in light airs close to the equator required full speed for launching and recovery, and so consumed enormous amounts of fuel oil. Admiral Nimitz released both to him. *Lexington* and *Yorktown,* the latter wearing the flag of Rear Admiral Frank Jack Fletcher, were the carriers.

For this planned two-carrier raid Admiral King [1] issued the simple order, "Attack Enemy." The object was not only to keep the Japanese guessing and inflict damage but to cover a movement of United States troops from Australia to Nouméa between 7 and 12 March.

The only practicable place to hit, it seemed, was Rabaul, and a plan was drawn up accordingly. But, while *Lexington* and *York-town* were proceeding thither, from the southward in order to avoid snoopers, news arrived that the enemy on 8 March had effected landings, against only token Australian resistance, at Lae and Salamaua on Huon Gulf, the bight of New Guinea facing the Bismarck Sea. [2] Both places had airfields. As Captain Turner

---

[1] Wilson Brown was then attached to Anzac Force and under direct operational control of Cominch.

[2] The name given in the course of the war to the body of water between New Britain, Papua, the Trobriand Islands and the Northern Solomons.

Joy, Admiral Brown's operations officer, remarked, this was an "answer to prayer" — an opportunity to hit the enemy in a new position before he was well dug in, and to halt a new southward advance that threatened Australia. For most of the night Brown's staff discussed with Captain "Ted" Sherman of *Lexington* whether they should venture into the Bismarck Sea to launch, or fly planes from the Gulf of Papua over the 15,000-foot Owen Stanley mountain range. Fortunately they chose the latter; the Bismarck Sea was virtually uncharted and much nearer to the headquarters of the Japanese 25th Air Flotilla at Rabaul. Admiral Crace, again loudly protesting at missing a chance to "shoot Japs," was ordered to patrol south of Rossel Island with his four cruisers and four destroyers, and to escort the oilers to a fueling rendezvous at lat. 15° S, long. 159° E. The other four cruisers and nine destroyers accompanied *Lexington* and *Yorktown*.

This strike was well planned and neatly executed. The carriers launched from a point about 45 miles off the south shore of Papua. Commander W. B. Ault of the *Lexington* air group, who had already flown to Port Moresby to supplement the meager knowledge available on board ship of New Guinea geography, flew a scout bomber to a position over the highest point of the pass over the Owen Stanley Range, and orbited there all the morning, transmitting weather and other information to planes and ships. By 0840 March 10 (East Longitude date and local time) the entire attack group of 104 planes was in the air. *Lexington's* torpedo squadron carried aërial torpedoes over a mountain pass some 7500 feet high. The Owen Stanleys were crossed successfully, plenty of merchant and combat shipping was found off Lae and Salamaua, and the aviators had a field day "remembering Pearl." No air resistance was encountered, but their task was much more difficult than that of Nagumo's aviators on 7 December, as the enemy ships, though surprised, were able to maneuver. Only one plane and pilot out of the 104 was lost. The aviators were eager to make another strike that afternoon; but Admiral Brown did not dare risk his ships any longer in that advanced position, where they might become targets for the enemy air force at Rabaul.

The usual over-optimistic accounts of ships sunk and damaged were discounted at Pearl Harbor, because Army Flying Forts from Townsville which attacked Lae and Salamaua next day reported that everything was still afloat; but a check-up after the war showed that the carrier planes had sunk a large minesweeper, a 6000-ton transport and a 6500-ton converted light cruiser, *Kongo Maru*.[3]

This was something, although Admiral Brown was under no illusion as to having greatly retarded the enemy's advance. The task force made its scheduled rendezvous with Admiral Crace and the oilers, and entered Pearl Harbor on 26 March after fifty-four days at sea, an unprecedented war cruise for 1942 that would seem short enough before the war was over.

## 2. *The Halsey–Doolittle Raid on Tokyo, 18 April*[4]

> For the actual strike East Longitude date and
> Zone minus 9 time, that of Tokyo, is used.

President Roosevelt in a dispatch to Winston Churchill remarked that Wilson Brown's raid on Lae and Salamaua was the most cheering thing that had happened in the Pacific so far. Something even more cheerful was already under way — Halsey's carrier raid on Tokyo with "Jimmy" Doolittle's Army bombers.

One day in January, 1942, Admiral King and his operations officer, Captain Francis S. Low, were discussing how the Navy might pull off a really spectacular diversionary raid on Japan. Marcus, Kwajalein and the like were all very well, but something better was wanted — a proper retaliation for Pearl Harbor. Tokyo,

---

[3] Apparently this was the "light cruiser of the *Natori* or *Tenryu* class" claimed by *Yorktown* air group; the other two, evaluated as transports, were sunk by *Lexington* planes.

[4] Based largely on Col. S. L. A. Marshall's excellent account, written for the War Department Historical Division, Pacific Section; and on *Hornet* Action Report 28 Apr. 1942. The account of the planning on which this is based was written especially for this work, from memory, by Vice Admiral Donald B. Duncan in 1947. Owing to the imperative need of secrecy, no written record of it was made at the time.

of course, was the answer; but how could Tokyo be reached? The enemy had shore-based aircraft capable of operating 300 miles off shore, and picket boats patrolling 500 miles off Tokyo Bay. How could we get striking power inside this double guard, without subjecting our carriers to the fate of the *Prince of Wales?* Our own carrier bombers lacked the range. The Army Air Force Mitchells, medium bombers known as B–25s, had the range and the punch. Could they be launched from carriers? Perhaps. Could they be recovered by the carriers? Most certainly not. Well then, why not have them launched outside picket-boat range, bomb Tokyo, and continue right through to friendly fields in China?

Admiral King ordered his air operations officer, Captain Donald B. Duncan, to study the problem, and put it up to the Commanding General of the Army Air Force, "Hap" Arnold, who agreed with enthusiasm to organize and equip the air units. So, while details of ship movements and Task Force Organization were being worked out by Captain Duncan, the aircraft were prepared and the aviators trained under Lieutenant Colonel James H. Doolittle USA.

In late March, 1942, when plans had been approved by King and Arnold and training was well advanced, Captain Duncan presented the plan to Admiral Nimitz at Pearl Harbor and made final arrangements with Admiral Halsey, whose task force was selected for the honor of executing this raid. Coöperation between the two services could not have been better, and the secret was well kept. Up to within a few days of sailing only six officers were cognizant of the plan. Even Captain Mitscher of the *Hornet* did not know what was up until a few days before the planes were hoisted on board his ship.

Sixteen B–25s, all that the carrier could handle,[5] were chosen for the strike; 70 officers and 130 enlisted men of the Army Air Force volunteered to operate and service them.

---

[5] Their wingspread was much too great for the carrier's elevators, so only a deck load could be taken. They belonged originally to 17th Bombardment Group, U.S.A.A.F.

The planes had to be given special equipment for carrier launching, and the men had only a month's training, under Colonel Doolittle. A strip of Eglin Field, Florida, was marked off in the dimensions of *Hornet's* flight deck, and under the instruction of Lieutenant Henry L. Miller USN, the pilots practiced taking off from that restricted space. They never had even one practice take-off from a real carrier's deck.

The planes were flown across the continent to Sacramento, then to Alameda Air Station on San Francisco Bay, and there loaded on the deck of *Hornet*, 1 April 1942. The carrier sailed next day, escorted by cruisers *Vincennes* and *Nashville*, four destroyers and fleet oiler *Cimarron*. Information of the mission and the target was first given out late in the following afternoon, when the force was well clear of shore. "Cheers from every section of the ship greeted the announcement and morale reached a new high, there to remain until after the attack was launched and the ship well clear of combat areas."[6]

With the target announced, various problems could be worked out. Detailed instructions were given on the basic plan, tactics, and, in the event of capture, "how to make friends and influence Japs," as the lectures by Lieutenant Stephen Jurika, formerly assistant Naval Attaché at Tokyo, were called. *Hornet's* crew gladly turned to, and helped the Army men with their work. The carrier-plane pilots, eager to substitute for the Army aviators in the strike, played poker with them assiduously in every spare hour, each Navy flyer hoping to run up an enormous credit before D-day, which he would generously discharge in return for being allowed to fly a B-25! It was perhaps fortunate that the A.A.F. proved to be as expert in this great American game as the U.S.N.

Exposed as the B-25s were to the elements on the flight deck, they required constant checking and inspection to insure against vibration damage to the control surfaces, and there was constant anxiety lest they break loose in the heavy seas that the *Hornet* encountered.

[6] *Hornet* Action Report.

To make place for the Army bombers, *Hornet* had struck her own planes below. Wildcats and Devastators, with wings folded, and dismantled SBDs were packed into every available space, even hung from the overhead. So, except for her few guns, the carrier was defenseless until she rendezvoused with Task Force 16 on the morning of 13 April. *Enterprise*, flying the flag of Admiral Halsey, met the *Hornet* group at a point between Midway and the western Aleutians, and provided combat air patrol for both carriers. The united Task Force was now organized thus: —

## TASK FORCE 16

Vice Admiral William F. Halsey, Jr.

ENTERPRISE        Capt. George D. Murray

*Air Group*, Lt. Cdr. Clarence W. McClusky, Jr.

| | | |
|---|---|---|
| VB–6: | 18 SBD–2&3 (Dauntless) | Lt. Richard H. Best |
| VF–6: | 27 F4F–3&4 (Wildcat) | Lt. James S. Gray, Jr. |
| VT–6: | 18 TBD–1 (Devastator) | Lt. Cdr. Eugene E. Lindsey |
| VB–3:[7] | 18 SBD–2&3 | Lt. Cdr. Maxwell F. Leslie |

HORNET        Capt. Marc A. Mitscher

*Air Group*, Cdr. Stanhope C. Ring

*Strike Group*, 16 B–25s (Mitchells), Lt. Col. James H. Doolittle USA

The following Army officers[8] commanded the B–25s: —

| | |
|---|---|
| Lt. Col. Doolittle | 1st Lt. Richard O. Joyce |
| 1st Lt. Travis Hoover | 1st Lt. Harold F. Watson |
| 1st Lt. Robert M. Gray | Capt. Charles R. Greening |
| 1st Lt. Everett W. Holstrom | 1st Lt. William M. Bower |
| Capt. David M. Jones | 1st Lt. Edgar E. McElroy |
| * 2nd Lt. Dean E. Hallmark | Maj. John A. Hilger |
| 1st Lt. Ted W. Lawson | 1st Lt. Donald G. Smith |
| 1st Lt. Edward J. York | * 2nd Lt. William G. Farrow |

* Shot by the enemy after capture.

*Cruisers*, Rear Admiral Raymond A. Spruance

| | |
|---|---|
| NORTHAMPTON | Capt. William D. Chandler |
| SALT LAKE CITY | Capt. Ellis M. Zacharias |
| VINCENNES | Capt. Frederick L. Riefkohl |
| NASHVILLE | Capt. Francis S. Craven |

[7] From *Saratoga* to replace VS–6 which was at Pearl Harbor training.
[8] Listed in order of takeoff.

Destroyers, Capt. Richard L. Conolly (Comdesron 6)
Desdiv 12, Capt. Edward P. Sauer

| | |
|---|---|
| BALCH | Lt. Cdr. Harold H. Tiemroth |
| BENHAM | Lt. Cdr. Joseph M. Worthington |
| ELLET | Lt. Cdr. Francis H. Gardner |
| FANNING | Cdr. William R. Cooke, Jr. |

Desdiv 22, Cdr. Harold R. Holcomb

| | |
|---|---|
| GRAYSON | Cdr. Thomas M. Stokes |
| GWIN | Cdr. John M. Higgins |
| MEREDITH | Lt. Cdr. Harry E. Hubbard |
| MONSSEN | Cdr. Roland N. Smoot |

Oilers, Cdr. Houston L. Maples

| | |
|---|---|
| SABINE | Cdr. Maples |
| CIMARRON | Cdr. Russell M. Ihrig |

After the carriers and cruisers had been refueled on 17 April, at a point about 1000 miles from Tokyo, they dropped the destroyers and oilers behind and made best speed forward.

Negotiations for landing fields had to be vague and indirect, as the Chinese government was notoriously "leaky." Generalissimo Chiang Kai-shek was told merely that a number of Army bombers were flying over to help China, and must have fields to land on; but he did not get around to designating the fields until 14 April. Colonel Doolittle had to assume on the voyage that the Chuchow [9] airdrome, the nearest known to be in Chinese hands, would be his final destination; but owing to a solid week of bad weather that field could not be prepared in time. This information was sent to the United States much too late to be transmitted to the task force, because of the danger that the enemy would intercept and decode it.

It was calculated that, in order to reach the Chinese airfield, which was 1093 nautical miles distant from Tokyo, the Mitchells, armed with four 500-lb. bombs each and carrying their maximum load of 1141 gallons of gasoline, would have to take off within 500 miles of the coast of Japan. Halsey's plan called for launching at that distance on the afternoon of 18 April, for a night attack.

[9] Chuchow, called Lishui on some maps, is in Chekiang Province, about 50 miles inland from Wenchow.

Thirteen planes were to concentrate on the Tokyo area, while three were to by-pass the capital and strike, respectively, Nagoya, Osaka, and Kobe. Colonel Doolittle was to precede the rest of his squadron by three hours and drop incendiary bombs on Tokyo in order to light fires which would serve as beacons to the rest.

The planes were spotted for the takeoff as early as 16 April, the tail of the last B–25 projecting over the after edge of *Hornet's* flight deck. All went well until the morning of the 18th. At 0210, when the force was still over 700 miles from land, the radar screen showed that two ships were ahead — very disturbing! Nobody suspected that the Japanese patrolled so far out. Task Force 16 altered course to avoid, and at first light *Enterprise* launched reconnaissance planes. At 0500, they reported another vessel 42 miles ahead, and believed that she had sighted them. That was correct; this picket boat sent in the first warning. After a third vessel had been sighted at 0644 this time visually from the *Hornet* (and eventually sunk by *Nashville*), Admiral Halsey knew that surprise had been lost. He was still 650 miles from Japan, 150 miles short of his intended launching position; and at that distance it was doubtful whether the B–25s would have gas enough to reach China. *Hornet* must launch at once and retire, or retire without launching; for Halsey could not risk a land-based bombing attack on his carriers. But he would not give up when there was hope of hitting Japan. With Doolittle's concurrence, he made the bold decision to launch as soon as bombing plans could be changed and adapted to a daylight attack.

So, at a point 623 miles from the nearest land and 668 miles from the heart of Tokyo, the B–25s were launched.[10] "The wind and sea were so strong that morning," recalled Admiral Halsey, "that green water was breaking over the carriers' ramps. Jimmy led his squadron off. When his plane buzzed down the *Hornet's* deck at 0725, there wasn't a man topside in the Task Force who didn't help sweat him into the air. One pilot hung on the brink of a stall until we nearly catalogued his effects, but the last of the sixteen

[10] Lat. 35°45′ N, long. 153°40′ E.

B–25s on flight deck of *Hornet*

A Group of B–25 Pilots and Crewmen
Captain Mitscher of *Hornet* talking to Lieutenant Colonel Doolittle, at left

*The Halsey-Doolittle Strike on Tokyo*

The launching, 18 April 1942
A B–25 has just taken off from *Hornet*

*Sabine* fueling *Enterprise*, 17 April
*The Halsey-Doolittle Strike on Tokyo*

was airborne by 0824, and a minute later my staff duty officer was writing in the flag log, 'Changed fleet course and axis to 90°, commencing retirement from the area at 25 knots.' " [11]

It happened that Tokyo was alerted for a big air raid with mock attacks by Japanese planes as the last B–25 was launched, and just as the mock attack ended the real one began. Consequently the great majority of the population, including even the interned Americans, thought that the B–25s and consequent anti-aircraft fire were the second act of the show, and never knew until it was all over that Tokyo had really been attacked. This circumstance lessened any psychological effect that the raid might have had on the local population, but assisted the B–25s to make a safe getaway.

The bombers arrived over the city at noon 18 April. Despite warnings received from picket boats, the authorities were caught unprepared. Not knowing that Army bombers were being used, they estimated that the carriers would have to continue their approach for several hours and attack next morning, if indeed they did not retire after being discovered.[12] So the B–25s met little opposition. They approached Tokyo from various quarters, skimmed in at rooftop level, and rose again before releasing bombs to avoid being damaged by the explosions.

Although the first bombs were dropped at 1215, no air alert was sounded for fifteen or twenty minutes. By 1235 all thirteen B–25s were over the city, encountering a few fighter planes and anti-aircraft fire of considerable volume but slight accuracy. The planes were kept at a respectful distance by the dummy machine guns mounted in the Mitchells' tails for that very purpose.

All assigned targets were strictly of a military nature, such as munitions, steel, gas and chemical plants, power stations and truck and tank factories. Specific instructions had been given not to attack civilian targets; but two or three of the planes made the mistake, almost inevitable in air warfare, of hitting the wrong building,

---

[11] *Admiral Halsey's Story* (1947) p. 103, with times converted to Zone minus 9.
[12] Capt. Ohmae supplementary interrogation, USSBS 495.

for which three of their comrades who were captured paid the supreme penalty.

The three planes assigned to Nagoya, Osaka and Kobe carried only incendiary bombs. The Nagoya plane succeeded in making a run through heavy fire from ground batteries, and the crew believed that all targets were squarely hit. The one assigned to Osaka probably attacked Nagoya instead. Kobe was easy for the third plane: no pursuit, no anti-aircraft fire and only a partial alert.

The actual damage inflicted on the Japanese cities was not great by subsequent bombing standards, and, as all bombed areas were roped off to keep civilians from knowing what had happened, the population was not much impressed. Japanese officialdom, hard put to it to explain how such an attack could possibly have taken place, suffered considerable loss of face. So little information was given out that many Japanese naval officers, discounting the possibility of long-range bombers being flown off carriers, believed the B-25s had flown all the way from Midway Island.[13] Yet even the most thought-controlled and victory-drunk Japanese could see that his homeland was not unassailable by air.

Not one of the attacking bombers was lost over Japan. Lieutenant Edward J. York's B-25 developed fuel trouble and headed for the nearest "friendly" airfield at Vladivostok, where his plane was impounded by the Russians and the crew interned; they escaped to Persia thirteen months later. The fifteen others made for China and kept flying until fuel was exhausted. Some actually flew over Chuchow, but that field had no homing device, and the Chinese, mistaking them for enemy, sounded the air raid alarm and extinguished field lights. Four planes made crash landings; crews of the other eleven bailed out in the black night, dropping down onto wet and slippery crags or into lakes. One man was killed in the parachute descent and four were drowned. Others were cut or had limbs broken as they hit the slopes. Those who made safe land-

---

[13] Capt. Watanabe in *Inter. Jap. Off.* I 66. This may seem strange in view of the picket boats' reports, but the pickets did not know that the planes in *Hornet* were B-25s, so it was assumed that the carriers were for an independent follow-up strike, and had been frightened away before launching.

ings wisely stopped in their tracks and rested the night through.
"Landing in a tree," wrote Lieutenant Cole, "I stretched my 'chute
between it and another tree, making a hammock, and proceeded to
go to sleep." Bombardier Sergeant Bither lighted a cigarette on
landing, calmly smoked it, flicked the stub away, watched the spark
fall into bottomless space, and decided that he, too, would sleep
right there. When day came these men made their way cautiously
down the slopes to the nearest village where most of them were
tenderly cared for by Chinese peasants and eventually passed on to
Chungking.

One plane, running out of fuel earlier than the others, splashed
off the China coast near Ningpo; the pilot and two crewmen who
managed to swim ashore were captured, as were the entire crew of
another plane that bailed out near Nanchang. All eight men were
tried by a military court and sentenced to die. Five of these sen-
tences were "graciously" commuted to life imprisonment, but Lieutenants Hallmark and Farrow and Sergeant Harold A. Spatz were
executed and a fourth died in a Japanese prison. Thus, 71 of the
80 pilots and crewmen, including Colonel Doolittle, survived the
raid on Japan.

Halsey made good his retirement without molestation, although
the Japanese dispatched both planes and ships in pursuit. Within
three hours the combat air patrol from *Enterprise* attacked sixteen
enemy patrol craft and sank several of them; one surrendered to
*Nashville* and the crew were taken prisoner. One of them told a
grimly humorous story. He had aroused his sleeping skipper to look
at "two of our beautiful carriers." The skipper came on deck, stud-
ied *Enterprise* and *Hornet* through his binoculars, and remarked
"They're beautiful all right, but they're not ours." He went below
and shot himself.[14]

*Hornet* took over combat air patrol from *Enterprise* about five
hours after the last B–25 was launched, and within thirty-six hours
the wings of the SBDs had been assembled by employing produc-
tion-line methods. Both carriers entered Pearl Harbor on 25 April,

[14] *Admiral Halsey's Story* p. 103.

hoping for a little rest; but they were urgently wanted in the Coral Sea.

This raid gave a tremendous lift to American morale, which badly needed assistance at that moment. No event in the war prior to the Battle of Midway gave the American people so much satisfaction as the news that Tokyo had been bombed; and, although the public would have liked to have known what planes were used and how they got there, President Roosevelt's humorous announcement that they flew from "Shangri-La," the mysterious Tibetan city of Hilton's *Lost Horizon,* added to the general hilarity.

The practical results, too, were important. Four Japanese Army fighter-plane groups, urgently needed elsewhere, were pinned down in Japan. The higher command, disconcerted, expedited plans for an overextension which led directly to the Battle of Midway. That alone was well worth the effort put into this operation by the Navy, and by the indomitable Army aviators who had volunteered to help even the score.

"In my opinion," wrote Admiral Halsey, "their flight was one of the most courageous deeds in all military history." [15]

[15] *Admiral Halsey's Story* p. 104. Owing to the secrecy of the Armed Forces in this respect — well justified in view of the Japanese puzzlement over the source of the B–25s — the Navy never got any popular credit for the operation, which was generally known as "Jimmy Doolittle's Raid."

Index

# Index

Names of Combat Ships in SMALL CAPITALS
Names of Merchant Ships in *Italics*

The following lists of ships and commanding officers are not indexed:
Japanese Navy July 1941, pp. 26–7; Ships in Pearl Harbor, 7 Dec. 1941, pp. 104, 213n; U.S. Asiatic Fleet, 8 Dec. 1941, pp. 158–60; Japanese Invasion Forces for Philippines, pp. 161–3; Abda Command January–February 1942, pp. 271–3; Japanese Naval Forces in Southwest Pacific Operation, January–March 1942, pp. 273–6; Abda Combined Striking Force, pp. 332–3; Japanese Java Invasion Forces, pp. 333–4; Task Force 16 in Raid on Tokyo, pp. 392–3.

## A

ABC–1 Staff Agreement, 51–3
Abda Combined Striking Force, 297, 332–3; Makassar, 299–303; Banka Str., 309–11; Badung Str., 321–30
Abda Command, 277; organization, 271–3, 278–9; strategy, 281–2, 292, 297–8; reorganized, 311–13; disintegrates, 335–8
Abda Western Striking Force, 340, 365
Abe, Rear Adm. H., 245, 253
ABUKUMA, 87, 382
ADB Conference, 53–6, 74, 129, 152
*Admiral Halstead,* 319
Aircraft, British, see R.A.F., R.A.A.F.
Aircraft carriers, 22, 27, 31, 83, 210–12, 259–68, 382–98
Aircraft, Jap., carrier-based, 22, 27, 85, 102n, 163, 263–4, 309–10, 316–18, 373, 378, 383–6; in strike on Pearl, 94n; tender- and land-based, 267, 299–302, 315–18, 361
Aircraft, U.S. Army, 123; types and losses at Pearl, 124; build-up, 221–2; B–17, 133, 138, 153, 156, 170, 177–8, 182, 259, 281, 320–1; B–24, 389; B–25, 390–7; fighters, 170, 201, 214, 314, 318; no. sent to Java, 305n
Aircraft, U.S. Marine Corps, 122 210–11, 214, 228–33, 236, 246–7

Aircraft, U.S. Navy, carrier-based, 120–1, 211–12, 217, 262–4, 267, 387–9; tender- or land-based, see Catalinas; losses at Pearl, 122–3, 212; build-up, 221
Air power and strategy, in invasion Phils., 167–74; in Malay Barrier, 292–3, 314–16, 359
AKAGI, 22, 85–8, 93, 382, 384
AKEBONO, AKIGUMO, 87
Alaska, 32–3
ALDEN, 331–3, 352, 375
ALLEN, 100
*AM–2,* 369
*AM–15,* 288
Ambon, 197, 296–7, 315; Jap. occupation force, 274
Amphibious forces wanting to U.S., 257
Amphibious warfare, Jap. development and technique, 165, 180, 293, 315–16
Anambas Is., 335, 338
Andaman Is., 381
Anderson, Lt. (jg) E. L., 217
ANTARES, 96, 137, 240n
Anti-Comintern Pact, 40, 49
Antrim, Lt. R. N., 373
Anzac Area, 277
Anzac Force, 261, 265–6, 387n
AOBA, 185, 245
Aparri, 174–6
ARASHIO, 329